IBE STUDIES ON EDUCATION
VOL. 3

HIGHER EDUCATION IN AN INTERNATIONAL PERSPECTIVE

GARLAND REFERENCE LIBRARY
OF SOCIAL SCIENCE
VOL. 1102

HIGHER EDUCATION IN AN INTERNATIONAL PERSPECTIVE

Critical Issues

edited by

Zaghloul Morsy
Philip G. Altbach

International Bureau
of Education

GARLAND PUBLISHING, INC.
New York & London / 1996

Library of Congress Cataloging-in-Publication Data

Higher education in an international perspective : critical issues /
edited by Zaghloul Morsy and Philip G. Altbach.
    p.   cm. — (Garland reference library of social science ; vol.
1102. IBE studies on education ; v. 3)
    "International Bureau of Education."
    Includes bibliographical references and index.
    ISBN 0-8153-2336-0 (Garland : alk. paper). — ISBN 9291450014
(Unesco : alk. paper)
    1. Education, Higher—Cross-cultural studies.   2. Comparative
education.   I. Morsy, Zaghloul.   II. Altbach, Philip G.
III. International Bureau of Education.   IV. Series: Garland reference library of social science ; v. 1102.   V. Series: Garland reference library of social science.   IBE studies on education ; v. 3.
LB2322.2.H53   1996
378—dc20   95-26399
                                                           CIP

Printed on acid-free, 250-year-life paper
Manufactured in the United States of America

CONTENTS

II Case Studies

PREFACE

True internationalism requires paying attention to perspectives from different parts of the world—especially in the current period of dramatic change. This book has a comparative and international perspective, not only in its contents but also with regard to its contributors and editors. It shows that scholars from many different countries and regions can work to create an interesting and significant volume.

Higher Education in an International Perspective stems from two special issues of *Prospects*, UNESCO's quarterly review of education (Numbers 78 and 79, 1991). The idea came originally from Zaghloul Morsy, at that time editor of *Prospects*. He asked me to collaborate with him in editing an imaginative collection of essays on key issues facing higher education, with authors reflecting differing perspectives and areas of the world. All too often, knowledge networks bulge with the writings of Western scholars; views from the developing nations are seldom included.

We were able to locate authors on all continents. UNESCO's "invisible college" of scholars around the world was instrumental in permitting us to expand beyond the usual confines of Western scholarship. Further, UNESCO's translation facilities permitted us to reach out to authors writing in Arabic, French and Spanish, as well as English. This book is, therefore, unusual, both in the range of topics considered and in the diversity of authors. We are convinced this variety is one of its important strengths.

We are indebted to Mr. Colin Power, UNESCO's Assistant Director-General for Education, and to the UNESCO Publishing Office for permitting us to publish these essays in book form. Hyaeweol Choi prepared the index. This volume is a cooperative effort of the Center for International Higher Education at Boston College and UNESCO.

Philip G. Altbach

INTRODUCTION
Zaghloul Morsy

To speak about higher education on a universal scale in a brief introduction is no easy task. The mesh of the net thrown over such a complex reality can be either too fine, catching, at best, a mass of detail, or so large that it can barely retain more than well-known generalizations. Nevertheless, keeping in mind the most penetrating arguments and the emerging new trends presented in the sixteen studies of this book, an attempt can be made to isolate the key problems from which most of the others spring.

A Kaleidoscopic Reality

A brief glance at higher education throughout the world reveals a wide range of academic systems, from the highly centralized (China and France) to those which are almost completely decentralized (India and Canada); from federal systems (Germany and the United States) to systems where the private sector is in competition with the public sector (Latin America and Japan); from systems which, until quite recently—and even today—are fragmented, with numerous and overly specialized establishments (the former Communist countries of Europe) to systems that are virtually carbon copies of others (some countries in Africa and the Arab states).

In addition, we are looking at some highly dynamic university systems (most of the countries of the European Union, the United States and Canada) that are driven by a spirit of competition and concern for "excellence"; at fast-changing systems in the process of constructive change (the Republic of Korea, Malaysia, and Taiwan); and at others that are still stagnating (the Arab states, Africa, Latin America, and many countries in Asia). Naturally there are also exceptional universities which stand out but do not challenge the prevailing national or regional trends.

Two examples may be given to illustrate the diverse circumstances of universities around the world. It is increasingly obvious, for instance, that the university systems in Eastern and Central Europe are seriously run down, paralyzed by forty or seventy years of subservience and bureaucracy. When faced with the challenge of renovation, they have found themselves forced, almost overnight, to create syllabi and types of training that were formerly forbidden or that existed in name only—such as management, political science, environmental studies, international law, sociology, commercial law, human rights, statistics and computer science—but which are indispensable in a modern world. Given the general pace of reforms, one must leave it to time and political will to perform the miracle.

The second example is typical of many developing countries or regions, especially Africa. As the Director-General of UNESCO has observed:

> The interrelated problems of poverty, hunger, disease, unemployment, illiteracy, debt, adverse terms of trade, foreign currency shortage, inflation, civil strife . . . have limited the means and to some extent sapped the capacity of the universities to adapt creatively. The effects are apparent in the deterioration of university facilities, in the decline in the quality of teaching and research and of graduate output, in shortages of books and equipment, in the brain drain, and even in tensions between the university body and state authorities.[1]

While Africa may have the excuse that its university system is relatively young, what can we say about many much older universities which, under the veneer of a so-called combination of tradition and modernity, follow a medieval-type model that persists in its own right and resists any change? Such an institution is a mere illusion of a university.

To highlight the diversity described so far, it is clear that both industrialized and developing countries present other contrasts, with postsecondary institutions in a barely embryonic state alongside mega- and multiuniversities that provide a vast array of quantitative and qualitative services in teaching and research and meet a number of challenges.

What is more, these diverse configurations—and no doubt others—are operating simultaneously, superimposing or juxtaposing themselves in such a way that it is impossible to include them in a single paradigm. But all of them, to varying degrees, are characterized by a set of dilemmas and paradoxes, most of which are illustrated in the different chapters of this book.

Democratization/Diversification

One of the primary problems in contemporary higher education stems from the extraordinary growth in enrollments that took place mainly in the industrialized countries in the 1960s and later appeared in most Third World countries. This explosive increase heralded the well-known transition, analysed by Martin Trow,[2] from élitist education to mass education and finally to universal higher education. The process may have slowed down before completion in the industrialized countries, but it is continuing relentlessly elsewhere. India, for instance, had a growth rate in student enrollments of more than ten percent a year in the 1970s. Total numbers were generally greater for the industrialized nations, but the rates of expansion were often larger in the Third World.

The changes in just one statistic give an idea of the extent of this unusual growth: worldwide, the number of students in higher education was 28.2 million in 1970, 58.4 million in 1988 and in 1990 appeared to be about 61 million.[3] In other words, enrollments more than doubled in twenty years, with inevitable consequences. This growth responds to a demand for democratization and is evidence of access to higher education by new groups and breaks with centuries of élitism, challenging the age-old or more recent "mandarinate." It has nevertheless diverted efforts towards training at the expense of research and produced an assortment of degrees which, because of their number, have unquestionably been devalued. Even worse, this rapid growth has contributed directly to unemployment, since, as is well known, while universities have the privilege of awarding countless degrees, they also turn out unemployed graduates, not to mention those who abandon study in their first or second year. Clearly, though, the universities are not solely to blame.

Carrying this line of thinking a little further, we must have the courage to say, along with Federico Mayor, then Rector of the University of Granada, that "we must not confuse the democratic ideal of egalitarianism with what is a danger of misunderstood democracy—mediocrity."[4]

Rather than labeling the problem one of "mediocrity" per se, it can be argued that the first stage of higher education is largely a "secondarized" education in very many places, and for that reason doomed to large-scale failure. In systems where university entrance is open to anyone who has completed secondary education, students find themselves lost in overcrowded lecture halls where the teacher does not have the slightest opportunity—partly because of constraints imposed by the obligatory curriculum, partly due to lack of time, partly because of the huge number of students—of passing on to students working method(s) that will enable them to acquire intellectual autonomy. Many of these same students will not have acquired any method of working or thinking during their secondary education either, where, unfortunately, rote learning frequently prevails. Consequently, in the initial stage of higher education students do not learn to structure their thinking, "to learn how to learn." This, of course, does not apply to the happy few who are from affluent and attentive families and will enter institutions of excellence, public or private. Moreover, since the criteria of evaluation are not same for secondary and higher education, there is nothing surprising about the present critical situation, in which so many students drop out or fail during the first years of higher education.

Obviously, in order to develop, all countries, especially in the Third World, need top-level, outstanding graduates who have earned their diplomas through genuine work: scholars of all kinds, doctors, engineers, university teachers, managers, and other higher-level professionals. But they also need nurses, factory supervisors, schoolteachers, and accountants. This is true for all sectors of the life and development of a nation, including technology, administration, health, education, agriculture, and industry. Harsh as it may seem to say so, it is an illusion—or pure demagogy—to think that everybody can be at the top of the ladder at the same time. Thus, although access to traditional higher education may in many cases be open to everyone, it is clear that in most countries this education—given the way it is structured and the way it functions—does not offer equal opportunities, either at the university or in later working life. There is certainly some hypocrisy inherent in this situation.

What, then, can be done, or what should be done instead? The word "selection" is taboo, even though selection is a widespread if surreptitious practice. It strikes in covert ways, for example, minimum pass marks, admission on the strength of written records, placing limits on the number of times a student may repeat a class. Curiously, it seldom operates through a clear institutional and agreed-upon system of guidance.

The solution, the alternative widely adopted by many industrialized countries, is diversification of the training available, especially in the early stages of higher education. This offers everyone the best chance of finding the path that corresponds most closely to their talents and desires. It would be economically, socially, culturally, and humanly wise to introduce diversification as early as the second stage of secondary education onward in order to guarantee students a more successful transition to higher education instead of letting them court failure and marginalization, which are as certain as they are foreseeable.

It has been clear since the 1960s that traditional universities could no longer cope on their own with the extraordinary growth in the demand for postsecondary education or with the demands made by economic development. Many countries in the industrialized world devised and put into operation a separate, nonuniversity sector. In addition, short courses and new types of postsecondary educational institutions with new functions were set up in the United Kingdom, the Federal Republic of Germany, France, the United States, Japan, the Republic of Korea, Iran, Pakistan, Venezuela, Mexico, and Thailand, and other countries. On the other hand, the emergence and implementation of lifelong education, recurrent education,[5] and the creation of open universities and distance education[6] began to offer people a second or third chance, at any age, to complete their education as they wished, and to improve their living conditions, without following the traditional university path, which, comparatively speaking, was no longer as exceptional as it was when the "alma mater" alone had the monopoly on education and the handing out of degrees. Why has this solution not been more systematically and more widely adopted in developing countries? Interest— in every sense of the word and correctly understood—and realism call for it in any case.

Autonomy/Commitment

Another problem is that of the sanctity of autonomy, in its many facets and claims. Autonomy is understood to imply, and this is not negotiable, that university teachers have the right to decide their own intellectual and research options. It further implies that the university is free to set its own objectives, curricular structure and content, and graduation criteria, and that it is entitled to defend its vocation to create new knowledge and to transmit and develop culture. Above all, it implies that the university assumes and exercises its most critical mission in society—whether accepted or not—far from the customs of, and compromises with, the political and/or spiritual powers that be.

However, what was once, not long ago, entirely true and valid cannot remain so forever. The university is surely, and increasingly, one of the major components of the society to which it belongs and whose real needs— development, among other things—it must be aware of, anticipate, and serve, regardless of the reluctance that it might still feel about the concepts of economic rationality, competition, and profit, which are universally recognized and accepted outside universities as being the keys to a modern economy and to development itself. In short, the university can no longer claim to serve society from an aloof position, in an indirect way. The university was once an ivory tower, jealously guarding its independence. This can no longer be so, if for no other reason than the equally legitimate concern of the group that finances it—society—to have a say in how the university uses the resources it is given and a stake in the results, in terms of practical contributions to the process of development that the society in question has a right to expect in return. From now on, autonomy is inconceivable without accountability (and not only in administrative and managerial terms) and the duty to provide services, according to a balance to be sought between autonomy and accountability and to an agreement between the university and the society in which it operates.

This partnership is all the more necessary given that in many industrialized countries, and in some Third World countries as well, the university has come to acknowledge two facts. The first of these is that it no longer holds the monopoly in the production of knowledge, training, or research. It thus knows that it can no longer live in a distant and self-contained autarchy, choosing only the larger academic community as its equal and its partner. Society and government are there questioning and demanding accountability from the individual university and the academic community as a whole. Thus, the university knows that its self-contained autarchy is only possible thanks to the generosity of society, which receives practically nothing in return. The second fact is that, by accepting some flexibility in its conception of autonomy, opening up to society and agreeing to listen to its demands and its needs, the university obviously can no longer simply juxtapose itself or place itself in opposition to, for example, the laboratories of large enterprises and companies and the public or semipublic applied research bureaus, both of which are increasing in number in the industrialized and developing countries.

If the university does not wish to suffocate through an even more drastic reduction of the resources it receives from society, and if it does not want to find itself more and more marginalized precisely because of the theoretical and applied research activities and the practical, immediately operational training that is going on outside its walls, it must, instead, use its intellectual freedom and its critical vocation as a basis from which to open up, cooperate, and enter into partnerships with other sectors, such as industry. These sectors are all accountable and submit to the rule of evaluation—a fundamental requirement—regarding their activities and performance, so why not the university? Only in this way can it reinforce its legitimacy in the eyes of society. It also must cease to revert to the monopolies of another era, which are in fact gradually crumbling away, if they are not already mere illusions. Its critical mission, like its role in transmitting and enriching culture, would be enhanced as a result, and no one would dare to claim that by opening up to its environment, it would lose its soul. Furthermore, such an opening up and such cooperation in the elaboration of new types of training, as well as the offer of services relating to research and continuing or recurrent education, would secure for it the extra resources it sorely needs. It would be fair to repeat that "these contacts . . . are already a reality in a number of universities in the developed world and to ask the question: 'Why not share them with the universities in the developing countries?'"[7]

Imitation/Dependency

The third problem is less universal. It is the cultural and linguistic gap that exists between most universities in developing countries and the milieu they are supposed to be serving, the gap being widened by another gap between the knowledge and skills produced by higher education and the needs of the societies around it. Let us quote once again from the address given in Accra by UNESCO's Director-General, in which what he says about Africa is also broadly applicable to many other countries:

> An imposed history appears to weigh heavily at many points on African higher educational institutions, which appear far from organically adapted to the societies of which they are a part . . . The persistence of inappropriate structures can give the impression that—despite the progress towards the development of an African academic identity . . . the special relationship with the European universities that nourished many of the independent African institutions at their origin lingers on like an unwanted dependency.[8]

This is in fact one of the great dilemmas of education in general, and of higher education in particular, in many Third World countries, and it will continue to be a problem until it is recognized as such and dealt with in medium- and long-term planning. Today's necessity can easily become tomorrow's constraint or irreversible dependency. In education, imitation or the reproduction of foreign models is in itself a kind of cultural dependency, and imitation that borrows only the form without paying attention to the spirit behind it cannot function correctly; sooner or later, stagnation occurs or great harm is caused. Objections can be made by pointing to examples of borrowed systems that succeeded where transplanted, such as the American system borrowed from Europe in the nineteenth century (but within the framework of the same culture), or Japan, in the Meiji era, which also borrowed from Europe. The latter example, an exception at that time, is no doubt more relevant and one that all the countries of the Third World should ponder upon. But it seems that history and much closer international interdependence in today's world will not give to borrowing countries the same opportunities that existed in the nineteenth century to develop themselves while at the same time preserving their own cultures and languages. It is not at all easy to free oneself completely from models that have already taken root, at least not in the short term. This is where, for example, university-level scientific research that has been given a firm orientation and is unreservedly backed by the national political will can and must play a decisive role.

Incidentally, this problem is not restricted to Third World countries; it certainly includes many Spanish-speaking ones.[9] The problem is hinted at in a document from the Netherlands Ministry of Education and Science that states: "Dutch is and remains the language of education in the Netherlands for all studies and examinations."[10]

The reason for the new rule stems from

a whole series of untruths printed in the foreign press . . . implying that the Dutch language is in danger of disappearing as a national language *(to the benefit of English)*. . . . On a number of different occasions, the Minister has found himself faced with the following dilemma: on the one hand, he is strongly committed to a flourishing Dutch culture and consequently, to the survival of Dutch as the language of instruction in schools, the government and the courts. On the other hand, the internationalization of higher education and research make the use of other languages besides Dutch indispensable.[11]

If the danger is real, and perceived as such in a developed country that is historically, culturally, and linguistically strong, the threat weighs all the more heavily on more vulnerable countries.

What Kind of Research?

The point has already been made that a modern, integrated university is an essential and necessary component in the process of national development. In this regard, one of its main functions is scientific research, whose value in the short, medium and long term is widely recognized for the training of highly qualified professionals and for development. For this reason, it has become, and rightly so, a priority in all the world's universities.

But what kind of research are we talking about? While in the industrialized countries a certain balance has been reached between fundamental and applied research and between research in the natural sciences and in the human sciences, and while bodies outside the university have applied the results of university research to develop technological products, this is not the case in the developing countries, except for a few noteworthy exceptions. Two examples, one of which may be apocryphal, illustrate this view.

In the 1970s, a brilliant student from Country X in Africa, which was in no way a "subservient" country, was preparing a Ph.D. on Pushkin at the Patrice Lumumba University in Moscow. Pushkin is certainly one of the great writers of all time and a considerable innovator, whom everyone should know and read. To be able to read his works in the original, for those who master Russian, is an enviable privilege. But did Country X, at the time ranked among the least advanced countries, really need to invest so much time and money in a research topic of dubious usefulness, research that was of even less use since neither then nor now was Russian taught in that country and there was no department of Russian at its university?

Another example is that of Egyptians studying the secret of mummification or Mexicans studying urban planning under Cuauhtémoc. Such research is carried out by scholars, using scientific methods. It can have positive effects such as academic interdisciplinarity and employment for researchers, but no one would expect these studies to make the production or processing of Egyptian cotton more competitive on the world market or to lead to cleaner air in Mexico City today.

It is generally agreed that, due to either misguidance or to the lack of flexible planning for research at national levels, many Third World scholars embark upon research they have little or no opportunity to make use of at home. These scholars will look for opportunities elsewhere, thus swelling the ranks of the tens of thousands of "brains" that have left their own countries. Looking at sub-Saharan Africa alone, "it is estimated, for instance, that between 1984 and 1987, 30,000 African graduates left their countries and work mostly in the industrially developed world."[12] Consider the outright loss in material, technical, and human resources that accompanies such migration.

This does not mean that in developing countries there should be no research in nontechnical fields. Humanistic and historical research have a legitimate place in all academic systems, including the Third World, when, for instance, such research aims at regaining and consolidating cultural identity or where it is concentrated on the revival and modernization of national languages. However, there is certainly insufficient technological focus in scientific research in most Third World countries, where a better balance is yet to be found and implemented between social sciences-oriented research and research aimed at the production sectors.

In quite a different context, we should not forget the countries of Central and Eastern Europe. To put it succinctly, they must now rejoin the mainstream of international research, after having been cut off from it for decades. This cannot be a painless task, since they must completely reshape their concept of research, change their methods and techniques, and learn and apply international rules regarding, for instance, the collection, processing, and analysis of data. In this regard, more than other countries, they without doubt need international cooperation.

After this rapid review of some of the major problems in higher education, the question arises: What about the future? The call of the future haunts every university in the world. But, all things considered and contrary to what many people say, the university is not in crisis nor is it ailing. It is only in transition and under close observation, even if the transition is inevitably slow and the observation wary. Its critical function, which is also one of its most creative missions, is already being applied to itself, as evidenced by the sixteen studies contained in the present book, all written by academics.

"Publish or perish" remains the dictum for academics. We could paraphrase that by saying to the university: "Play the game or be left out of it." The university will change, it will join in and perhaps again lead the game, because it is already trying, here and there, because it is fully conscious of the threats and the challenges that face it, and because it has no other choice.

Notes

1.   F. Mayor, Address given at the opening of the UNESCO–African Association of Universities Seminar on the Institutional Development of Higher Education in Africa, Legon University, Accra (Ghana), 25 November 1991, p. 3 (DG/91/43).

2.   M. Trow, "Problems of the Transition from Élite to Mass Higher Education," *Policies for Higher Education*, Paris, OECD, 1974.

3.   See UNESCO, *Statistical Yearbook 1991*, Table 3.10, and *World Education Report 1991*, Table 8, pp. 134–137, Paris, UNESCO.

4.   F. Mayor, "¿Universidad, todavia?" *Educación, ciencia y cultura Iberoamericana* (Madrid), Supplement to Vol. 4, No. 4, July–October 1987, p. vi.

5.   See A. Tuijnman, "Emerging Systems of Recurrent Education," *Prospects* (Paris, UNESCO), Vol. XXI, No. 1, 1991, pp. 17–24.

6.   See the two Open Files on distance education in *Prospects*, Vol. XVIII, Nos. 1 and 2, 1988.

7.   F. Mayor, "Universality, Diversity, Interdependence: The Mission of the University," Address given to the Ninth General Conference of the International Association of Universities, Helsinki, 6 August 1990, p. 8 (DG/90/28).

8.   F. Mayor, Address given at the opening of the UNESCO–African Association of Universities, op. cit., p. 2.

9.   See, and project to the year 2020 or 2050, the facts, analyses and trends of the Open File "Intercultural Bilingual Education in Latin America," *Prospects*, Vol. XX, No. 3, 1990.

10. Ministry of Education and Sciences, Netherlands, *Information on Education*, No. 0-02-F, February 1992.

11. Ibid.

12. E. Ngara, "Making the Most of Limited Resources," *UNESCO Sources*, No. 32, December 1991, p. 14.

PART I

Situation, Challenges and Prospects

The idea
of the university

Changing roles, current crisis

and future challenges

Torsten Husén

Before the 1950s, higher education was hardly a field of scholarly studies, which is paradoxical given the fact that institutions of higher learning were the places where most of the research activities were taking place. There was 'institutional research' at some American universities, in most cases focused on pedagogical and/or instructional problems, but not on studying universities as institutions and the social settings within which they were operating. However, since the late 1960s, higher education has become a rapidly growing field of research, to a large extent, comparative in orientation. A survey and bibliography by Altbach and Kelly (1985) contains 6,901 entries, most of them from the 1970s and early 1980s. Several research

Torsten Husén (Sweden). *Professor Emeritus of International Education at the University of Stockholm and President of the International Academy of Education. Former Director of the Institute of Educational Research (1971–82), Chairman of the Governing Board of the International Institute for Educational Planning (1970–80) and Chairman of the International Association for the Evaluation of Educational Achievement (1962–78). He is the author of some fifty books and hundreds of articles.*

centres have specialized in comparative studies in higher education. A communication network for the exchange of experiences and research has been established by organizations such as the International Council for Educational Development (ICED).

The Carnegie Commission on Higher Education, followed by the Carnegie Council on Policy Studies in Higher Education, dealt primarily with problems of higher education in the United States, but commissioned several comparative studies, such as the one by Ben-David (1977). The Commission dealt with problems of undergraduate education in a long series of reports.

Given this proliferation of material, it would be utterly presumptuous to try to present within the framework of an article like this a more detailed picture of the state of the art in this field. The goal set for the present article has been to present some of the major issues and trends. In order to put the present situation in perspective it has been necessary to begin with a short historical background. In preparing this work I have drawn from my paper on global education written in 1985/86 for the United Nations University.

The concept of the university – a brief historical review

The university as an institution has to be conceived in its historical, cultural and economic setting. From the present vantage-point, in our high-technology, information-based society, it differs enormously from the university established in medieval Europe. It does not, as an organization and with regard to its functions, have much in common even with the German, French or British universities of the mid-nineteenth century. But there are, as we shall see, certain features which are concerned with academic ethos and freedom and which have survived the changing conditions.

In order to obtain a proper perspective of the current situation and the issues that universities in both developed and developing countries must face, it is useful to indicate briefly the main stages in their development process, covering some 800 long years.

The medieval university – a community of masters and students – was a typical example of the guild system. Students wanting access to advanced learning flocked as apprentices to men known for their scholarship. The term 'chair', designating a teaching chair, has been used for centuries to mean a full professorship. Wisdom was, in the beginning, literally lectured *ex cathedra*.

The next stage in the development of the university was inextricably connected with its role in shaping the national state, which needed professionally trained civil servants. Students from countries like Sweden and Norway on the periphery of Europe were sent to continental universities, just as developing countries today send their students to Europe or the United States. Latin established itself as the *lingua franca*. In the 1630s, Comenius (Jan Amos Komensky) produced a widely used textbook entitled *Janua linguarum reserata* (*The Door to the Languages Opened*). An international academic culture with Latin as the medium of communication dominated scholarly Europe.

The idea of cross-national co-operation in culture, science and, not least, education, was indeed a hallmark of the seventeenth century. Francis Bacon, for example, spelt out a plan for such co-operation. In his book *Seminarium universum*, published in 1701, German educator August Wilhelm Francke advanced the idea of internationalizing teachers' education.

The activities of the very respected educationist Comenius should be viewed in such a context. Comenius was convinced that a prerequisite for international co-operation, as well as for educational reform, was a fundamental change in language instruction, that is, in teaching Latin. His concept of '*pansophia*' was closely related to this.

Well into the nineteenth century, universities were solely teaching and training institutions. Research played only an accidental role. But the founding by Wilhelm von Humboldt of a research university in Berlin in the early nineteenth century set an example that was emulated all over the world. Research in most European countries had until the end of the eighteenth century been conducted under the auspices of the academies, such as the Royal Society in Great Britain. The German research university model was emulated in the United States, particularly by the private universities such as Johns Hopkins (which provided only graduate teaching and research), Harvard, Stanford and the University of Chicago.

Before the turn of the present century, a good many American students went to Germany for graduate studies that were not available in the United States. College was the American counterpart of the European upper secondary school. The American secondary school the high school – had developed as an extension of the elementary school, which was further emphasized by the fact that it was run by the local community, whereas the European grammar school – *lycée* or *Gymnasium* – usually was governed by the state. High school, much earlier than the European junior secondary school, became a mass institution.

Until the mid-twentieth century, the university in Europe was an élite institution, typically enrolling 2 to 4 per cent of the relevant age-group. A qualified technical work-force, required by emerging industry and commerce, was trained by tertiary institutions outside the university system, for example by institutes of technology for the training of engineers. Such a binary system was more prevalent in Great Britain than in Germany, where institutes of technology could more easily gain university status. In the United States the Morrill Act of 1862, and the founding of the so-called land grant colleges, opened the doors of universities to 'practical' studies relevant to agriculture and industry.

The transition after the Second World War from an industrial to a service and welfare society, which gave rise to a rapidly growing public sector, has led to a corresponding demand for highly trained manpower in different occupations – social workers, office workers and teachers. During the period from 1950 to 1975 university enrolment 'exploded' in several European countries, the United States and in some developing countries. The university changed from an élite to a mass institution. In his taxonomy of university development Trow (1973) distinguished between three stage: élite, mass and universal. He the dividing line between the élite and mass system at 15 per cent enrolment of the relevant age-group.

The enrolment increase was accompanied by the diversification and specialization of training programmes and research activities and the appearance of the 'multiversity' – a term coined by Kerr (1963) in a book on the development of the large state universities in the United States. 'Practice' entered a scene that had previously been dominated by 'theory', which had enjoyed much higher prestige (*Oxford Review of Education*, 1985). Discussion began on what should be the real objectives of the university in a society where, for example, 20–25 per cent of an age-group went on to tertiary studies. The matter was seriously considered by the Robbins Commission in the United Kingdom in the 1960s and by the U68 Commission in Sweden (Husén, 1977).

During the last few decades a new role for the university has been considered – to provide 'recurrent' education (Tuijnman, 1989) within a strategy of a 'triple alliance' between the world of employment, the government (both local and central) and the education service (Ball, 1985). The National Advisory Body and the University Grants Committee in the United Kingdom a few years ago issued a joint statement about objectives. After taking notice of the fact that specific knowledge quickly becomes outdated, and that the context in which it is applied changes rapidly, it is underlined that 'initial higher education, particularly at diploma and first degree level, should . . . emphasize underlying intellectual, scientific and technological principles rather than provide too narrow specialist knowledge'. The abilities required in modern industry and business include (Ball, 1985, p. 232):

the ability to analyse complex issues, to identify the core problem and the means of solving it, to synthesize and integrate disparate elements, to clarify values, to make effective use of numerical and other information, to work co-operatively and constructively with others, and above all perhaps, to communicate clearly both orally and in writing.

At some American universities centres for continuing education had already benn founded in the 1950s, where professionals were given the opportunity, for a few days or a couple of weeks, to upgrade their competences with the assistance of faculty members.

By and large, the universities in advanced industrial countries have increased the proportion of part-time students who take carefully chosen courses in order qualify for more demanding tasks in their vocational life and to be promoted.

This sketchy review has followed the development of the university in Europe. Third World countries, some of them referred to as 'developing', have followed different northern models, which in some instances have been imbued with indigenous traditions, for example in Japan. After the Second World War, when a great many countries changed their status from colonies to autonomous nations, an enormous need for graduates to run the administration and the professions in the independent countries emerged. Young, promising people who came out of the indigenous secondary schools were sent to Europe or the United States for, in the first place, basic tertiary education. They were thereby educated in the prevailing intellectual and cultural traditions of the host countries.

The universities founded in Africa, Asia and Latin America were often established according to European models. Graduates from these continents were sent to Europe and the United States for advanced degrees in order to provide indigenous faculty to replace expatriates. Those who studied abroad and were assigned teaching positions after the completion of their studies quite naturally emulated the practices established at the institutions where they conducted their studies.

Curricula at universities in the Third World countries have usually been patterned on European models. The 'eurocentric' system of university education has been hampering universities in these countries in releasing endogenous creativity and seeking their own cultural roots. There is, however, a tension between the orientation toward indigenous values and problems, on the one hand, and addressing global problems, on the other, a tension that can only be alleviated or resolved by communication across cultural boundaries.

Irrespective of whether a university is in a high-technology, information-based society or in a developing society still dominated by a subsistence economy, we can identify certain pervasive, and even universal features of higher education, which make higher education, in fact, 'higher'. Can we identify a common core that constitutes 'the idea of the university'? The main part of the present article is devoted to this exercise.

The university as a social system

The university as an institution has always been rigid and conservative, but its ethos of inquiry and pursuit of truth has been radical in the literal sense of the word – that is, going to the roots. This appears as a paradox. How can an institution be conservative *per se* but radical in its mission to the extent of coming into conflict with power centres such as the state or the Church? The explanation lies in the scope of freedom that in spite of everything has been given to the university. Intellectuals, whether they be single authors or linked to some other institution, cannot enjoy the institutional protection that the university can give its inmates. Typically, in important matters the European university for a long time operated under its own jurisdiction.

Attempts from the outside to introduce deep-seated institutional changes have been met with fierce resistance, which has been seen as a conservatism rooted in self-interest. But in this case, self-interest happens to coincide with interests to protect the freedom to search for knowledge.

The university was once established as a community of scholars and students, as a loose, but intimate, association with no hierarchical or bureaucratic superstructure. From the outset, the communicative link between the professor and the students who flocked around his 'chair' was an outstanding feature of the institution. The university could operate within a relatively wide ideological and financial margin set by the state and/or the Church.

Professors at leading universities have today been characterized as 'prima donnas', and the model of traditional university governance as 'professional feudalism' or, more recently as 'organized chaos' or 'garbage'. Universities differ fundamentally from other organizations in society. They are not, as are large commercial enterprises, guided by instrumental and economic rationality towards common, well-defined goals. Maximization of expected values is fundamental to rational action. But an academic organization, such as a university, has no common goals. The goal structure, to say the least, is extremely diffuse.

But the single units, the institutes, departments and 'chairs' represented by individual 'prima donna' scholars, which together constitute a university, possess an ample amount of what the university as a collectivity lacks, namely clear goals. Thus, the university can be conceived as a 'container' for a number of rather independent units (institutes, departments, and, not least, individuals). Each unit pursues goals of its own. The structure is atomistic. Decisions taken at the university level have to be settled by the governing board. The rationality has its focus at the basic operational level where individual academics strive for recognition by finding out better solutions to problems than their colleagues.

Goals of university education

Against the background given above, what could be conceived as the proper goals of the university education? The purpose is not to espouse any particular educational philosophy but rather to try to synthesize certain aspects of the debate that has been going on over the last century and to pinpoint programmes aiming to achieve learning of a more integrative and liberal arts nature. We are here primarily interested in university programmes that try to equip students with what is referred to as liberal or general education. What traditional subjects should be included in a core curriculum? Should these traditional subjects be rearranged so as to achieve the cross-disciplinary mix that would prepare the students to tackle practical problems with which they will be confronted in real life? Is disciplinary structured knowledge more useful in the long run than an ad hoc reorganization that helps tackle actual problems but not unforeseen ones? Thus, the very exposure to problems and information relevant to their solution is a pedagogical issue of the highest importance.

The pedagogical approach conducive to liberal arts education has to be considered. That the 'cognitive map', in terms of specific pieces of information, tends to change rapidly so as to make today's 'approved' knowledge obsolete by

tomorrow is an important fact. This has led to greater emphasis on general cognitive skills, such as problem-solving, rather than on mastery of specific facts. It has also led to greater emphasis on skills to find and sift new knowledge in an era of information explosion to promote the ability to keep up with the changes taking place on the cognitive map.

In order to obtain a perspective on the Western university of today, we could start with the Humboldtian university in Berlin, established with emphasis on research and graduate training which first spread to other parts of Germany and then was emulated in other countries. When John Henry Newman held his famous lecture in 1852 on 'The Idea of a University', making a plea for 'knowledge being its own end' and refuting the Baconian concept of utilitarianism, the idea of research and teaching being conducted in close connection began to materialize at German universities, with institutes and seminars being established around university chairs.

The idea of a university, with research and training of researchers as a main mission, materialized in the United States at Johns Hopkins, which was founded in 1876 and began as a pure graduate school with emphasis entirely on research and training of researchers. Shortly before that, the Land Grant Act (the Morrill Act) had been passed in Congress, which was a breakthrough for a new utilitarian conception of the university, followed some decades later by the extension services that revolutionized agriculture in the United States. In the 1930s, the young President of the University of Chicago, Robert M. Hutchins, launched a 'counter-reformation' which he said should 'take the university back to Cardinal Newman, to Thomas Aquinas, and to Plato and Aristotle'. He succeeded, according to Kerr (1963, p. 17), in reviving the philosophical dialogue, but 'Chicago went on being a modern American university'.

The undergraduate programme introduced by Hutchins was one designed by 'secular absolutists'. Students should be acquainted with absolute and timeless truths. Worthwhile knowledge was to a large extent embodied in a set of

Great Books, which could be listed and identified as what every educated person should know. Thanks to the devoted work by the faculty and a good selection of students, the Chicago undergraduate programme was successful for quite some time in training young people to become 'generalists', to give them a well-rounded liberal education.

Schematically we can distinguish four models on the European and North American scenes, models that have been more or less emulated in the rest of the world (Ben-David, 1977):

The Humboldtian *research university*, where research and teaching were expected to interact from the very beginning of university studies. Studies were to gain experience from the frontiers of knowledge and how these frontiers were extended in order to be prepared as pioneers in their respective professional fields.

The British *residential model* – the 'Oxbridge' model – is built on close informal contacts between students and professors. Such contacts are considered as important for the development of young people as is the attendance of formal lectures and seminars, and have at Oxbridge been formalized by tutorials.

The French *grandes écoles model*, epitomized a state-directed meritocratic society, where professionals with a particular education are regarded as an exquisite élite. These institutions (where no research is conducted) are intellectually and socially highly selective.

The *Chicago model*, developed by Hutchins, was a programme with a strong liberal arts orientation. The ideal was to make students familiar with the thinking of leading personalities in the humanities, sciences and social sciences, and to promote their ability to pursue further studies on their own and to train them to be independent and critical in their study and thinking.

Traditions of the Western university

For centuries, the university, as it emerged in medieval Europe, changed little and slowly. It embodied, as mentioned above, the paradox of being conservative as an institution, but with regard to its intellectual orientation it has tended to be a hotbed of new ideas and innovations, and very often of political radicalism. It was originally created to educate an élite for the Church and the state. It has always tried to establish both a certain distance and autonomy between the two. Briefly, the Western university has been characterized by the following:

It has made a more or less sharp distinction between theory and practice.

It has put a premium on autonomy and aloofness to the extent of complete irrelevance.

It has been both socially and intellectually an élitist institution.

It has tried to be an 'ivory tower', as an institution whose main purpose is to 'seek the truth'.

These four characteristics have also loomed large in universities in other regions of the world, where the European model or models have been emulated.

In 1984, on the occasion of the fiftieth anniversary of the New School for Social Research in New York City, a special issue of its journal *Social Research* reprinted an article by the outstanding political scientist Hans Morgenthau entitled 'Thought and Action'. The article is typical of how a European academic, a German professor no less, sees the university. Morgenthau begins his article with the following dictum (Morgenthau, 1984, p. 143):

Theoretical thinking and action as typical modes of human behaviour are irremediably separated by way of their logical structure. Since politics are in their essence actions, there exists with the same necessity an unbridgeable chasm, an eternal tension between politics and a theoretical science of politics.

Theory tries to understand the empirical world by observing it but without changing it. Practice tries to interfere in the empirical world with the prime purpose of changing it. The *vita contemplativa* (theoretical analysis) is the very negation of the *vita activa* (political action). Morgenthau refers to the *Nichomachean Ethics*, where Aristotle makes a distinction between *theoria* which is the highest form of human activity and is incompatible with *praxis*, which belongs to the realm of politics.

The same views have in a more elaborate way been spelt out by Lobkowicz (1983), Rector of the University of Munich, in an anthology of papers entitled *The Western University on Trial*. At the core of 'the idea of the university', Lobkowicz sees the pursuit of truth. The crisis of the Western university is due to its failure to ask itself the basic question: 'What is the university good for?' The very expression 'the idea of the university' goes back to Cardinal Newman, and his 1852 lectures as founding rector of Dublin University.

The *raison d'être* of universities is usually defended by pragmatic arguments, for example the competitive power of a nation on the world market. But most of the disciplines taught at the university have little, if any, direct bearing on the economic efficiency of a country and its standing in international trade and military competition. Its faculty and researchers feel an overriding obligation to contribute to the extending of the frontiers of knowledge which they see as its fundamental and distinctive mission.

A university is a comprehensive institution with a wide range of disciplines and specialties. The very multiplicity of subjects enables the university to combine professional training with cultural enlightenment. The fact that humanities, social sciences and natural sciences are studied in the same institution gives it the resources to educate well-rounded professionals and not just narrow technocrats. It is particularly important to bridge the gap between humanists and scientists, the 'two cultures' that C. P. Snow spoke about.

According to Lobkowicz, (1983, p. 34):

'The university, as originally conceived, is the only human association in which men can come together solely for the purpose of knowing . . . [it] represents institutionalized theory.' The search for truth is what ultimately justifies the existence of the university. In this view the university serves society best by being itself 'a place for tranquil, disciplined and objective thinking', which is the best way of preparing for any profession.

Most advocates of the ivory-tower model of a university pay at least lip service to the idea that the university should serve society by pursuing things relevant to that society. But these functions, they say, can also and more effectively be fulfilled by other pragmatically oriented institutions. Universities are easily distracted from their tasks, which require a high level of originality and detachment from practical concerns.

The traditional European philosophy about the proper role of the university has had its strongholds at the great research institutions and on the whole at élite universities. But not even at those institutions, depending upon how they perceive their mission, has this philosophy remained unchallenged. One example is the Massachusetts Institute of Technology, which for a long time has played an important role in contributing to policy-making in both technology and economics in the United States. The stance taken by Morgenthau, for example, has increasingly been repudiated by academics determined to break away from the idealistic philosophy of a line of demarcation between *theoria* and *praxis*.

A similar development can be seen in Third World countries where the role of universities in promoting social and economic development has become a major task (see, for example, Thompson et al., 1977). In this study, the focus was on 'promising experiments' going on in LDCs with the purpose of having higher education play a pivotal role in social change.

Crisis and reappraisal
of higher education

Western universities went through a period of
soul-searching self-examination after the period
of trials and tribulations that reached a peak with
the 'events' of 1968. Those who defended the
traditional idea of the university felt that it was
under fire from those who wanted to politicize,
moralize and reform an institution whose 'primary allegiance is to cognitive rationality' (Chapman, 1983, p. 1).

The re-examination was also partly epistemological. Much of the quest for a hermeneut-
ic (understanding) approach was a revulsion
against analytic and utilitarian causal rational-
ism and a call for spiritual unity and moral significance. Here, there was of course an inherent
ambiguity between the two approaches, which
required a delicate balance between them. It was
felt that the Western universities primarily committed to intellectual objectivity and using the
criterion of competitive excellence in their internal promotion did not quite adequately meet
the needs of Third World countries.

Agencies concerned with human and social
development took a much more pragmatic view
of the role of the university in Third World
countries. UNESCO noted that science, being a
product of history and society, 'owes as much to
the social environment as to the work of scientists'. Science interacting with the surrounding
society implies that the developing societies
should try to work out their own scientific and
technological development strategy. Although
the application of science on a long-term basis
calls for analyses of global problems, it has to recognize the importance of local cultures and the
needs of the people who share that culture. In its
Medium-Term Plan for 1977–82 the Organization points out that the new concept of development puts man in the centre of development. A
major objective should be the 'promotion of the
formulation of a global, multidisciplinary interpretation of development, having regard to the
interrelations between the various factors contri-

buting to this, and which are, in return, affected
by it'. In a presentation to an African audience
the Director-General of UNESCO pointed out
that in the developing countries the university
has a key role where students and teachers from
a wide variety of background can work together,
'combining training and research, study and
production, tradition and progress, attachment
to one's identity and responsiveness to the
world, in the work of pursuing the objectives of
the community' (Sanyal, 1982, p. 8). In 1986,
within the framework of the UNESCO Medium-Term Plan, the Division of Higher Education adopted certain principles of action, among
them giving priority in higher education to endogenous national development, avoiding élitism and giving national policies precedence over individual options, and promoting institution
co-operation, as a means of bridging the gap between countries at different stages of development.

The ivory-tower philosophy has, as we have
seen, been challenged over the last couple of decades. The 'ecology' of higher education has
changed rapidly since the early 1950s. University enrolment has multiplied manifold. It thereby
changed from an élite to a mass institution
(Trow, 1973). Research began to be supported
by governments on a massive scale. People began to talk about 'mega-science'. The increased
financial support from public sources gave rise
to demands for accountability and influence on
the part of public interest groups on university
governance. Whether the academics wanted it
or not they became closely involved with government and industry, not least by undertaking
large-scale commissioned projects. The body of
research grew and was greatly enriched as new
areas of study were introduced. *Verwissenschaft-
ligung* ('scientification') created hopes that research would add a new dimension of rationality
to decision-making in public affairs. Hopes were
high for what science could achieve in improving the human condition (see, for example,
Lundberg, 1947). The tendency to 'vocationalize' university education at a time when demand
for highly trained manpower was greater than
the supply was met by opposition on the part of

students who wanted 'genuine education', and also reacted against the neglect they felt they were being subjected to in an era of rapidly increasing resources for research, when professors cared more about their research projects than about their teaching.

The uproar at the University of Paris in 1968 illustrated what can happen when student disenchantment reaches an explosive level. The then Minister of Education Edgar Faure, architect of the *loi d'orientation* (guideline legislation) of 1968, outlined in a book his diagnosis of the French situation and the objectives of the new law (Faure, 1969). The book includes a presentation given by him at the General Conference of UNESCO in 1968. He regarded the student upheaval as a crisis of communication, at the root of which, politically, was the double problem of autonomy and participation. He quotes a UNESCO report on how young people, who learn, through modern news media, about different cultures tend to form a separate international youth culture in opposition to adult cultures, locked into traditional schemes. The protesters were concerned about the war in Viet Nam and violently opposed to the consumer society which was seen as depriving individuals of their self-determination. Faure also pointed out the imbalance, in terms of enrolment, between faculties and disciplines. In France, six students out of ten were enrolled in the humanities and social sciences, and only one out of four in the natural sciences. The planning document prepared by the Commissariat du Plan pointed out that at least twice as many science graduates were needed.

The new university, guided by the principles of autonomy and participation, needed a new pedagogy based on a dialogue and not just a transfer of knowledge which, once it has accumulated a certain stock, was assessed by 'punctual examinations'. Furthermore, universities should realize that teamwork was called for, because in the real world this was a basic mode of work, not least in the field of management. The new category of students who, to a large extent, come from homes without a tradition of advanced education, would gain most from such

changes in teaching strategies. More emphasis had to be put on learning how to learn in university courses, as well as on teaching how to teach.

Foreign study, cultural authenticity and internationalization

The number of students attending universities outside their home countries has increased more than tenfold worldwide over the last thirty years. The motive for studying abroad is, in the first place, to obtain good professional training that either cannot be had in the home country or, if available, is considered inferior to that of the foreign country. Graduate studies at leading institutions in other countries is, at the very least, a means of transferring competence and knowledge essential for economic and social development in the home country. Study abroad has been an appropriate educational remedy for the human capital needs of developing countries.

Even though foreign study has gone through a period of spectacular expansion over the last few decades, it has a long history. Leading universities established themselves on the European continent much earlier than in countries on the periphery, where they were unable to reach the level of quality of the continental ones. Students from peripheral countries flocked to the universities of Germany and France. Latin served as the *lingua franca* and had the same instrumental value for international communication in the academic world as English and French have today.

In addition to the pragmatic goal of obtaining useful profession training, a period of study abroad contributes to a broader cross-cultural perspective for the student. A deepened knowledge of the human condition in other cultures contributes to promoting international discourse and understanding.

Until the early 1970s, international and other agencies dealing with development believed that higher education was the key to economic take-off in countries newly liberated from colonial rule. A few highly trained individuals would have a multiplier effect and were expected to bring about a take-off in the education system as well. Foreign study would be the fastest route for replacing expatriate manpower and making provisions for rapid economic development.

In the 1970s there was a shift in priorities, noticeable for example in the World Bank's educational policy for the Third World, which changed from giving priority to post-secondary education to meeting the basic educational needs of the poor. At the same time, doubts were being raised about the value of the advanced higher education provided at leading universities in the North. The categories of thinking imparted at foreign universities were those of 'normal science' in these countries. The relevance of the subject matter presented and the frame of reference for it was called into question. Students from the developing world coming to 'central' countries for graduate studies were incorporated into the scientific-technological, market-dominated infrastructure of these countries. Underlying all this were the epistemological and philosophical foundations of the Western countries with a research orientation and attitudes towards teaching and curricula which reflected highly developed and affluent economies. The emulation of the professional models of countries at the 'centre' did not always contribute to liberating indigenous creativity and self-reliance.

Given this background, the very idea of studying in central countries has been challenged. Weiler (1984, p. 177), for example, sees the dependence on academic training provided by central countries as 'the more significant obstacle to cultural authenticity'. We are faced here with a serious dilemma that looms large. How can bright students from developing countries be given an opportunity to develop their potential without being sent to the best central universities?

How can cultural authenticity and the cultivation of local and/or national traditions and paradigms of inquiry be preserved in higher education in a world of increasing interdependence? The modes of inquiry and the entire intellectual orientation of universities have traditionally, since the seventeenth century, been universal in character. Scholars have been searching for universal truths and universally valid principles. Latin was, as pointed out above, in spite of linguistic, cultural and other differences, the language of scholarly communication. Students from the backward and underdeveloped countries in the North went to Paris, Prague and Leyden for their studies, which were conducted in Latin. One could easily find parallels in earlier centuries to countries at the 'centre' and 'periphery' respectively.

The idea of the university as it is still espoused in Europe and North America has dominated Western science. In his Introduction to *The Western University on Trial*, Professor J. W. Chapman, a political scientist, points out in considering the predicament of Western universities by 1980: 'No other civilization – not the Chinese, Indian or Islamic – invented an institution specialized for intellectual education; this is unique to the West' (Chapman, 1983, p. 1). But he is keenly aware of the tension between individualistic rationality and the desire for spirited unity and moral significance. This internal ambiguity calls for a delicate balance between truth-seeking and relevance.

Comenius was convinced that the main prerequisite for educational reforms of international proportion was a common language of instruction in higher education. To this effect, in 1631 he published his *Janua linguarum reserata*. It was a phenomenal success and was translated into twelve European languages as well as Arabic, Persian and Mongolian. Alfred North Whitehead once referred to the seventeenth century as the 'century of genius' with outstanding scientists, such as Bacon, Galileo, Kepler and Locke. He could just as well have referred to it as the century of genius in the realm of international relations, where scientists and philosophers were able to communicate with each other through the *bona officia* of the new academies, such as the British Royal Society and the Académie Royale des Sciences in France. Intellectual communications were established between scholars in Europe and the Far East. Along with internationalism went growing pluralism and religious tolerance in countries like the Netherlands, spurred by the expulsion of religious dissenters from other countries.

Internationalism in the seventeenth century was marked by more than a dozen proposals for a universal language. There was almost the same number of cultural utopias and schemes for educational co-operation, such as Bengt Skytte's 'Sophopolis' (Brickman, 1983/84). Inspired by Comenius he spelt out the idea of establishing centres or cities of learned and wise men drawn from many countries. Such centres were conceived as islands in a world of intolerance, censorship and persecution. At least two universities, Padua and Leyden, had multinational faculties and student bodies. The idea of cross-national co-operation in culture, science and, not least, education was indeed a hallmark of the seventeenth century. Francis Bacon developed a plan for such co-operation.

Revising the undergraduate curriculum

Before the Age of Enlightenment both the school and the university curriculum were based on faith – reverence for the past and firm trust in authority. Already before the impact of the Enlightenment a change was elicited by the Cartesian mode of thought. It proceeded with Sir Isaac Newton and was completed by the Encyclopedists, a development that led to nineteenth-century positivism. Even though there was a decline in the dominance of the Scriptures, the classical heritage, with Latin and Greek playing key roles, prevailed for a long time. Classical studies were considered to be the core of *culture générale*.

A curriculum is often perceived in terms of subjects that should be studied for so many years and for so many periods a week, as well as in terms of the sequence of topics within each subject. The choice of subject areas and their relative importance, as reflected in how much teaching should be devoted to them, is usually controversial because it is concerned with the relative importance and power of the various academic organizations. Thus, territorial conflicts easily flare up. The problem of composing a well-rounded curriculum becomes particularly difficult and vexing because the academic reward system promotes narrow specialization and therefore works against the cross-disciplinary approaches necessary for a concerted effort in tackling real-life problems. There are always difficulties in trying to achieve a consensus on what subjects should constitute the core curriculum in studies organized to achieve the aims of a 'liberal' or 'general' education.

If an institution of higher learning wishes to turn out graduates with a well-rounded education with the dual aim of preparing them both as professionals and as educated persons, a difficult selection has to be made from the considerable choice of courses offered. Each of the various departments are offering many courses from which the selection has to be made. The great variety of such courses, each with a rather diluted body of information, easily leads to what could be called multidisciplinary illiteracy. Superficial knowledge replaces study in depth, and the great many short courses easily prevent the development of analytical skills and of critical, independent study which ought to be the by-products of in-depth study.

On two occasions, in 1943 and 1978, Harvard University appointed committees, with the mission of inquiring into the problem of devising a curriculum of well-rounded general education for undergraduate students. The Red Book, as the 1946 Harvard report, *General Education in a Free Society*, is known, went to some length to put the issues of undergraduate curricula into the framework of modern, democratic society. Given its premises, democracy evidently carries the germ of 'discord and even fundamental divergence of standards'. On the other hand, democracy cannot function unless there are some 'binding ties of common standards'. This dilemma has to be resolved by the educational institution, which must help establish a common frame of reference of standards and beliefs without which democracy cannot survive.

Thus an undergraduate curriculum would have to achieve two overriding objectives – heritage and change, and communality in outlook and diversity. In their discussion of the principles upon which a core curriculum 'for survival' should be based, Boyer and Kaplan (1978) point out that every core curriculum in the past has been guided by a vision of communality. To be sure, all the students should be equipped with some basic, discipline-structured competence. But they should also learn to be self-conscious in relation to tradition. This goes beyond 'knowing', it means knowing *how* and *why* we know. The core curriculum they propose is 'built on the proposition that students should be encouraged to investigate how we are one as well as many (*e pluribus unum*)' (Boyer and Kaplan, 1978, p. 58).

Boyer and Kaplan consider the following three domains as the commonality, the 'core' of a common undergraduate 'survival' curriculum. First, history that makes students aware and knowledgeable about the common heritage, a history taught without bias and with a minimum of national ideology. Second, exposure to the broad range of issues raised by our common existence. This means 'comprehensive literacy' in terms of mother-tongue and various 'languages', including computer language and mathematics. It also means studies of institutions in present society and their impact on us as individuals and on our roles as producers and consumers. Finally, preparation for the future on the basis of knowledge about the present situation. Depletion of natural resources, proliferation of nuclear weapons, overcrowding and mass starvation, and unbalanced economic distribution are some of the main problems faced by a world of increasing interdependence.

In 1978 the second Harvard Committee produced a *Report on Core Curriculum*. Out of 100 courses, the committee proposed a selection of eight, with the intent of equipping undergraduates with a common core of learning but *not*

with a body of common teaching. The committee proposed that every undergraduate student should take at least one course in each of the following areas: literature and the arts, history, social and philosophical analysis, and foreign languages and cultures. Emphasis in the teaching and learning in these fields should be put on the 'mode of understanding' in the respective fields. In the discussion on the core curriculum, many participants pointed out the importance of putting emphasis on the modes of inquiry in the major fields of intellectual discourse instead of trying to present comprehensive courses with a large amount of more or less unstructured and unanalysed information.

Dilemmas in preparing an undergraduate curriculum

In preparing its curricula, the university is faced with a dual task: on the one hand, it is expected to prepare its students to generate new knowledge. On the other hand, it is in charge of imparting already-existing knowledge to a new generation of professionals. These two tasks easily come into conflict with each other, since most students do not intend to go in for research and are not interested in it. Those aiming for a research career are more interested in transforming existing knowledge than accepting what already exists.

Another dilemma has to do with specialization as against general or comprehensive overviews. Evidently, in-depth study in a given field generates solid competence in that particular field but easily leads to a narrow perspective and weakens the ability to acquire new knowledge when the subject matter learned becomes obsolete. One solution to this dilemma has been to recommend a core curriculum that provides a common frame of reference for all students. It gives them an opportunity to test their interests and abilities and can thereby serve as a launching pad for subsequent specialization. The danger of too much specialization at the undergraduate level has been given much attention. But considering the exponential growth of research, coupled with enormous specialization, there is ample reason to be concerned about too much specialization at the graduate (doctoral) level as well.

A well-rounded, general education is concerned not only with cognitive objectives but also with emotional and moral development. It is also concerned with the cultivation of values. When, in 1943, James B. Conant, the President of Harvard University, appointed a committee on 'General Education in a Free Society' with the task of looking into the proper curriculum for the 'great majority' of young people and not only the 'comparatively small minority that attends the universities or colleges', he said in the Introduction to the report (Harvard Committee, 1945, pp. viii et seq.):

The heart of the problem of a general education is the continuance of the liberal and humane tradition. Neither the mere acquisition of information nor the development of special skills and talents can give the broad basis for understanding which is essential if our civilization is to be preserved. No one wishes to disparage the importance of being 'well-informed'. But even a good grounding in mathematics and the physical and biological sciences, combined with an ability to read and write several foreign languages, does not provide sufficient educational background for citizens of a free nation. For such a program lacks contact with both man's emotional experience as an individual and his practical experience as a gregarious animal. It includes little of what was once known as the 'wisdom of the ages', and might nowadays be described as 'our cultural pattern'. It includes no history, no art, no literature, no philosophy. Unless the educational process includes *at each level of maturity* some continuing contact with those fields, it must fall short of the ideal. The student in high school, in college, and in graduate school must be concerned, in part at least, with the words 'right' and 'wrong' in both the ethical and the mathematical sense. Unless he feels the import of those general ideas and aspirations that have been a deep moving force in the lives of men, he runs the risk of partial blindness.

These words were spoken in 1945, before the real enrolment explosion had begun in the United States, not to mention Europe. But the massification at the undergraduate level with the accompanying diversity among students with regard to background, intellectual ability, interest and expectations, has created a situation where major changes are called for. One of the strategies developed to cope with the new situation has been the establishment of the comprehensive university, the 'multiversity' Clark Kerr referred to in his Godkin lectures in 1963, or the *Gesamthochschule* that hardly took off in Germany after the unrest of the late 1960s. The establishment of the comprehensive university occurred for various motives. In the Swedish U68 reform, the bringing of all students to large comprehensive institutions of higher learning, a *högskola*, was considered to be beset with the same virtues as the setting up of comprehensive secondary schools. In addition to providing a common frame of reference one would also be able to inculcate egalitarian values.

Closely related to comprehensivization as a response to 'massification' were, in many countries, systematic attempts to vocationalize the programmes, particularly those in the faculties of arts and sciences. Every university programme should lead to a given vocational sector; this was, for example, the case in Sweden. In this context, attempts were made to disconnect teaching from its disciplinary orientation and incorporate cross-disciplinary approaches as learning strategies.

It is perhaps too early to pass more definitive judgement on the policy of comprehensive institutions introduced in Europe in the 1970s. As pointed out by Cerych (1980), there has been an 'appreciable loss of momentum in certain ambitious reforms', and the late 1970s have been a period of 'reform dissolution'. He makes particular reference to the French 'orientation law' of 1968. He refers to the time-honoured belief that one cannot change institutions that have existed for many centuries overnight (Husén, 1986).

Goal conflicts

The modern university is expected to work towards many different goals. It has to fulfil its traditional goal of training professionals. It is expected to promote equality of educational opportunity by giving access to university education to underprivileged groups. It is expected to contribute to the extension of the frontiers of knowledge by high-quality research. It is expected to serve the national economy by carrying out research which will benefit national industry and trade. In some countries it is also expected to let different interested parties participate in its governance. Evidently, all these goals are far from compatible with each other. Some are in direct conflict, such as competence and quality with participation, or equality with quality. We shall elaborate here on the former goal conflict.

Research cannot be organized within the same managerial straitjackets that have been adopted for undergraduate programmes in rapid expansion, or in an emergency situation of enrolment explosion. There is a fundamental conflict between research, on the one hand, which needs plenty of elbow room for discretionary decisions to be taken by individual scholars or assemblies of qualified scientists and, on the other hand, the bureaucratic and hierarchical control of work and the output. This conflict has become aggravated by other conflicts since the 1960s. Thus we have witnessed the conflict between the application of intellectual criteria in academic appointments and the exercise of important power by being elected to serve on decision-making bodies, representing particular interest groups. Academic competence has been forced to yield to the power of numbers. If such a conflict pertains to matters in which academic qualifications are indispensable, the solution may damage the standard of work at the university, be it research or teaching.

Centralized government of universities with detailed control exercised through an administrative hierarchy has grown stronger in recent decades in several countries. This has come into conflict not only with academic freedom but also with vociferous demands for student or junior faculty participation.

Perhaps the most serious conflict of roles is the one between competence and participation. On one side, we have the insistence on collegial autonomy exercised by scholars whose competence has been thoroughly assessed in peer reviews and, on the other, we have hierarchical decision-making machinery that takes decisions in assemblies constituted by representation of interest groups and executed through a hierarchical administration.

Present trends
and future challenges

As pointed out above, well into the twentieth century the university mainly served as an institution training professionals for the state or the Church – lawyers, priests and physicians. The faculty of philosophy had a preparatory function – to lay the foundations of general competence needed in order to be able to absorb more specialized knowledge.

In the late twentieth century, higher education has assumed new important functions, such as in-service training of professionals. At the same time enrolment, in terms of the proportion of the relevant age-group enroling, has increased enormously. As late as 1950 the typical percentage entering the university in the industrial countries was 2 to 4 per cent. Over three decades it has increased to typically 15–20 per cent. The university was transformed from an élite to a mass institution. Before the onset of the financial crisis in the 1970s it seemed as if the third stage, universal higher education, would soon be reached. Three features stand out today.

First, a university degree has become a prerequisite for an increasing number of occupations, which thereby have become professionalized. By the fact of being trained in institutions where research is conducted, a professional status has been conferred to, for example, social workers and certain categories of teachers.

Second, a well-rounded general, liberal arts-oriented education has established itself at the undergraduate level. This has particularly been the case in the United States, where the college was established as a substitute for the European *lycée* or *Gymnasium*. In many countries, university studies have traditionally been very pragmatic and goal-oriented. They train civil servants, secondary-school teachers, medical practitioners, etc. In a rapidly changing society, where specific competencies easily become obsolete, both the public and the private sectors have realized the usefulness of employing well educated 'generalists' who are trained to employ analytical techniques in problem-solving.

Third, whereas before the end of the nineteenth century research played a subordinate role or was even non existent at the university, it has today (with the United States taking the lead) become professional. Research institutes have a staff of full-time researchers who have considerably reduced or even eliminated teaching loads. This applies particularly to the best universities. Can we expect these trends to prevail in the future? There are many indications that they will. We will point out some of them below.

Professionalization in terms of research-based vocational education will increase in a high technology and information-based society. This will result in an increased enrolment in tertiary institutions both of young people of 'normal' university age and adults who have already spent a considerable number of years working. Recurrent or lifelong education will become a pervasive element in the life of the majority, particularly among those who already have received further formal education. The collaboration between the university and business and industry will gradually increase in terms of enterprises buying complete packages of courses for their employees.

The need for 'generalists' with well-rounded education in leading positions, persons with good analytical training, keen receptivity and independence, will increase. In a rapidly changing society there is a need for leaders with a wide margin of adaptability who also possess the ability and the moral power to steer changes towards desired goals.

Research and development will play an increasingly dominant role and permeate both productive and social life. The role of the university is primarily to produce fundamental knowledge that can then be applied not only in the training of professionals but also in the development of new techniques and products.

To what extent should the university provide its students with moral and ethical guidance? Such a task is, of course, extremely delicate in a pluralistic society. But if there is such a thing as an academic ethos, the core of it is the pursuit of truth which traditionally is the guiding ethical principle for research.

Closely related to the task of providing ethical guidance is the critical function of the university. This is a radical task in the literal sense of the word. Academic freedom in terms of freedom of expression has often brought the university into conflict with centres of power, the state or the Church. It is difficult for the state to accept that those who eat from its hand may also sometimes bite it!

Modern society is dominated by industrial mass production of goods and by increased public services in health, education and welfare. There is an expanding body of information that the ordinary citizen must master in order to survive. Such a society needs a tertiary system of education with widened functions and expanded enrolment. Whether the mega-institutions emerging are called universities or not is a matter of taste. The 'multiversity' has come to stay, at least in advanced high-technology societies.

If higher education develops to become not only a mass but almost a universal good, we can begin to ask what is 'higher' in higher education. But all social systems have a tendency to adapt themselves to new frameworks. We can note how, by differentiation, an élite sector in a mass system is emerging. Certain institutions or programmes stand out as more demanding, and therefore became more prestigious, such as the study of medicine. In the United States and Ja-

pan the co-existence of public and private universities has brought about a differentiation and
a 'pecking order' within the system. In the United States the private universities have taken the
lead, whereas in Japan the 'imperial', that is, the
state universities, are the most prestigious.

In a pluralistic society moving towards increased specialization and differentiation, the
need for a common core of learning becomes
more urgent than before. The more specialization goes on and the earlier in life it is introduced, the more the individual is doomed to sol-
itude. Thus, more than ever, the goal for
institutions of higher learning is to education
generalists – a professional élite with a common
core of learning that provides them with a common frame of reference.

Growing research and development, particularly in modern high technology industry, has
given rise to partnerships between universities
and private enterprises with regard to training,
retraining of staff and research. Universities
have begun to play an important role in in-service training of professionals and in providing
educational services to labour-market organizations.

However, partnerships between universities and corporations are not without their problems. The common denominator of these is
that university resources are easily diverted from
the traditional tasks – the education of students
and the conducting of fundamental research.
Authorities and students are asking whether the
enterprises really are footing the entire bill, particularly for contracted research. It is difficult to
estimate how much of the costs are covered by
the public purse from which a university is financed. Another problem is that of continuity.
Research contracts imply employing staff for
projects over a short time span. When a project is
finished, the head of a department is faced with
the problem of finding a means of livelihood for
those who worked on the project. Short-term involvement in 'applied' projects with its effects on
continuity is a disadvantage for basic research
which works with a distant time horizon.

Innovation in business corporations is not
an end in itself, whereas it is usually the case in
university research where scholars seek knowledge for its own sake. Corporations operate under the competitive pressure of the marketplace. Their goal is to serve consumer needs
with products, to improve means of production,
enhance technical know-how and to meet dea-
dlines. Pursuing research for its own sake, as is
the custom in universities, is done without the
restrictions of the market. The 'market' is the international community of scholars where the value of research results is assessed according to
internal science-specific criteria.

The partnership between university and
government is beset with the same problems,
which have become more acute over the last few
decades, when universities have contracted
large projects with central or local governments.
A major challenge for the future seems to be to
maintain fundamental research as a principal
function of the university. It is the only place
where activities aiming at the extension of the
frontiers of knowledge is institutionalized.

The university plays an important role in
the establishment and preservation of cultural
and historical identity. The national leaders in a
newly independent country are often university-
educated, and the creation of at least one national university has usually been a top priority when
a former colonial territory has gained national
independence. Studies and research in the humanities, particularly in history, are often of ut-
most importance in the establishment and preservation of national identity.

Academic freedom and autonomy, particularly *vis-à-vis* the state, will continue to be an
overriding issue. This relationship is delicate
and has to be discussed making a distinction between 'dependency' and 'intervention'. Universities in most countries are financially highly dependent on the state, and in many cases teaching
staff are appointed by the Ministry of Education.
But the scope for intervention can be very limited, most often due to the civil-service status of
professors with life tenure.

The academic ethos at Western universities, according to which the overriding objectives of the university is 'to seek the truth', an activity seen as separate from the total

responsibility for social and human affairs of the surrounding society or the world as a whole, represents an issue that has become particularly relevant in modern 'risk' societies with their close relationships to research. This issue is closely related to the dichotomy between theory and practice.

A balance has to be struck between endogenous creativity and independence of the dominant intellectual streams from Europe and North America and the universalist orientation necessary in science and technology in attempts to tackle pressing global problems.

Universities in Third World countries, both in their teaching and research, have to address social and human development in their own regions and countries, but must also help open up the perspectives of their students to problems of a universal character. This again is a problem of a delicate balance between parochialism and internationalism.

General or 'liberal' versus specialized education will continue to be a pervasive issue. It cannot be resolved by comprehensive courses in various disciplines but by the style of learning adopted in the field of specialization. It is concerned with learning, which goes beyond any encyclopedic knowledge in a particular field, a learning centred around intellectual skills and academic values. ∎

References and bibliography

ALTBACH, P. G. (ed.). 1975. *The University's Response to Societal Demands*. New York, International Council for Educational Development.

ALTBACH, P. G.; KELLY, D. H. 1985. *Higher Education in International Perspective: A Survey and Bibliography*. London/New York, Mansell Publishing.

ASPEN INSTITUTE FOR HUMANISTIC STUDIES. 1984. *European and American Universities – Their Responsibilities at the End of the 20th Century*. Berlin, Aspen Institute for Humanistic Studies. (Report No. 4.)

BALL, C. 1985. The Triple Alliance: What Went Wrong? What Can Be Done? *Oxford Review of Education*, Vol. II, No. 3, pp. 227–34.

BEICHMAN, A. 1983. Is Higher Education in the Dark Ages? *The New York Times Magazine*, 6 November.

BEN-DAVID, J. 1977. *Centers of Learning: Britain, France, Germany, United States*. New York, McGraw Hill.

BERGENDAL, G. 1981. *Higher Education and Knowledge Policy: A Personal View*. Malmö, School of Education.

——. 1983/84. Knowledge Traditions in Higher Education. *Western European Education*. Vol. XV, No. 4.

BLACKBURN, R., et al. 1976. *Changing Practices in Undergraduate Education*. Berkeley, Carnegie Council for Policy Studies in Higher Education.

BOTKIN, J. W.; ELMANDJRA, M.; MALITZA, M. 1979. *No Limits to Learning: Bridging the Human Gap*. Oxford, Pergamon Press.

BOYER, E. L.; KAPLAN; M. 1977. *Educating for Survival*. New Rochelle, N.Y., Change Magazine Press.

BRICKMAN, W. W. 1983/84. Swedish Supernationalist in Education, Science and Culture: Bengt Skytte (1614–1683). *Western European Education*, Vol. XV, No. 4.

BURN, B. B. 1980. *Expanding the International Dimension of Higher Education*. San Francisco, Jossey-Bass.

CERYCH, L. 1980. Retreat from Ambitious Goals? *European Journal of Education*, Vol. 15, No. 1.

CHAIT, E. F. 1975. *The Useful Arts and the Liberal Tradition*. New York, McGraw-Hill.

CHAPMAN, J. W. (ed.). 1983. *The Western University on Trial*. Berkeley, University of California Press.

Comparative Education Review. 1984. Special issue: *Foreign Students in Comparative Perspective*. Vol. 28, No. 2. University of Chicago Press.

DIRKS, W., et al. 1983. *Existenzwissen*. Frankfurt/Main, Neue Verlagsgesellschaft. (Frankfurter Hefte, Extra, 5.)

FAURE, E. 1969. *La philosophie d'une réforme*. Paris, Pont.

FAURE, E., et al. 1972. *Learning to Be*. Paris/London, UNESCO/Harrap.

FOUCAULT, M. 1966. *Les mots et les choses*. Paris, Gallimard.

HARVARD COMMITTEE. 1945. *General Education in a Free Society. Report of the Harvard Committee*. With an Introduction by James Bryant Conant. Cambridge, Mass., Harvard University Press.

HEILBRONNER, R. 1974. *An Inquiry into the Human Prospect*. New York, Norton.

HUSÉN, T. 1976/77. Swedish University Research at the Crossroads. *Minerva*, Vol. 14, No. 4, pp. 419–46.

——. 1979. General Theories in Education: A Twenty-five Year Perspective. *International Review of Education*, Vol. 25.

——. 1980. A Marriage to Higher Education. *Journal of Higher Education*, Vol. 51, No. 6.

——. 1985. International Education. *International Encyclopedia of Education: Research and Studies*. Oxford, Pergamon Press.

——. 1986. *The Learning Society Revisited*. Oxford, Pergamon Press.

HUSÉN, T.; KOGAN, M. (eds.). 1984. *Educational Research and Policy: Research and Studies*. Oxford, Pergamon Press.

HUTCHINS, R. M. 1969. *The Learning Society*. New York, Praeger.

INKELES, A.; SIROWY, L. 1985. Convergent and Divergent Trends in National Educational Systems. *Social Forces: An International Journal of Social Research.* Vol. 62, No. 2.

JENCKS, C.; RIESMAN, D. 1968. *The Academic Revolution.* New York, Doubleday.

KAYSEN, C. (ed.). 1973. *Content and Context: Essays on College Education.* New York, McGraw-Hill.

KERR, C. 1963. *The Uses of the University.* New York, Harper & Row.

KUHN, T. 1962. *The Structure of Scientific Revolutions.* Chicago, University of Chicago Press.

LEVINE, A. 1978. *Handbook on Undergraduate Curriculum.* San Francisco, Jossey-Bass.

LOBKOWICS, N. 1983. Man, Pursuit of Truth and the University. In: J. W. Chapman (ed.), *The Western University on Trial.* Berkeley, University of California Press.

LUNDBERG, G. A. 1947. *Can Science Save Us?* New York, Longmans, Green.

MORGENTHAU, H. 1984. Thought and Action in Politics. *Social Research 50th Anniversary.* New York, New School for Social Research.

MULLER, R. 1985. A World Core Curriculum. In: V. Yogendra (ed.), *Future Education.* Warwick (Australia), Centre Publications.

NEAVE, G. (ed.). 1978. *Recession and Retrenchment. Review of New Trends in European Higher Education.* Special issue of *Paedogogica Europaea,* Vol. 13, No. 1.

NEWMAN, J. H. 1947. *The Idea of a University.* New York, Longmans, Green.

Oxford Review of Education. 1985. Special issue: *Higher Education, the State and the Economy: An Anglo-American Symposium.* Vol. II, No. 3.

Prospects, Vol. III, No. 4, 1973. Special issue on the European University in Change.

RIESMAN, D. 1980. *On Higher Education.* San Francisco, Jossey-Bass.

ROSENGREN, F. H., et al. 1983. *Internationalizing Your School.* New York, National Council on Foreign Language and International Studies.

RUDOLPH, F. 1977. *Curriculum: A History of the American Undergraduate Course of Study Since 1636.* New York, McGraw-Hill.

SANYAL, B. C. (ed.). 1982. *Higher Education and the New International Order: A Collection of Essays.* London, Pinter.

SEABURY, P. (ed.). 1975. *Universities in the Western World.* New York/London, The Free Press.

SIMMONS, A.; WILSON, J. Q. 1980. Harvard's Revision: Two Views. *Dialogue,* Vol. 13, No. 1.

SOEDJATMOKO. 1985. The International Dimension of Universities in an Interdependent World. Address given at the eighth General Conference of the International Association of Universities, UCLA, 12 August.

TEICHLER, U. 1983. Hochschule und Beschäftigungssystem. *Enzyklopädie Erziehungswissenschaft,* Vol. 10. Stuttgart, Klett Kotta.

THOMPSON, K. W.; VOGEL, B. R.; DANNER, H. E. 1977. *Higher Education and Social Change.* New York, Praeger.

TROW, M. 1973. *Problems in the Transition from Élite to Mass Higher Education.* Berkeley, Carnegie Commission on Higher Education.

——. 1981. Comparative Perspectives on Access to Higher Education. Paper prepared for the Leverhulme Seminar on Demand and Access, Edinburgh.

TUIJNMAN, A. 1989. *Recurrent Education, Earnings and Well-being.* Stockholm, Almqvist & Wiksell International.

WEILER, H. 1984. Political Dilemma of Foreign Study. *Comparative Education Review.* Vol. 28, No. 2.

Western European Education. 1976. Special issue: *Mass Higher Education and the Élitist Tradition.* Vol. VIII, No. 1/2.

Patterns in higher education development

Towards the year 2000*

Philip G. Altbach

Universities are singular institutions. They have common historical roots yet are deeply embedded in their societies. Traditionally élite institutions, modern universities have provided social mobility to previously disenfranchised groups. Established in the medieval period to transmit established knowledge and provide training for a few key professions, universities over the centuries have become the most important creators of new knowledge through basic research.[1] The contemporary university stands at the centre of its society, an institution which is crucial to every modern society. It is the most important institution in the complex process of knowledge creation and distribution, not only serving as home to most basic science but also to the increasingly complex system of journals, books and data bases which communicate knowledge worldwide.[2]

Universities are the key to providing training in an ever-increasing number of specializations that are important for modern societies. Universities have also taken on a political function in society – they often serve as centres of political thought, and sometimes of action, and they train those who become members of the political élite. This article is concerned with discussing the patterns of higher-education development evident in the post-Second World War period throughout the world and in analysing some of the reasons for these trends and will point to likely directions for universities in the coming decades. Questions such as autonomy and accountability, the role of research and teaching, reform and the curriculum and the implications of the massive expansion that has characterized universities in most countries are of primary concern here. Universities are simultaneously international institutions, with common historical roots, and are also embedded in national cultures and circumstances. It is worth while to examine the contemporary challenges to higher education in both a historical and comparative perspective.

Philip G. Altbach (United States of America). *Professor, Director of the Comparative Education Center, State University of New York at Buffalo. He has written widely on higher education, and is most recently Editor of* International Encyclopedia of Comparative Higher Education *(1990). Former Editor of* Comparative Education Review.

* The author is indebted to Robert Arnove, Gail P. Kelly and Lionel Lewis for their comments on this article and to Lalita Subramanyan for her assistance with editing.

A common heritage

There is only one common academic model worldwide. The basic European university model, which was established first in France in the thirteenth century, has been significantly modified but remains the universal pattern of higher education. The Paris model placed the professor at the centre of the institution and enshrined autonomy as an important part of the academic ethos. It is significant that the major competing idea of the period, the student-dominated University of Bologna in Italy, did not gain a major foothold in Europe, although it had some impact in Spain and later in Latin America.[3] The university rapidly expanded to other parts of Europe – Oxford and Cambridge in England, Salamanca in Spain, Prague and Krakow in the Slavic areas and a variety of institutions in Germany were established in the following century.

Much later, European imperialist nations brought universities to their colonies. The British, for example, exported academic models first to the American colonies and later to India, Africa and South-East Asia;[4] the French in Viet Nam and West Africa; the Spanish and Portuguese throughout Latin America; the Dutch in Indonesia. Other colonial powers also exported academic institutions. Colonial universities were patterned directly on institutions in the mother country, but often without the traditions of autonomy and academic freedom that the latter enjoyed.[5]

The university was by no means a static institution. It changed and adapted to new circumstances. With the rise of nationalism and the Protestant Reformation in Europe, the universal language of higher education, Latin, was replaced by national languages. Academic institutions became less international and more local in their student bodies and orientations. Universities were significantly affected by their national circumstances. Protestant Amsterdam differed from Catholic Salamanca. Fledgling Harvard, although patterned on British models slowly developed its own traditions and orientations. Academic institutions have had their ups and downs. Oxford and Cambridge, strongly linked to the Church of England and the aristocracy, played only a minor role in the development of the Industrial Revolution and the tremendous scientific expansion of the late eighteenth and nineteenth centuries.[6] In France, universities were abolished after the Revolution in 1793. They were gradually re-established and the Napoleonic model became a powerful force not only in France but also in Latin America.[7] German universities were severely damaged during the Nazi period by the destruction of autonomy and the departure of many of their professors, permanently losing their scientific pre-eminence.[8]

For our purposes, two more recent modifications of the Western academic model are relevant. In the mid-nineteenth century, a newly united Germany harnessed the university for nation-building. Under the leadership of Wilhelm von Humboldt, German higher education was given significant resources by the state, took on the responsibility for research aimed at national development and industrialization, and played a key role in defining the ideology of the new German nation.[9] The reformed German universities also established graduate education and the doctoral degree as a major focus of the institution. Research became for the first time an integral function of the university. The university was reorganized as a hierarchy based on the newly emerging scientific disciplines. American reformers took these German innovations and transformed higher education even more by further stressing the links between the university and society through the concept of service and direct relationships with industry and agriculture, democratized the German chair system[10] through the establishment of academic departments and the development of the 'land grant' concept for both high-level research and expanded access to higher education.[11] Institutions which seem deeply embedded in the national soil have in fact been significantly influenced by international ideas and models.

The world's universities follow institutional patterns which are basically derivative of these Western models. There are virtually no exceptions. The one remaining fully non-Western institution, the Al-Azhar University in Cairo, focuses mainly on traditional Islamic law and theology. Significantly, its science faculties are now organized along European lines.[12] There are many variations, including post-secondary polytechnic institutions in the United Kingdom, the Soviet Union and other countries, Open Universities in the United Kingdom, Israel, Thailand and elsewhere and even the two-year community colleges in the United States and similar institutions, often following the American model, in other countries.[13] While the functions of these institutions may differ from those of traditional universities, their basic organization, patterns of governance and ethos remain remarkably linked to the basic Western academic ideal.

Networks of knowledge and higher education

There are many explanations for the domination of the Western academic model and the lack of alternatives in the modern world. The fact that the Western university institutionalized the study of science and later its production is a key factor. The link between universities and the dominant world economic systems no doubt is a particularly important reason for Western domination. For significant parts of the world, academic institutions were imposed by colonizers. There were few possibilities to develop independent alternatives. In many cases, traditional indigenous institutional forms were destroyed by the colonizers, as in India when in the nineteenth century the British imposed European patterns and no longer recognized existing traditional institutions.[14]

It is significant that none of the formerly colonized nations have shifted from their basically European academic models. The contemporary Indian university resembles its pre-Independence predecessor. Japan, never colonized, recognized after 1868 that it had to develop scientific and industrial capacity and jettisoned its traditional academic institutions in favour of Western university ideas. It imported ideas and models from Germany, the United States and other countries in the development of its universities.[15] Other non-colonized nations, such as China and Thailand, also imported Western models and adapted them to local needs and conditions.[16]

Western universities were seen to be successful in providing advanced education, in fostering research and scientific development and in assisting their societies in the increasingly complex task of development. Universities in both the United States and Germany were active in fostering industrial and agricultural development in the nineteenth century. The harnessing of higher education to the broader needs of national economic and social development was perhaps the most important innovation of the nineteenth century. The idea that higher education should be generously supported from public funds, that the university should participate in the creation as well as the transmission of knowledge and that academic institutions should at the same time be permitted a significant degree of autonomy was behind much of the growth of universities in this century.

Further, Western universities were at the centre of a knowledge network that includes research institutions, the means of knowledge dissemination such as journals and scientific publishers, and an 'invisible college' of scientists. It is worth noting that the bulk of the world's scientific literature now appears in the English language. Even scholars in such industrialized nations as Sweden and the Netherlands often find it necessary to communicate their research findings in English. The large Dutch multinational publishers, Elsevier and Kluwer, publish virtually all of their scholarly and scientific books and journals in English.

The circulation of scholars and students worldwide, and in a sense even the 'brain drain' is an element of the international knowledge system, helping to circulate ideas and also maintaining the impact of the major 'host' countries and their research hegemony. There are more than one million students studying outside their home countries. The large majority of these students are from Third World nations and they are studying in the industrialized nations, with the United States, the United Kingdom, Germany and the Soviet Union among the major 'host' countries.[17] They gain expertise in their studies, but they also learn the norms and values of the academic system in which they are located, often returning home with a zeal to reform their universities in a Western direction. Frequently, foreign graduates have difficulty readjusting to their home countries, in part because the advanced training they learned abroad may not be easily assimilated into less well-developed economies. Such frustrations, along with the blandishments of significantly better remuneration, leads to the brain drain. However, in the contemporary world, the brain drain is often not permanent. For one thing, members of the Third World scientific diaspora often maintain contact with their colleagues at home, contributing advanced knowledge and ideas. They frequently return home for periods of time and work with local academics. And in an increasing number of instances, they return home permanently when academic – and sometimes political – conditions are favourable. They bring with them considerable expertise and often assume leadership positions in the local scientific and academic communities. Without question, the massive circulation of highly educated personnel has a great influence on the transfer of knowledge. With few exceptions, the knowledge and institutional patterns that are transferred are from the major industrialized nations to the Third World – or even to other more peripheral industrial countries – with very little traffic in the other direction.[18]

The knowledge network is complex and multifaceted, and there is evidence that while its centres remain extraordinarily powerful, there is a movement towards greater equalization of research production and use. Japan, for example, already has a powerful and increasingly research-oriented university system and some of the newly industrialized countries of East and South-East Asia are building up research capac-

ity in their universities.[19] While hegemony may be slowly dissipating, inequality will remain endemic to the world knowledge system.

Expansion: hallmark of the post-war era

Post-secondary education has dramatically expanded since the Second World War. Expansion has taken place in virtually every country in the world to differing extents. The growth of post-secondary education has in fact been, in proportional terms, more dramatic than that of primary and secondary education. Writing in 1975, Trow spoke of the transition from élite to mass and then to universal higher education in the context of the industrialized nations.[20] While the United States enrolled some 30 per cent of the relevant age cohort in higher education in the immediate post-war period, European nations generally maintained an élite higher education system with fewer than 5 per cent attending post-secondary institutions. By the 1960s, many European nations educated 15 per cent or more of the age-group: Sweden, for example, enrolled 24 per cent in 1970, and France 17 per cent. At the same time, the United States increased its proportion to around 50 per cent, approaching universal access.

In the Third World, expansion was even more dramatic. Building on tiny and extraordinarily élitist universities, Third World higher education expanded rapidly in the immediate post-independence period. In India, enrolments grew from approximately 100,000 at the time of Independence in 1947 to over 3.5 million in 1986. Expansion in Africa has also been dramatic, with the post-secondary student population growing from 21,000 in 1960 to 437,000 in 1983.[21] Recent economic difficulties in much of sub-Saharan Africa have meant that per-student expenditure has dropped significantly, contributing to a marked deterioration in academic standards.

Similar trends can be seen elsewhere in the Third World. In a few instances, such as the Philippines, where more than one-third of the age cohort enters post-secondary education, Third World enrolment ratios have reached the levels of many of the industrialized nations, although in general the Third World lags far behind in terms of proportions of the population attending higher education institutions. For example, despite China's student population of more than 2 million, only about 1 per cent of the age cohort attends post-secondary institutions – about 4 per cent of those graduating high school. Expansion in the Third World has, in general, exceeded that in the industrialized nations, at least in proportional terms, although there are significant variations among Third World nations – some countries maintain small and relatively élitist university systems while others have expanded more rapidly.

Regardless of political system, level of economic development, or educational ideology, the expansion of higher education has been the most important single post-war trend worldwide: about 7 per cent of the relevant age cohort (20 to 24 years) attend post-secondary educational institutions – a statistic that has shown an increase each decade since the Second World War. Higher education expanded dramatically first in the United States, then in Europe; currently the main focus of expansion is in the Third World. There are, of course, significant variations in enrolment statistics and ratios. Women, in general, attend university less frequently than men – although they now constitute approximately 40 per cent of enrolments – with considerable variations by country. The industrialized nations, with a few exceptions, have a higher proportion of the age cohort in post-secondary education than Third World countries. Generalized statistics concerning enrolments in post-secondary education mask many key differences. For example, many industrialized nations have a higher proportion of students in technological and scientific fields than in the traditional liberal arts, which tend to predominate in the non-socialist developing nations.

There are many reasons for the expansion of higher education. A key factor has been the increasing complexity of modern societies and economies, which have demanded more highly trained personnel. Post-secondary institutions have, almost without exception, been called on to provide the needed training. Indeed, training in many fields that had once been imparted 'on the job' have become formalized in institutions of higher education. Entirely new fields, such as computer science, have come into existence and rely on universities as a key source of research and training. Nations now developing scientific and industrial capacity, such as the Republic of Korea and Taiwan, have depended on academic institutions to provide high-level training as well as research expertise to a greater extent than was the case during the first Industrial Revolution in Europe.[22]

Not only do academic institutions provide training, they also test and provide certification for many roles and occupations in contemporary society. These roles have been central to universities from their origins in the medieval period but have been vastly expanded in recent years. A university degree is a prerequisite for an increasing number of occupations in most societies. Indeed, it is fair to say that academic certification is necessary for most positions of power, authority and prestige in modern societies. This places immense power in the hands of universities. Tests to gain admission to higher education are key *rites de passage* in many societies and are major determinants of future success.[23] Competition within academe varies from country to country, but in most cases there is also much stress on high academic performance and tests in the universities. There are often further examinations to permit entry into specific professions.

The role of the university as an examining body has grown for a number of reasons. As expansion has taken place, it has been necessary to provide increasingly competitive sorting mechanisms to control access to high-prestige occupations. The universities are also seen as meritocratic institutions which can be trusted to provide fair and impartial tests that will honestly measure accomplishment and therefore access.

When such mechanisms break down, as in China during the Cultural Revolution, or where they are perceived to be subject to corrupt influences, as in India, the universities are significantly weakened. The older, more informal and often more ascriptive means of controlling access to prestigious occupations, are no longer able to provide the controls needed nor are they perceived as fair. Entirely new fields have developed where no sorting mechanisms existed and academic institutions have frequently been called upon not only to provide training but also examination and certification.

Expansion has also occurred because growing segments of the population of modern societies have demanded it. The middle classes, seeing that academic qualifications were increasingly necessary for success, demanded access to higher education. Governments generally responded by providing access.[24] When governments did not move quickly enough, private initiative frequently established academic institutions in order to meet the demand. In countries like India, the Philippines and Bangladesh, a majority of the students are educated in private colleges and universities.[25] At present, there are worldwide trends towards imposing user fees, increasing the stress on private higher education, and raising tuition fees in public institutions. These changes are intended to reduce the cost of post-secondary education for governments while maintaining access, although the long-term implications for quality, access and control of higher education are unclear.

In most societies, higher education is heavily subsidized by the government and most, if not all, academic institutions are in the public sector. While there is a growing trend towards private initiative and management sharing responsibility with public institutions, there is little doubt that the government will continue to be the main source of funding for post-secondary education.[26] The dramatic expansion of academic institutions in the post-war period has proved very expensive for governments worldwide.[27] None the less, the demand for access has proved to be an extraordinarily powerful one.[28]

There have been significant variations in higher education expansion. For example, many analysts writing in the 1960s assumed that the world, and particularly the Western industrialized nations, would move from élite to mass and finally to universal access to higher education, generally following the American pattern.[29] This has not occurred. In much of Western Europe, the expansion that characterized the 1960s slowed and in some countries came to a complete halt, although there are now signs of renewed expansion. The causes for this situation were in part economic, with a slowdown of the Western economies following the 'oil shocks' of the 1970s; in part the causes were demographic, resulting from a significant drop in the birth rate and a smaller cohort of young people; and in part philosophical, as countries were less sympathetic to further growth of public institutions, including universities.

Generally, the proportion of the age cohort going on to higher education in Western Europe stabilized at under 20 per cent.[30] With the exception of the Soviet Union, most Eastern European countries also enroll under 20 per cent of the relevant age-group in higher education, thus maintaining relatively élitist academic systems. Similar trends are also evident in the United States, where access is considered to be 'universal' and enrolments have stabilized at around 50 per cent of the age-group.

In sharp contrast to the Western industrialized countries, Third World universities have, in general, continued to expand without stopping, despite the fact that, at least in Africa and Latin America, there have been serious economic problems in the past two decades. While with only a very few exceptions, such as the Philippines, Third World enrolment ratios remain significantly lower than those in the industrialized nations, there continues to be a strong commitment to continued expansion and access. This is the case even in countries like India, where there is severe unemployment of graduates and where there is a significant brain drain of university graduates abroad. In sub-Saharan Africa, there has been a slowing of expansion, not so much because demand for higher eduction has decreased but due to severe economic problems which have limited the ability of governments to pay the costs of continued growth. In many Third World countries, it remains impossible for local universities to absorb all of those qualified to attend, thus creating an exodus of students abroad. This is the case in Malaysia, where about half of the country's enrolments are abroad.[31]

It is necessary to analyse the prospects for continued expansion of higher education from several perspectives. While there are common worldwide trends, such as the increasingly important role of technology, there are also important differences among countries and in different parts of the world. The Third World presents a specific set of circumstances. While it is likely that its pace in some Third World countries will slow in the coming decade, expansion will continue to be a key factor in higher education. Regional variations will be important, with economic factors dominating. Universities will very likely grow more slowly in less-successful economies. Rapidly expanding economies, such as those of the newly industrializing countries in East Asia, will have resources to expand higher education and at the same time there will be a demand for graduates. Taiwan and the Republic of Korea, for example, can easily absorb university graduates as well as the expenditures needed for large and better-equipped universities. Yet, even where there is evidence that higher educational growth should slow or even stop, it is unlikely that this will take place since popular demand for post-secondary education will remain high and political authorities will find it easier to provide access than to limit it.

The situation in the Western industrialized nations is more difficult to predict. A variety of factors argues for a resumption of growth, although probably not at the levels of the 1960s. There is evidence of a modest upturn in population in some age categories in some Western nations although demographers predict that this will be relatively short-lived. The large numbers of graduates trained in the 1960s and now occupying positions in schools and universities as well as in government and in industrial enterprises will be retiring in large numbers in the

coming years, triggering a significant demand for university-trained personnel. There is also a recognition that university-based research is an important ingredient for scientific and technological strength in an increasingly competitive world economy. Much, however, will depend on broader economic trends. It is also difficult to predict whether resistance to governmental spending in general and for education in particular will continue to be an important political factor in many Western countries.

Despite imponderables, it is likely that in general there will be increased support for higher education spurred by demographic and market factors and continued demand for access by an ever-widening segment of the population. Whether there will be a resumption of the growth of access to wider segments of the population – both of the traditional age-group and of 'non-traditional' students – remains to be seen.[32]

Change and reform: the legacy of the 1960s

The demands placed on institutions of higher education to accommodate larger numbers of students and expanding functions resulted in significant reforms in higher education in many countries. There was much debate concerning higher education reform in the 1960s – and a significant amount of change did take place.[33] It is possible to identify several important factors which contributed both to the debate and to the changes that took place. Without question, the unprecedented student unrest of the period contributed to a sense of disarray in higher education. Further, the unrest was in part precipitated by deteriorating academic conditions which resulted from rapid expansion. In a few instances, students demanded far-reaching reforms in higher education although, generally, they did not propose specific changes.[34] Students frequently demanded an end to the rigidly hierarchical organization of the traditional European university, and significant changes were made in this respect. The 'chair' system was weakened and the responsibility for academic decision-making, formerly a monopoly of the full professors, was significantly expanded – in some countries to include students. At the same time, the walls of the traditional academic disciplines were broken by various plans for interdisciplinary teaching and research.

Reform was most dramatic in several very traditional Western European academic systems. Sweden's universities were completely transformed in the most far-reaching of the reform movements. Some of the changes effected in Sweden resulted in democratizing decision-making, decentralizing the universities, expanding higher education to previously under-served parts of the country, providing for interdisciplinary teaching and research and vocationalizing the curriculum.[35] Significant changes also took place in France and in the Netherlands. Reformers in both these countries stressed interdisciplinarity and a democratization of academic decision-making. In Germany, the universities in areas dominated by the Social Democratic Party were also significantly altered, with the traditional structures of the university giving way to more democratic governance patterns.

But in many industrialized nations, structural change was not dramatic, and in many instances very limited. In the United States, for example, despite considerable debate during the 1960s, there was very limited change in higher education.[36] Japan, the site of significant unrest and a large number of reports on university reform, saw virtually no basic change in its higher education system although several 'new model' interdisciplinary institutions were established, such as the science-oriented Tsukuba University near Tokyo. The United Kingdom, less affected by student protest and with an established plan for expansion in operation, also experienced few reforms during the 1960s.[37] It is also the case that some of the changes implemented in the 1960s were criticized or abandoned. In Germany, for example, reforms in governance that gave students and junior staff a dominant position in some university functions were ruled unconstitutional by the German courts.[38]

Vocationalization has been an important trend in changes in higher education in the past two decades. Throughout the world, there has been a conviction that the university curriculum should provide relevant training for a variety of increasingly complex jobs. The traditional notions that higher education should consist of liberal, non-vocational studies for élites or that it should provide a broad but unfocused curriculum, have been widely criticized for lacking 'relevance' to the needs of contemporary students. Students, worried about obtaining remunerative employment, have pressed the universities to be more focused. Employers have also demanded that the curriculum be more directly relevant to their needs. Enrolments in the social sciences and humanities, at least in the industrialized nations, have declined because these fields are not considered vocationally relevant.

Curricular vocationalism is linked to another major worldwide trend in higher education: the increasingly close relationship between universities and industry.[39] This relationship has implications for the curriculum, as industrial firms have sought to ensure that the skills that they need are incorporated into the curriculum. It also has significant implications for academic research, since many university–industry relationships are focused largely on research. Industries have established formal linkages and research partnerships with universities in order to obtain help with research that they find important. In some countries, such as Sweden, representatives of industry have been added to the governing councils of higher education institutions. In the United States, formal contractual arrangements have been made between universities and major corporations to share research results. In many industrialized nations, corporations are increasingly providing focused educational programmes for their employees, sometimes with the assistance of universities.

University–industry relations have significant implications for higher education. Technical arrangements with regard to patents, confidentiality of research findings and other fiscal matters have assumed importance. Critics also have pointed out that the nature of research in higher education may be altered by these new relationships as industrial firms are not generally interested in basic research. University-based research, which has traditionally been significantly oriented toward basic research, may be increasingly skewed to applied and profit-making topics. There has also been some discussion of the orientation of research, for example in fields like biotechnology, where broader public policy matters may conflict with the needs of corporations. Specific funding arrangements have also been questioned. Pressure on universities to serve the immediate needs of society and particularly the training and research requirements of industry is currently a key concern for universities and one which has implications for the organization of the curriculum, the nature and scope of research and the traditional relationship between the university and society.[40] Debates concerning the appropriate relationship between higher education and industry are likely to continue, as pressures grow even stronger on universities to provide direct service to the economy.

Universities have traditionally claimed significant autonomy for themselves. The traditional idea of academic governance stresses autonomy and universities have tried to insulate themselves from direct control by external agencies. However, with the increase in the size, scope, importance and cost of universities, there has been immense pressure by those providing funds for higher education – mainly governments – to expect accountability from universities. The conflict between autonomy and accountability is one of the flashpoints of controversy in recent years, with the result that there has been an increase in accountability from academic institutions, again with significant implications for them.[41] The issue takes on different implications in different parts of the world. In the Third World, traditions of autonomy have not been strong and demands for accountability, which include both political and economic elements, are especially troublesome.[42] In the industrialized nations, accountability pressures are more fiscal in nature.

Despite the varied pressures on higher edu-

cational institutions for change and the significant reforms that have taken place in the past two decades, basic institutional patterns have remained and there have been few structural alterations in universities. One of the few has been in Sweden as part of the dramatic reform that has taken place there. Elsewhere, curricula have been altered, expansion has taken place, and there have been continuing debates concerning accountability and autonomy, but universities as institutions have not changed significantly. As Edward Shils has argued, the 'academic ethic' has been under considerable strain, and in some ways it has been weakened, but it has survived.[43]

Towards the 1990s

The university as an institution in modern society has shown considerable durability. It has maintained key elements of the historical models from which it evolved over many centuries. At the same time, it has successfully evolved to serve the needs of societies.[44] There has been a significant convergence of both ideas and institutional patterns and practices in world higher education. This has been due in part to the implantation of European-style universities in the developing areas during and after the colonial era and because universities have been crucial in the development and then the internationalization of science and of research.

Despite remarkable institutional stability over time, universities have significantly changed and have been subjected to immense pressures in the post-Second World War period. Many of the changes which have been chronicled here have come as the result of great external pressure and despite considerable opposition from within the institution. Some have argued that the university has lost it soul.[45] Others have claimed that the university is irresponsible because it uses public funds and does not always conform to the direct needs of industry and government. Pressure from governmental authorities, militant students or external constituencies have all placed great strains on academic institutions.

The period since the Second World War has been one of unprecedented growth – and of the increasingly central role of higher education in virtually all modern societies. While growth may continue, the dramatic expansion of recent decades is at an end. It is unlikely that the place of the university as the most important institution for training personnel for virtually all of the top-level occupations in modern society will be weakened. The role of the university in research will also continue, although as has been noted, there are significant pressures concerning the nature and focus of university-based research and perhaps a weakening of the commitment to basic research.[46]

Internationally, there may well be some further convergence as science becomes even more international and as the circulation of academic élites continues through foreign study. While significant national variations will remain, universities have increasingly similar roles throughout the world and research is increasingly communicated to an international audience.

The challenges are, none the less, significant. The issues discussed below, no doubt among others, will be of concern in the present decade and beyond.

ACCESS AND ADAPTATION

Although in a few countries, access to post-secondary education has been provided to virtually all segments of the population, there is in most countries a continuing demand for higher education. Progress towards broadening the social class base of higher education has slowed and in many industrialized countries stopped in the 1970s. With the emergence of democratic governments in Eastern Europe, the possible re-emergence of demand in Western Europe and continuing pressure for expansion in the Third World, it is likely that there will be heightened demand for access and thus expansion of enrolments in many countries. Limited funds and a

desire for 'efficient' allocation of scarce post-secondary resources will come into direct conflict with demands for access. These demands for access by previously disenfranchised groups will continue to place great pressure on higher education. In many countries, racial, ethnic or religious minorities play a role in shaping higher education policy. Issues of access will be among the most controversial in debates concerning higher education. This topic may be especially volatile since there is a widespread assumption that all segments of the population should be able to obtain a university education – yet, the realities of higher education in most countries do not permit this level of enrolment.

ADMINISTRATION, ACCOUNTABILITY AND GOVERNANCE

As academic institutions become larger and more complex institutions, there will be increasing pressure for a greater degree of professional administration. At the same time, the traditional forms of academic governance will be under increasing pressure not only because they are unwieldy but because in large and bureaucratic institutions they are inefficient. The administration of higher education will increasingly become a profession, much as it is in the United States. This means that there will be the growth of an 'administrative estate' in many countries where it does not now exist. The demands for accountability will increase and will cause academic institutions considerable difficulty. As academic budgets increase, there will be inevitable demands to monitor and control expenditures. There is, at present, no general agreement concerning the appropriate level of governmental involvement in higher education. The challenge will be to ensure that the traditional – and valuable – patterns of faculty control of governance and the basic academic decisions of universities are maintained in an increasingly complex and bureaucratic environment.

KNOWLEDGE-CREATION AND DISSEMINATION

Research is an increasingly important part of the mission of many universities and of the academic system generally. Key decisions concerning the control and funding of research, the relationship of research to broader curricular and teaching issues, the uses made of university-based research and related issues will increasingly be in contention. Further, the system of knowledge dissemination, including journals and books and increasingly computer-based data systems, is rapidly changing and hotly debated. Who should control the new data networks? How will traditional means of communication, such as the journals, survive in this new climate? How will the scientific system avoid being overwhelmed by the proliferation of data.?[47] The needs of peripheral scientific systems, including both the Third World and smaller academic systems in the industrialized world, are increasingly important.[48]

While the technological means for rapid knowledge dissemination are available, issues of control and ownership, the appropriate use of data bases, problems of maintaining quality standards in data bases, and related questions are very important. It is possible that the new technologies will lead to increased centralization rather than wider access. It is also possible that libraries and other users of knowledge will be overwhelmed by both the cost of obtaining new material and the flow of knowledge. At present, academic institutions in the United States and other English-speaking nations, along with publishers and the owners of the communications networks stand to gain. The major Western knowledge producers currently constitute a kind of OPEC of information, dominating not only the creation of knowledge but also most of the major channels of distribution. Simply increasing the amount of research and creating new data bases will not ensure a more equal and accessible knowledge system. Academic institutions are at the centre but publishers, copyright authorities, funders of research and others are also necessarily involved.

THE ACADEMIC PROFESSION

The professorate has found itself under increasing strain in recent years in most countries. Demands for accountability, increased bureaucratization of institutions, fiscal constraints in many countries, and an increasingly diverse student body have all challenged the professorate. In most industrialized nations, a combination of fiscal problems and demographic factors led to a stagnating profession. Now, demographic factors and a modest upturn in enrolments are beginning to turn surpluses into shortages.[49] In the Newly Industrialized Countries (NICs), the professorate has significantly improved its status, remuneration and working conditions in recent years. In the poorer nations, however, the situation has, if anything, become more difficult with decreasing resources and ever-increasing enrolments. Overall, the professorate will face severe problems as academic institutions change in the coming period. Maintaining autonomy, academic freedom and a commitment to the traditional goals of the university will prove a challenge.

In the West, there will be difficulties in luring the 'best and brightest' into academe in a period when positions will again be relatively plentiful: in many fields, academic salaries have not kept pace and there has been a deterioration in the traditional academic life-style. The pressure on the professorate not only to teach and do research but also to attract external grants, do consulting and the like is significant. In the United Kingdom and Australia, for example, universities have become 'cost centres', and accountability has been pushed to its logical extreme. British academics entering the profession after 1989 will no longer have tenure, but will be periodically evaluated. In the NICs, the challenge will be to create a fully autonomous academic profession where traditions of research and academic freedom are only now developing. The difficulties faced by the poorer Third World countries are perhaps the greatest: to maintain a viable academic culture in deteriorating conditions.

PRIVATE RESOURCES
AND PUBLIC RESPONSIBILITY

In almost every country, there has been a growing emphasis on increasing the role of the private sector in higher education. One of the most direct manifestations of this trend is the growing role of the private sector in funding and, in many cases, directing university research. In many countries, there has been an expansion of private academic institutions. And there has been an emphasis on students paying an increasing share of the cost of their education, often through loan programmes. Governments have tried to limit their expenditures on post-secondary education while at the same time recognizing that the functions of universities are important. Privatization has been the means of achieving this broad policy goal.[50] There are, of course, important implications of these trends. Decisions concerning academic developments may move increasingly to the private sector, with the possibility that broader public goals may be ignored. Whether private interests will support the traditional functions of universities, including academic freedom, fundamental research and a pattern of governance which leaves the professorate in control is unclear. Some of the most interesting developments in private higher education can be found in such countries as Viet Nam, China and Hungary, where private institutions have recently been established. Inevitably, private initiative in higher education will bring with it a change in values and orientations. It is not clear that these values will, in the long term, be in the best interests of the university.

DIVERSIFICATION AND STRATIFICATION

While diversification – the establishing of new post-secondary institutions to meet new needs – is by no means an entirely new phenomenon, it is a trend that has been of primary importance in recent years and will continue to reshape the academic system. In recent years, the establishment of research institutions, community colleges, polytechnics and other academic institutions designed to meet specialized needs and serve specific populations has been a primary characteristic of growth. At the same time, the academic system has become more stratified: once individuals are within a segment of the system, it is difficult to move to a different segment. And there is often a high correlation of social class and other variables with selection to a particular segment of the system. To some extent, the reluctance of the traditional universities to change is responsible for some of the diversification. Perhaps more important has been the belief that it is efficient and probably less expensive to establish new limited-function institutions. An element of diversification is the expansion of the student population to include larger numbers of women and other previously disenfranchised segments of the population. Women now constitute 40 per cent of the student population worldwide and more than half in fifteen countries.[51] In many countries, students from lower socio-economic groups and racial and ethnic minorities are entering post-secondary institutions in significant numbers. This diversification will also be an important challenge for the coming decades.

ECONOMIC DISPARITIES

There are substantial inequalities among the world's universities and it is likely that these inequalities will grow. The major universities in the industrialized nations generally have adequate resources to play a leading role in scientific research – in a context where it is increasingly expensive to keep up with the expansion of knowledge.[52] At the same time, universities in much of the Third World simply cannot cope with the combined challenges of continuing pressure for increased enrolments and budgetary constraints and in some cases fiscal disasters. For example, universities in much of sub-Saharan Africa have seen dramatic budget cuts and find it difficult to function, let alone improve quality and compete in the international knowledge system.[53] In the middle are academic institutions in the Asian NICs, where there has been significant academic progress and it is likely that these institutions will continue to improve. Thus, the economic prospects for post-secondary education worldwide are mixed, with considerable challenges ahead.

Universities worldwide share a common culture and reality. In many basic ways, there is a convergence of institutional models and norms. The key issues identified here are experienced worldwide. At the same time, there are significant national differences which will continue to be felt. There is little chance that the basic structures of academic institutions will significantly change, although some of the traditional academic ideologies and practices are threatened and alterations are likely, for example concerning the continuing growth of an administrative cadre in universities. Unanticipated developments are also possible. For example, while conditions for the emergence of significant student movements, at least in the industrialized nations, do not seem likely at the present time, circumstances may change.[54] In the Third World, student movements continue to be an important political and academic force.

This article has pointed to some key factors that have affected academic institutions worldwide. The past decade has not been an especially favorable one for higher education, yet academic institutions continue to be very important institutions, if anything expanding their impact on both science and society. The future presents significant challenges but the very centrality of the university in modern society creates a degree of optimism. ∎

Notes

1. For a historical perspective, see C. Haskins, *The Rise of Universities*, Ithaca, N.Y., Cornell University Press, 1957.
2. P. G. Altbach, *The Knowledge Context: Comparative Perspectives on the Distribution of Knowledge*, Albany, N.Y., State University of New York Press, 1987.
3. For further discussion of this point, see A. B. Cobban, *The Medieval Universities: Their Development and Organization*, London, Methuen, 1975.
4. The history of British higher education expansion in India and Africa is described in E. Ashby, *Universities: British, Indian, African*, Cambridge, Mass., Harvard University Press, 1966.
5. I. Gilbert, 'The Indian Academic Profession: The Origins of a Tradition of Subordination', *Minerva*, No. 10, July 1972, pp. 384–411.
6. For a broader consideration of these themes, see L. Stone (ed.), *The University in Society*, Princeton, N.J., Princeton University Press, 1974, 2 vols.
7. J. Ben-David, *Centers of Learning: Britain, France, Germany, the United States*, pp. 16–17, New York, McGraw-Hill, 1977.
8. F. Lilge, *The Abuse of Learning: The Failure of the German University*, New York, Macmillan, 1948.
9. C. E. McClelland, *State, Society and University in Germany, 1700–1914*, Cambridge, Cambridge University Press, 1980. See also J. Ben-David and A. Zloczower, 'Universities and Academic Systems in Modern Societies', *European Journal of Sociology*, Vol. 3, No. 1, 1962, pp. 45–84.
10. In the German-originated chair system, a single full professor was appointed in each discipline. All other academic staff served under the direction of the chair-holder, who held a permanent appointment to the position. Many other countries, including Japan, Russia and most of Eastern Europe, adopted this system. In time, it was criticized as too rigid and hierarchical.
11. L. Veysey, *The Emergence of the American University*, Chicago, University of Chicago Press, 1965. For a somewhat different analysis, see E. T. Silva and S. A. Slaughter, *Serving Power: The Making of the Academic Social Science Expert*, Westport, Conn., Greenwood, 1984.
12. In Egypt, the Al-Azhar University still offers Islamic higher education in the traditional manner. There are virtually no other universities which fundamentally diverge from the Western model. For a discussion of the contemporary Islamic university, see H. H. Bilgrami and S. A. Ashraf, *The Concept of an Islamic University*, London, Hodder & Stoughton, 1985.
13. P. G. Altbach, 'The American Academic Model in Comparative Perspective', in: P. G. Altbach (ed.), *The Relevance of American Higher Education to Southeast Asia*, pp. 15–36, Singapore, Regional Institute for Higher Education and Development, 1985.

34   Philip G. Altbach

14. For a case-study of British higher education policy in India, see D. Lelyveld, *Aligarh's First Generation: Muslim Solidarity in British India*, Princeton, N.J., Princeton University Press, 1978.

15. M. Nagai, *Higher Education in Japan: Its Take-off and Crash*, Tokyo, University of Tokyo Press, 1971.

16. For case-studies of a variety of Asian universities, see P. G. Altbach and V. Selvaratnam (eds.), *From Dependence to Autonomy: The Development of Asian Universities*, Dordrecht (Netherlands), Kluwer, 1989.

17. For a full discussion of the issues relating to foreign study, see P. G. Altbach, D. Kelly and Y. Lulat, *Research on Foreign Students and International Study: Bibliography and Analysis*, New York, Praeger, 1985.

18. A telling example in this respect is that the number of American students going abroad is only a small proportion of foreigners coming to the United States – and the large majority of Americans who do study in other countries go to Canada and Western Europe and not to the Third World. See also R. Arnove, 'Foundations and the Transfer of Knowledge', in: R. Arnove (ed.), *Philanthropy and Cultural Imperialism*, pp. 305–30, Boston, Mass., G. K. Hall, 1980.

19. For a discussion of higher education development in the NICs, see P. G. Altbach et al., *Scientific Development and Higher Education: The Case of Newly Industrializing Countries*, New York, Praeger, 1989.

20. M. Trow, 'Problems in the Transition from Elite to Mass Higher Education'. Paper prepared for a conference on mass higher education held by the Organisation for Economic Co-operation and Development (OECD), Paris, 1975.

21. For documentation concerning African higher education, see World Bank, *Education in Sub-Saharan Africa: Policies for Adjustment, Revitalization and Expansion*, Washington, D.C., World Bank, 1988, particularly Chapter 6.

22. Altbach et al., *Scientific Development and Higher Education . . .*, op. cit.

23. M. A. Echstein and H. J. Noah, 'Forms and Functions of Secondary School Leaving Examinations', *Comparative Education Review*, No. 33, August 1989, pp. 295–316.

24. It is also the case that academic institutions serve as important 'sorting' institutions in modern society, sometimes diverting students from highly competitive fields. See, for example, S. Brint and J. Karabel, *The Diverted Dream: Community Colleges and the Promise of Educational Opportunity in America, 1900–1985*, New York, Oxford University Press, 1989.

25. R. L. Geiger, *Private Sectors in Higher Education: Structure, Function and Change in Eight Countries*, Ann Arbor, Mich., University of Michigan Press, 1986. For a focus on Latin America, see D. C. Levy, *Higher Education and the State in Latin America*, Chicago, University of Chicago Press, 1986.

26. It is significant that private higher education institutions are being established in Viet Nam and in China. At the same time, Malaysia has rejected proposals for the establishment of private universities.

27. D. B. Johnstone, *Sharing the Costs of Higher Education: Student Financial Assistance in the United Kingdom, the Federal Republic of Germany, France, Sweden and the United States*, Washington, D.C., The College Board, 1986.

28. It is worth noting that agencies such as the World Bank have strongly argued against continued expansion of higher education, feeling that scarce educational expenditures could be much more effectively spent on primary and secondary education. See *Education in Sub-Saharan Africa: Policies for Adjustment, Revitalization and Expansion*, Washington, D.C., The World Bank, 1988.

29. Trow, op. cit.

30. See L. Cerych and P. Sabatier, *Great Expectations and Mixed Performance: The Implementation of Higher Education Reforms in Europe*, Trentham (United Kingdom), Trentham Books, 1986. See, in particular, Part 2 for a consideration of access to higher education in Western Europe.

31. J. S. Singh, 'Malaysia', in: P. G. Altbach (ed.), *International Encyclopedia of Comparative Higher Education*, New York, Garland, 1990.

32. There will also be some significant national variations. For example, the United Kingdom, under Margaret Thatcher's leadership, consistently reduced expenditures for post-secondary education, with significant negative consequences for higher education. See, for example, Sir Claus Moser, 'The Robbins Report 25 Years After: and the Future of the Universities', *Oxford Journal of Education*, Vol. 14, No. 1, 1988, pp. 5–20.

33. For broader considerations of the reforms of the 1960s, see L. Cerych and P. Sabatier, *Great Patterns of the Higher Education System*, London, J. Kingsley, 1989; P. G. Altbach (ed.), *University Reform: Comparative Perspectives for the Seventies*, Cambridge, Mass., Schenkman, 1974; and P. G. Altbach, *Perspectives on Comparative Higher Education: Essays on Faculty, Students and Reform*, Buffalo, N.Y., Comparative Education Center, SUNY-Buffalo, 1989.

34. For an example of an influential student proposal for higher education reform, see W. Nitsch et al., *Hochschule in der Demokratie*, Berlin, Luchterhand, 1965.

35. J. E. Lane and M. Murray, 'The Significance of Decentralization in Swedish Education', *European Journal of Education*, Vol. 20, No. 2/3, 1985, pp. 163–72.

36. See A. Astin et al., *The Power of Protest* (San Francisco, Jossey-Bass, 1975) for an overview of the results of the ferment of the 1960s on American higher education.

37. 'The Legacy of Robbins', *European Journal of Education*, Vol. 14, No. 1, 1988, pp. 3–112.

38. For a critical viewpoint, see H. Daalder and E. Shils (eds.), *Universities, Politicians and Bureaucrats: Europe and the United States*, Cambridge, Cambridge University Press, 1982.

39. See, for example, 'Universities and Industry', *European Journal of Education*, Vol. 20, No. 1, 1985, pp. 5–66.

40. Of course, this is not a new concern for higher education. See T. Veblen, *The Higher Learning in America: A Memorandum on the Conduct of Universities by Business Men*, New York, Viking Press, 1918.

41. See K. Hufner, 'Accountability', in: P. G. Altbach (ed.), *International Encyclopedia of Comparative Higher Education*, op. cit.

42. P. G. Altbach, 'Academic Freedom in Asia: Learning the Limitations', *Far Eastern Economic Review*, 26 June 1988, pp. 45–84.

43. E. Shils, *The Academic Ethic*, Chicago, University of Chicago Press, 1983.

44. A classic discussion of the development of the modern university is Ben-David and Zloczower, op. cit.

45. See, for example, R. Nisbet, *The Degradation of the Academic Dogma: The University in America, 1945–1970*, New York, Basic Books, 1971. A. Bloom, in his *The Closing of the American Mind* (New York, Simon & Schuster, 1987) echoes many of Nisbet's sentiments.

46. It is significant to note that in those countries that have located much of their research in non-university institutions, such as the Academies of Sciences in the Soviet Union and some Eastern European nations, there has been some rethinking of this organizational model, as well as a feeling that universities may be more effective locations for the major research enterprise. See A. Vucinich, *Empire of Knowledge: The Academy of Sciences of the USSR (1917–1970)*.

47. See T. W. Shaugnessy et al., 'Scholarly Communication: The Need for Action – A Symposium', *Journal of Academic Librarianship*, Vol. 15, No. 2, 1989, pp. 68–78. See also *Scholarly Communication: The Report of the National Commission*, Baltimore, Johns Hopkins University Press, 1979.

48. These issues are discussed in P. G. Altbach, *The Knowledge Context . . .*, op. cit. See I. L. Horowitz, *Communicating Ideas: The Crisis of Publishing in a Post-Industrial Society* (New York, Oxford University Press, 1986) for a different perspective.

49. For an American perspective, see H. Bowen and J. Schuster, *American Professors: A National Resource Imperiled*, New York, Oxford University Press, 1986.

50. D. C. Levy, *Higher Education and the State in Latin America: Private Challenges to Public Dominance*, Chicago, University of Chicago Press, 1986. See also R. L. Geiger, *Private Sectors in Higher Education: Structure, Function and Change in Eight Countries*, Ann Arbor, Mich., University of Michigan Press, 1986.

51. G. P. Kelly, 'Women in Higher Education', in: P. G. Altbach (ed.), *International Encyclopedia of Comparative Higher Education*, op. cit.

52. A possible exception to this situation are the universities in the United Kingdom, where a decade of financial cuts by the Thatcher government has sapped the morale of the universities and has made it difficult for even such distinguished institutions as Oxford and Cambridge to continue top-quality research. See G. Walford, 'The Privatization of British Higher Education', *European Journal of Education*, Vol. 23, No. 1/2, 1988, pp. 47–64.

53. *Education in Sub-Saharan Africa . . .*, op. cit., pp. 68–81.

54. For a survey of student movements, see P. G. Altbach (ed.), *Student Political Activism: An International Reference Handbook*, Westport, Conn., Greenwood Press, 1989.

Autonomy and accountability in higher education

Orlando Albornoz

The concepts of *autonomy* and *accountability* are closely linked. However, there would also appear to be an additional relationship between these and other related concepts, such as economic and social development, academic freedom and the specific political role of the university, both within its own confines and in relation to the world outside. From the standpoint of the concept of development, it would seem that as a country achieves a higher level of development, interest in the autonomy of the university diminishes and interest in its accountability grows. Academic freedom for its part is indissolubly bound up with autonomy because of the fundamental criterion that academic freedom cannot exist without autonomy. University

Orlando Albornoz (Venezuela). *Professor at the Universidad Central de Venezuela and visiting professor at the Universidad de Oriente (Venezuela) and at the Facultad Latinoamericana de Ciencias Sociales in Buenos Aries. President of the Committee of Educational Research in Sociology and the International Association of Sociology. Member of the Steering Committee of the International Association of Universities and consultant for a number of international organizations. Among his recent works are:* La educación en el Estado democrático; Juventud y educación en Venezuela; La educación bajo el signo de la crisis; *and* La reforma educativa. *He is co-author (with Miguel A. Escotet) of* Educación y desarrollo desde la perspectiva sociológica.

autonomy seems in turn to depend on the prevailing political system, since democracy by its nature guarantees autonomy, while the authoritarian forms of political organization deny the concept of autonomy; under an authoritarian system, the activities of the state are centralized and the universities are treated as appendages of the government. On the other hand, the same concept of autonomy is often used to support the claim that any form of accountability negates the principle that the university must manage its own affairs without external interference.

Any discussion of the concepts of autonomy and accountability is therefore bound to be extremely complex, especially as the way in which these concepts are used and handled varies as a function of place and time. Hence it is unlikely that we can consider these two concepts 'universal', though, technically speaking, there can be no doubt of their conceptual characteristics in each case. If a chart were to be drawn up of the way in which each of these two concepts is applied in each university throughout the world, there would in all probability be total agreement on the concept of autonomy, but disagreement on the possibility of implementing norms of accountability in the universities. In a society like that of the United States, for example, the notion of accountability involves a reference to issues of public order, since higher education is not alone in being subject to this kind of accountability; the same principle applies to the activities of politicians and to institutions in general. In a Third World society, on the other hand, accountability is not an issue of public order, but a subject that remains to all intents and purposes secret. The private lives of politicians are generally preserved in this way without any need for details to be known to public opinion; it follows that many institutions and activities are considered to be exempt from public accountability, such as the payment of taxes and other matters; even the curriculum vitae of the persons who occupy public functions is habitually treated as a 'confidential matter' and one that is kept out of the public domain.

At all events, it is appropriate to analyse the concepts of autonomy and accountability separately to begin with, before looking at the associations between them. That at least is the approach that we propose to follow in this study, faithful to the criterion indicated at the outset that these are closely related concepts, but nevertheless issues that must be dealt with separately.

Autonomy

In the words of Perkins (1978): 'From the earliest beginnings of the university in the Middle Ages, down to the present century, autonomy or self-government has been a key ingredient in the ideology of institutions of higher learning'. However, it seems very likely that the notion of autonomy will be seriously called into question in the post-industrial world since society tends, as it progresses in that direction, to integrate its various functions more closely; that being so, the university will no longer be able to claim that it lives confined in an ivory tower. In the contemporary world, autonomy therefore seems to involve striking a delicate balance between the need to respond to the requirements of society, while at the same time satisfying the needs specific to the institution itself, such as academic freedom. In that sense, the final decade of the twentieth century is clearly an excellent vantage point from which to observe the development of

the concept of autonomy, with regard to the far-reaching political changes that we have witnessed at the beginning of this decade, symbolized by the reunification of Germany and the resurgence of democracy in the countries of Eastern Europe.

This equilibrium of functions is highly unstable. On the one hand, the university is unable to adapt fully to the demands made by society, namely the training of human resources or the generation and dissemination of knowledge; neither can it permit its members to work in complete and absolute independence from those needs of society. The literal meaning of the concept of autonomy is self-government. Different social groups, the nation as a whole and professional or university associations, may thus be described as autonomous when they are capable of controlling their own affairs. There is a general impression that institutions such as universities are excessively autonomous, but what is certainly implied by this is that they must be accountable to society at large, or to those affected by their decisions.

The different dimensions of the concept of autonomy are apparent from the interpretation placed on it by Berlin (1958):

I wish my life and decisions to depend on myself, not on external forces of whatever kind. I wish to be an instrument of my own, not of other men's acts of will. I wish to be a subject, not an object; to be moved byreasons, by conscious purposes, which are my own, not by causes that affect me, as it were, from outside. . . . I wish, above all, to be conscious of myself as a thinking, willing, active being, bearing responsibility for my choices and able to explain them by references to my own ideas and purposes.

It follows from the foregoing that autonomy presupposes a strong component of moral responsibility and a close relationship between autonomy and liberty. The university must be autonomous, but it must equally assume a profound moral responsibility and apply the notion of liberty within the limits that may be imposed by this moral responsibility. Autonomy, in other words, is not an abstract right, but a concrete rationale. It is accordingly not neutral but rather a concept related to a specific reality – in this instance, society and its demands and expectations. The university naturally seeks to optimize and maximize the exercise of its autonomy, but society has the right to control that autonomy and so autonomy must inevitably be restricted when conflicts arise between the rights of society and those of the university. Autonomy may thus be referred to as an unstable equilibrium.

Experience of university autonomy enables us to define its different levels. It is a generally accepted fact that this concept involves, at the very least, the following categories, as suggested by Durham (1989): autonomy of research, teaching autonomy, administrative autonomy and autonomy of financial expenditure. I should like to add one further category: that of physical or spatial autonomy. However, each of these particular categories must be analysed in relation to the type of university involved since, in the case of Venezuela, to quote the example with which I am most familiar, there are at least four types of university and the concept of autonomy varies in practice as a function of the type of institution concerned. These types are as follows: the autonomous university in the strict sense of the term, and the governmental university, both of them being in the public sector, together with two other categories in the private sector that I might define as the private university with a primarily academic function and the private university with commercial objectives. The autonomous Latin American university is seeking to extend the forms of autonomy referred to above to include that of physical or spatial autonomy. At the end of 1990, a polemic developed in Venezuela on the subject of whether or not the police force should have access to the precincts of the university, especially if the members of the university community were facing a risk to their personal safety. The argument centred on the question as to whether the police force was entitled to enter the grounds of the university or whether the autonomy of the university was such that this territory could not under any circumstances be violated, the concept of autonomy thus being extended to the university campus itself.

If autonomy implies self-control, it is clearly apparent that when the university itself is unable to exercise that control, it must be imposed by those who have the means of maintaining public order. Any contrary claim would amount to a *reductio ad absurdum,* though the same criterion is acceptable in the case of a nation, according to the principle of territorial integrity. Intervention by bodies external to the university is not justified in any other case, but it does occur under authoritarian and dictatorial forms of government, because university autonomy then ceases to exist. Within a liberal democracy, the prevailing principle is that of non-interference with university autonomy, but it is obvious that when fundamental human rights, such as the right to life, are violated, university autonomy becomes a secondary concept as otherwise we should have to interpret it as an absolute principle. In that sense, it would seem appropriate to consider the principle of equality of both individuals and institutions before the law as the only absolute. Mention should, however, be made at this point of the issue of the integrity of the individual versus the integrity of the institution. If a tyrannical administration is established in a university, in a democratic society the members of that society have the right to intervene, just as if a tyrannical government is established in a nation, the university is entitled to fight against it to defend its own autonomy.

The question of autonomy of the university may therefore be approached by reference to the categories defined above. Scientific autonomy implies the fact that the originators of knowledge must be able to deploy their efforts according to their own agenda, subject only to evaluation by their peers and without external interference of any other type. Similarly, teaching autonomy implies that the university must have the capacity to decide within its own frame of reference which knowledge should be transmitted and which techniques should be used for that purpose. As to the question of administrative autonomy, the university must be in a position to control the admission of students and teaching and research staff, to draw up its own curricula, confer academic degrees and establish relations with other institutions within the country and abroad, while also encouraging the production and subsequent dissemination of knowledge on the scale which it deems appropriate. Finally, the university must be free to manage its own budget within the limits of the funds available, and to collect new funds needed for its activities, though it must remain subject to institutional forms of administrative, academic and financial control. The autonomy of the university must therefore not be allowed to bring it into conflict with such forms of accountability as may be defined. University autonomy may of course be considered relative, while academic freedom is an absolute. It follows that the university itself may be accountable, but not this freedom which transcends any possibility of measurement by concepts of accountability, such as efficiency and efficacy, output and performance . In that sense it deserves to be emphasized that university autonomy can only operate and function within the limits of political democracy; otherwise when 'authoritarian cultures' arise, this concept, like that of academic freedom, disappears (Brunner, 1981). Similarly, when market forces dominate within democratic societies, the autonomy of the university will be diminished by the application of the laws of competition.

The theme of autonomy might of course be approached in other ways. Berdahl (1971), cited by Lindly (1986), has done so by postulating two categories which enable the concept to be defined in more concrete terms. He speaks of the two dimensions of autonomy – procedural and substantive. In the first case, the mechanism of control stems from decisions of an administrative nature while, in the second, fundamental academic matters are involved, whose control affects the academic dynamic of the university. The interesting feature of Berdahl's approach is that it teaches us that the concept of autonomy must be categorized to understand its full significance, in his case as a dichotomy, or in Durham's approach, through a set of different categories to which must be added the notion of the specific territory of the university, which is how autonomy is understood in Latin America in

particular. In this sense, the concept of autonomy has been associated with that of sovereignty in Latin America. This distinction has been postulated in precise terms (Gabaldon, 1982, p. 155):

Sovereignty is the supreme and independent power of the public authorities as representatives of the state or, in other words, it is the characteristic feature that the political power of one particular state is not subject to that of any other state. Autonomy is the authority that specific entities within a state and belonging to it may enjoy in order to regulate the particular interests of their internal affairs by means of norms and organs of government that have been granted to them and therefore belong to them.

To understand the full practical implications of the sovereign version of autonomy, it is interesting to analyse the political climate experienced by many countries of the Third World in recent decades. In this broad process of the construction of political democracy, the territory of the university has often been the scene of a struggle against dictatorship and authoritarianism so that the concept of autonomy has acquired a significant political colouring and become an aspect of the struggle for power. However, the political powers always seek to control the academic authority, especially in or under forms of authoritarian government of which history has given us so many examples – such as the rise to political power of National Socialism in Germany or of the Cuban *guerilleros* in their country. Similar examples can be observed today in connection with the Palestinian universities or the universities in the countries of the Third World in general where the academic authorities have no autonomy and certainly no sovereignty of their own. In the developed countries this is, of course, a debate that has little meaning and it might almost be maintained that a higher level of development and political stability is accompanied by no discussion of the territorial sovereignty of the university whatsoever because this is an issue that does not even arise, just as at a higher level of development and political stability the concept and actual implementation of university autonomy are more permanent and better identified; at the same time, when a higher level of development and greater political stability are achieved, the degree of accountability is also greater and the level of interference by the political power with the academic authorities is correspondingly reduced.

However, techniques have progressively been developed to regulate autonomy, as Volkwein (1987) has made clear with reference to the North American example. This would seem to be the consequence of a process of negotiation between the political and academic authorities, so that the state and the university are constantly engaged in the redefinition of their mutual relations, but without either power imposing its own predetermined criteria on the other, except as a result of this process of negotiation. In other words, the pressure from society is reflected in action by the state to regulate the university in such a way that it becomes more efficient and effective, in conformity with the demands made by society and by the state. The regulatory techniques correspond in brief to the elaboration of a macro-policy that enables the political and academic powers to define their fields of action and preserve their own institutional integrity. When Volkwein suggests new areas of research into the topic of the relations between the state and the academic world, he asks two questions that I consider particularly relevant at this juncture: What is the proper balance between the competing interests of state accountability and campus autonomy? Is there an identifiable point at which state policies and control practices become disincentives to effective management? A similar question might also be formulated in the light of the experience of the autonomous Venezuelan university, for example (the autonomous university is also sovereign to the extent that it is founded on the principle that the university includes territoriality in the concept of its autonomy): to what extent does the state impede the efficient functioning of the university when it applies absolute deregulatory procedures on the assumption that any other attitude would constitute an encroachment on the autonomy of the university?

In the case of Venezuela, the state has certainly been tending to limit the autonomy of the universities, but it has done so indirectly, without discussing negotiating procedures with the academy, by taking its own decisions. In the example mentioned above, the government took action affecting the autonomous university in 1970 when it created mechanisms for the diversification of higher education, thus enabling the role of the autonomous universities which had hitherto been essential in the Venezuelan system of higher education to be reduced. This educational policy proved successful and, at the time of writing (1990), nearly 20 per cent of students following courses of higher education in Venezuela attend non-university institutions, while some 30 per cent more attend universities that have been created without an autonomous statute – in other words they are under governmental control. As a result, enrolments in the autonomous universities have fallen to 50 per cent of the total; it should be noted that universities separate from the autonomous establishments were not created in Venezuela until 1953, the year in which two private universities were opened.

However, to return to the central topic, the question of autonomy remains one of the most important issues affecting the university. Pope John Paul II, for example, issued a series of norms relating to the operation of Catholic universities in 1990, but these standards still upheld the principle of autonomy, despite the expression of the hope that the Catholic universities would respect 'the authority of the Church in matters of faith and morality'. The situation prevailing in the stable British democracy is equally interesting; here the managerial model of education, inspired by the Conservative Government, maintains that 'higher education outcome should or ought to be determined and judged outside itself and in terms of social rather than intellectual criteria', thus endorsing Kogan (1989) in the belief that the universities had been treated 'like religious houses in the early sixteenth century, full of libidinous abbots and corrupt nuns and most in need of reform'.

In any event, the words of Kerr (1990) hold true:

Their autonomy [of the universities] to respond to the internationalization of learning, as to other initiatives they wish to carry out, is affected by their ownership: public or private or some combination; by their governance: external or internal or some combination; by their financing: single sources or multiple sources, and private or public funds distributed as though they were private, for example, through grants or loans to students. How far national purposes may impose their unwanted will on academic purposes depends substantially, country by country, on the long-run strategic situation of institutions of higher education.

In fact, as Levy (1986) has pointed out, this is the case in Latin America and the Caribbean area; in some countries of this region, institutional autonomy is greater in the case of private universities created as a consequence of the growth of this sector in the last three decades. The creation of private universities does admittedly require statutory authorization from the state, but once they have been established they develop criteria of autonomy which are practically absolute. Moreover, some private universities in the region manage to function without statutory recognition, benefiting from the lack of rigorous standards of accreditation. This is the case of the Universidad de la Tercera Edad (University for Senior Citizens) in Venezuela which has been operating at various centres throughout the country since 1985 without legal recognition by the appropriate authority, at least up to the time of writing. However, therelationship between autonomy and the private university is delicate, since in the latter case the immediate interests are much closer to the decision-making process, so that academic freedom can easily be infringed through interference by the proprietors of the universities in their internal affairs. It might be put forward as axiomatic that the autonomous university is alone in being able to achieve acceptable levels of academic freedom, at least in Latin America, because private universities enjoy only a limited and restricted form of academic freedom.

One aspect to which little reference has been made in literature on the autonomy of universities in the strictly academic sense, is the extent to which internationalization of knowledge in reality impinges on the intellectual sovereignty of the universities. As a consequence of technological advances and of the international policies of consensus which are developing in the 1990s, the national academic space is becoming part of a global, universal context where the capacity of the individual universities for autonomy is tending ostensibly to diminish. It is true that the universities are institutions dedicated to universal knowledge, but until very recently that was no more than a rhetorical proposition, a principle and an objective; today, in our global village, this new world dimension is giving rise to an interesting intellectual practice which permits the dissemination of knowledge on an authentic international scale. What Altbach (1987, p. 186) has described as 'knowledge networks in the modern world' are becoming extremely active entities in our contemporary world. He suggests that a better understanding of the way in which knowledge networks function might provide a stimulus for the attainment of autonomy:

The knowledge network is complex. Those who currently dominate the network have considerable advantages. To a considerable extent, they control the copyright system, existing distribution networks and the major international languages. Yet there is room for manoeuvre. A careful understanding of the nature of the network, the interrelationship of its elements and the possibilities for independent action will yield not only understanding of one of the most important aspects of postindustrial society, but may also provide considerable autonomy.

However, this process may obviously engender the opposite effect, namely a loss of autonomy by the universities to the extent that they are caught up in these mechanisms for the international production and dissemination of knowledge that originate essentially in the metropolitan academic centres and reach out to the academic centres of the Third World through the intermediary of rigorous procedures for the transfer of knowledge. In fact, inter-university communication continues to be a North–South relationship and South–South communication only occurs in exceptional cases.

This is easy to observe in the statistics for international student movements from which it emerges that students from almost all the countries of the Third World are present in the metropolitan countries, but there are very few exchanges between Third World countries themselves; this situation is obviously explained by the keen desire to acquire the new technologies which are produced in the industrialized world, but it is often forgotten that when the need arises to solve common problems, as is the case today in the Third World, it inevitably involves the acquisition of familiarity with new technologies as a specific means of resolving common problems.

But these issues of the international relations of a university and its corresponding academic autonomy are affected by the habitual mechanisms of industrial power. We may speak of three levels of pressure on university autonomy: the level of national society, the level internal to the institution itself and this third level of international pressure that follows the pattern of relations between the developed metropolitan countries and the countries of the Third World; however, the latter is certainly not a homogeneous entity since some Third World countries do try to maintain their university autonomy through control of these knowledge networks which are of such vital international importance.

Mention should be made here of the fact that, in the case of Latin America at least, university autonomy is essentially a political conquest, as is apparent from the principles underlying the creation of an autonomous university for the first time in Córdoba, Argentina, in 1918. In fact, the preservation or abolition of university autonomy has been a key indicator for any understanding of the political mechanisms that govern the university. In practice the first action that de facto regimes take is to abolish university autonomy, which is always restored when the country concerned reverts to a state of law. In the Third World countries, the concept of autonomy is thus intimately bound up with the nature of the political regime and with the concept of freedom itself.

There is a general impression that if a distinction is drawn between research universities and teaching universities, the former are in greater need than the latter of their institutional autonomy because in general, as Schwartzman (1989) points out 'the question of university autonomy is always associated with the prestige of science and its indissoluble ties with teaching and the dissemination of knowledge, the issue of democracy being much less important here'. This endorses our point of view that the research universities (described by Parsons as cognitive complexes) are created at an advanced stage of development when autonomy becomes binding in the context of intensive processes of modernization; in that situation the university is, relatively speaking, less dependent on the forms of political government.

Accountability

The subject of accountability is closely bound up with that of autonomy, but may be said to have essentially practical implications. It is a relatively new concept in the modern academic world. However, viewed from the historical angle, university institutions have always been subject to some kind of control. When Bernard de Clairvaux visited Paris in 1139, he spoke in dramatic terms of the need for scholars to preserve their moral standards and good habits, thus giving them an indirect warning that if they did not themselves control their academic lives, others would do it for them (Ferruolo, 1985). Be that as it may, universities have undergone periodic reforms and this procedure no doubt constitutes a form of accountability. Today, however, rather than saving souls, there is a real need for efficient use to be made of public funds and also for the private universities to satisfy the demands of society rather than those of the groups that promote them. Accountability thus becomes a concept involving evaluation and measurement of performance, and monitoring of all the functions of a university. In the strictly technical sense, accountability means rendering accounts not only in the book-keeping sense of the term, but also with reference to the relationship between the objectives and the means, in conformity with the needs of society and of the university itself.

Mortimer (1972) draws a clear distinction between external and internal accountability, that is to say with reference to society at large and to the institution as such. In his view, the need for some form of control by society over the universities exists because this level of education has ceased to be a privilege and become instead an established right in our mass society. But the question then arises as to who in society is to exercise this controlling function in such a way that it effectively meets the abstract needs of society and not those of one particular power group in that society. In democratic societies with anadequate level of pluralism, the answer may take various forms since control may be effected equally by the executive of the country and by professional associations, but in cases where the level of pluralism is less pronounced, society ends up by being synonymous with small power groups. In a pluralistic society, most of the controls are effected through forms of accreditation and institutional authorizations to enable the universities to function, together with general official recognition in particular of academic degrees and diplomas. But in a modern society of that kind, public opinion serves as a permanent factor of accountability, in such a way that the institutions fall into line with certain trends and manifestations of social pressure, often of an innovative nature *vis-à-vis* the university; society itself has mechanisms for change that generally precede changes within the university, for example, changes that enable minority rights to be defended or changes in the representation and role of the sexes.

Unfortunately, however, these mechanisms of public opinion do not exist in many societies of the Third World and institutional control tends to take the form of political repression. This is the reason for the enormous resistance on the part of universities in this part of the world against accepting accountability to a body external to the university itself. This does not mean that the universities are unaware of their relative inefficiency or the need for forms of control. In Brazil, for example, the Rector of Rio de Janeiro University points out that 'in an underdeveloped country like ours, universities end up doing everything, including services that are the state's responsibility. But lack of assessment and control allows much inefficiency' (*The Chronicle*, 11 July 1990). In Mexico, when approval was obtained for mechanisms of control and evaluation of the universities, the opinion was voiced that these were 'government mechanisms to control us', just as the Rector of the National Autonomous University of Mexico stated in an interview that he agreed with the idea of a general evaluation of the Mexican universities, but was well aware that some university administrators viewed this evaluation as a kind of 'inquisition' (*The Chronicle*, 1 August 1990). Similarly there is a trend, even in the developed countries, to reject any external evaluation of higher education. For example, in the United Kingdom a report by the House of Commons sought to establish strict forms of control which met with the disapproval of public opinion. An editorial in *The Times Higher Education Supplement* (14 September 1990) argued two critical issues here:

Universities are public institutions but they are not state institutions . . . the second is that such strict line-by-line financial accountability goes against the spirit certainly, and the letter arguably, of the Education Reform Act. This makes it clear that the Government's and Parliament's control is confined to the public funds given to universities. Their other income is their own business.

At all events, as Mortimer rightly observes:

It is clear that colleges and universities are held accountable to a variety of external interests and agencies: they are accountable to society for the functions they perform, they are accountable to the executive, legislative and judicial branches of government for efficiency in their operations, for controlling excessively deviant faculty and student

behaviour, and for essential fairness and due process in their internal decision-making process.

This view may of course be peculiar to North
American society where such a network of controlling mechanisms does exist. It would be difficult to envisage the concept of accountability
in this form in any other type of society where
the controls often lean towards political and social repression.

Mortimer refers in the second place to internal forms of accountability. Although he does
not refer directly to the following interpretation,
it might be said that internal accountability is
much more necessary and has to do with the
measurement of factors such as the performance
and activities within the university of members
of the teaching and research staff in relation to
their actual function within the institution; the
measurement of the academic and personal performance of students from the standpoint of the
institution, and the performance of the administrative and manual personnel (these being the
categories of staff in any university). Similarly, it
may be appropriate to measure all the other
functions of the university, especially scientific
research, relations with industry and with the
community, dissemination and coverage. In this
internal sense, the university needs a definition
of accountability, and we are told that 'accountability is the guarantee that all students, without
respect to race, income or social class, will acquire the minimum school skills necessary to
take full advantage of the choices that accrue
upon successful completion of public schooling'
(Porter, 1971). However, in societies where educational inequality is relatively great, all the students in effect form part of the whole so that the
first appropriate form of accountability is external in order to ensure that a majority of the persons needing to do so do in fact gain access to
the system of higher education.

Internal resistance to the procedures for the
evaluation of academic performance is extremely strong. In the case of the Venezuelan university for instance, internal evaluation is extremely
difficult to implement because the members of
the teaching and research staff are not an in-

tegral part of the whole, but are members of the
powerful teaching associations that define and
regulate the role of such staff and the number of
working hours that they are required to put in
each week; any form of evaluation is refused unless it can rely on the approval of the Association
of University Teachers which in reality systematically rejects the notion of evaluation in any
shape or form. The rector, who is the highest
university authority in Venezuela, in fact has his
hands tied. The Rector of the Central University
of Venezuela governs but has no power in relation to the academic community. Edward Holyoke, President of Harvard University, said on
his deathbed in 1769: 'If any man wishes to be
humbled and mortified, let him become President of Harvard College'; the rector of an autonomous Venezuelan university might paraphrase Holyoke and say that there is no position
of greater importance in Venezuela from which
it is possible to do absolutely nothing than that
of a rector. He certainly has no authority to organize any evaluation of the teaching and research staff, the students, employees and manual
workers, because each of these groups is protected by rigorous employment contracts which are
to all intents and purposes inviolable. Suffice it
to say that a member of the teaching and research staff in the Venezuelan autonomous universities has a job for life, and no authority exists with the right to change this situation. So
much so that any evaluation tends to be seen as a
restriction of acquired rights and a threat to the
privileges won through many years of struggle
for power. Nothing short of an 'inquisition', to
repeat the words of one Mexican academic. At
the other end of the scale, in the private Venezuelan universities, the contracts of members of
the teaching staff (few staff are engaged in scientific research which is in any case oriented almost exclusively towards semi-professional activities) are renewed annually, so that there is in
effect an internal process of accountability, albeit strictly confined to teaching performance.

Clark (1983) writes that 'almost any educated
person could deliver a lecture entitled "The
Goals of the University". Almost no one will lis-

ten to the lecture voluntarily.' The same adage holds good for the concept of autonomy, especially in Latin America where it is a tenet of academic faith. In effect, much of the rhetorical thinking on the subject of the university in this part of the world turns on the concept of autonomy, though it is not an exclusive feature of this region. In India, for example, the same principle is treated with some reverence in official documents formulating the policy for higher education. Similarly, in the United Kingdom, discussion of university autonomy has become an important feature of educational debate in that country, while the universities of the former German Democratic Republic were obliged, following the unification of Germany, to espouse the concept of autonomy following the pattern that applied in the West.

The concept of accountability is of enormous interest, especially because it presupposes that it will be accompanied by specific techniques to control and regulate the university, a matter in which governments take an excessive interest, though the universities do at the same time believe that suitable forms of accountability could increase their internal efficiency. Many kinds of resistance to accountability do exist and some have already been mentioned. In North America, this resistance stems from certain actors in the educational process and more specifically from the members of the teaching and research staff as

some teachers may not support the accountability concept because it implies that their work is being evaluated – and this is disconcerting to some individuals. In addition, some teachers' associations may oppose the concept on the basis that it implies an evaluation of the entire teaching profession.

Accountability as a principle thus involves innovation, while autonomy is an inherent feature of the traditional concept of the university. Determining how these two issues can be reconciled for the greater benefit of the universities and of the vital process of national and international development, is an interesting challenge to the contemporary academic world. ∎

References

ALTBACH, P. G. 1987. *The Knowledge Context, Comparative Perspectives on the Distribution of Knowledge*. Albany, State University of New York Press.

BERDHAL, R. 1971. Quoted by R. Lindly. 1986. *Autonomy*. Atlantic Highlands, N.J., Humanities International Press Inc.

BERLIN, I. 1958. Quoted by R. Lindly. 1986. *Autonomy*, p. 7. Atlantic Highlands, N.J., Humanities International Press Inc.

BRUNNER, J. J. 1981. *La cultura autoritaria en Chile*. Santiago de Chile, Facultad Latinoamericana de Ciencias Sociales.

CLARK, B. R. 1983. *The Higher Education System. Academic Organization in Cross-national Perspective*. Berkley, Calif., University of California Press.

DURHAM, E. R. 1989. *A autonomia universitaria, O princípio constitucional e suas implicações*, pp. 1–16. São Paulo, Nucleo de Pesquisas sobre Ensino Superior, Universidade de São Paulo.

FERRUOLO, S. C. 1985. *The Origins of the University; The School of Paris and their Critics, 1100–1215*. Stanford, Calif., Stanford University Press.

GABALDON, A. 1982. *La enfermedad latinoamericana de la educación superior*. Caracas, Fondo Editorial para el Desarrollo de la Educación Superior.

KERR, C. 1990. The Internationalization of Learning and the Nationalization of the Purposes of Higher Education: Two 'Laws of Motion' in Conflict? *European Journal of Education*, Vol. 25, No. 1, pp 5–22.

KOGAN, M. 1989. Managerialism in Higher Education. In: Denis Lawton (ed.), *The Education Reform Act: Choice and Control*, pp. 67-81. London, Hodder & Stoughton.

LEVY, D. C. 1986. *Higher Education and the State in Latin America: Private Challenges to Public Dominance*. Chicago, University of Chicago Press.

LINDLY, R. 1986. *Autonomy*. Atlantic Highlands, N.J., Humanities International Press Inc.

MORTIMER, K. P. 1972. *Accountability in Higher Education*. Washington, D.C., American Association for Higher Education.

PERKINS, J. A. 1978. Autonomy. *The International Encyclopedia of Higher Education*, Vol. 2A, pp. 578–83. San Francisco, Jossey-Bass.

PORTER, J. W. 1971. Accountability in Education. In: L. M. Lessinger and R. W. Tyler (eds.), *Accountability in Education*, pp. 42–52. Worthington, Ohio, Charles A. Jones Publishing Co.

SCHWARTZMAN, S. 1989. *Ciencia, profissões e a questão da autonomia*, pp. 1–18. São Paulo, Nucleo de Pesquisas sobre Ensino Superior, Universidade de São Paulo.

VOLKWEIN, J. F. 1987. State Regulations and Campus Autonomy. In: J. C. Smart (ed.), *Higher Education. Handbook of Theory and Research*, Vol. III, pp 120–54. New York, Agathon Press.

Open universities

A comparative approach

Tony Kaye and Greville Rumble

This article is an analysis of the use of distance education methods for post-secondary education, written shortly after the fifteenth World Conference of the International Council for Distance Education (ICDE), held in Caracas in November 1990. The proceedings (Croft et al., 1990; Villaroel and Pereira, 1990) of this meeting, attended by representatives from a very large number of distance teaching institutions and open learning projects throughout the world, demonstrate clearly the great diversity of pedagogies, resources, curricula, media, and organizational structures which characterize the uses of distance education methods in post-secondary education. It has become customary, since a review published by UNESCO some sixteen years ago (MacKenzie et al., 1975), to group such diverse projects together under the banner of 'open learning'; since then a number of new institutions called 'open universities' have been

Tony Kaye (United Kingdom). *Senior Lecturer in the Open University's Institute of Educational Technology. He is currently involved in a number of distance education developments in Europe, and is particularly interested in the potential of new communications technologies for improving the quality of distance learning.*

Greville Rumble (United Kingdom). *Directs the provision of student support services in the East Anglian Region of the Open University. He was previously the university's Planning Officer, and has consulted widely on distance education, particularly in Third World countries, and written widely in the field.*

established (some following the lead of the British Open University) to cater specifically for external or distance students. This article reviews these developments, and makes some predictions about likely future trends. It also points out the limitations of trying to draw comparisons between educational projects which are, in reality, often very different from each other, even within a single country or region.

We do not develop lengthy definitions of the terms 'distance education' and 'open learning' in this article. This has been done elsewhere (for recent reviews, see Kaye, 1988, and Rumble, 1989). It is sufficient to say that we consider distance education as including any organized forms of education in which attendance at a class, tutorial, lecture, or any other form of face-to-face interaction between students and teachers carried out at the same time and in the same place, is *not* the primary learning mode. Should this sound too negative, we could turn it on its head and define distance education as encompassing those forms of instruction in which independent study of specially prepared learning materials is the primary learning mode, and in which the roles of 'teacher' are split between course developers, who design and prepare the learning materials, and tutors, who provide support for the distance student, act as mediators between the institution and the student, and usually evaluate and grade students' work. Distance education institutions can be described as more 'open' than many traditional institutions for a number of reasons specifically arising from the emphasis on independent study: easier access for geographically remote students, flexibility of self-paced study, publicly available learning materials, etc. However, they are not necessarily more 'open' in terms of entry requirements, registration fees, curricula, or any other policy-related matters.

The main purpose of this article is to draw some comparisons between the different ways in which distance education methods have been used for post-secondary education (regardless of whether the words 'open' or 'university' appear in the title of the organizations concerned). We do not attempt to compare the relative quality or effectiveness of distance education systems and campus-based systems. Quality and effectiveness are complex issues. Direct comparisons between traditional and distance teaching institutions are often hard to make: there are curricular differences; the nature of the student population is different; the teaching and learning methods and the conditions of study are different; mature students may be admitted with non-traditional or even no prior educational qualifications, and may have very different expectations as to their educational aims and the way in which they will satisfy them.

Distance teaching methods have been used for over a century for post-secondary and higher education, and the ICDE has recently estimated that there are over 10 million students currently taking degree courses at a distance. There is no question that these methods can be effective, provided that the materials are of adequate quality, the course developers and tutors are competent, the students are motivated, and the necessary resources are made available. In these respects, the picture is little different from that in the traditional education sector – essentially the same variables determine success or failure.

The development of distance education

The first generation of distance education (largely based on correspondence tuition), saw a number of purpose-built distance teaching institutions at the post-secondary level: an Insti-

tute for Teaching by Correspondence was established in Russia as early as 1850, and a number of correspondence-teaching polytechnical institutes came into existence in the Soviet Union in the 1920s and early 1930s. Other early examples of purpose-built providers of post-secondary distance education courses include the Toussaint and Langenscheidt Institute in Berlin (established in 1856, and a pioneer in language teaching by correspondence) and the Swedish Liber Hermods Institute, established in 1898, and at times enrolling over 150,000 students each year.

In addition to institutions exclusively devoted to distance teaching, for many years universities whose main task was to teach traditional students by traditional means, using lectures, seminars and tutorials, had sought to extend their boundaries to meet the needs of part-time adult students and those of normal entry age who for one reason or another – geographical, social, or personal – could not study on-campus. The first tentative steps were made by the University of London which from 1858 allowed qualified candidates to be admitted for degree studies without the necessity of following a course of instruction at one of its approved colleges. This left it open for 'external students' (as they came to be called in 1898) to seek tuition from private correspondence colleges such as University Correspondence College and Wolsey Hall. The logical development was for the university itself to provide correspondence tuition to 'external' students. The first steps were taken not by the University of London but by universities in the United States (Illinois State University, 1874; University of Chicago, 1891; University of Wisconsin, 1906), Canada (Queen's University, 1889), Australia (University of Queensland, 1911) and subsequently copied by many hundreds of higher education institutions both in these and other countries (witness the development of Correspondence Directorates at Indian universities, external studies at Australian and anglophone African universities, *universidades abiertas* in Latin American universities, and independent studies at universities in the United States.

A new pattern of distance education was first given visibility in the higher education world by the establishment of the British Open University over twenty years ago. Given the subsequent development of open universities in other countries, it is easy to forget how innovative the British Open University seemed at the time. As Cyril Houle, Professor of Education at the University of Chicago commented: 'For some not-easily-defined reason, the Open University instantly became a worldwide topic of concern . . . among both educators and the general public' (Houle, 1974, p. 35). The originality of the British Open University lay in the fact that it gave prominence to a second generation of distance education for home-based students, based on the combination of correspondence tuition, face-to-face tutorials, and the use of broadcast media as well as print, within the framework of a publicly funded institution offering its own degrees.

In making general statements about distance teaching at university level, one should bear in mind that there are major differences in scale, curricula, pedagogical approaches and resource levels, between the many different institutions involved throughout the world (see Daniel (1987) for a recent 'world tour' of distance education). One could even ask whether it makes sense to draw any comparisons at all between, say, the Chinese Central Radio and Television University (which teaches hundreds of thousands of students mainly through broadcasting TV recordings of lectures to viewing groups in factories and offices), the Soviet universities operating a 'consultation' model (with around 1.5 million students spending 30 per cent of their study time in face-to-face meetings), and the German Fernuniversität (which uses print-based courses, some backed up with audio and video cassettes, for 37,000 home-based independent learners), simply on the grounds that they happen to be 'distance teaching' institutions. Any generalizations made in the remainder of this article should be understood in this context.

Some achievements of distance higher education

In many ways institutions of the kind referred to by Rumble and Harry (1982) as 'distance teaching universities' (i.e. institutions mandated to teach by distance means, and often called 'open universities') have received a disproportionate amount of attention, compared to the far more common 'mixed mode' institutions which teach by both distance and traditional means, and thus reach both remote and campus-based students. Together, these very different kinds of institutions, operating in diverse social, cultural and economic environments, have achieved remarkable successes.

The use of distance teaching methods has enabled universities to teach far more students than they would otherwise have been able to do. Once courses have been written, they can over a number of years be used to teach many thousands of students. Distance education methods thus open up opportunities. A quarter of all university and college graduates in the former German Democratic Republic had attained their qualifications through distance studies (Möhle, 1988, p. 325). In Asia, the late 1970s and 1980s were marked by the foundation of new distance teaching universities such as the Sukhothai Thammathirat Open University in Thailand, which has had an accumulated enrolment of over 500,000 students, and produced over 78,000 graduates; the Allama Iqbal Open University in Pakistan, which had almost 120,000 students in 1986; and the Indira Gandhi Open University in India, which has a potential annual enrolment of 700,000 students (Taylor and Sharma, 1990). These and other similar institutions increased access to higher education.

While distance teaching methods enable universities to teach students who live at a great distance from the institution, geographical remoteness from students is not a necessary feature of this kind of education. The main characteristic is that learning takes place in the absence of a teacher, so that teaching needs to be in some ways mediated. There is nothing intrinsically odd in a campus-based student studying by distance means, i.e. the bulk of learning is from media and not from sitting in the presence of the teacher. If we think in these terms, we can see how distance education methods can greatly increase the number of students traditional institutions cater for.

Nevertheless, distance education methods do enable institutions to overcome barriers to access, arising from geographical remoteness (e.g. the University of Queensland External Studies Division and the Universidad Nacional de Educación a Distancia, Spain) and inability to attend traditional campus-based universities. The British Open University, for example, has over 3,000 students with disabilities. Many would be unable to attend a traditional university. The Allama Iqbal Open University meets the needs of women in purdah. The Extension Course Institute of the Air University, Montgomery, Alabama (established in 1950) offered technical and professional correspondence courses to US Air Force reservists and personnel on active duty. Above all, distance education systems, by utilizing methods which allow students to study in a place and time of their own choosing, have enabled many millions of individuals who could not have attended a traditional day- or evening-based system to take higher education courses.

Universities using distance teaching methods have thus provided opportunities to qualified school-leavers who, for whatever reason, were unable to take traditional higher education courses at the normal time (ie. post-school), and who have welcomed the opportunity to have a 'second chance' at higher education.

In China the establishment of the Central Radio and Television University was seen as a means of providing a way of educating the many young people whose natural educational development had been disrupted during the cultural revolution (Dieuzeide, 1985, p. 42), while the College of Adult and Distance Education at the University of Nairobi, Kenya, has as its primary objective the education of 'the large majority of adults who were denied higher education opportunities during the colonial circumstances' (Otiende, 1988, p. 351).

The commitment to openness may be linked to the removal of the normal minimum educational qualifications for entry to higher education, as in the case of the British Open University, although, in fact most higher distance education throughout the world is not 'open learning' in this sense. However, distance teaching universities have often implemented innovative academic policies, including modular course structures, a choice of paced and unpaced courses, mixed assessment based on both continuous and final assessment, and considerable freedom for students to choose courses of their own liking, rather than follow heavily prescribed curricula.

Distance education has played a major part in the in-service training and professional upgrading of teachers. Particularly in Asian, African, and Latin American countries, the expansion of education in response to population growth and increasing participation rates has posed major problems for educational planners. The population of Kenya is expected to double in 18 years, that of the United Republic of Tanzania in 20 years, that of Nigeria and the Philippines in 25 years. (In contrast, it will take 462 years for the population of the United Kingdom to double at its current rate of growth.) Distance education is one way of training untrained teachers – or upgrading existing teachers – without taking them out of the classroom, and many countries have been quick to seize the opportunity presented them, with in-service teacher training projects to be found, for example, in Botswana, Costa Rica, Nigeria, Pakistan, Swaziland, Thailand and the United Republic of Tanzania. In many, though not all, of these countries the responsibility for delivery of such projects rests with the universities. Similar in-service training courses are also to be found in many of the wealthier countries.

Universities also have a significant role to play in other areas of vocational training. For example, in the former German Democratic Republic 'the main factor influencing higher education . . . is its applicability to economic activity' (Möhle, 1988, p. 326). In China current policy in regard to higher education at a distance is based on the principle that 'the only goal of higher correspondence education' is 'to serve economic reconstruction' (Jianshu, 1988, p. 451). In the United Republic of Tanzania the National Correspondence Institute was established *inter alia* to contribute to manpower development in the country, and to help accelerate national development (Kiyenze, 1988, p. 284). The National Open University, Taiwan, founded in 1986, has as one of its aims the provision of on-the-job training at university level (Chen, 1988, p. 164).

Distance education is believed to be a means of reducing the costs of education and training. Although the establishment of distance teaching institutions and their infrastructure, and the investment in the development of course materials, can be very significant, these costs can be spread over very large numbers of students. The direct costs of teaching are, however, generally lower than those found in traditional systems. As a result the high capital investment can be offset by reduced expenditure on teachers (labour), with the result that, provided student numbers are high enough, average costs are lower than (perhaps up to a third of the value of) those found in traditional institutions. A number of studies have shown that distance education can be cheaper than traditional methods of higher education: for example, Wagner (1980) on the British Open University, Muta and Sakamoto (1989) on the Japanese University of the Air, Guadamuz Sandoval (1988) on the Universidad Estatal a Distancia, Costa Rica, and Nielsen (1990) on the effectiveness of in-service teacher training projects in a number of countries.

However, these results should be interpreted with great care, for a wide range of reasons. Firstly, one is not always comparing like with like (distance learners may be older, or more highly motivated than campus-based students; curricula may be different; distance learning may be the *only* way of reaching certain groups such as practising teachers etc.). Secondly, it is not always clear how infrastructure costs for dis-

tance learning should be allocated (the British Open University uses existing postal and broadcasting services, and the staff and facilities of other universities and polytechnics, at marginal cost to itself). Finally, of course, the cost of a distance learning system – as of a conventional system – depends in large measure on the resources invested. The British Open University is much better resourced, and hence more costly than, say, the Allama Iqbal Open University in Pakistan, even though both institutions cater for comparable numbers of students. Even though the British Open University's unit costs per graduate are less than those for a traditional university student, they are probably not very much less than those of a graduate taking a degree course at a polytechnic in the United Kingdom.

The evidence on effectiveness is mixed. For years, correspondence education had a bad reputation. Drop-out rates were often higher than in traditional forms of education. The foundation of distance teaching universities was often greeted with considerable scepticism. On the other hand, individual distance teaching universities have produced many thousands of graduates, notwithstanding the fact that, in some cases, a higher proportion of their students fail to graduate than is the case in traditional institutions offering similar courses. However, amongst the factors determining completion or success rates, it is virtually impossible to isolate those which are specifically related to the *form* of education (distance or campus-based), even when similar curricula and assessment procedures are being compared. Student characteristics (age, motivation, location, economic level) may differ, as may the level of involvement (campus-based students are often studying full-time, distance learners generally are part-time students). Drop-out and repeater rates can be high in both distance and campus-based institutions: the factors which influence their level are more likely to be associated with assessment policies and the quality and extent of student support than the teaching method *per se*. Clearly, a correspondence student getting no help from a tutor or other students is more likely to drop out than a student taking an equivalent course at a well-staffed campus university; by the same token, a distance learner working with good quality self-study materials, with a tutor and other students available over the telephone and at regular study centre meetings, may be less likely to drop out than a student whose sole source of education is attendance at overcrowded lectures.

Some significant issues facing higher distance education

A number of criticisms can be made of current distance education methods, especially if one is comparing them to some idealized campus-based provision (small groups of students learning from motivated and experienced teachers, with access to libraries, laboratories, computers, etc.). The strength or significance of these criticisms will vary from one culture or situation to another, but they can be summarized as follows:

The limited opportunities for discussion, both between students and with tutors and other resource people: even when opportunities for discussion with tutors are provided, the people filling the tutor roles are rarely the same as the people who prepared the distance study materials, so opportunities for discussion with 'master teachers' are rare.

The relative inflexibility of distance learning courses in catering for individual needs, interests and experiences: the distance learner, once embarked on a course, has little or no opportunity to change its direction, or influence what is taught (this may also, in fact, be the case in many conventionally taught courses, but in a distance system, it is a constraint of the teaching method *per se*, rather than of institutional policy or the teacher's inclination).

The high cost of producing, modifying and up-dating mass-produced print and audio-visual distance learning materials; the higher the quality of these materials, the more they cost to produce, and the greater is the temptation to enrol as many students as possible on the same courses, and to re-use the materials in the same form for many years; indeed, the entire cost structure of distance education is based on the resultant economies of scale.

The need to rely on infrastructure for communications (post, telephone, transport, etc.) and for some aspects of materials production (printing, broadcast production, etc.), which are outside the control of the institution and of its teachers, and whose malfunctioning can jeopardize the quality and effectiveness of provision.

The extent to which these factors – endemic to many current distance teaching universities – are seen as disadvantages will vary from one context to another, and will depend very much on the ultimate purpose of the distance education project. The second and third factors above might not be drawbacks for a country-wide in-service teacher training programme in a new national curriculum, planned to run over a five-year period, although they would be in the context of, say, an information technology course for up-dating managers from different types of organizations and companies. And the importance assigned to dialogue in formal educational systems varies significantly from one culture to another – as it does from one educational philosophy or discipline to another within the same culture.

DIALOGUE AND INTERACTIVITY

The limited provision for dialogue in many distance education systems is seen as a major disadvantage by those with a humanistic vision of education, and is more difficult to remedy than in a traditional campus-based system where it is in principle possible to re-arrange teaching methods to allow for more seminars and other group activities, if the need arises. Harris (1987, p. 137) has argued that the 'conventions of "good writing" and "good broadcasting" found in distance education systems pre-construct a largely passive student'. What is important in higher education 'is argument between people, unconstrained discussions which raise "validity claims" of several types, and which settle these claims only by the force of the better argument'. For Harris, 'the most obvious medium for these discussions is face-to-face contact' – although he acknowledges that the mere presence of such discussion does not guarantee 'democratic discussions' of the kind which he identifies 'as the kernel of the critical role of the university'.

Distance education course developers can build in self-assessment questions which can encourage students to enter into a discussion with themselves. Holmberg (1989, pp. 43–6) writes of the need to incorporate what he calls guided didactic conversation into distance teaching materials. However, Harris (1987, p. 119), and Lockwood (1989, pp. 210–14) have challenged the extent to which students do in fact make use of self-assessment questions and student activities to engage in a 'discourse' with their materials. And in any event, such self-testing procedures, although possibly useful for checking on acquisition of skills and knowledge, are no substitute for interactive discussion with other students and teachers.

In this context, the feedback provided by correspondence tuition gains considerable importance. Unfortunately, the quality and extent of such written feedback may not be very good, and it may arrive too long after the event for the student to be able to incorporate it into his understandings. Research (Rekkedal, 1983) also shows that the longer the delay between the submission of an assignment and receipt of comments on it the higher the drop-out rate.

Recognition of the importance of more immediate forms of two-way communication than can be provided by the postal service has led many distance teaching institutions to incorporate some face-to-face teaching into their systems. This is often used as a means of ensuring that the students have understood the teaching materials and are as prepared as can be for the examination. A similar function is undertaken by telephone teaching (either one-to-one, or, using conference call systems, one-to-a number of students), and, in some instances, by computer-me-

diated communication, through one-to-one electronic mail and group-based computer conferencing (Mason and Kaye, 1989).

Unfortunately, the costs of interacting are high. As the amount of face-to-face and technology-mediated tuition and interpersonal communication increases, so the direct cost per student increases. Ultimately this will undermine the potential cost advantage of distance education, which stems from the substitution of capital (locked up in the development of course materials and the technical infrastructure needed for production and distribution) for the labour of classroom teachers.

MATERIALS DEVELOPMENT AND INFRASTRUCTURE

In countries where distance education is being used to meet high priority development needs, concern over the level of dialogue in the system, or the cost of updating material, or of tailoring it to individual needs, might seem at first sight a luxury, especially if there are not enough teachers available to meet educational needs through traditional methods. However, as Zahlan has pointed out, 'one of the difficulties faced by Third World countries is the weakness of the activities that digest, criticize, process, and market knowledge' (Zahlan, 1988, p. 83). The temptations can be strong to import, often without adaptation, distance teaching material produced elsewhere. In some cases, where the courses are relevant to local needs, such an approach might be defensible (e.g. the Open Learning Institute of Hong Kong). In other cases, the course materials may be irrelevant to these needs, the process of adapting them might be too complex, and they might not be accompanied by the student support services for which they were designed. Nevertheless, where local expertise and resources for producing multi-media distance teaching materials at university level do not exist, the temptation to buy in and adapt material produced elsewhere can be great.

But the origin or development of teaching materials is only one problem faced by many countries wishing to expand educational provision through distance education methods. Speaking of distance education in Africa, Jenkins (1989, p. 48) has indicated that 'few politicians and ministry of education officials have demonstrated any strong commitment to distance education. Despite its intensive use, in most countries it has low status and remains on the periphery'. As a result, funding is often insufficient. As Jenkins comments elsewhere, 'the barriers to improvement in distance education in many cases are to do with resources' (Jenkins, 1990, p. 38).

Such poverty is reflected in the lack of printing capacity, the poor maintenance of printing machinery, and the problems posed by the high cost of paper referred to by Kiyenze (1988) in respect of distance education in the United Republic of Tanzania and the problems of understaffing referred to by Siaciwena (1988, p. 202) in respect of the distance teaching system at the University of Zambia. Further problems may be engendered by the poor communications infrastructure within a country: in Zambia, for example, the majority of roads are not all-weather roads, and the telephone system cannot be relied upon to provide an effective student support system (Siaciwena, 1988, pp. 203, 204). Travel may be expensive and time-consuming, as in Indonesia (Setijadi, 1988, p. 194). The recruitment and training of qualified staff may be difficult, as in Indonesia (Setijadi, 1988, p. 195) and Zambia (Siaciwena, 1988, p. 205). Finally, not all systems are cost-effective, high quality, mass education systems. The number of students on the University of Papua New Guinea extension studies programme was so low that it 'operates like a handicraft industry rather than a mass production device' (Kaeley, 1978, p. 33). Nor are all systems necessarily cost-effective, in comparison with traditional systems. Yet, despite such reservations, there is plenty of evidence that distance education has contributed much to the development of higher education. Daniel (1987, pp. 30–1) points out that 'both individual countries and international organizations such as the World Bank appear satisfied with the results of investment in higher distance education' and the very fact that distance education projects have a commitment to formative evaluation of their programmes means that 'most programmes have an impressive array of statistics about their operation and can often be shown to be self-improving systems'.

Likely future trends

It is, of course, difficult to look into the future, but in this final section we shall attempt to identify what we see as some of the trends in the development of higher education at a distance over the next few years.

A PHASE OF CONSOLIDATION AND LIMITED GROWTH

Firstly, it seems likely that the well-established national open universities to be found in many European, Asian and Latin American countries will continue to function in much the same way as they have done in the past, with the addition of new programmes and target groups in response to social, economic, political and market needs. The same applies to the extension/correspondence studies departments of conventional universities. In some cases, existing institutions may be merged with others (as has happened with the creation of the Open Learning Agency in British Columbia – an amalgam of three pre-existent distance teaching organizations).

In some countries, however, the established distance teaching universities will be competing for students with campus-based institutions trying to increase their economic viability by widening access to part-time study, through evening classes, open learning courses, and various forms of distance education. Competition for the part-time (paying) adult student has increased recently, as governments reduce funding for education. So institutions will have to decide whether to reduce their expenditure, widen their student base, or increase their fees to compensate for loss of government support. The last course of action will undoubtedly reduce the ability of deprived sectors of the community to take advantage of a form of education which, above all others, seems to cater for their needs. More significantly, institutions will find themselves offering those courses for which there is a ready commercial market. Examples might include business studies, law and languages. The broad-based curriculum found in many distance teaching universities may be threatened.

The pressure to reduce costs may lead to changes in the range of media used for distance education, which will become apparent in different ways. Precisely at the time when the potential range of media is increasing rapidly, we already see institutions in some poorer countries who cannot afford to make use of the media now available in the wealthier countries, and for whom print and correspondence tuition, supported by audio, is likely to remain the basic strategy in the immediate future. In other cases, budgetary pressure is likely to lead to a reduction in the level and quality of student support services such as tutorials, correspondence tuition and counselling, which in turn will lead to an increase in drop-out rates (Paul, 1988) and an overall lowering of the effectiveness of the system.

The generally depressed economic climate will, of course, have other effects. For some years now, educational budgets have been reduced or have had to be spread further, with consequential falls in the unit of resource (the average amount of money provided for education per student). It seems unlikely that this will change. On the face of it, this appears to make distance education, with its potential economies of scale, an attractive proposition. Yet there are financial reasons why this may not happen. Firstly, this would imply a switch in resources, from traditional to distance education sectors. Powerful vested interests will resist such moves. Unless more politicians begin to see distance education as a viable alternative to traditional forms of higher education, the change is unlikely to occur. Secondly, the high initial cost of setting up new institutions makes it likely that

there will be further pressure on traditional universities to engage in distance education – this will be seen as a cheaper and less risky alternative. So, with a few isolated exceptions such as the Vietnamese Peoples' Open University (Arger and Tran, 1990), we do not feel that there is likely to be, in the 1990s, the appearance of a second wave of new 'open universities' comparable to that of the last two decades.

NETWORKING AND THE 'DISTRIBUTED CLASSROOM' MODEL

The dominant pedagogy of many distance teaching universities and institutions is based on independent study of print (and some multi-media) materials, with fairly minimal levels of student support through correspondence tuition and occasional face-to-face meetings. Alongside the continuing (if economically restricted) activities of the institutions based on this model, we think it is likely there will be an increase over the next few years in the number of projects using different pedagogical models of distance education – models which put more emphasis on learning in groups, on networking (in the broad sense), and in a more central role for the individual teacher. In this last respect, they contrast strongly with the conventional 'open university' model, where the individual teachers are subsumed into the relative anonymity of the course team (the course developers who prepare the self-study materials), and local tutors play essentially a remedial and evaluative role.

The growth of this new generation of projects – most of which are appearing in the economically developed countries – can be related to a number of factors:

Wider access to new technology for students (e.g. telephones, home computers, modems, facsimile machines) and for course developers and teachers (desk-top publishing, networking services, satellite broadcasting).

Growing demand from industry and many service organizations for continuing education, re-training and updating of their staff.

Increasing competition for part-time adult students, which has encouraged many traditional universities to widen their target audiences, often through the use of new technologies and/or through the establishment of consortia with industry and with training organizations.

A move towards a 'post-Fordist' society, in which products are produced in more limited numbers aimed at increasingly segmented markets, and there is an increased consciousness of the need to respond to the individual consumer; for distance learning,[1] this presupposes a greater commitment to addressing the needs of the individual learner, as flexibly as possible (Rumble, 1990). What many of these projects are doing, effectively, is to use communications technology to 'distribute' the classroom teacher, through radio, audio-conferencing, satellite TV transmissions of lectures, and, more recently, computer conferencing (see, for example, Bacsich et al., 1986). This is not new – the model of groups of learners coming together during a radio or TV broadcast, and then discussing the broadcast material amongst themselves under the guidance of a local *animateur* or tutor, is one that has been used for many years at a variety of levels. Examples include the use of radio in Nicaragua, Mexico, the Dominican Republic, Senegal and Kenya (Jamison et al., 1978), and in the Canary Islands (Cepeda, 1982); examples at the higher education level include the use of satellite television to broadcast lectures to groups distributed over a wide area, such as at the Chinese Central Radio and Television University and the China TV Teacher College (Fuwen Gao and Weiwei Li, 1990; Zhao Yuhui, 1988), or the National Technological University in the United States (Sarchet and Baldwin, 1990). The University of Wisconsin has been using audio-conferencing for nearly thirty years (recently supplemented with slow-scan TV) through a state-wide Educational Telephone Network to allow groups of up to 10 students to interact with teachers from 170 different learning sites.

In the last few years, there has been a resurgence of interest in 'technology-based' distance education projects. Examples cited in a recent study (Open University, 1990) include:

IBM's use of two-way video via satellite for in-house training and up-dating, both in the United States and in Europe.

Rio Salado Community College in Arizona, which has distance classes linked both through audio-conferencing and computer conferencing.

The Open Learning Agency in Vancouver, which runs networks for both audio-conferencing and audio-graphic conferencing.

The French Conservatoire National des Arts et Métiers, which uses school computer rooms for networked evening classes, enabling students to download teaching material from a central computer in Nantes, and to interact with their teacher through electronic mail.

A course for health care professionals in Denmark, run entirely through computer conferencing, with students and teachers connecting to the system from personal computers in homes and offices.

Other examples could be cited, especially in the domain of computer networking (see, for example, Mason, 1990). Computer conferencing has been heralded as 'third generation distance education', based on the active creation of new knowledge and understandings by groups learning together (Nipper, 1989), or as representing a 'new domain' for education, qualitatively different from both classroom instruction and traditional distance education (Harasim, 1990).

One of the attractions of such technology-based projects is that – assuming the students have access to the necessary equipment – it is possible for teachers in traditional institutions (or company training departments) to introduce and run new courses and programmes far more rapidly and flexibly than would otherwise be possible, either through traditional face-to-face teaching or through traditional distance education. This is a key factor for EuroPACE, for example, which (like the National Technological University) produces and transmits by satellite to reception sites throughout Europe up-to-date videos of lectures and demonstrations by experts in fields such as engineering, electronics and telecommunications. These transmissions are supported by desk-top published print materials and a computer conferencing network. Much less time and investment is required to film experienced teachers in their classrooms, or to ask them to teach a group using computer conferencing or audio-conferencing, than is needed to assemble a course team to produce a package of self-study materials for independent learners.

Distance educators from open universities wedded to the course-team approach – and the quality control that this can guarantee – might be sceptical about the pedagogical and academic quality of 'talking head' television programmes, of the often meandering discussions which are common in computer conferences, or of the speed and ease with which individual teachers can now produce professional-looking print materials with desk-top publishing packages on a personal computer. However, the fact that courses based on these technologies are generally for *groups* of learners, who can easily discuss the course amongst themselves and with a tutor, means that the same painstaking attention to detail that is required in self-study material for isolated learners is perhaps not so critical. Furthermore, as in a classroom situation, adjustments can be made relatively easily – something which is much more problematic in the conventional mass distance education course.

Conclusion

Learn one-fourth from the teacher,
One-fourth from self-study,
One-fourth from fellow-pupils and
One-fourth while applying knowledge
from time to time.
(Sanskrit verse quoted by Gomathi Mani, 1990, p. 129.)

In general, we believe that the existing distance teaching universities will continue to thrive wherever they fill a clear need which is not being met by other institutions. Many of these institutions will probably continue teaching successfully in the ways they have done in the past – whether the main emphasis in particular cases is on the use of print-based independent study materials, or on group viewing of broadcast lectures, or on face-to-face meetings supplemented with private study.

However, we believe that there will be increasing pressure from conventional higher education institutions for a share of the adult, part-time student market – in fact it is the very success of distance education and open learning methods over the last two decades that has encouraged other institutions to adopt them. It may well be the case that the increasing use of self-study and distance or open learning materials in campus-based institutions illustrates a convergence of distance education and traditional classroom-based pedagogies (Smith and Kelly, 1987). One thing is clear: many conventional institutions are now embarking on distance teaching, producing their own flexible open learning materials (print, audio-visual and computer-based), and using new technologies to provide 'distributed classrooms'. And a significant number of traditional open universities in Europe and elsewhere have started using electronic publishing, computer networking, and satellite delivery technologies in ways which might eventually lead to major changes in the 'industrial' (mass production and delivery) model of distance education. The convergence of these technologies means, for example, that it is possible to use the same electronic medium for teacher-produced text and graphics, conferencing and information exchange between participants in a course, and data-bases of reference information. This is likely to have a major influence in the future on the cost structure of distance education, and on the potential for inter-institutional collaboration in course production and teaching.

We think it unlikely that a significant number of new 'open universities' (on the model of those set up in the 1970s and 1980s) will appear in the current decade. It is more likely that some new distance teaching universities will be set up as networked consortia, which, in the econom ically advanced countries at least, will make some use of computer networking and/or satellite technologies. In the European context, a number of such initiatives are already on the drawing board: these include a proposed French open university, and even a 'European Electronic University' (a pilot project of the Commission of the European Communities' DELTA programme). Whether such technological star-gazing will also result in a truly *global* university (Utsumi and Urbanawicz, 1990) remains to be seen! But the challenge is there, and it is one which calls into question the economic basis of many of the established distance teaching universities, for new technology developments, with their emphasis on flexibility and increased responsiveness to student needs, are often likely to lead to increases in student-related costs. This implies a shift in funding from front-end course materials development and production to better and more comprehensive support services for students. If this results in greater flexibility and a more balanced mix of independent study, group interaction and student–teacher contact than is to be found in either the conventional lecture-based mode of higher education, or in the traditional independent-study mode characteristic of many 'open universities', then the overall quality of students' learning experiences will be improved. The challenge in achieving this goal will be to maintain the best features of the 'industrial' model of distance education (quality control, cost-effectiveness, attention to the needs of the independent learner) with the best features of the new technologies – particularly those of flexibility, interactivity, co-operation and immediacy. ∎

Note

1. Distance education institutions on the Open University model, with their mass production and delivery systems, have been seen as 'Fordist' organizations – that is, 'economic organizations designed to exploit economies of scale in assembly-line factories making standardized goods for homogeneous mass markets' (Hirst, 1989, p. 18).

References

ARGER, G.; TRAN, D. T. 1990. *ZIPOU Vietnamese People's Open University: The Evolution of an Ideal.* In: M. Croft, I. Mugridge, J. S. Daniel and A. Hershfield (eds.), *Distance Education: Development and Access.* Caracas, International Council for Distance Education/Fondo Editorial Universidad Nacional Abierta.

BACSICH, P.; KAYE, A.; LEFRERE, P. 1986. *An International Survey of Information Technologies for Education and Training.* (Oxford Surveys in Information Technology, 3.)

CEPEDA, L. 1982. Radio ECCA, Canary Islands. In: A. Kaye and K. Harry (eds.), *Using the Media for Adult Basic Education.* London, Croom Helm.

CHEN, S.-M. 1988. Creating the National Open University in Taiwan: The Influence of Cultural and Educational Factors. In: D. Sewart and J. S. Daniel (eds.), *Developing Distance Education.* Oslo, International Council for Distance Education.

CROFT, M.; MUGRIDGE, I.; DANIEL, J. S.; HERSHFIELD, A. (eds.). 1990. *Distance Education: Development and Access.* Caracas, International Council for Distance Education/Fondo Editorial Universidad Nacional Abierta.

DANIEL, J. S. 1987. World Trends in Higher Distance Education and Opportunities for International Cooperation. In: UNESCO, *Higher Level Distance Education*, pp. 17–42. Paris/Victoria (Australia), UNESCO/Deakin University.

DIEUZEIDE, H. 1985. Les enjeux politiques. In: F. Henri and A. Kaye (eds.), *Le savoir à domicile. Pédagogie et problématique de la formation à distance.* Sainte-Foy (Canada), Presses de l'Université du Québec/Télé-Université.

FUWEN GAO AND WEIWEI LI. 1990. Speeding Up the Development in China by Distance Education. In: M. Croft, I. Mugridge, J. S. Daniel and A. Hershfield (eds.), *Distance Education: Development and Access*, pp. 40–42. Caracas, International Council for Distance Education/Fondo Editorial Universidad Nacional Abierta.

GOMATHI MANI. 1990. Problems Unique to Distance Education. In: M. Croft, I. Mugridge, J. S. Daniel and A. Hershfield (eds.), *Distance Education: Development and Access*, pp. 127–9. Caracas, International Council for Distance Education/Fondo Editorial Universidad Nacional Abierta.

GUADAMUZ SANDOVAL, L. 1988. Universided Estatal a Distancia. In: J. B. Oliveira and G. Rumble (eds.), *Educación a Distancia en América Latina.* Washington, D.C., Economic Development Institute of the World Bank, 1991.

HARASIM, L. (ed.) 1990. *On-line Education – A New Domain.* New York, Praeger.

HARRIS, D. 1987. *Openness and Closure in Distance Education.* Lewes (United Kingdom), Falmer.

HIRST, P. 1989. After Henry. *New Statesman and Society*, 21 July, pp. 18–19.

HOLMBERG, B. 1989. *Theory and Practice of Distance Education.* London, Routledge.

HOULE, C. O. 1974. *The External Degree.* San Francisco, Jossey-Bass.

JAMISON, D. T.; KLEES, S. J.; WELLS, S. J. 1978. *The Costs of Educational Media: Guidelines for Planning and Evaluation.* Beverly Hills/London, Sage.

JENKINS, J. 1989. Some Trends in Distance Education in Africa: An Examination of the Past and Future Role of Distance Education as a Tool for National Development. *Distance Education*, Vol. 10, No. 1, pp. 41–63.

——. 1990. A Response to the Article by Geoff Arger on 'Distance Education in the Third World'. *Open Learning*, Vol. 5, No. 3, pp. 37–9.

JIANSHU, Z. 1988. The Development of Higher Distance Education in China. In D. Sewart and J. S. Daniel (eds.), *Developing Distance Education.* Oslo, International Council for Distance Education.

KAELEY, G. S. 1978. The Impact of Distance Education in Papua New Guinea. *ICDE Bulletin*, No. 14, pp. 18–36.

KAYE, A. R. 1988. Distance Education: The State of the Art. *Prospects*, Vol. XVIII, No. 1, pp. 43–54.

KIYENZE, B. K. S. 1988. Distance Education and National Development in Tanzania. In D. Sewart and J. S. Daniel (eds.), *Developing Distance Education.* Oslo, International Council for Distance Education.

LOCKWOOD, F. 1989. A Course Developer in Action: A Reassessment of Activities in Texts. In: M. Parer, *Development, Design, and Distance Education*, pp. 205–16. Churchill (Australia), Centre for Distance Learning, Gippsland Institute.

MACKENZIE, N.; POSTGATE, R.; SCUPHAM, J. (eds.). 1975. *Open Learning: Systems and Problems in Post-secondary Education.* Paris, UNESCO.

MASON, R. 1990. *The Use of Computer Networks for Education and Training.* Sheffield (United Kingdom), The Training Agency.

MASON, R.; KAYE, A. (eds.). 1989. *Mindweave: Communication, Computers and Distance Education.* Oxford, Pergamon Press.

MÖHLE, H. 1988. Social Development in the GDR: Consequences of Higher-level Distance Education. In: D. Sewart and J. S. Daniel (eds.), *Developing Distance Education.* Oslo, International Council for Distance Education.

MUTA, H.; SAKAMOTO, T. 1989. The Economics of the University of the Air of Japan Revisited. *Higher Education*, No. 18, pp. 585–611.

NIELSEN, H. D. 1990. *Using Distance to Extend and Improve Teaching in Developing Countries.* Paper presented to the World Conference of Education for All, Jomtien, Thailand, 5–9 March 1990.

NIPPER, S. 1989. Third Generation Distance Learning and Computer Conferencing. In: R. Mason and A. Kaye (eds.), *Mindweave: Communication, Computers and Distance Education.* Oxford, Pergamon Press.

OPEN UNIVERSITY (United Kingdom). 1990. *State of the Art in Open and Distance Education.* Report prepared for the PRECISE project of the DELTA programme. Brussels, Commission of the European Communities, Directorate-General XIII.

OTIENDE, J. E. 1988. Distance Education and National Development: The Case of the External Degree Programme of the University of Nairobi, Kenya. In: D. Sewart and J. S. Daniel (eds.), *Developing Distance Education.* Oslo, International Council for Distance Education.

PAUL, R. 1988. If Student Services Are so Important, then Why Are We Cutting Them Back? In D. Sewart and J. S. Daniel (eds.), *Developing Distance Education.* Oslo, International Council for Distance Education.

REKKEDAL, T. 1983. The Written Assignments in Correspondence Education. Effects of Reducing Turn-around Time. *Distance Education*, Vol. 4, No. 2, pp. 231–52.

RUMBLE, G. 1989. 'Open Learning', 'Distance Learning', and the Misuse of Language. *Open Learning*, Vol. 4, No. 2, pp. 28–36.

——. 1990. Tomorrow's Education and Training: The Challenge for Distance Education. In: M. Croft, I. Mugridge, J. S. Daniel and A. Hershfield (eds.), *Distance Education: Development and Access.* Caracas, International Council for Distance Education/Fondo Editorial Universidad Nacional Abierta.

RUMBLE, G.; HARRY, K. (eds.). 1982. *The Distance Teaching Universities.* London, Croom Helm.

SARCHET, B.; BALDWIN, L. 1990. The National Technological University Meets a World-wide Need. In: M. Croft, I. Mugridge, J. S. Daniel and A. Hershfield (eds.), *Distance Education: Development and Access.* Caracas, International Council for Distance Education/Fondo Editorial Universidad Nacional Abierta.

SETIJADI. 1988. Indonesia: Universitas Terbuka. *Prospects*, Vol. XVIII, No. 2, pp. 189–97.

SIACIWENA, R. M. C. 1988. The External Degree Programme at the University of Zambia. *Prospects*, Vol. XVIII, No. 2, pp. 199–206.

SMITH, P.; KELLY, M. 1987. *Distance Education and the Mainstream.* London, Croom Helm.

TAYLOR, J. C.; SHARMA, K. 1990. Distance Education in South Asia: Towards Regional Cooperation. In: M. Croft, I. Mugridge, J. S. Daniel and A. Hershfield (eds.), *Distance Education: Development and Access.* Caracas, International Council for Distance Education/Fondo Editorial Universidad Nacional Abierta.

UTSUMI, P.; URBANAWICZ, C. F. 1990. Inexpensive Methods of Global Education for Third World Countries. In: M. Croft, I. Mugridge, J. S. Daniel and A. Hershfield (eds.), *Distance Education: Development and Access.* Caracas, International Council for Distance Education/Fondo Editorial Universidad Nacional Abierta.

VILLAROEL, A.; PEREIRA, F. (eds.). 1990. *La educación a distancia: desarrollo y apertura.* Caracas, International Council for Distance Education/Fondo Editorial Universidad Nacional Abierta.

WAGNER, L. 1980. Costs and Effectiveness of Distance Learning at the Post-secondary Level. In: UNESCO, *The Economics of New Educational Media.* Vol. 2: *Cost and Effectiveness*, pp. 225–55. Paris, UNESCO.

ZAHLAN, A. 1988. Issues of Quality and Relevance in Distance-teaching Materials. *Prospects*, Vol. XVIII, No. 1, pp. 75–83.

ZHAO YUHUI, 1988. China: Its Distance Higher Education System. *Prospects*, Vol. XVIII, No. 2, pp. 217–28.

The privatization
of higher education

Jandhyala B. G. Tilak

The context

Privatization of higher education is not a new phenomenon in the world economy. In many countries of the world, the private sector has come to play either a limited or predominant role in higher education. In some countries, the origin of privatization can be traced back a few centuries. But privatization has assumed greater significance as a policy strategy of the development of education in recent times, essentially, but not wholly, due to stagnating – and in some countries declining – public budgets for education, on the one hand, and on the other, increasing social demand for higher education, manifested in slogans like 'higher education for all' (Roderick and Stephens, 1979).

There has been remarkable growth in privatization during the last two to three decades in several countries of the world, as shown in Table 1. The number of private colleges and universi-

ties has increased, and enrolments in private institutions increased at a much faster rate than in public institutions. enrolments in private institutions increased by several times in many countries – for example, in Colombia, by 1.7 times the rate of growth of public education and 2.03 times in Peru from the mid-1960s to the mid-1970s (Brodersohn, 1978, p. 176). In a good number of countries the share of enrolments in private education and the number of private institutions as a proportion of the total number of institutions are more than half of the total (see Tables 2 and 3).[1]

Private education has grown for several reasons, which can be summed up in two categories: excess demand and differentiated demand for higher education (James, 1987). First, the social demand for higher education exceeds the public supply, and the private market seeks to

Jandhyala B. G. Tilak (India). *Professor and Head of the Educational and Finance Unit at the National Institute of Educational Planning and Administration (New Delhi); previously with the World Bank. He has also taught at the University of Delhi, the Indian Institute of Education and the University of Virginia. His publications include:* Economics of Inequality in Education; Educational Finances in South Asia; Education and Regional Development; Education, and its Relation to Economic Growth; Poverty and Income Distribution; *and* Political Economy of Education in India.

TABLE I. Privatization trends in selected countries (percentage of enrolments in private higher education)

Country	Earlier Year		Latest Year		Change
Colombia	1953	33.6	1983	60.4	+26.8
Japan	1950	57.0	1980	81.3	+24.3
Republic of Korea	1955	55.2	1986	76.9	+21.7
Latin America	1955	14.2	1975	33.7	+19.5
Thailand	1967–71	1.9	1977–81	5.5	+3.6
Argentina	1970	14.6	1987	9.8	–4.8
United States	1950	49.7	1988	24.7	–25.0

Sources: Colombia: Patrinos, 1990, p. 163; Japan and United States: Kaneko, 1987, p. 27, Cohn and Geske, 1990, p. 73; Republic of Korea: Lee, 1987, p. 56; Latin America: Levy, 1985; Thailand: Malakul, 1985, p. 56; Argentina: Balan, 1990, p. 14.

TABLE 2. Enrolments in public and private higher education (percentages)

Country	Year	Public	Private	Total[1]
Philippines	1984/85	15.3	84.7	1 504
Republic of Korea	1986	23.1	76.9	1 262
Japan	1989	24.4	72.6	2 067
Indonesia	1985/86	33.3	66.7	900
Colombia	1983	39.6	60.4	356
Cyprus	1986/87	41.9	58.1	3.5
Burma	mid-1980s	42.0	58.0	–[2]
Bangladesh	mid-1980s	42.0	58.0	–
India	mid-1980s	43.0	57.0	–
Pakistan	1968	49.0	51.0	151
Chile	1986/87	54.5	45.5	233
Brazil	1983	64.8	35.2	693
Malaysia	mid-1980s	76.0	24.0	–
United States	1988	75.3	24.7	8 500
Argentina	1987	91.2	9.8	7 531
Papua New Guinea	mid-1980s	94.0	6.0	–
Thailand	mid-1980s	94.0	6.0	–
Spain	1981/82	97.0	3.0	–
China	mid-1980s	100.0	0.0	–
Sri Lanka	mid-1980s	100.0	0.0	–

1. In thousands.
2. Not available.

Sources: Philippines: Elequin, 1990, p. 312; Republic of Korea: Lee, 1987, p. 56; Japan: Nishihara, 1990, p. 26; Indonesia: Toisuta, 1987, p. 73; Colombia: Patrinos, 1990, p. 163; Cyprus: Koyzis, 1989; Pakistan: Jiménez and Tan, 1987*b*, p. 178; Chile: Schiefelbein, 1990; Brazil: Schwartzman, 1988, p. 100; United States: Cohn and Geske, 1990, p. 73; Argentina: Balan, 1990; Spain: McKenna, 1985, p. 461; other (Asian) countries: Tan and Mingat, 1989, p. 202.

meet the unsatisfied demand.[2] Secondly, demand for different quality (presumably high quality) and content in education (such as, for

TABLE 3. Percentages of public and private sectors in higher education: institutions

Country	Year	Public	Private	Total[1]
Republic of Korea	1986	19.6	80.4	256
Philippines	1985/86	27.6	72.4	1 158
Japan	1985	28.8	71.2	1 103
Brazil	1983	83.9	16.1	124
United States	1980	84.5	15.5	–[2]
Pakistan	1976/77	96.1	3.9	433

1. Actual numbers.
2. Not available.

Sources: Republic of Korea: Lee, 1987, p. 56; Philippines: Elequin, 1990, p. 340; Japan and United States: Kaneko, 1987, p. 23; Brazil: Schwartzman, 1988, p. 100; Pakistan: Jiménez and Tan, 1987*a*, p. 178.

example, religious education) also contributes to the growth of privatization. On the supply side, private entrepreneurs are ready to provide higher education either for philanthropic or other altruistic motives, or for profit. The dividends could be social and political gains, or quick economic profits.

Diversities in privatization

Higher-education systems in the world present enormous diversity. Two major categories of higher education can be found in this context: predominantly public higher-education systems, where higher education is provided and funded by the state (as it is in socialist countries, for example), and mixed higher-education systems with varying roles by both public and private sectors (as found in the rest of the world). Again under the latter category, there is significant diversity from country to country. Some systems are dominated by the private sector, which can be termed as 'mass private and restricted public sectors' as in several market economies (e.g. Japan, Republic of Korea, Philippines, and Latin American countries such as Colombia). Then there are mixed systems dominated by the state sector, as in several developing countries of South Asia (including India), Africa, and Western Europe. These systems can be aptly described as 'parallel public and private sectors'. In some welfare states such as the Netherlands and Belgium, both coexist under state funding. Systems where the private sector has a very limited role, as in Sweden, the United Kingdom, France, Spain, Thailand, etc., can be described as 'peripheral private sector' (Geiger, 1987*a*).

In practice, the public/private distinction of a higher-education institution is not very clear. If the criterion used to define it is its source of funding, a private university may be receiving substantial financial resources from the government; and a public university may generate large amounts of resources from private sources. On the other hand, if it is to be defined on the basis of management, a private institution may be effectively controlled by the state, and may be administered according to government regulations. Alternatively we may prefer to define institutions in terms of their character, that is, whether they be 'profit-making' or 'non-profit making'. All this shows how ambiguous the term 'privatization' can be.

Several forms of 'privatization' of higher education may be noted and classified into four categories (Tilak, 1991).

First, an extreme version of privatization implying total privatization of higher education, colleges and universities being managed and funded by the private sector, with little government intervention. These pure or 'unaided' private institutions do provide financial relief to the government in providing higher education, but at huge long-term economic and non-economic cost to the society.

Second, there is 'strong' privatization, which means recovery of full costs of public higher education from users – students, their employers or both. Due to the externalities associated with higher education, privatization of this type may not be desirable, and of course not empirically feasible.

Third, there is a moderate form of privatization implying public provision of higher education but with a reasonable level of financing from non-governmental sources. Since higher education is a quasi-public good, 100 per cent public financing of education can be seen as economically unjustified. Since private individuals also benefit, it is reasonable that they share a proportion of the costs. So the state, students/ families and the general public pay for higher education. This will be discussed in more detail below.

Lastly, there is what can be termed 'pseudo-privatization', which cannot be really called privatization. higher-education institutions under this category are private but government-'aided'. They were originally created by private bodies, but receive nearly the whole of their expenditure from governments. Thus these institutions are privately managed but publicly funded. A substantial number of private higher-education institutions in several countries belong to this category, and they receive government aid to meet almost all their recurrent expenditure. Hence strictly from the financial point of view, such private colleges do not play any significant role.[3]

Despite these diversities, a broad generalized analysis of the role of the private sector in higher education can be made. However, the generalizations made below refer mostly to the first and the fourth categories of privatization, as described above. Some of the following general features may also fail to take account of certain particularities of some private institutions which are exceptions to the rule.[4]

Myths and facts about privatization

The case for privatization of higher education exists mostly on the basis of financial considerations. Public budgets for higher education are at best stagnant, and are indeed declining in real terms, more particularly in relation to other sectors of the economy. Privatization is also favoured on the grounds that it would provide enhanced levels of internal and external efficiency of higher education, and higher quality of education; and as the private sector would have to compete with the public sector, the competition would result in improvement in quality and efficiency not only of private education but also even public higher education. In the long run, due to economies of scale, private institutions provide better quality education at lower cost than public institutions, as in Japan. Furthermore, by reducing public subsidies to higher education, the 'perverse effects' of public subsidization of higher education on income distribution could be reduced, and, through privatization, inequities in funding education would be substantially reduced (see Psacharopoulos, 1986; Psacharopoulos and Woodhall, 1985; Roth, 1987; James, 1987).

TABLE 4. Expenditure per student in higher
education (private/public)

Country	Year	Ratio
Thailand	1977–81	0:25
Republic of Korea	1985	0:71
Japan	1980	0:72
United States	1988	1:60

Sources: Thailand: Malakul, 1985, p. 59; Republic of Korea: Kim, 1990, p. 240; Japan: Kaneko, 1987, p. 29; United States: Cohn and Geske, 1990, p. 73.

On the other hand, privatization is opposed on at least three sets of grounds. The existing market system does not ensure optimum social investment in higher education, as externalities exist in the case of higher education, which is a 'quasi-public good' (Tilak, 1991). The market system also fails to keep consumers well informed of the costs and benefits of higher education. It is likely that the costs of private education are much higher than public education as in the United States and the Republic of Korea. Finally, a private system of higher education is also insensitive to distributional considerations, and in fact contributes to socio-economic inequalities. Accordingly, public education is not only superior to private education, but private institutions cannot even survive without state support.

All these arguments for and against privatization, by its defenders as well as its opponents, are open to empirical verification, without which they may be brushed aside by the opposing side as merely politico-ideological arguments. Sophisticated arguments based on hard core evidence are rarely made in favour of privatization (Breneman and Finn, 1978, p. 6). Without empirical evidence, all the arguments, however well-formulated and articulated, remain as 'myths'. With this in mind, a few of these myths are empirically examined below, by examining the scanty evidence available, with examples drawn from diverse countries.

THE FIRST MYTH

There is huge demand for private higher education, as private education is qualitatively superior to public education.

The facts

The evidence shows that the higher quality of private education compared with public higher education is exaggerated. In Japan, public higher education provides better facilities, which are significantly related to quality, than private universities and colleges. The number of pupils per teacher in public universities is only eight, compared with twenty-six in private universities (James and Benjamin, 1988). While more than 75 per cent of students enrolled in higher education in the country are in the private sector, teachers in this sector constitute less than half the total. The pupil/teacher ratio in private institutions is three times the ratio in state institutions in Indonesia and the Philippines, and more than double in Thailand. The difference is not as high in Brazil, but the ratio clearly favours public higher education, the ratios being fourteen and ten respectively in private and public universities. Private universities are found to employ more retired, part-time, and under-qualified teachers in Japan, Colombia, Brazil, Argentina, Indonesia and in several other countries. The teachers are also paid less. Only government subsidies could raise the salary levels of teachers in private universities in Japan. On the whole, teachers in private institutions have less academic prestige.

Even the availability of space per student and other facilities are reasonably higher in public universities than in private universities in Japan. In all, private universities spend less than half of what public universities spend per student (see Table 4). For example, in Japan, in 1980, expenditure per student was 1,982,000 yen in public universities, compared with 848,000 yen in private universities (Kaneko, 1987). It is only in the United States that the difference is in favour of private universities.[5] All this should indicate that quality differences are indeed more favourable to public than to private universities.

Yet private universities may sometimes show better results in final examinations, as essentially they admit only the best prepared students. However, 'graduation of the "best" graduates is not by itself proof of the "best" education' (Levy, 1985, p. 454).

Even if the quality of output is taken into consideration, that is, internal efficiency, measured in terms of academic achievement, success rates, drop-out rates, failure rates, etc., private education does not compare favourably with public education. The large body of evidence available on this issue refers to the school sector, and not to higher education. Even with respect to the school sector, recent studies (Willms, 1987) have found that the advantage of private schooling with respect to academic achievement for an average student is not significant, as reported earlier (Coleman et al., 1981). The limited information available on higher education leads us to question the beliefs regarding the superiority of private education. drop-out rates are higher in private colleges than in government colleges in Thailand (NEC, 1989, p. 287), and in the Philippines (Arcelo and Sanyal, 1987, p. 154), and the rates of failure are high in Colombia (Patrinos, 1990). The productivity of private universities in Indonesia is found to be much lower than public universities (Pramoetadi, 1985, p. 33).

In the Philippines, while the private sector increased accessibility to education to the people, it was found to have contributed to a deterioration in the quality and standards of higher education to such an extent that many people argued for a halt of the public laissez-faire policy in the growth of higher education and for the expansion of state supported institutions (Tan and Alonzo, 1987, p. 159). In Brazil and Peru, the quality of private higher education was described as 'disgraceful' (Levy, 1985, p. 453).

In India, except for those institutions recognized by the public sector, private colleges, which receive no aid from the government, have been increasing in number essentially due to the existence of excess demand for higher educa-

tion, particularly from the upper classes and those who fail to gain admission to government colleges. Rarely is the quality of these institutions regarded as superior. Their growth also has to do with the fact that people tend to equate high fees with a high quality of education (Breneman, 1988). Above all, many non-élite private universities and colleges were created, as is the case in some Latin American countries, to provide job-related training, rather than higher education *per se.*

It is also argued that as the private sector has to compete with the public sector, the efficiency of the former and, equally important, the efficiency of all higher education, including public, improve significantly. But in countries where mass private sectors prevail, or in countries where private sectors play a peripheral role, there is little scope for competition, and as a result, the private sector may turn out to be very inefficient, and even economically corrupt.[6] Thus the arguments on efficiency and quality of private higher education do not withstand close scrutiny.

THE SECOND MYTH

It is widely believed that graduates from private universities receive higher rewards on the labour market in the form of lower unemployment rates, better paid jobs and consequently higher earnings (Jimenez and Tan, 1987b; Patrinos, 1990). In short, the external efficiency of private higher education is argued to be greater than public higher education, which would explain the growth of privatization.

The facts

The empirical evidence does not support these assumptions. Unemployment rates among graduates from private universities are about 2.8 times higher than those from public universities in the Philippines (Arcelo and Sanyal, 1987, p. 190). This is also the case in Thailand where 27 per cent of graduates from private universities are unemployed during the first year after graduation, compared with 13.3 per cent of the grad-

TABLE 5. Percentage rates of return to private versus public higher education

	Private	Public
United States		
Private rates of return	15.0	18.0
Thailand		
Private rates of return	10.46	19.51
Social rates of return	9.75	9.48
Philippines	8.75	12.55
Japan		
Private rates of return		
Social sciences	7.5	9.0
Engineering	7.0	9.0
All higher[1]	6.7	7.1
Social rates of return		
Social sciences	7.8	7.6
Engineering	7.1	6.6
All higher[1]	6.9	5.4

1. Yano and Maruyama, 1985, p. 80.

Sources: United States: Leslie and Brinkman, 1988, p. 64; Thailand: National Education Commission, 1989, p. 169; Philippines: Arcelo and Sanyal, 1987, p. 169; Japan: James and Benjamin, 1988, pp. 77, 106.

uates from national universities (Setapanich et al., 1990, p. 420). Private universities in Cyprus are found to be fuelling the diploma-inflation problem, leading to a serious problem of graduate unemployment (Koyzis, 1989, p. 18).

Estimated rates of return, a summary statistic of the external or labour-market efficiency of education (presented in Table 5), show that public higher education pays better than private higher education, particularly from the point of view of individuals in several countries, including Japan, the Philippines, and Thailand. Social rates of return for public and private university education are close in Thailand, showing little significant advantage for private higher education, even from the point of view of the society.[7]

THE THIRD MYTH

Private institutions provide considerable relief from financial burden to the governments, as they are self-financing.

The facts

States such as Malaysia allocate huge investments – more every year – to prop up dubious private institutions, while growth and expansion of public institutions are frozen. In Thailand, while 30 per cent of students attend private institutions, the ratio of government expenditure to private expenditure on higher education is 97:3 (Malakul, 1985). Explicit appropriations may be not be very high; but implicit subsidies or indirect government support to the students to purchase higher education is an important source of funding for private universities in the United States. State scholarships have exposed the myth of the pure privateness of universities like Harvard, Columbia, Yale, etc. (Levy, 1986*b*, p. 171).[8] Around 85 to 90 per cent of scholarship money in California goes to students in private universities, while private enrolments form only 10–12 per cent of the state's total (Levy, 1986*b*, p. 174). In Japan, 21.5 per cent of private higher-education expenditure is covered by state subsidies (this figure was nil in 1951). State subsidization of private institutions in Japan originated due to the bankruptcy of private higher education. The resources of the private institutions are boosted 'through infusion of significant amounts of public funds' in several countries (Geiger, 1987*b*, p. 18). In many countries, state subsidies cover more than 90 per cent of the recurrent expenditure of private institutions. In Sweden and Canada, the government provided the capital needs of the private institutions. More than 77 per cent of the government budget on higher education in Uttar Pradesh in India goes as aid to private colleges (Muzamil, 1989, p. 247). Whatever the reasons, private and public universities in Belgium and the Netherlands receive equal funding from the state (Geiger, 1988). All this leads us to conclude that most private institutions are not totally private, at least from a financial standpoint.

THE FOURTH MYTH

The private sector responds to the economic needs of the individual and society, and provides

TABLE 6. Percentage of specialization of private and public sectors in higher education in Latin America

	Bolivia	Colombia	Ecuador	Mexico	Peru	Argentina[1]
Commercial						
Private	58	37	23	35	47	–[2]
Public	10	10	18	20	23	–
Humanities						
Private	12	5	9	1	7	9
Public	2	7	6	2	0	–
Law						
Private	0	16	6	6	5	2
Public	8	4	6	9	4	–
Medicine						
Private	0	4	1	20	1	7
Public	21	9	11	20	7	–
Exact Sciences						
Private	0	4	3	1	6	–
Public	15	12	5	4	4	–
Engineering						
Private	0	17	8	17	8	–
Public	23	26	17	24	29	–

1. Balan, 1990, p. 16.
2. Not available.
Source: Levy, 1985, p. 456.

relevant types of education. 'The major advantage of private universities has been in responding more quickly or efficiently to market demands' (Balan, 1990, p. 17).

The facts

In most countries, private higher-education institutions offer mainly low capital-intense disciplines of study. It is true that not only are there few private universities involved in research activities, but they are also involved in providing cheap commercial and vocational training as in the case of several Latin American countries, or in the case of 'parallel' colleges in Kerala in India (Nair and Ajit, 1984). As can be seen in Table 6, no private institutions in Bolivia offer higher education in law, medicine, exact sciences, engineering; 58 per cent specialize in 'commercial' courses, and 12 per cent in the humanities. In Peru, Colombia and Ecuador, a negligible proportion of private institutions offer courses in medicine and exact sciences. However, when the potential for economic profit is high, the private sector entered into professional fields

and opened engineering and medical colleges, as in India (Kothari, 1986). On the whole, research and broad educational needs of the economy are barely served by the private sector. Private institutions tend to provide more personal and fewer social benefits to students. The private sector responds to market demands, but only in the short term, while 'improvement of schools requires long-term planning – not the quick alteration of a commodity to meet changing fashions' (Ping, 1987, p. 21).

THE FIFTH MYTH

It is generally believed that private enterprise has genuine philanthropic motives in opening private colleges and universities, which are by definition part of the 'non-profit sector'. They also make huge investments in higher education.

The facts

Private institutions are largely funded either from students' tuition fees and charges or from public subsidies. Very few private institutions make any investment from their own resources. These institutions are in fact operated in a kind of seller's market, recovering the full costs plus profits from some source or other. For instance, in Japan 70 per cent of the costs of higher education in private institutions are met from tuition fees, while the corresponding proportion is 82 per cent in the Republic of Korea. The role of private finances other than fees, such as donations, endowments etc., is not at all significant. In the United States, however, tuition charges account for only slightly more than one-third of the total costs. Private institutions are involved in disguised profit-making operations in almost all countries, including Brazil and India.

The private colleges that receive little public support in India expect huge donations and capitation fees, and charge abnormally high fees, ten to twenty times higher than those charged by government colleges. While universities and colleges are, by definition, non-profit institutions, these private institutions do not merely cover their costs, they also make huge 'quick profits', which are not necessarily reinvested in education. Educational considerations hardly figure in this context (Tilak, 1990). As a result, higher education is subject to vulgar commercialization.

THE SIXTH MYTH

It is generally noted that private education is élitist, and caters to the needs of the wealthy. For example, I have hypothesized earlier (Tilak, 1986), largely based on evidence on the school sector, that the benefits of education in private institutions – costly and presumably of high quality – accrue largely to the élite (as the private sector caters mainly to the needs of the élites), while the benefits of education in public schools – which are generally compelled to choose quantity rather than quality and, accordingly, provide inexpensive education – mostly for the masses.

The facts

Private universities generally serve a privileged clientele. In Colombia private universities are dominated by high-income groups. Barely 2 per cent of the students are from the bottom quintile and 13 per cent from the bottom 40 per cent of the income group population. The picture is similar in Japan. In Thailand, students in private universities have parents with, on average, one and a half times the income of those of students in public universities. The democratization of public higher education has reduced considerably the élitist character of higher education. The social élitism attached to private higher education was found to be one of the most important factors in the growth of an élite private sector in higher education in Latin American countries (Levy, 1985). The private institutions lent an élitist or secular-élitist character to higher education.

In countries characterized by 'mass private and restricted public sectors' such as Japan, the Philippines and Brazil, the evidence is not clear cut, as there are significant diversities within private universities. Some private universities are highly élitist and selective, while others are not. In these countries, there are a few élite private universities, and a large number of low-quality, low-cost private universities and colleges – for example, in Colombia and Brazil.

On the whole, however, as fees in private universities are very high compared with public universities, only the relatively well-to-do opt for private higher education. In the United States and Thailand, for example, fees per student in private universities are five times those in public institutions; the corresponding ratio in Japan is 2.5:1. But as access to public higher education is restricted, students from the upper and professional classes are more or less forced to go to private universities. However, 'public universities continue to be the first choice for many' for educational and financial reasons (Levy, 1985, p. 454).

Most public higher-educational institutions are politicized. Only private institutions are apolitical.

The facts

Basically the inadequacy of public policies results in the growth of the private sector. In some Latin American countries, as public policies favoured leftist political activism in public universities, private universities have grown to counter these forces. But to argue that private institutions are free of political forces is not true. Private education has been found to strengthen a given political ideology and to help in reproduction of class structure (Salter and Tapper, 1985). In several countries, state support to private universities is based on political and ideological factors, which can be called 'political-economic' factors. In India, for example, more than half the private engineering colleges in Maharashtra are owned by politicians, and used for political purposes. Motives of profit, influence and political power explain the growth of these private colleges (Rudolph and Rudolph, 1987, p. 296; Kothari, 1986).

Privatization of higher education improves income distribution, as public funding of higher education, with all its 'perverse effects' is generally found to be regressive (Psacharopoulos, 1977; Blaug, 1982).

The facts

As evidence from Japan – one of the few countries to have carried out elaborate investigations on this issue – shows, public universities seem to have slightly higher redistributive effects than private universities in transferring resources from the top income quintile to the others. The advantage enjoyed by public institutions is greater in the school sector (James and Benjamin, 1988, p. 127). In the case of India, it has been found that the private education system contained forces that contribute to disparities, and that the state sector was not adequate enough to counteract these forces. As a result, the whole education system was found to be a contributing factor towards accentuating income inequalities (Dasgupta, 1979).

An assessment of pros and cons

Previously, I classified privatization into four categories: (a) extreme privatization (total or pure private institutions); (b) strong privatization (full cost recovery); (c) moderate privatization (partial cost recovery); and (d) pseudo-privatization (government-aided private sector). The above analysis largely refers to the first and last forms of privatization only. Based on available evidence on a few major countries of the world, this analysis has exploded some of the myths.

In many countries, the growth of privatization can be attributed largely to the failure of public universities, while private universities have certainly made positive contributions. Private universities in some countries, such as the United States, have contributed in important and unique ways to diversity, independence, quality, efficiency and innovation (Breneman and Finn, 1978, p. 6). In countries like Japan, each private university has its own identity, tradition, culture, etc. In contrast, public universities hardly offer any diversity or individual choice. In this sense, privatization increases the possibilities for individual choice in the type and quality of higher education. But 'the stress upon individualism – upon individual preference – at the expense of social responsibility and cohesiveness must be a matter of concern' (Ping, 1987, p. 291).

In many countries private higher education eases the impending financial burden faced by the public authorities. One noteworthy example is Chile, where total public expenditure on higher education was reduced from $171 million in 1981 to $115 million 1988 (Schiefelbein, 1990) as private education grew. Without this, governments would either have to suppress the huge demand for higher education, or find themselves in deeper financial deficit. In fact, political and economic stability would have been threatened in some Latin American countries, if it were not for the role of private sector (Levy, 1985, p. 451). In most cases, however, resources come from students, not from other private sources. Private institutions supplied manpower not only to the private but to the public sector of the economy as well. Private universities are also believed to reduce the number of students going to foreign universities, as in the case of Greece (Psacharopoulos, 1988).

But the goals and strategies of the private sector in higher education are on the whole highly injurious to the public interest. First, the private sector has turned the 'non-profit sector' into a high-profit-making sector not only in terms of social and political power, but also in terms of financial returns, and as profits are not allowed in educational enterprises in several countries, private educational enterprises have resorted to illegal activities in education. When governments attempted to regulate profits by allowing state subsidies and restricting fee levels, all the private institutions found they had one thing in common – a demand for subsidies. In the first instance, state subsidies eased the financial crisis of the private universities, as in Brazil, and in the long run contributed to 'private enrichment at public expense'. As a result of all this, many countries today have 'bastard' private-sector colleges, either illegally set up to do legal business, or legally created to do illegal work (Singh, 1983).

Secondly, by concentrating on profit-yielding, cheap, career-related commercial studies, the market-oriented private universities provide vocational training under the name of 'higher education' and ignore 'broader higher education'. Private universities also totally ignore research, which is essential for sustained development of higher education.

Thirdly, by charging high fees, private institutions create irreparable socio-economic inequities between the poor and rich income groups of the population. As a World Bank study noted, private education turns out to be 'socially and economically divisive' (Psacharopoulos and Woodhall, 1985, p. 144). Access to higher education by lower income groups is negatively affected by the rapid growth of privatization.

It is generally felt that 'even if one assumes that the private sector is generally superior to the public sector, it does not logically follow that proportional expansion of the private sector would make for a better system' (Levy, 1985, p. 458). In short, private education is not found to be economically efficient, qualitatively superior, and socially equitable. Accordingly, it is feared that increased privatization of higher education would present more problems than solutions, as in case of Colombia (Patrinos, 1990, p. 169). Thus the inappropriateness of the market metaphor in higher education is abundantly clear.

Towards a desirable pattern of privatization

Privatization of the second and third categories mentioned above may not be characterized by so many problems. As higher education is a quasi-public good, 100 per cent cost recovery may not be desirable. In other words, the second type is neither desirable nor practically feasible. At the same time, since individuals do benefit from higher education, it is natural that they are required to pay for their education (Tilak, 1991). The dwindling economic abilities of governments also make it necessary. Hence the notion of choice relates only to the third category.

Under this category, privatization implies provision of public education, but with reasonable levels of costs recovered from the users. In other words, it means private purchase of public education at less than full cost. In this context, there are a few major proposals being discussed in several countries, such as increase in fees, student loans, graduate tax, etc. (World Bank, 1986). Some of these are being tried out in a few countries. The experience of those countries makes it clear that each of these alternatives has its own strengths and weaknesses (see, for example, Tilak and Varghese, 1991). A tax on graduates would be efficient if there were a strong relationship between education, occupation and productivity, and a low degree of substitution between different layers and types of higher education, so that those with higher education do not find themselves unemployed. Student loans transfer the burden from the present to the future, and for the loan schemes to work effectively, well spread credit markets to float educational loans are required, without which the recovery of loans would be a serious problem. Of these three measures, fees seem to be the most effective. The experience of the Republic of Korea is encouraging in this regard: nearly half the costs of public higher education are met by students in the form of fees (Table 7). However, instead of a uniform increase in fees, selective pricing (Tilak and Varghese, 1985; Jimenez, 1987; Tilak, 1990) may be more efficient and equitable.

TABLE 7. Fees as percentage of total expenditure on higher education

Country	Year	Public	Private	Total
Colombia	mid-1980s	5.0	85.0	–
Republic of Korea	1985	49.6	82.3	73.4
Japan	1980	13.3	70.4	54.0
United States	1986/87	14.5	38.7	22.4

Sources: Colombia: Jimenez and Tan, 1987b, p. 134; Republic of Korea: Lee, 1987, p. 61; Japan: Kaneko, 1987, p. 24; United States: Williams, 1990, p. 9.

Under selective pricing, students belonging to different socio-economic groups would be required to pay different rates of fees, which would be related to the ability of the students to pay and the costs of courses. Privatization of this type would be more efficient, generating additional private resources for higher education, and also more equitable, as it would not create dual structures of higher education, as do the other forms

described above – one for the élite and another for the masses. As Ping (1987, p. 291) noted, 'All children matter, not just those whose parents have learnt to play the market effectively.' In fact, privatization of this form will be free from most of the evils of other forms discussed above, and may assimilate the diverse strengths of privatization. ∎

Notes

1. However, even though the private market mechanism is, in general, strong, the share of the private sector in higher education in enrolments in the United States decreased from about half in 1950 to a quarter in 1988.
2. For example, in 1988 the rapid growth of demand, including overseas demand, for higher education in Australia, led to privatization of hitherto public higher education (Stone, 1990).
3. Other types of classification have been proposed. (See, for example, Khadira, 1990.)
4. Universities, colleges and other higher-education institutions, either public or private, vary in size and other characteristics. Here they are referred to as if they were homogeneous.
5. The private higher-education system in the United States seems to be distinct from others with respect to several other characteristics.
6. While Latin American countries may present an excellent example of the first kind, countries like India provide examples for the second category.
7. In Kenya, government schools are found to yield returns 50 per cent higher than private (*harambee*) schools, both to the individual and to society (Knight and Sabot, 1990, p. 291). See also Psacharopoulos (1987) for similar data on Colombia and Tanzania.
8. Voucher schemes also come under the same category.

References

ARCELO, A. A.; SANYAL, B. C. 1987. *Employment and Career Opportunities after Graduation. The Philippine Experience.* Manila, Fund for Assistance to Private Education, for IIEP.

BALÁN, J. 1990. Private Universities within the Argentine Higher Educational System, Trends and Prospects. *Higher Education Policy,* Vol. 3, No. 2, pp. 13–17.

BLAUG, M. 1982. The Distributional Effects of Higher Education Subsidies, *Economics of Education Review,* Vol. 2, No. 3, pp. 209–31.

BOYD, W. L.; CIBUKALA, J. G. 1989. *Private Schools and Public Policy, International Perspective.* London, Falmer.

BRENEMAN, D. W. 1988. *College Cost and Tuition, What are the Issues? Proceedings from a National Conference.* Washington, D.C., National Center for Postsecondary Governance and Finance.

BRENEMAN, D. W.; FINN JR, C. E. 1978. An Uncertain Future. In: D. W. Breneman and C. E. Finn Jr (eds.), *Public Policy and Private Higher Education*, pp. 1–61. Washington, D.C., Brookings.

BRODERSOHN, M. S. 1978. Public and Private Financing of Education in Latin America. A Review of its Principal Sources. *The Financing of Education in Latin America*, pp. 146–76. Washington, D.C., Inter-American Development Bank.

COHN, E.; GESKE, T. G. 1990. *Economics of Education*, 3rd ed. Oxford, Pergamon Press.

COLEMAN, J. S.; HOFFER, T.; KILGORE, S. 1981. *Public and Private Schools.* Chicago, National Opinion Research Center.

DASGUPTA, A. 1979. Income Distribution, Education and Capital Accumulation. Washington, D.C., World Bank.

ELEQUIN, E. T. 1990. Survey Report – Philippines. In H. Muta (ed.)., *Educated Unemployment in Asia*, pp. 305–72. Tokyo, Asian Productivity Organization.

GEIGER, R. L. 1987a. *Private Sectors in Higher Education, Structure, Function and Change in Eight Countries.* Ann Arbor, University of Michigan Press.

——. 1987b. Patterns of Public-Private Differentiation in Higher Education, An International Comparison. In: RIHE, *Public and Private Sectors in Asian Higher Education Systems: Issues and Prospects*, pp. 7–20. Hiroshima, Hiroshima University.

——. 1988. Public and Private Sectors in Higher Education, A Comparison of International Patterns. *Higher Education*, Vol. 17, No. 6, pp. 699–711.

——. 1990. The Dynamics of Private Higher Education in the United States, Mission, Finance and Public Policy, *Higher Education Policy* Vol. 3, No. 2, pp. 9–12.

HAERTEL, E. H.; JAMES, T.; LEVIN, H. M. (EDS.). 1987. *Comparing Public and Private Schools.* Vol. 2: *School Achievement.* New York, Falmer.

JAMES, E. 1987. The Public/Private Division of Responsibility for Education, An International Comparison, *Economics of Education Review*, Vol. 6, No. 1, pp. 1–14.

JAMES, E.; BENJAMIN, G. 1988. *Public Policy and Private Education in Japan.* London, Macmillan.

JIMÉNEZ, E. 1987. *Pricing Policy in the Social Sectors.* Baltimore, Johns Hopkins/World Bank.

JIMÉNEZ, E.; TAN, J.-P. 1987a. Decentralized and Private Education. The Case of Pakistan. *Comparative Education*, Vol. 23, No. 2, pp. 173–90.

——. 1987b. Selecting the Brightest for Post Secondary Education in Colombia: The Impact of Equity. *Economics of Education Review*, Vol. 6, No. 2, pp. 129–35.

KANEKO, M. 1987. Public and Private Sectors in Japanese Higher Education. In: RIHE, *Public and Private Sectors in Asian Higher Education Systems, Issues and Prospects*, pp. 21–34. Hiroshima, Hiroshima University.

KHADIRA, B. 1990. Privatization of Higher Education, *Main stream*, Vol. 28, 24–25, 7–14, April, 25–26, Vol. 35; and 24–28.

KIM, T.-C. 1990. Survey Report – Republic of Korea. In H. Muta (ed.), *Educated Unemployment in Asia*, pp. 223–304. Tokyo, Asian Productivity Organization.

KNIGHT, J. B.; SABOT, R. H. 1990. *Education, Productivity and Inequality, The East African Natural Experiment.* New York, Oxford/World Bank.

KOTHARI, V. N. 1986. Private Unaided Engineering and Medical Colleges: Consequences of Misguided Policy. *Economic and Political Weekly*, Vol. 21, No. 14, pp. 593–96.

KOYZIS, A. A. 1989. Private Higher Education in Cyprus: In Search of Legitimacy, *Higher Education Policy*, Vol. 2, No. 2, pp. 13–19.

LEE, K. 1987. Past, Present and Future Trends in Public and Private Sectors of Korean Higher Education. In: RIHE, *Public and Private Sectors in Asian Higher Education Systems, Issues and Prospects*, pp. 49–70. Hiroshima, Hiroshima University.

LESLIE, L. L.; BRINKMAN, P. T. 1988. *The Economic Value of Higher Education.* New York, Macmillan/American Council on Education.

LEVY, D. C. 1985. Latin America's Private Universities, How Successful are They? *Comparative Education Review*, Vol. 29, No. 4, pp. 440–59.

——. 1986a. *Higher Education and the State in Latin America – Private Challenges to Public Dominance.* Chicago, University of Chicago Press.

——. 1986b. 'Private' and 'Public', Analysis Amid Ambiguity in Higher Education. *Private Education: Studies in Choice and Public Policy*, pp. 170–92. New York, Oxford.

——. 1986c. Alternative Private-Public Blends in Higher Education, International Patterns. In: D. C. Levy, (ed.), *Private Education: Studies in Choice and Public Policy*, pp. 195–213. New York, Oxford.

——. (ed.). 1986d. *Private Education: Studies in Choice and Public Policy.* New York, Oxford.

MALAKUL, P. 1985. Prospects and Problems in Higher Education Expansion in Thailand. In RIHE, *Higher Education Expansion in Asia*, pp. 52–65. Hiroshima, Hiroshima University.

McKENNA, J. B. 1985. University Reforms in Spain, *Comparative Education Review*, Vol. 29, No. 4, pp. 460–70.

MUTA, H. (ed.). 1990. *Educated Unemployment in Asia.* Tokyo, Asian Productivity Organization.

MUZAMIL, M. 1989. *Financing of Education.* New Delhi, Ashish.

NAIR, R. G.; AJIT, D. 1984. Parallel Colleges in Kerala. *Economic and Political Weekly*, Vol. 19, No. 42/43, pp. 1840–7.

NEC (NATIONAL EDUCATION COMMISSION). 1989. *Costs and Contributions of Higher Education in Thailand.* Bangkok, NEC.

NELSON, S. C. 1978. Financial Trends and Issues. In: D. W. Breneman and C. E. Finn Jr (eds), *Public Policy and Private Higher Education*, pp. 63–142. Washington, D.C., Brookings.

NISHIHARA, H. 1990. Private Colleges and Universities in Japan, Glittering Prizes. *Higher Education Policy*, Vol. 3, No. 2, pp. 26–30.

PATRINOS, H. A. 1990. The Privatization of Higher Education in Colombia, Effects on Quality and Equity. *Higher Education*, Vol. 20, No. 2, pp. 161–73.

PING, R. 1987. Privatization in Education, *Journal of Education Policy*, Vol. 2, No. 4, pp. 289–99.

PRAMOETADI, I. S. 1985. Higher Education Development in Indonesia. In RIHE, *Higher Education Expansion in Asia*, pp. 13–35. Hiroshima, Hiroshima University.

PSACHAROPOULOS, G. 1977. Perverse Effects of Public Subsidization of Education or How Equitable is Free Education? *Comparative Education Review*, Vol. 21, No. 1, pp. 69–90.

——. 1986. Welfare Effects of Government Intervention in Education, *Contemporary Policy Issues*, Vol. 4, No. 3, pp. 51–62.

——. 1987. Public versus Private Schools in Developing Countries: Evidence from Colombia and Tanzania, *International Journal of Educational Development*, Vol. 7 , No. 1, pp. 59–67.

——. 1988. Efficiency and Equity in Greek Higher Education, *Minerva*, Vol. 26, No. 2, pp. 119–37.

PSACHAROPOULOS, G.; WOODHALL, M. 1985. *Education for Development*. New York, Oxford/World Bank.

RIHE (RESEARCH INSTITUTE FOR HIGHER EDUCATION). 1985. *Higher Education Expansion in Asia*. Hiroshima, Hiroshima University.

——. 1987. *Public and Private Sectors in Asian Higher Education Systems, Issues and Prospects*. Hiroshima, Hiroshima University.

RODERICK, G.; STEPHENS, M. (eds.). 1979. *Higher Education for All?* London, Falmer.

ROTH, D. C. 1987. *The Private Provision of Public Services in Developing Countries*. New York, Oxford/World Bank.

RUDOLPH, L. I.; RUDOLPH, S. 1987. *In Pursuit of Lakshmi: The Political Economy of the Indian State*. Chicago, University of Chicago Press.

SALTER, B.; TAPPER, T. 1985. *Power and Policy in Education, The Case of Independent Schooling*. London, Falmer.

SAMOFF, J. 1990. The Politics of Privatization in Tanzania. *International Journal of Educational Development*, Vol. 10, No. 1., pp. 1–15.

SCHIEFELBEIN, E. 1990. Chile: Economic Incentives in Higher Education. *Higher Education Policy*, Vol. 3, No. 3, pp. 21–6.

SCHWARTZMAN, S. 1988. Brazil, Opportunity and Crisis in Higher Education. *Higher Education*, Vol. 17, No. 1, pp. 99–119.

SETAPANICH, N.; PRASATVETAYAKUL, V.; KOHENGKUL, S.; CHANG-JAI, K. 1990. Survey Report – Thailand. In: H. Muta (ed.), *Educated Unemployment in Asia*, pp. 373–442. Tokyo, Asian Productivity Organization.

SINGH, N. 1983. *Education Under Siege*. New Delhi, Concept.

STONE, D. L. 1990. Private Higher Education in Australia, *Higher Education*, Vol. 20, No. 2, pp. 143–59.

TAN, E. A.; ALONZO, R. P. 1987. The Philippine Experience in Manpower Planning and Labour Market Policies. In: R. Amjad (ed.), *Human Resource Planning: The Asian Expe-*

rience, pp. 151–80. New Delhi, ARTEP/International Labour Office.

TAN, J.-P.; MINGAT, A. 1989. Educational Development in Asia. Washington, D.C., World Bank. (Report No. IDP51.)

TILAK, J. B. G. 1986. A Comment on 'Differences in the Role of the Private Educational Sector in Modern and Developing Countries' by Estelle James. *International Conference on Economics of Education*. Dijon, IREDU.

——. 1990. *Political Economy of Education in India*. Buffalo, State University of New York.

——. 1991. Financing Higher Education. Research Seminar on Reform and Innovation in India Higher Education. Buffalo/Bombay, State University of New York/SNDT Women's University,

TILAK, J. B. G.; VARGHESE, N. V. 1985. Discriminatory Pricing in Education. New Delhi, National Institute of Educational Planning and Administration. (Occasional Paper No. 8.)

——. 1991. Financing Higher Education in India, *Higher Education*, Vol. 21, No. 1.

TOISUTA, W. 1987. Public and Private Sectors in Indonesian Higher Education. In: RIHE, *Public and Private Sectors in Asian Higher Education Systems, Issues and Prospects*, pp. 71–9. Hiroshima, Hiroshima University.

WALFORD, G. (ed.). 1989. *Private Schools in Ten Countries, Policy and Practice*. London, Routledge.

WILLIAMS, G. 1989/90. Changing Patterns of Finance, *OECD Observer*, No. 161.

WILLMS, J. D. 1987. Patterns of Academic Achievement in Public and Private Schools, Implications for Public Policy and Future Research. In: E. H. Haertel, T. James, and H. M. Levin (eds.), *Comparing Public and Private Schools*. Vol. 2: *School Achievement*, pp. 113–34. New York, Falmer.

WORLD BANK 1986. *Financing of Education in Developing Countries, An Exploration of Policy Options*. Washington, D.C., World Bank.

YANO, M.; MARUYAMA, J. 1985. Prospects and Problems in Japanese Higher Education. In: RIHE, *Higher Education Expansion in Asia*, pp. 68–84. Hiroshima, Hiroshima University.

University, research, development

Abdallah Laroui

In this article I shall not deal with the general problem of scientific research and development, and the role of universities in these areas. Rather, I shall confine myself to giving an account of the problem as I have experienced it during my university career over the past twenty years. Although this is my personal experience, which may or may not bear generalization, it is still, in my opinion, not without significance if we look seriously at the problem under discussion: how can scientific research – and academic research in particular – support economic development?

University research: supporting development?

At first, it used to be thought that development was an inevitable consequence of research which, in turn, was a natural adjunct of higher

Abdallah Laroui (Morocco). *Professor of history at the Faculty of Letters, Mohamad V University, Rabat. Member of the Royal Academy of Morocco. Author of numerous works, including:* L'idéologie arabe contemporaine *(Modern Arab Ideology);* The History of the Maghreb: An Interpretive Essay; The Crisis of the Arab Intellectual: Traditionalism or Historicism; Islam et modernité *(Islam and Modernity). Also author of many articles and studies, among them 'Europe et non Europe' (Europe and non-Europe) in the* Encyclopedia Universalis.

education, and that what had happened in a number of developed countries would automatically happen in those that were not, whatever the intention of governments. If there were many university graduates, some of them would inevitably be engaged in research in laboratories and university institutes, either following their natural inclinations or as a way of earning a living. If research culminated in success, then, for sure, some or all of the results would find their way into production. However, what actually came to pass was the very opposite of these expectations. We are all aware of what happened and there is no need for me to dwell on it here.

I shall discuss only what is relevant to the topic at hand: just as with primary and secondary schools, the vast increase in student numbers turned the universities into inward-looking and inbred institutions. As a result, they formulated their own concept of scientific research, criticizing and negating the notion of economic development. All this came about not through opposition to research, as we might imagine, but through research itself.

The ineffectiveness of research

How did this strange turn of events unfold? Let me illustrate with an example. Suppose that a country pioneered something called 'production development science'. People saw its benefits and wondered how and why it had arisen in that particular country and at that time. They then agreed to devote enormous resources to study this cosmic event so that all humanity might benefit thereby. Of course, they asked the country in question to undertake all necessary studies with help from the international community. The topics were defined, special teams were assigned to each one, ways and means were studied, and so on. For a long time, the country devoted its energies to nothing but this project: it was done as well as it could be done and everybody benefited. But what about the country itself? Without a doubt, it would find itself sliding down the league table of the developed and innovative countries. And why? Because the sophisticated equipment it needed for the task was supplied free by other countries, which thus gained experience they were subsequently able to use in their own industrial production.

Was the study undertaken a scientific one? Were the methods adopted scientific? Were the people in charge scientists? Were the results scientific and applicable in the economic field? The answer to all these questions is 'yes'. And yet it is clear that the effort involved, though it indirectly helped other countries, did not help to develop the potential of the country undertaking the project. It is highly likely that the study resulted in the invention of new methods for laboratory and administrative organization; new forms of recreation were provided, giving individuals a psychological stability never experienced before; unemployment levels were reduced and so on. While all these things may benefit individuals and society in general, they do not, however, increase material wealth. If, in our search for the origins of scientific research *per se*, we assigned to the task scientists relying on their tried and tested equipment and methods, how is it that their intellectual effort and its attendant psychological and social benefits could not be translated into economic development – new material wealth – despite the fact that everything was done within a scientific framework, that is, one that is modern, empirical, objective, purposeful and planned?

The reason is clear. The focus of the study had shifted from the object being studied to the act of studying itself and from future probabil-

ities to past certainties. The conclusion is equally clear: research with objectives other than the discovery of the laws of nature – the search for '*hiyal*' (devices and contrivances) as they were called, in Arabic, in times of old – to save time and effort, does not directly and immediately contribute to visible development, that is, to the increase in consumable wealth. This type of research may be honourable, valuable, worthy, appropriate. However, it cannot be expected or seriously be claimed to increase wealth except by chance and at the cost of additional time, effort and expense. This conclusion is self-evident; it does not even need to be demonstrated. Nevertheless, it is this very conclusion that the universities refuse to accept, not deliberately or by design but as a result of a natural progression imposing its negative results without encountering any opposition.

Some examples

I shall now illustrate the problem with a number of examples but without going into great detail or presenting a huge number of arguments.

HISTORY

It is hardly surprising that history dominates the humanities and even the social sciences. I personally have defended and continue to defend the adoption of an historical approach to the understanding of the past in all their various aspects against the fallacies constantly put forward by pseudo-philosophers of the intuitive-aesthetic school. What, however, are we to say about the dominance of history over the science of production and development – and the natural sciences associated with it?

It is for this reason that I prefaced my argument with an example relating to the same topic. The history of science is a science but it is not science itself! There are good reasons for studying it – and benefits as well – even in paving the

way for genuine inventions, an argument usually put forward by its practitioners. However, it is
evident that it does not contribute directly – in
the shortest possible time and at the least expense – to the development of wealth.

LINGUISTICS

A new linguistic theory (or an old one in modern
dress) emerges from an institute of technology
(that it should emerge from such an establishment rather than one of the ancient universities
is in itself significant) as a result of advances in
informatics intended to provide a framework for
research into problems involving language acquisition and competence, and code-switching.
The study is essentially empirical and procedural both in its concerns and its orientation. So-
mehow or other, it was expected that this theory
could be uprooted and transplanted elsewhere
for application in educational research to solve
problems specific to our societies. However,
what happened, was that it was transformed into
a philosophical issue, into the burrowing of
bookworms into obscure roots and precedents
concealed in the works of ancient grammarians.
From the realm of the empirical, a domain that
may, in the long run, contribute to the development process, we shift to comparative translation, interpretation, etc., and thus are drawn into
labyrinths of futile argument.

EPISTEMOLOGY

Scientists isolated in their laboratories scorn any
reference to the logic of science. In the Anglo-
Saxon world, however, it can be observed that
there are epistemologists who are experts in certain sciences and not just parasitic concerning
them. Their concern is to draw attention to the
dangers of enshrining theory in stone. When
this happens, researchers are so preoccupied
with the prevailing theory that they are blind to
all the natural phenomena contradicting it. The
epistemologist would argue that the apparatus
used in experiments devised in accordance with

the logic of such a theory observes, registers and
measures only those phenomena that fit. The
role of epistemologists is, essentially, to free researchers from blind loyalty to any one view.
They criticize theories in order to free research
from any limitations and constraints. However,
when criticism is divorced from its underlying
motivation and concerns, experimental science
is reduced to blind-man's buff, no different from
the groping in the dark of other disciplines. It is
then dismissed as rhetoric myth. At the level of
principle, an analogy may be drawn between yo-
ga and the language used by some modern epistemologists; this analogy may help us to evolve
important scientific theories. However, the analogy can only be seen when minds are freed from
the weight and role of the modern laboratories,
for it is they, rather than any associated theories,
that contribute to the development of resources.
The significant relationship (one that, in the
case of the comparisons we referred to, is deliberately obscured) is the link between concept
and invention, between the logic of science and
the laboratory structure. The fact that we have a
glut of epistemologists does not necessarily her-
ald the dawn of a scientific research which will
ensure economic development.

ECONOMICS

Nowadays, historical analysis of the main economic sectors tends to be based on statistics for
production, investment and savings. This trend
has come to be known as economic aggregation,
that is, the study of the cultural influences
passed on through methods of work and channels of exchange. There is no doubt that this development is symptomatic of a deep concern in
economic circles about the chronic crises experienced not only by Third World countries but
also by others, each according to its means and
as a function of its wealth. The significant point,
however, is that the ideas prevailing in the 1960s
were themselves based on 'economic criticism'
and the introduction of social and political concerns, with emphasis being placed on the role of
the state and state institutions. Economic aggre-

gation, therefore, is nothing new and excess activity in this direction is perhaps one of the reasons for the crisis. The current development is not so much an inclination towards but an extension of that very trend which denies that economics, the science of wealth production and distribution, is even relatively independent of social systems and the laws governing their cohesion. So far has this idea been pushed that we are now in the strange position of seeing the fundamental link between production and savings – a principle established since the fifth century B.C. – either forgotten or neglected while a principle as basic as the connection between production and distribution has been altered to such an extent as to become meaningless or negative.

ELECTRONICS

Let us suppose that a department is established for the study of the electronics industry and the application of electronics in the field of data processing. If those graduating from the department confine their research to the field of numismatics or devising better methods to catalogue the treasures of the national heritage, what role will they have to play in development in its currently accepted sense? I do not deny the fact that they have some role; but what I am saying is that this role has to be judged in cost-benefit terms.

MATHEMATICS

It has been observed that many science graduates are slow to adapt to changes in the economic environment and end up as teachers, who then impart what they themselves have learned, both in form and content, to students who will in turn teach it to others in exactly the same way. This is what I referred to when I spoke of the university as a closed institution. Faced with this problem, we look for the causes and blame it on pedagogy, language, the poor quality of practical work, the sorry state of university laboratories,

and so on. However, if we turn our attention to the experience of other countries, we find that: (a) criticism is expressed with regard to the current rage for so-called modern maths (a highly abstract discipline closely linked to formal logic); (b) a strong case is made for the sciences of observation; (c) there are calls for a revival of mechanics ('*hiyal*'); and (d) from within mathematics itself, there is demand for a doubling of geometry courses at the expense of algebra. Thus, we find that the problem is deeper and more widespread than we had thought and that the root of the problem lies perhaps in our natural inclination to favour the subjective over the objective, which confirms the observations I made about the hypothetical example given at the beginning of this article.

At this point, I would like to make an observation of a general nature, namely that the adoption of a theoretical approach, even if pushed to its limits, is not usually detrimental in countries where an experimental science establishment already exists. On the contrary, it increases their power. For this very reason, although the American model is often held up as an example to follow, it seems to me that it is an inappropriate one because, in my view, the United States today is more in need of philosophers than scientists.

The theoretical approach, however, is harmful in countries that lack experience in the field of natural science and laboratory experimentation. This is because they are held captive by their own subjectivism, under the influence of ideas which, though outwardly scientific and modern, are in fact other-worldly and antiquated. It is no surprise that there are Indians and Arabs who excel in modern algebra, however remote this discipline might now be from its older form. Neither is it surprising to see them discover hidden truths in new-found schemes of numbers and letters. However, within the context of wealth creation, what they need is practice in trigonometry and the like, that is, to translate numbers of all kinds into geometrical shapes. Rather than mere verbal expression, therefore, what is required to achieve this result is comprehensive and balanced training of the mind, the eye and the hand.

The logic of teaching
and the logic of research

I am quoting, in the 'counter-bibliography' at
the end of this article, the article by Llibouty on
the teaching of physical mechanics. According
to the author, this discipline has been abandoned because it no longer offers 'good subjects'
for research. Does it follow then that there are
two kinds of logic in research – one for universities and the other for non-university laboratories? Let us begin with some observations.

In the universities themselves, the scientific disciplines are not organized in the same way
everywhere; an American physics book for first-
year students is different from a French book
written for an equivalent level. European competitive examinations in mathematics have
shown that the English are stronger in geometry
and the French in analysis – more attention to
precision in the first case, more creativity in the
other. The classification of the sciences is also
different: based on theoretical principles in one
instance, on subject of study in the other. Interdisciplinarity is difficult to implement in a
Comtian-type classification system. This has two
major consequences: on the one hand, basic
contradictions pass unnoticed – a concept pro-
pounded by I. Prigogine and I. Stengers, authors
of *Order out of Chaos: Man's New Dialogue with
Nature* (London, Bantam Books, 1984) – on the
other hand, ad hoc solutions, so important to research, are played down, if not rejected, on principle. In the rational system of classification, any
solution that is not directly deduced from the
original theory is called empirical.

These are, strictly speaking, academic observations. But let us take a look at the results.
The training of an engineer or a researcher does
not begin at the age of 20, but very much earlier.
We could go so far as to say that it is virtually a
method of thinking that stems directly from general culture and from the teaching and learning
system.

It is natural that in certain cases – through
force of habit and intellectual discipline – the ad

hoc solutions are not immediately apparent:
who in fact teaches in engineering schools if not
lecturers whose only thought is of joining a university?

Of course, we should be careful when making generalizations about trends, especially
when we are not referring to specific cases. It
may be deduced, however, that such antitheses
as basic versus applied research and university
versus industrial research conceal a much more
significant contradiction, one that separates
technologists from epistemologists, even though
this antimony (Galileo versus Descartes) has
been brought to light in recent years chiefly
through studies of the history of science.

Let us say that the university is shifting naturally in the direction of theoretical science,
which just as naturally becomes philosophical.
Let us also say that ad hoc solutions are born in
laboratories, and that, in the universities, theories of reorganization prevail. When the latter
are cut off from laboratories and industry, then
science truly becomes a philosophy. Therefore,
the next step is scientism, which can certainly
play a positive cultural role, but can also be the
source of a paralysing ideological conflict.

In these circumstances, science is only preserved from scientism by an influence coming
from outside the university (the state, transnational economic groupings, large companies). If
the university chooses to withdraw behind its
privileges of autonomy where the state cannot
reach it, the latter will turn towards other specific institutions, which it creates or expands, or it
may prefer to operate through military research.
Every day we can witness examples of one or
another of these options.

But they too are only ad hoc solutions;
there can be no real progress until technologists
and epistemologists are brought face to face, until the latter are forced to reexamine their expla-
natory systems and the classification of the
sciences is completely overhauled. In this way,
and only in this way, can university scholars be
fully liberated and recover the ability to observe
and innovate and to solve problems instead of
being content just to back up established results.

Reform of teaching, education and information is therefore a matter of urgency.

A number of studies on the logic, on the history of science and on educational methods lead to similar results: the university, whether it is public or private – long considered the temple of the spirit of research, a place where critical abilities are developed and dialogue encouraged – has become a temple of dogma, of perpetuation of the status quo, of the defence and illustration of established scientific theory. As a result, the university restricts innovation and inhibit the motivation to solve problems.

This helps us to understand the statements about why the university is on the decline or at a standstill. It is certainly no accident that the research we have mentioned was carried out in the United States, which is concerned about aggressive Japanese competitiveness. The university is by its very nature dogmatic, simply because it systematizes and reorganizes results obtained elsewhere; it finds itself somewhat at a disadvantage when compared with other institutions less preoccupied with standards of accuracy. Basic research, in this perspective, is not what it is usually thought to be: it seeks to unify a branch of knowledge; it need not have any practical application and may not even be in a position to offer concrete solutions.

The logic of research, where it flourishes, is different. It is essentially open, empirical, opportunistic, even anarchistic according to some, that is to say, without guiding rules. That is why the terms 'revolution' and 'breakthrough' are frequently applied to it; but it is only in exceptional cases that we can make such generalizations about these terms and apply them to university science. Surely it is no coincidence that from Aristotle to Descartes and Comte 'scientific' has been synonymous with 'systematic'?

Distortion of the aims of university research?

With the examples and observations discussed thus far, I will rest my case. Although, as I have said, the illustrations are particular and may not apply to many industrially advanced countries, the general conclusion to be drawn is that, by its very nature, the orientation of the university does not necessarily promote research designed to develop material wealth. The fact that universities are not confined to a single role is demonstrated by the current debate over the division of research between industrial institutions and universities.

Over the past twenty years, I have observed how the concepts of research and development have been transformed in university education. Research has moved from the objective to the subjective, from examination of nature to analysis of the self behind the study. The concept of development, meanwhile, has been pushed beyond its usual sense of increasing material wealth to mean developing talent. Thus, emphasis has shifted from production to consumption, from supply to demand, from meeting needs to examining their origin.

Despite the impression that may be given by some of the terms used, I should like to stress that I am not making any value judgement here, nor am I saying that the present state of affairs is right or wrong. I am merely stating the most obvious of conclusions, namely that university research, in its present conception and practice, cannot directly contribute to the development of wealth because that is not its role, even if it sometimes happens. I would not deny that research into the self, in all its aspects, may lead to an increase in production, whether in the short or the long term. This is because the self in question is the producer, because producers content with themselves and their environment and in control of their instincts and needs may become responsible agents. Though positive, this role of the university is expensive and open to question.

Reorienting university research and culture

Having said all this, I find myself in a somewhat difficult situation when it comes to putting forward practical proposals that might remedy the state of affairs described above. The problem is that the ideas upon which my argument has been based are nowadays branded as outmoded and belonging to the nineteenth century – curiously enough by critics who normally speak in praise of authentic cultural traditions. The twin pillars of my case are, first, that development means, above all, the increase of consumable material wealth and, secondly, that scientific research conducive to development means discovery of the riddles of nature. I am well aware of all the arguments that may be made against these simplified definitions. However, when the obvious is denied, we are forced to go back to basics and rejection of my twin pillars only makes the problem worse. What is the point at issue? The problem is not that the university does no research but that the research it does do, from all the evidence, fails to contribute sufficiently to development. And what we are discussing here is not the development of talent and personality – this is an accepted fact or it should be. We are saying that there is a crisis, because although the university helps to develop personality, it does not sufficiently prepare graduates to participate effectively in the field of material production, through intellectual work.

The issue, therefore, is one of orientation rather than of material means and numbers. There is no point in increasing the number of teachers, building laboratories, organizing sabbaticals, improving communications and so on unless someone teaches the teachers. If university education remains as it is, without any change in orientation, all this effort will be counter-productive. As long as research costs have no yield in terms of wealth production, they are not a useful investment. Although the results may raise a smile from those who advocate self-fulfilment, they will bring tears to the eyes of whoever is responsible for the balance sheet.

Comparisons of figures for funds allocated to research in terms of GNP ignore the differences in education, especially at university level, even though this point is among the findings of the subjective research which I discussed above. If only such findings were put to good use!

There are those who argue that no good can come of trying to reform university education. Justifying their position with long lists of examples, they suggest that research should be organized outside the university and even outside government control altogether. Many old-established universities have rejected or impeded research aimed at industrial exploitation, claiming that such action is intended to preserve their independence and freedom. This is only natural since the university – as its very name suggests – aims to provide a general education, to impart knowledge rather than specialization and professional training. The example of the United States, which is sometimes used in counter-argument, does not apply here because American public education has always been technical and practical. It originated as one of the means that created a nation, a fact observed by various nineteenth-century visitors to that country and, foremost among them, Alexis de Tocqueville. Although those in charge are loud in their praise of the role of the university, the truth of the matter is that this – whether openly or tacitly – is their real position.

There are others who would like to save the university from the fate which threatens to transform it into a substitute for general secondary education and to make it the bastion of national heritage and traditions. They must surely conclude that the university has no role in promoting genuine research (in its obvious sense) and supporting development without a review of its academic components and an educational revolution to change its focus from subjective to objective, to put the past behind it and to lead it into the future. This reverse transformation back to its original nature cannot be applied to or undertaken by the university on its own. The involvement of the state is necessary, not in planning research programmes but in creating a general educational curriculum which would begin by reformulating educational methods and subjects at the primary and secondary levels and which, with proper orientation of the mass media, would end by systematizing relationships between university institutes and private sector laboratories and industrial establishments. Such a programme will not succeed unless it is the concern of the nation as a whole, without reservation and without one side competing against another. Although some may fear that any spiritual aspiration will be strangled by the tentacles of materialism and the grip of the scientific community, should we be swayed by this prospect of a putative danger when there is a real one at hand? The argument might be stronger if we had already set out upon this road and the negative effects were beginning to show. However, as we have not even begun to conceive how we might tread such a road, scaremongering about the likely outcome is nonsense. Indeed, it indicates a deep-rooted scepticism as to people's ability to realize the error of their ways and to safeguard their beliefs and the things they hold sacred. For such pessimism, there is no justification.

Neither I nor anyone else is claming that a philosophy of development alone is enough to bring about development: there is an abundance of examples, both old and new, to refute any such claim. Development is linked to material and financial factors, with the ability to organize and plan, with the selection of objectives and priorities. However, even if all these factors are present, they will be to no avail unless they are embodied in such a philosophy. How can development come about unless it proceeds from a will – in the ordinary everyday meaning of the word – to that end? ■

Counter-bibliography

BOUGHALI, M. *La représentation de l'espace chez le Marocain illètrè.* Paris, Anthropos, 1974.

FERGUSON, E. S. The Mind's Eye: Non-verbal Thought in Technology. *Science*, 1977, pp. 827–36.

FEYERABEND, P. *Contre la méthode*, Paris, Seuil, 1979.

HILL, D. R. Article on '*Hiyal*', *Encyclopédie de l'Islam*, 2nd ed., supp., pp. 371–4.

LLIBOUTY, L. La mécanique physique: une grave lacune de notre enseignement. *La Recherche*, No. 208, March 1988, pp. 391–2.

SHEAKAWAT, V. Alternative Models of Scientific Rationality: Theorisation in Classical Indian Science. *Diogenes*, No. 144, 1989, pp. 32–51.

SCHAFER, P. The New World Order: A Contribution to the World Decade for Cultural Development. Paris, UNESCO, 1989. (Studies and Documents, 41.)

YACHIR, F. La nouvelle problématique du développement. Paris, UNESCO, 1989. (Études et Documents, 43.)

Universities and national development

Issues and problems

in developing countries

Lawrence J. Saha

If the relationship between education and national development is complex, the contribution of various levels of education to development, that is, primary, secondary and tertiary, is even more perplexing. Each level has to be seen in the context of the target population relevant to its function, the curriculum, the expectations of its products, the recruitment and training of its teachers, and the costs and funding of its operations. During the past decade, there has been disagreement among planners and researchers about the appropriate priorities for the educational strategies of countries wishing to promote development. The difficulty increases when questions about development are addressed, such as: What kind of development? For whom? For what purpose? How?

This article will not attempt to discuss these questions for all levels of education, but will focus specifically on one, the tertiary level and, to be more precise, on universities. The relationship between universities and national development will be addressed in the context of a multidimensional concept of national development. Although the term 'development' is often used with a taken-for-granted meaning (most often as economic development), Fägerlind and Saha (1989) argue that greater precision is needed to isolate the various paths of development, paths which are often contradictory, each with its own determinants and consequences. These three dimensions are the economic, the sociocultural and the political. Following this distinction, it can be shown that universities play distinct roles for each dimension of national development. Furthermore, as will become clear, it is possible that in given country contexts, it will be impossible for all three dimensions to be pursued simultaneously.

Thus in the following pages we will examine the relevance and contribution of universities for national development for each of the three dimensions. Within each of these dimensions specific issues will be addressed as appropriate – for example, rates of return, employment and unemployment, vocational and academic curricula, equality and ideology.

Lawrence J. Saha (United States). *Reader in the Department of Sociology, the Australian National University, Canberra. Co-author with Ingemar Fägerlind of* Education and National Development: A Comparative Perspective *(2nd ed., 1989), and co-editor with John P. Keeves of* Schooling and Society in Australia: Sociological Perspectives *(1990).*

Universities and economic development

In so far as the economic growth model has tended to dominate most research and debate about development, much of the assessment of the contribution of universities to development has been in this context. Thus ultimately the contribution of universities has been evaluated in the context of increases in per capita income, shifts in the base and structure of economic systems (for example, from agricultural to industrial and service-based economies), and rates of return to society and to individuals. Although these indicators of economic growth are generally accepted by all countries, their relevance and character will differ between the developed and less developed countries. They will also differ between regions such as Africa, South-East Asia and Latin America (Hallak, 1990).

The disparity between countries in primary, secondary and tertiary enrolments is taken for granted: in all countries, primary enrolments are highest while tertiary enrolments are lowest. Furthermore, these enrolments (at all levels) are lowest for the least developed countries and highest for the most highly developed countries. For example, in 1985 the average enrolments for low-income economies at the primary level was 67 per cent, at secondary level 22 per cent and at the tertiary level 5 per cent. Conversely, in the industrial market economies, there was 100 per cent enrolment at the primary level, 93 per cent at the secondary level, and 39 per cent at the tertiary level (World Bank, 1988b).

The increase in enrolments at all levels from 1965 to 1985 is also revealing (see Table 1). Low-income countries increased primary enrolments by 52 per cent, secondary by 144 per cent and tertiary by 400 per cent. For the industrial market economies, the increases were 0 per cent (100 per cent primary enrolments had already been reached by 1965), 48 per cent and 86 per cent, respectively. For countries at all levels of development, the increases at the tertiary level were the highest.

TABLE I. Percentage increase of enrolments by levels of education and of development, 1965–85

Country classification	Level of education		
	Primary	Secondary	Higher
Low income	52	144	400
Lower middle income	37	163	225
Upper middle income	8	97	128
Industrial	0	48	86

Source: World Bank, 1988b.

Although it stands to reason that expansion will be the greatest where there is room for it, there are other considerations which are equally relevant. First, in the less developed countries, expansion at the tertiary level has increased rapidly, and well before universal primary and secondary education have been attained. This would suggest that tertiary-level education is both highly valued and much in demand in the less developed countries, and that the rapid expansion might be indicative of attempts to emulate the prestige of universities in the industrial societies. At the same time it has been argued that tertiary education, at least in sub-Saharan Africa, might be over-expanded (World Bank, 1988a). One interpretation of this 'higher-education paradox' is that the expansion has lowered the quality of output, with the result that there has been an actual increase in the shortage of highly skilled graduates.

A second, and much more important, consequence of rapid growth in the tertiary sector is cost. Of the three levels of education, the unit cost of higher education exceeds by many times the unit cost of primary and secondary education. For example, in 1981 the unit cost of secondary education for African countries was seven times that of primary education, while the unit cost of higher education was fifty-seven times higher (Cocco and Nascimento, 1986, p. 257). In French-speaking Africa the unit cost of universities in 1983 was nine times the cost of a secondary pupil and forty times that of a primary pupil (Diambomba, 1989).

Furthermore, the relative cost of higher

TABLE 2. Returns to education for selected countries: rates of return by educational level

Country	Survey year	Private returns			Social returns		
		Primary	Secondary	Higher	Primary	Secondary	Higher
Ethiopia	1972	35.0	22.8	27.4	20.3	18.7	9.7
Kenya	1971	28.0	33.0	31.0	21.7	19.2	8.8
Nigeria	1966	30.0	14.0	34.0	23.0	12.8	17.0
Mexico	1963	32.0	23.0	29.0	25.0	17.0	23.0
Greece	1977	20.0	6.0	5.5	16.5	5.5	4.5
Yugoslavia	1969	7.6	15.3	2.6	9.3	15.4	2.8
Canada	1961	–[1]	16.3	19.7	–	11.7	14.0
Sweden	1967	–	–	10.3	–	10.5	9.2
United Kingdom	1977	–	11.7	9.6	–	3.6	8.2
United States	1969	–	18.8	15.4	–	10.9	10.9

1. Figures not available.

Source: Psacharopoulos and Woodhall, 1985, pp. 56–7.

education for the less developed countries is higher than for the industrialized countries. In the early 1970s the per cent GNP per capita for a unit cost of higher education in less developed countries was 1,405, compared with 55 for the OECD countries (Fägerlind and Saha, 1989).

These relatively high costs of higher education pose serious problems for the less developed countries of the world, particularly during times of diminishing revenue and declining economies. In setting priorities regarding the maintenance of these education systems, one consideration must be the social and individual returns to investment in education for each of these levels.

The individual costs of education include fees, books and, most importantly, forgone earnings. For society the costs include 'the costs of teachers and other staff, books, other goods and services such as heating and lighting, and the value of buildings and equipment' (Psacharopoulos and Woodhall, 1985). The benefits to the individual are almost exclusively calculated in terms of higher income as a result of educational attainment, whereas for society the benefits are in terms of the increase in productivity due to education credentials. Although the calculations of rates of return are complex and subject to a number of assumptions (see Psacharopoulos, 1985), the general patterns appear clear. A

selection of rates of individual and social rates of return for the less developed and advanced countries are given in Table 2.

On the basis of these figures, Psacharopoulos and Woodhall (1985, p. 58) conclude that the private rates of return are higher than the social rates of return, that both social and private rates of return are higher for primary education, and that the rate of return is higher in the developing countries than the developed countries. Furthermore, in the developing countries the social rates of return to higher education are lower than the returns to primary and secondary education (27, 16 and 13 per cent, respectively).

These figures clearly indicate that the social rates of return to education are the lowest for the most expensive level of education, at least for the developing countries. Therefore, at least in terms of economic development, it would appear that universities and other forms of higher education should have the lowest priority for educational planning and expansion. Furthermore, because the private rates of return for higher education are greater than the returns to society, the financing of higher education becomes problematic. For example, why should a government subsidize universities and other forms of higher education when the main beneficiaries are the individuals and not the rest of society? This is precisely why recent policy recommendations have argued that the consumers of higher education should be the ones who pay, rather than the government.

The consequences of reverting to user-pays or cost-recovery policies are not completely known, and in any event are highly complex. For example, would universities and other forms of higher education be underfunded (and under-invested)? Would the demand for universities decline? Would universities become accessible only to the wealthy and the élite?

Ultimately, these questions bear directly on issues of equality and efficiency. If governments continue to fund universities at a level needed to maintain quality and meet the social demand, will the main beneficiaries be those who are already advantaged, or will those from less privileged backgrounds also gain access? Although the wealthy usually choose to send their children to private primary and secondary schools (Schiefelbein, 1983), this is less likely to be the case for universities, even if private universities were available alternatives, which in many countries they are not. As Diambomba (1989) observes, entry to universities, in Africa at least, has served only to produce graduates who later receive high salaries, therefore not only reproducing privilege in society, but also imposing extremely high costs on society as a whole.

Although a number of mechanisms have been suggested to equalize opportunities for university and higher education attendance (for example, vouchers and loan systems), none that would equitably transfer the high costs of universities to the user has been adopted.

Efficiency and national development

Carnoy et al. (1982) note that one explanation for the apparent decline in relative spending per student in higher education has been economies of scale and the ability to increase enrolments at less cost per student. For those countries that have reduced their costs per student, increases in enrolments have been possible. Although the reduction in government expenditure on universities and higher education might be seen as more equitable because the user and main beneficiaries carry most of the cost, the 'privatization' of universities may turn out to be inefficient. In this respect efficiency is evaluated in terms of the provision and delivery of higher education in those areas, in those fields, and for a wide range of able students who are seen as beneficial for society as a whole. A privatized university system is more likely to respond to market forces rather than the benefit of society (unless the two are defined as the same). This could mean that universities will be found mainly in urban areas, in pleasing climates, and will recruit from the affluent and able students (Schiefelbein, 1983, p. 15).

Diambomba (1989) suggests that the key factors for the inefficiency of higher education in Africa have been the inadequate links between universities and job markets, the imbalance between enrolments in specific disciplines, and finally the lack of appropriate training for the skills needed in the labour market. In other words, by following too closely the demands of students, the African universities have not produced the kinds of graduates needed by society. In particular, the aspirations of university graduates are not only inordinately high, a pattern consistent with findings related to the education systems in less developed countries as a whole (Saha, 1991), but graduates' attitudes toward work make them unable to seek out, or take on other kinds of occupation, such as entrepreneurial activities.

Overall, then, because of the high cost of universities, their inequity and inefficiency, and low rate of return compared with primary- and secondary-level education, it could be said that higher education in general and universities in particular are obstacles rather than agents for economic development. Unless universities and other forms of higher education can be made less costly to society (as compared with costs to individuals), and unless they can be better integrated to the needs of their countries, at the risk of becoming more marginal to the international university community, and unless the social rate of return can be increased through a combination of reduced costs and cost-recovery mechanisms, then universities in developing countries will have a lower priority in educational planning policies.

As stated at the outset, economic development is only one dimension according to which we can assess issues related to universities and national development. While economic considerations are certainly essential, particularly in the context of diminishing economic resources, there are other dimensions which may be less tangible and less amenable to quantitative analysis, but nevertheless provide alternative bases for the evaluation of the contribution of universities to the national development of society. One of these is the social and cultural dimension.

Universities and social aspects of national development

Although it would be erroneous to suggest that concerns with economic aspects of development are motivated only by investment in human capital considerations, it has been said that since Schultz's 1960 address there has occurred a 'human investment revolution in economic thought' (Sobel, 1978). Yet a preoccupation with economic development runs the risk of overlooking and neglecting other important dimensions in the development process. Furthermore, there are limits to the economic development perspective with respect to education (Klees, 1986), and it would seem that this is particularly true with respect to universities.

Therefore, following the three dimensions outlined above, it is appropriate to consider the extent to which universities are related to the social and cultural development of a society, and thus to national development and nation-building. In other words, the contribution of universities to national development must be evaluated

according to criteria in addition to cost-benefits, rates of return or increases in productivity, all of which regard education as a form of investment in human capital.

A focus on higher education and the social and cultural dimensions of national development include, first, an examination of the modernizing effects of universities, that is, changes in values, attitudes and life-styles. Second, we will examine the extent to which universities in developing countries represent the interests of their own country, or conversely represent colonial or international interests, which are mostly Western in tradition.

UNIVERSITIES, VALUES, ATTITUDES AND LIFE-STYLES

One of the best documented research findings is that, compared with those with no higher education, persons who have attended some form of higher education tend to be less traditional, less family-oriented, more secular and more change-oriented in attitudes, values and behaviour. Although it is debated whether or not attendance at university 'causes' these modernizing effects, or whether a self-selection is the cause, the association is nevertheless clear.

The modernizing impact of universities on students, in some respects, is nothing more than an extension of the effects of education generally. Higher education in general, and universities in particular, exercise impacts on society as well as on individuals. With respect to society, the impact affects the mobilization and the use of human resources, and also the way that society is stratified (Bergendal, 1985). Although the mobilization of human resources is more closely linked to questions of economic development and work productivity, there is also an impact on the values, attitudes and life-styles of individuals in society.

Because those persons who attend universities are more likely to come from higher-status and higher-income family backgrounds, the graduates of universities are more likely to attain social and occupational levels comparable to their origins. To this extent, universities serve to reproduce social structures, not only in the sense that the occupational and income distribution in a given society is likely to remain the same, but because the inequalities will be inherited from one generation to the next. However, this effect of universities is likely to be greater in countries where a larger proportion of an age cohort, such as 25 or 30 per cent, attends university, as compared with countries where only 5 per cent do (Bergendal, 1985). Thus this particular impact is likely to be greater in Western advanced countries rather than the developing countries, which have small proportions of age cohorts attending university.

A further way that universities have an effect on values, attitudes and life-styles is through the inculcation of a body of legitimate knowledge to students. The cognitive impact of university attendance on students has been well documented: students who take courses in certain subjects, at least in a factual sense, know more about those subjects compared with those who have not taken them (Dahlgren, 1985, p. 2224). However, the long-term effects of these cognitive gains suggests that over time, the deterioration of this factual knowledge is 'dramatic'.

An additional problem with respect to the acquisition of knowledge by university students is the question of what knowledge is learned. Although there has been considerable concern about the legitimation of knowledge by school and university curricula in all societies, both developed and the less developed, the legitimation of knowledge poses more serious issues for developing countries.

Much of what is valued and taught in the universities of developing countries is imported from the developed countries. This is particularly the case with science and technological knowledge, 95 per cent of which is produced in the industrial countries (Ahmed, 1985). A major difficulty of most developing countries is that while science and technological knowledge is seen as important for solving a country's problems, such as poverty, disease and illiteracy, its importation from the industrial countries poses difficulties of adaptation and use. The reason is that this knowledge is not neutral but Western in value-orientation and application. As Ahmed (1985) notes, the Western version of science and technology has been largely irrelevant for solving the problems of developing countries, and Third World universities that use books, curricula and materials from the industrial countries succeed only in producing graduates suited for employment in those industrial countries.

The type of inappropriate science and technology education in developing countries results in experts who do not understand, do not appreciate or are not committed to the solution of problems in their own countries. Because they look to scientists and technologists in the developed countries as their reference group, they choose inappropriate research topics, publish in overseas journals, and where possible, take higher-paid and possibly more prestigious jobs overseas. Their own countries lose the very talent that it has inappropriately educated and trained. Ahmed (1985, p. 4476) argues that universities in developing countries can counter this tendency by introducing courses 'where the learner is engaged in tasks of creative and divergent thinking as well as in constructive actions to implement scientific and technological ideas in the surrounding society'. Research opportunities and facilities in the universities of developing countries must be improved, and research productivity rewarded. Only then will universities in developing countries produce graduates who are committed to the solution of their own countries' problems and not join the brain drain which has been so characteristic of many graduates of Third World universities.

Altbach (1990) develops these same observations further, and perhaps more optimistically, in his analysis of universities and scientific development in four countries: Malaysia, Singapore, Republic of Korea and Taiwan. Because science represents an 'international' knowledge system, Altbach shows how the dominance of English and the frequency and prestige of overseas university training and degrees serve as important links between Third World scientists and 'mainstream' science in the industrialized world. There are both advantages and disadvantages in these pressures on the universities and scientists in the developing countries to emulate and keep up with the mainstream. Nevertheless, with respect to the four countries under consideration, a sufficiently indigenous scientific base was developed so that science and technology as taught and researched in local universities have made important contributions to the national development of these four countries.

How did this indigenous scientific base come about? First, by sacrificing the desire to have the national language dominate throughout the education system and in science teaching and research, these countries to a greater or lesser extent allowed English to dominate. Thus the commitment to the international scientific community has meant the development of a strong international scientific community, but at the cost of furthering the decline in the importance of indigenous languages and cultures. As Altbach notes, Singapore has taken the most extreme commitment to the internationalization of local science by using English throughout the educational and professional scientific community. On the other hand, while supporting an indigenous scientific community, the Republic of Korea nevertheless has used English as the medium for the most advanced work. In other words, although population size and the entrenchment of local and national cultures make possible a commitment to an indigenous science, the most advanced scientific teaching and research is invariably done in English. This is a hard fact that cannot be ignored in decisions about science and technology teaching and research in the universities of the developing countries.

A further issue in this context concerns both the proportion of academics who have received their training in overseas universities in the industrialized countries, and also the number who migrate to the industrialized countries to pursue their professional careers, that is, the brain drain. Although the brain drain from the developing to the developed countries is often interpreted in a negative way, Altbach takes a more optimistic perspective and identifies several dimensions whereby the process may in fact be beneficial for the home country. For example, many emigrants do maintain contact with their home country and serve as a source of contact for indigenous scientists. Furthermore, many of those who have allegedly migrated, do in fact return to make an important contribution to their home country.

The brain drain, however, should not be seen as a concern only for the developing countries. There is considerable movement between universities in all countries of the world, both developing and developed. The academic profession is, more than any other, an international profession. Apart from political and language considerations, it is often thought that academics should be free to pursue their careers in whatever locale they think appropriate and possible. Thus the brain drain occurs between the developed countries and between the developed and the developing countries. Although the presence of large numbers of expatriate academics are seen as detrimental to Third World universities, the pattern exists in some of the countries of the developed world as well. For example, a study of Australian universities between 1961 and 1974 found that a steady rate of about 40 per cent of academics were appointed from overseas, although about half of them were returning Australians (Saha and Klovdahl, 1979). Similar patterns occurred in Canada during the same period. Thus the presence of expatriate academics, and the brain drain itself, are not phenomena unique to the developing countries. Nevertheless the departure of trained academics from the developing countries to the developed represents a loss of human resources which could impede the maintenance of a relevant local university system and the attainment of national development objectives.

ASPIRATIONS AND EXPECTATIONS

It has been argued that the process of modernization has brought about an individualistic orientation as compared with the collectivist orientation commonly found in traditional cultures. In so far as universities represent an end point in the educational process, they are also responsible for modernizing and individualizing the orientations of students such that individual ambitions take priority over collective ones. There is considerable empirical evidence to support the notion that higher levels of educational attainment in the less developed countries result in inordinately high levels of both educational and occupational aspirations and expectations. For example, Biraimah (1987, p. 575) found in her study of 500 students at the University of Ife, Nigeria, that 57 per cent of the males and 33 per cent of the females expected to obtain doctorates, expectations which she regarded as 'inflated and unrealistic'.

This tendency, which has been observed in many Third World countries, has been even more dramatically shown in an analysis of the study of science knowledge in eighteen countries conducted by the International Association for the Study of Academic Achievement (IEA). Using a pooled sample from all eighteen countries, Saha (1991) found an inverse relationship between the level of socio-economic development of country and the level of educational and occupational aspirations of students. In other words, with home background and science knowledge controlled, students from the less developed countries had higher levels of educational and occupational aspirations than those from the developed countries.

There are a number of persuasive explanations for this pattern, for example the 'revolution of rising expectations' or the existence of strong links between educational credentials and occupational positions. Nevertheless the implications for universities in the developing countries, as agents for the promotion of national development, is important. In so far as inflated and blocked ambitions can be a source of frustration, political discontent and emigration (see Saha, 1991), the contribution of universities to national development in any country, but particularly the developing countries, has to be seen as problematic. Whether the solution lies in the dampening of inflated ambitions, the tolerance of the negative consequences, or the conscious loosening of the links between educational credentials and occupations, is a matter for educational and political policy-makers to consider.

Universities and national political development

One of the neglected areas of research on education generally has been its relationship to the political development of a country. By political development, Coleman (1965) means the institutionalization of political integration and participation. To the extent that an education system produces citizens who are politically aware, and who have a strong sense of national identity, and who are interested and participate in the political processes of their country, education can be said to contribute to its political development.

The processes of political integration and participation can take many forms, ranging from saluting the flag to voting, from a psychological sense of 'we-ness' to reading newspapers. From the point of view of education, however, these processes of integration and participation are reflected in the tasks of political socialization, the training of political élites and the promotion of a national political consciousness (Fägerlind and Saha, 1989).

Although universities clearly contribute to these processes of political development, with the exception of student political activism, little research attention has been directed to their unique political impact. This may in part be due to the smaller proportions of students in universities in the developing countries. However the role of universities in developing countries for political development, in many respects, is unique and crucial for a number of reasons.

First, the political systems in many developing countries are fragile and often not well established. Universities, because they expose students to a wider range of ideas and knowledge, are often seen as potential threats to the official political ideology of the government. The potential for university-based political activity is reflected in the frequency with which universities are closed by governments when their political security is threatened. It takes a secure regime to tolerate the articulate and sophisticated levels of criticism which often emanate from universities.

Because of the small proportions of the population enrolled in Third World universities, and the way that they are selected for entry, the students are already by definition members of an élite. Often they become members of a political élite as well, but it can happen that the university-educated élite can clash with the traditional élite, as in Papua New Guinea (Latukefu, 1988), resulting in tensions and conflict.

Therefore, rather than promote political integration, universities in some Third World countries may appear to threaten it. Third World universities, particularly those removed and detached from the indigenous culture of their societies, can therefore be divisive. However, it is important to keep in mind that in the case of totalitarian regimes, the role of dissent played by universities and their students may represent a contribution to national political development, if the dissent results in a move towards a more democratic and politically stable government.

Finally, the contribution of universities to the development of national political consciousness in Third World countries is equally problematic. On the one hand universities might be expected to inculcate political consciousness simply as an extension of political socialization generally. However, if universities in developing countries represent cultural outposts of the industrial societies, then it could happen that the opposite effect might occur. Universities would, in these circumstances, produce graduates whose orientations and political loyalties lie outside their own countries. The brain drain of graduates becomes, in part, the result of a displaced national political consciousness.

Thus the contribution of universities to national political development is problematic for all countries, but particularly for the developing countries. The latters' universities, by trying to emulate and compete with universities in the industrialized countries often become out of step with their own culture and insensitive to their own society's needs. In these circumstances the contribution to political development may be counter-productive. Furthermore, because many universities adopt a critical stance toward their own societies, conflicts occur between universities and governments, particularly when those governments are totalitarian, insecure and intolerant of dissent. This political dimension of universities with respect to national development is clearly one of the most sensitive, problematic and perhaps the most important of the three dimensions considered in this article.

The relationship between universities and the national development of societies is multidimensional and complex. However, irrespective of which dimension of national development one considers, the ambivalence of universities stems largely from the fact that in structure and history, they are both international and national institutions. Universities and their members have their feet in two worlds – that of their own country and that of the international university community. This dual membership does not pose the same problems for the universities of the industrial societies as it does for the universities of developing countries. There is greater divergence between the two in the developing-country context, and the contribution of these universities to the national development of their own countries must be balanced by their simultaneous participation in an international university community. Herein lies the major source of the issues and problems which they must continuously confront.   ∎

References

AHMED, R. 1985. Scientific and Technological Education in Developing Countries. In: T. Husén and T. N. Postlethwaite (eds.), *The International Encyclopedia of Education*, Vol. 8. Oxford, Pergamon Press.

ALTBACH, P. G. 1990. Higher Education and Scientific Development. *New Education*, Vol. XII, No. 1.

BERGENDAL, G. 1985. Higher Education: Impact on Society. In: T. Husén and T. N. Postlethwaite (eds.), *The International Encyclopedia of Education*, Vol. 4, Oxford, Pergamon Press.

BIRAIMAH, K. L. 1987. Class, Gender and Life Chances: A Nigerian University Case Study. *Comparative Education Review*, Vol. 31, No. 4.

CARNOY, M.; LEVIN, H.; NUGENT, R.; SUMRA, S.; TORRES, C.; UNSIKER, J. 1982. The Political Economy of Financing Education in Developing Countries. *Financing Educational Development*. Ottawa, International Development Research Council.

COCCO, I.; NASCIMENTO, G. 1986. Trends in Public Expenditure on Education: 1975–83. *Prospects*, Vol. XVI, No. 2, pp. 253–8.

COLEMAN, J. S. 1965. *Education and Political Development*. Princeton, N.J., Princeton University Press.

DAHLGREN, L. O. 1985. Higher Education: Impact on Students. In: T. Husén and T. N. Postlethwaite (eds.), *The International Encyclopedia of Education*, Vol. 4, Oxford, Pergamon Press.

DIAMBOMBA, M. 1989. Universities and Development in Africa: Problems and Challenges for Planning. In: F. Caillods (ed.), *The Prospects for Educational Planning*. Paris, UNESCO/International Institute for Educational Planning.

FÄGERLIND, I.; SAHA, L. J. 1989. *Education and National Development: A Comparative Perspective*. 2nd ed. Oxford, Pergamon Press.

HALLAK, J. 1990. *Investing in the Future*. Paris, UNESCO/International Institute for Educational Planning.

KLEES, S. 1986. Planning and Policy Analysis in Education:What Can Economics Tell Us? *Comparative Education Review*, Vol. 28, No. 3.

LATUKEFU, S. 1988. The Modern Elite in Papua New Guinea. In: M. Bray and P. Smith (eds.), *Education and Social Stratification in Papua New Guinea*. Melbourne, Longman Cheshire.

PSACHAROPOULOS, G. 1985. Cost-Benefit Analysis in Education. In: T. Husén and T. N. Postlethwaite. *The International Encyclopedia of Education*, Vol. 2, Oxford, Pergamon Press.

PSACHAROPOULOS, G.; WOODHALL, M. 1985. *Education for Development: An Analysis of Investment Choices*. New York, Oxford University Press.

SAHA, L. J. 1991. The Effects of Socio-Economic Development on Student Academic Performance and Life Plans: A Cross-National Analysis. (Unpublished MS.)

SAHA, L. J.; KLOVDAHL, A. S. 1979. International Networks and Flows of Academic Talent: Overseas Recruitment in Australian Universities. *Higher Education*, Vol. 8.

SCHIEFELBEIN, E. 1983. *Educational Financing in Developing Countries*. Ottawa, International Development Research Centre.

SOBEL, I. 1978. The Human Capital Revolution in Economic Development: Its Current History and Status. *Comparative Education Review*, Vol. 22, No. 2.

WORLD BANK, 1988a. *Education in Sub-Sahara Africa: Policies for Adjustment, Revitalization and Expansion*. Washington, D.C., World Bank.

——. 1988b. *World Development Report 1988*. Oxford, Oxford University Press.

Rethinking the financing of post-compulsory education*

Jean-Claude Eicher and Thierry Chevaillier

Throughout the world, the finance of education is in serious crisis. The crisis of educational finance is not limited to the problem of meeting the obligations of societies to provide some minimum amount of compulsory education for their students. This minimum does not assure the preparation of an appropriately trained labour force in a world that is increasingly technological and in which a competitive economy requires the replacement of traditional production processes with others based on sophisticated labour and capital. The rapid growth of post-compulsory systems of education is no longer a luxury, but a necessity for industrialization and economic development. Properly trained engineers, managers, professionals, and high level technical and administrative support personnel are crucial to the establishment of efficient industries and government services, and thereby to the generation of employment for those with only compulsory schooling.

This is not to say that top financial priority should be given now and in all countries to the higher levels of the school system. Basic education is still far from being universal in many less developed countries, especially in sub-Saharan Africa and, in many instances, its quality has been deteriorating, sometimes drastically. Where this is the case, basic education remains a priority and its share of the education budget should, if anything, increase.

But expansion and improvement of post-compulsory education (PCE) is considered as crucial in industrialized and semi-industrialized countries and is, in the long run, a condition for the development of the poorest countries, especially if we remember that PCE takes many forms, including not only university-level education but also, in many countries, upper-secon-

Jean-Claude Eicher (France). *Director of the Institut Universitaire de Formation des Maîtres (Institute of Teacher Training) of Burgundy (Dijon); founder of the Institut de Recherche sur l'Économie de l'Éducation (Research Institute on the Economics of Education) (IREDU) and its Director until 1987. Author of several studies on economics and the economics of education. Co-author of the three-volume* work, Économique de l'éducation; l'économie des nouveaux moyens d'enseignement.

Thierry Chevaillier (France). *Lecturer in economics at the Université de Bourgogne (Dijon), where he is also Vice-president, in charge of budgetary and personnel management; member of the Conseil d'Orientation de l'Observatoire des Coûts de l'Enseignement Supérieur (Advisory Board on Monitoring the Financing of Higher Education).*

* This study resulted from the work of a task-force set up by the International Academy of Education on 'Rethinking the Finance of Post-compulsory Education' in the framework of a project financed by the Volkswagen Stiftung.

dary-level education and post-secondary options such as short-course technological institutes, community colleges as well as training programmes run by industries or trade unions.

At all levels of education, the financing of post-secondary education can be considered as particularly problematic. This is because the funding crisis, much broader and deeper now than in the late 1960s when it was first announced by Philip Coombs, is made even more acute by a growing crisis of confidence that makes many governments less and less willing to subsidize education as generously as in the past. These crises have already led to many changes in the finance and administration of schools and especially of higher education institutions. The handful of models of institutional arrangements that could be observed in the 1960s are much less clear-cut today. A tendency towards a more mixed financing is apparent. Although most innovations have been implemented individually as emergency measures, there are many ingenious alternatives that are worth evaluating and considering as a starting point towards more comprehensive reforms.

The funding crisis

Since the 1950s in developed countries, and a little later in most developing countries, the demand for education has increased tremendously, often explosively. Both demographic factors and rising expectations of families have played important roles in the expansion of post-compulsory education especially in the Third World. Supply responded to this new situation and enrolments experienced a spectacular growth.

In higher education they reached levels never seen before. Growth was explosive in most developing countries. For instance, in the thirty years between 1955 and 1986, enrolments multiplied by a factor of 36 in Indonesia, 33 in Thailand, 63 in Venezuela, 60 in Congo, 87 in Madagascar, 103 in Kenya and 112 in Nigeria.

The increase was also very rapid in most developed countries, at least until 1980. Enrolments multiplied by 15 in Spain between 1955 and 1986, 9.7 in Sweden, 9.4 in Austria and 6.7 in France.

But growth has been slowing down everywhere since the late 1970s, with the exception of developing countries that created 'open universities', such as Indonesia, the Republic of Korea and Thailand.

This tremendous expansion implied formidable financial support for education. At first, public budgets for education were sharply increased. The share of gross domestic product (GDP) spent publicly on education increased very rapidly during the 1960s: on average, expenditure increased twice as fast as GDP during the first part of the decade and, albeit relatively a little more slowly, still more than half as fast again until 1970. Although a movement towards stabilization of the ratio was visible in the 1970s, it still increased in a majority of countries in every region of the world until around 1980. Since then, there has been a marked reversal of the trend so that today a large number of countries, both in the developed and in the developing world, have either stabilized or, more often, reduced their public support for education.

Beyond the general upward trend apparently slowing down and in many cases reversing itself towards the end of the period, six phenomena should be pointed out.

Although developing countries seem to be spending a smaller proportion of their resources on education, they are catching up with developed countries, which means that their effort has been more intense in the past and therefore will be more difficult to sustain in the long term.

A tendency towards stabilizing the effort was more noticeable in the former than in the latter group in the early 1970s (the average moved only from 3.63 to 3.69 per cent against 4.86 to 5.24 per cent in developed countries) which may reveal that, as foreseen by Philip Coombs in 1968, the financial crisis struck many of the developing countries sooner.

The economic difficulties that affected market economies after the first oil crisis of

1973, induced a sharp apparent increase in public support for education in both developed and developing countries. But it is difficult to conclude that it reveals the high priority given to it at a time of dwindling resources, because a more detailed analysis shows that it is mostly the result of inertia: it is due to the low income elasticity of education expenditure in the short run, made up as it is of wages and salaries in a larger proportion than most other public budgets.

The trend reversal was more visible in the late 1970s in countries where education was less strongly subsidized by the state. This was a consequence of both a greater flexibility in financing and of a quicker change of attitudes towards education.

In developing countries at all levels and in developed countries mostly at the tertiary level, stabilization of effort means less expenditure per student as enrolments increase faster than GDP and/or public budgets.

The willingness to spend public money for post-compulsory (and even more for post-secondary education) decreased more sharply than for compulsory education.

It is clear that the reversal of the upward trend, in some cases sharp enough to lead to a reduction, not only in the support for education but also in the amount spent was not caused by a lessening of the demand for education. In developed countries it is true that the decline of fertility since the mid-1960s has led to a decrease in the number of pupils, first in primary school, then in the whole compulsory cycle. But in post-compulsory education, this decline has been felt only recently and demand is still increasing. Statistical studies of youth unemployment show that the probability of unemployment is negatively correlated with the level of schooling. Young people are aware of this fact and try to continue their studies as long as they can.

In developing countries, with the notable exception of China, the slowdown of demographic growth is nowhere near important enough to lead to a decrease in the absolute number of school-age children. In Africa, the demographic revolution is still in its expansive phase and the number of potential students still

increases in most countries by 3 per cent a year. Present and expected future benefits of education, together with the low private cost involved, especially in periods of very high unemployment, induced large numbers of the secondary school-leavers to enrol at university.

At the same time, in all countries, the pressure on public budgets increased. On the one hand, the slowdown of economic activity had an unfavourable influence on tax revenues; on the other hand, competing expenditure like unemployment compensation, agriculture, health, foreign-debt servicing and sometimes military spending, tended to take precedence over education.

The conclusion is clear: there is a financial crisis in education in most countries; that crisis is much deeper than macrostatistics reveal and it is not going to disappear soon, especially in developing countries, if new solutions are not found. But the crisis has also been intensified by the fact that education is no longer considered as a panacea: there is a doctrinal crisis as well.

The doctrinal crisis

The tremendous expansion of education in the 1960s was made possible by the fact that most governments put more public resources into that sector. They reacted so positively and so quickly because the then dominant economic theory presented education as a highly profitable investment.

But by the mid-1970s this excessive optimism and the strong urge to give first priority to education in public budgets subsided substantially when, with the rise of graduate unemployment, the capacity of the education system to produce graduates geared to the needs of the labour market was questioned, especially in developing countries where many accused the existing school system of imitating the programmes of the former colonial power. The capacity and the willingness of public decision-makers to allocate resources according to social preferences was also challenged by new economic theories. All these new trends converged towards a more critical view of education and a reduced willingness to increase the public financial contribution to its development, thereby making the financial crisis more acute. Thus, pressed by the urgency of the situation, most countries have been experimenting with, or at least studying, new ways to finance education and new types of relationship between the state and the school system, especially at the post-secondary level.

As these countries started from quite different, and sometimes opposing, institutional and financial backgrounds, a clear tendency away from extreme solutions can be observed: countries with public financing and control are looking towards more private financing and more autonomy, at least at the higher levels of the system; countries, like Japan, where private institutions, unsubsidized by the state, were dominant, have tended to introduce or to increase public subsidies and public control of the private sector.

Although most of the measures implemented in the last twenty years, especially in higher education, have been more in the nature of emergency actions than of fully thought-out reforms, economic analysis unambiguously concludes that they should be supported so long as they lead to more mixed solutions in financing education.

But constraints are strong and manifold. History has moulded the various national school systems in different ways so that there is no unique optimal 'scientific' solution to the problem of the finance of post-compulsory education. We must be aware that it would be a dangerous mistake to impose radical changes without taking into account the practical and social constraints and the political process of each given society.

Taking these constraints into account, however, it is still possible to find solutions suitable to each given situation, so long as priorities and objectives are clear. Although each country has its own peculiarities and must find its own optimal set of rules, it is possible to make recommendations which are broadly valid for groups of countries sharing the same problems of management and funding.

It is necessary, however, to distinguish between the problems and the solutions applicable to higher education and those to post-compulsory secondary education because, in the latter case, public financing is likely to remain dominant and public control tight. Nevertheless, the same broad set of questions need to be answered in all cases.

The main questions

The first and the broadest of these questions is: Who should pay for education? Most innovations involving a broadening of the resource base through the contribution of a new group (or a larger contribution of an existing supporter) have actually been forced upon the system and/or its institutions by circumstances. There is no evidence that those moves were towards the optimum. We must therefore try to build upon what economics can tell us about the optimum financing of education. As we shall see, one broad conclusion is that *mixed financing is better than either pure public or pure private financing.*

This, in turn, raises a second question: Should mixed financing imply a dual system of schools, public schools being financed through public monies while private schools receive their support solely from private sources? Our conclusion is that *mixed financing is advisable for both public and private institutions.*

The next three questions relate more specifically to the financing of the educational services offered by schools.

First, assuming that these services should be subsidized by the state, should the money be given to the institutions or to the students who attend them?

Second, as other sources of finance – firms, philanthropy and, in LDCs, foreign aid – may be tapped, what should their respective contributions be and how should they be given and received? Choices are still more open but, at least as far as *financing by firms* is concerned, two conclusions seem warranted: (a) it could and should increase in many countries; (b) *it should be provided according to varied contractual arrangements.*

Third, is it possible to use resources in a more efficient way, thereby lowering unit cost? This question concerns the cost of education to students, including living expenses while studying. Assuming that the students should not be charged the total cost, how should they be helped? Should they receive grants or loans or a combination of both?

WHO SHOULD PAY FOR WHAT IN POST-SECONDARY EDUCATION?

Education is a process that changes the characteristics of those who go through it, thereby enabling them to benefit personally either immediately or later on. But education is also valued by society as a whole, which, for various reasons feels that it should not be bought and sold in the market on a purely commercial basis. In other words, a case can be made in favour of both public and private financing of education.

The case for public funding of education

In market economies, competition among buyers and sellers and between the two groups is supposed to lead to the best possible use of available resources. But economics textbooks also teach us that several conditions have to be met in order for this optimum result to be achieved. Some of them are not fulfilled in the case of education.

First, certain goods can be used by several people in a non-competitive way, that is, entirely and simultaneously consumed by each individual. Such goods will not be voluntarily purchased on a market if it is not technically or economically feasible to prevent anyone in particular from using them, since they are available to everyone as soon as they are produced. This difficulty, referred as the 'free-rider' problem, dissuades private firms from incurring the cost of producing them. If the goods in question

are considered important by society, they will then have to be financed through non-market devices such as by taxation or philanthropy and offered to all. Strictly speaking, education does not belong to that category of 'a pure public good' as it is always possible to forbid a potential student to sit in a classroom. It is however often argued that it combines the characteristics of both a public and a private good, the quality of education being indivisible, at least for a given institution. When more and more students are crowded into the same classroom, quality decreases, not just for the newcomers but also for those who were already there. This creates a case for public funding to produce or maintain quality in education. The students and their families have no way to evaluate accurately the quality of teaching. Private suppliers could therefore be tempted to increase the quantity, that is, the number of seats they offer, even though this has an adverse effect on quality.

Information available to students is imperfect in another way. The ultimate outcome of education is spread over time and could be affected by many events, most of which cannot be foreseen. It is often argued that this uncertainty leads many young people to underestimate the true future benefits of education and therefore to underinvest in their education if they have to pay the full cost of their studies. Along the same lines, it can be stated that uncertainty about the future earnings of graduates make lenders unwilling to finance education at the going market rate. This increases the cost of education for those who cannot finance it with their own resources and further reduces the demand for education.

Another point in favour of public financing of education is the existence of what economists call positive externalities. Most goods provide satisfaction or other advantages only to those who acquire them. Some entail benefits to other groups or to society at large, over the sum of individual benefits they bestow on their owners. These extra social benefits are attributed to external effects or externalities.

Education is supposed to produce such positive externalities both economic and non-economic. They range from the contribution to economic growth of the advance of knowledge and the increase in the flexibility of the labour markets to the transmission of literacy, aesthetic and cultural values and more efficient political participation. This wide consensus has led to the generally accepted conclusion that these positive externalities justify substantial government intervention.

Finally, public financing may be justified from quite a different point of view – that of the state. If we consider government not only as the representative of the whole community but as an institution trying to maximize its revenue, the influence of education on the graduates' ability to pay taxes out of the extra income they will earn has to be taken into account. If the government reckons that it will get more out of the future incomes and outlays of graduates than it is currently spending in order to expand or improve education, it is justified in maintaining a budget for education.

But we should note that if all the arguments examined above are in favour of some public contribution to the funding of education, they do not lead us to conclude that it should cover the whole cost.

The case for private financing of education

The main arguments for individuals (or their families) paying for the education they receive, at least beyond the compulsory level, are well known. Students acquire private benefits through higher income and social status, increased consumption, better health, higher political efficacy and greater access to, and better understanding of, culture, science and technology. Other arguments in favour of the payment of fees by students can be found on the supply side.

First, there is the well-known 'token user charge' argument. People are inclined not to appreciate what they receive free of charge and consume goods indiscriminately and wastefully. When a fee, however modest, is collected, rationality tends to increase.

Second, when the customer pays for what he gets, he is entitled to pass judgement on the product. When schools charge fees, they have to take into account students' preferences and organize the curriculum accordingly. This promotes 'internal efficiency' of educational institutions.

Third, fees represent extra revenue for publicly funded schools, thereby enabling them to maintain quality in time of budgetary squeeze.

But benefits from education are also gained by private enterprises: general education reduces the need for training and the cost of retraining when shifting to new products and technologies, while specific training and research programmes may increase productivity. There is no obvious reason why they should not pay for what will benefit them.

Finally, if philanthropists receive satisfaction from the development of education, they can be expected to provide funds towards it.

The above arguments show quite clearly that a convincing case can be made in favour of both public and private funding of education. *The optimal solution appears to be a mixed system.* But this leaves untouched a very important question: What should be the proportion paid by each participant?

On principle, the answer is simple: each participant should pay for education according to the benefits received. But many of those benefits are difficult or impossible to measure. Individual students do not know with a reasonable certainty what they will earn throughout their active life; neither are they able to quantify the non-monetary benefits they expect from going to school beyond the compulsory period. Firms tend to discount the advantages they get from graduates. Philanthropists have to choose between various competing uses for their money. They are interested in the cost-effectiveness of the funds they intend to donate but have no objective criteria to guide them in their choice.

All things considered, the choice of the precise mix depends more on the practical and social constraints of a given society and the political process than on the rational views of researchers and evaluators. But this does not mean that nothing can be said about the consequences of a given choice.

Different countries make widely different choices about the public/private division of responsibility for PCE, especially at the higher level. Moreover, there are good reasons to recommend both public and private financing of it. Does that mean that the optimal solution is a dual system comprising public institutions fully supported through public apportionment and private institutions charging full cost covering fees? Empirical observations show that this extreme solution is very seldom adopted and logic militates in favour of more mixed solutions.

There are several arguments in favour of public subsidies to private schools. Such subsidies could be a prerequisite for a large expansion of private education. The costs of PCE and still more of higher education are high. Few students (or their families) can afford to pay them in full. Private institutions can only hope to attract large numbers of students if they charge below cost fees. Subsidies may generate savings in public budgets if they divert more students from public schools than would unsubsidized private schools.

It may at the same time help to meet cultural and economic goals and to ensure political stability if it allows minorities to attend schools of their choice at a reasonable cost. Furthermore, it may help shift part of the financial burden to households when law or tradition prevents or hinders the levying of fees by public institutions. Finally, it may allow the state to impose controls on private schools in return for the subsidy, thereby making sure they do not disseminate subversive ideas or, more generally that they offer education of at least a minimal quality.

There are also strong arguments in favour of some private financing of public institutions: (a) the token-user-charge argument quoted above; (b) the rate-of-return argument, which questions students getting their education free when they will earn more after graduation; and (c) the autonomy argument to be developed below.

The conclusion is that the distinction between public and private education is not always as clear-cut as it seems. Private management does not always mean purely private financing. Letting a publicly subsidized private sector grow can alleviate budgetary strains; encouraging public institutions to seek other (private) sources of income will reach the same goal.

PUBLIC FINANCE OF EDUCATION: SUBSIDIES TO INSTITUTIONS OR STUDENTS

If there is a broad agreement that post-compulsory education should be subsidized by the state, institutional ways by which those subsidies are channeled differ widely from country to country (and from state to state in federal countries). These arrangements have differential effects on the working of the system which have to be clearly understood in order to guide public choices.

Broadly speaking, there are two 'pure' (polar) solutions. Either the support is offered to the institutions or it is given to the students. In the latter (pure) case the institution charges a fee covering the full cost of the services it offers and the student gets a grant or subsidized loan from the state. In the former, the institution determines the range and the quality of its services according to the state subsidy and the other resources it is able to gather (student fees, grants from firms, etc.).

Institutional support

This can take two forms – general and specific. In the first case, public funds are used to support the general educational functions of the institutions in the form of annual budgets calculated on the basis of a more or less complicated funding formula and provided through the normal budgetary allocations by the appropriate government bodies. In contrast, specific grants represent those that are given to institutions for specified purposes.

Traditionally, public money was given to institutions mainly in the form of specific or restricted grants. Staff wages and salaries were paid either directly by the state or, on a national scale, by each institution out of a state grant. This type of institutional arrangement tended not to induce innovation but rather bound the hands of the payer as well as those of the recipient.

Apparently, unrestricted block grants, when they existed, were generally so low that they offered no choice to the institutions. There was an exception in the United Kingdom where, for a long time, generous unrestricted grants were used to finance universities and left them a great deal of freedom. But it is generally considered that this arrangement did not promote more innovation and competition than restricted grants that were allocated to the other higher education institutions of the country, the polytechnics and colleges.

Neither solution leads to optimal results: unrestricted block grants do not provide incentives and tend to shrink through time. Specific grants do not ensure the long-term stability that institutions need and may be given more in accordance with the passing priorities and fancies of elected bodies than with a thought-out pattern of development.

The stimulus needed to urge institutions to innovate could be provided by a combination of a basic allocation with a funding formula linked to objective criteria like the number of students and specific grants towards development programmes agreed jointly by the institution and the funding body on a contractual basis and subject to evaluation. Such procedures are being tested or implemented in a few European countries and seem to give good results.

This combination may also increase total funding in two ways: first, by resulting in larger grants to the innovative institutions; and, second, by matching the specific grants with additional resources obtained from other public or private sources.

One condition that has to be fulfilled for these new procedures to yield the expected positive results is that leeway be given to institutions in their use of public money.

Student support

Student-oriented support can take the form of grants (such as scholarships or maintenance grants) or loans. Obviously, if the public authorities were to substitute student-oriented approaches for institutionally oriented ones, the budgetary subsidies to institutions would decline so that they would have to raise student charges. Students would pay higher tuition fees with the funds that they receive from the state. State institutions would still receive state support indirectly through the public funds provided to students for their education as well as any direct institutional funding that may exist.

This solution is supposed to increase students' range of choice, especially where private institutions are eligible to participate. It may also promote equity, as the amount of the subsidy can be tailored to students' economic circumstances and background. It creates competition for students between institutions. But this is not necessarily a good thing as it will not only increase diversity and in some sense productivity but also probably favour short-term strategy at the expense of long-range planning, and sometimes encourage faddism and poor-quality alternatives in order to attract students. Furthermore, it will probably induce a reduction of the programmes whose benefits accrue to society at large rather than to individual students.

Considering the mixed results of each 'pure' solution, it seems reasonable to recommend a combination of institutional and student support. To be more specific, so long as postsecondary educational institutions provide social benefits to the state besides to those received by students and their families, there is a rationale for some institutional support. Benefits that depend on student choices and participation should be funded through student support. But, on the whole, one thing is clear: There is a strong case in favour of shifting to more student-oriented subsidies in many countries, especially in Europe, where public support is overwhelmingly given to institutions. This of course leaves open the question of the type of support to be provided to students (grants or loans) and of how it should be administered, which will be examined below.

OTHER SOURCES OF FINANCE

Educational institutions do not have to rely exclusively on public subsidies and/or on student fees. It is generally considered that business at large has a legitimate interest in PCE which argues the case for firms to bear a proportion of its cost. But institutions, especially universities, may also derive income from their own assets. Philanthropists may be induced to provide additional resources. Lastly, international assistance should sometimes be solicited in developing countries.

Financing by business

Firms contribute to public funding of institutions or students through general taxation. But there are also specific ways in which they can be induced or forced to share the burden, like taxes earmarked for education and levied on turnover or on payroll or tax exemption on gifts. An interesting example is the French *taxe d'apprentissage*, a payroll tax of 0.6 per cent, which is waived if firms make a donation of the same amount to vocational- and technical-education institutions of their choice, either directly or through business associations.

They sometimes neither need incentive nor compulsion to contribute to the financing of education when they find a way of solving their own problems by contracting with educational institutions for specific services.

Business contributions related to teaching and training

In a rapidly changing technological environment firms need to provide their work-force with more training than before. On-the-job training is still important, especially in order to adapt newly employed workers to their jobs. But it is even more important to teach new skills, to adapt the work-force to new processes and to a new organization of labour.

Firms are not able to perform all these tasks

themselves; they have to contract with training institutions. Technical schools and universities can provide part of this training but most of the courses they offer are not adapted to this new demand. They have to set up continuing education departments, financed by fees paid by firms for their trainees. However, their teaching staff may be reluctant to enter these new and often more exacting teaching activities unless they receive some financial reward on top of their statutory salary. As far as the institution as such is concerned, there is an incentive to develop such departments only if some of the extra resources are likely to spill over to traditional teaching and research or if they help to develop links with business, thereby facilitating in-firm placement and eventually jobs for their students.

As a matter of fact, firms can also contribute to education by providing opportunities for students to bridge the gap between the abstract knowledge acquired in education and operational skills when they offer them practical work experience during their period of study.

These contributions are real but they must not be seen as a diversification of financial resources of higher education institutions but rather as a consequence of a diversification of their purposes and activities.

Research services to business

'Pure' research is conducted and financed either within the education system or independently with specific funding by the state or by philanthropists. Applied research bridges the gap between 'pure' research and production of goods and services. It is directly linked to the production process and can be considered as a specific type of productive investment by firms and public organizations. Training and applied research are closely linked and therefore firms and educational institutions can enter into mutually fruitful co-operation agreements that will only be efficient so long as they remain specific and limited in scope.

Applied research could generate extra resources if universities were to exploit their intellectual property rights by patenting or licensing to industry the fruits of their research laboratories, thus participating in the so-called transfer of technology. This is a very promising but difficult path to take. On the one hand, the tradition of academic research, free dissemination of new knowledge, is hardly consistent with the secrecy required when developing a new product in a competitive environment; publication of results is often considered as the ultimate aim of scientific activity. On the other hand, many universities lack the professionalism protect and market their ideas. But inventions hatched in university laboratories cannot go on making the fortune of private firms; despite the difficulties, higher education institutions should strive to turn their intellectual property rights into an additional source of finance.

Income from property, industrial or financial assets

Endowment of schools and universities with land or property has long been a simple way of securing their financial independence but can no longer be considered as the main funding method for all PCE institutions, for they would have to own a considerable share of the land, buildings and businesses of the country to be able to get enough resources to cover most of their current expenditure.

Some donors, however, prefer to make endowments for a specific purpose (like endowed chairs) and universities, even though they would prefer to spend the proceeds of donations immediately, sometimes have to set up and manage endowment funds.

In the latter half of the twentieth century, endowments have been increasingly turned into financial assets with a higher yield than property but more risky. Managing these assets requires costly expertise and may create problems for institutions designed for a different purpose. Because of the peculiar way they are governed, academic institutions may be tempted to exert pressure on enterprises in which they own stock to redirect their activities towards nobler or higher goals (for example, the campaigns against military research, nuclear power, pollution or apartheid in South Africa). They may also indulge in speculative or 'creative' finance by

using practices designed to increase revenue through tax-subsidy financing or legal devices that permit participation in equity growth from commercial enterprises (by creating subsidiaries or foundations for the sole purpose of benefiting from business tax provisions). Setting up a foundation could allow institutions to benefit from endowments without having to meddle in matters so distant from their original purpose.

However, universities should not hesitate to create or help to create various enterprises whenever they are related to their teaching or research activity: consultancy firms, run either by staff or students, science parks, incubators and joint ventures for developing university-produced inventions, service agencies for exploiting their unused facilities by organizing conferences, etc.

Philanthropists, benefactors and sponsors

Individual and business philanthropy flourishes in a specific environment made up of a favourable tax system and a national tradition of solidarity in the local community, as opposed to reliance on a central authority. Without these, even the best organized fund raising campaigns will not succeed in providing a sustained flow of resources to PCE institutions. Provided they meet certain conditions of financial soundness and accountability, post-compulsory education institutions should be treated as tax-exempt foundations and charities and be allowed to receive tax deductible donations from firms as well as from individuals. Each institution would then be able to appeal to one or several constituencies (alumni, business sponsors, etc.) according to the type of project it intends to finance from the proceeds of such donations.

International assistance

The financial situation of some developing countries is such that, in the short and middle term they will most probably not be able to maintain a minimum level of quality and accommodate demographic expansion without outside help. But in the past, disinterested international assistance has not always been forthcoming.

TABLE I. Evaluation of different methods of funding education

Method	Efficiency	Equity	Resource broadening	Administration cost
Specific grants to institutions	+	=	= or +	-
Vouchers to students	+	=	+	-
Tuition fees				
Token fees	+	=	+	-
Substantial uniform fees	+	-	+ +	-
Substantial variable fees	+ +	- -	+ +	-
Full-cost fees	+ +	- -	+ +	-
Financing by business				
Contribution to teaching	+	= or -	+	-
Research services	+	=	+	-
Educational payroll tax	+	= or -	+ +	-
Endowments and gifts	=	?	+	- -

These facts, by now well known, lead to the following conclusion: international assistance should increase, at least for some developing countries; but it should also be reorganized – fewer teachers on loan, fewer 'gifts', but more assistance to local programmes, and more subsidies to help cover the recurring expenses of key institutions (textbook printing presses, for instance).

Effects of financial innovations

All things considered, diversification of the sources of funding of PCE institutions is a distinct possibility, but it is not without consequences on their organization. It generally strengthens their autonomy but it also supposes a stronger management as diversification makes it more difficult to achieve consensus.

But it should be emphasized that changing the source of funds also strongly affects the working of the system as a whole or that of each member institution. The effects of various innovations introduced in a given system can be assessed according to four criteria: *efficiency* and *equity*, the two traditional criteria of welfare economics; *resource broadening* potential, that is, the capacity to generate new resources by bringing in new categories of fund providers or by inducing existing contributors to increase their funding; but new modes of financing may entail *administrative costs* which may lower the net in-

take. If we consider, for instance, a system financed mainly through public unrestricted grants to institutions, the average effects of the main financial innovations can be summarized in Table 1. In some case, the outcome cannot be foreseen without knowing more details about the way changes are implemented.

No single source scores high according to each one of the four criteria. The same conclusion would be reached if we started from a different inital arrangement. This means two things: first, the final choice depends on the weight the final decision-maker gives to each criterion; second, a combination of different sources is in most cases to be preferred to a single source of income.

CUTTING COSTS OR SHIFTING TO NEW
OPERATING METHODS

The problem for schools and universities in a crisis situation is to manage to increase or, at least, to maintain their output. Looking for new resources is not the only solution. Finding ways to use existing resources in a more efficient way should also be recommended. Two types of changes in financial arrangements may lead to an increase in efficiency (or at least in effectiveness).

First a tightening of public subsidies. If the amount of the public grant (and/or the number of posts) decreases sharply, institutions are strongly induced to curtail all expenditure non-essential to the day-to-day working of the institution and if they are allowed to do so, to reallocate staff members. But there is generally no close correlation between anticipated effects of restrictive financial policies and their effective consequences.

Evaluations of the consequences of policies of retrenchment in various European countries show that the effects of government policies were linked with the extent of the consultation between the ministry of education and the institutions, and with the degree of autonomy of the latter.

It can generally be observed that the results were more in keeping with expectations where the universities benefited from a real degree of autonomy and were closely associated in devising the reallocation plan (the case of the Netherlands) than where the rules were set up by a ministry or central agency without consultation (the case of the United Kingdom) and still more where the universities had very little autonomy, and therefore shortages of resources were often induced by the many structural rigidities of the system (the case of France).

Also, we must be aware of the fact that the increase in the efficiency of teaching and research cannot in most cases be documented as, in most instances, no reliable performance indicators have been developed.

Cost effectiveness can also be increased through changes in the way educational services are delivered. Traditional education is organized in such a way that its unit costs have a tendency to increase over time as its main input is highly qualified labour whose relative price goes up. But economic history has shown that it is possible to lower unit costs by substituting capital for labour. For a long time, technological innovations were of little use in education, owing to the characteristics of its 'product'. But, with the communication revolution, there are bound to be changes: what is generally considered to be the main objective of education, that is, to transmit knowledge, should be strongly affected by the availability of new media of communication,

which should also help research, another main objective of education.

Great expectations were placed on the first generation of those communication technologies – radio, television and, more generally, all types of audio-visual aids. The disappointment with the results was at least as strong. On the whole, these instruments were shown by evaluators to be costly, underutilized and often having no significant effect on learning. But most of these evaluations concerned projects developed within the system of compulsory education and taking place inside schools.

The balance sheet is much more positive when we look at post-secondary education and distance teaching. Evaluations made in developed countries in the late 1970s gave quite a sizeable advantage to open institutions. For instance, Israel's Everyman's University cost only 60 per cent of what regular universities in the country did, and the cost per student in the British Open University was estimated to be only 70 per cent of that in a comparable British university, at a time when the former had only 34,000 students, that is, at a time when it had not yet reaped the full benefit of the economies of scale connected with distance teaching.

Part of the difference is, of course, due to the fact that a much higher proportion of distance education students take up courses in the humanities or law where the cost per student is relatively low, but it remains true that the cost is much lower in every field.

The second generation of new communication technologies (microcomputers, videodiscs, cable TV, etc.) has a much greater potential than ever and will progressively transform higher education.

Potentially, the new technologies of information and communication (NTICs) have three effects which affect, directly or indirectly, the financing of post-compulsory education.

First, they allow students to receive high-quality teaching without leaving their place of residence. The best specialists in each field can be used to elaborate the courseware so that each student can attend, so to speak, lectures by the best teachers in the country. Furthermore, the student can choose to study according to his or her own schedule, in the evenings or at weekends, for instance. Besides being more convenient to the student, this contributes to the following.

Second, NTICs may contribute to lowering the cost of education. By allowing students to choose their schedule and study load, they avoid or reduce cases where adults must forgo earnings, as they can thereby study without giving up their regular occupation. Furthermore, if each recorded course is used by a large number of students, teacher costs per student will be very low compared with traditional education where there is a teacher in each classroom or, at best, for a small number of classrooms. Of course, the gain will be more important in school programmes where the same curriculum is followed by many students than in adult education where demand is much more diversified and in higher education where the students are much more autonomous than in secondary education where frequent contacts between teacher and students are still needed. It should also be remembered that extra costs are added, those of hardware, courseware, transmission, etc., but these tend to decrease through time.

Third, distance teaching using NTICs may be an opportunity to shift the financial burden of education, at least partially, onto the students. They will have to buy the hardware (microcomputers, peripherals, interfaces, etc.). They may be more willing to pay for the courses themselves, that is, to buy the courseware, for three reasons. If they are adults already engaged in professional activities, the fact that they do not forgo much or any of their earnings allows them to enjoy a higher disposable income. If they anticipate a rise in salary once they have obtained the degree or diploma they seek, their willingness to pay for their studies is still greater. They may, in some cases, receive financial help from their employer who may be prepared to buy the courseware. If they have not yet entered into active life, they may feel that this is the only opportunity they have of studying further if they do not have enough academic credentials to be admitted to regular courses, or if they are not will-

ing or able to move to the place where those courses are offered.

The new technologies may therefore, for all these reasons, be a way to lower the cost of PCE and/or to shift part of the financial burden onto students in countries where there are very low fees or none at all.

Two caveats are in order, however. First, evaluations show that there is still a wide gap between the potential and the practical effectiveness of NTICs, so that we may expect them to catch on much more slowly than anticipated by some. Second, these instruments are sophisticated, some of them highly so, and they may only function in an adequate environment. The hardware must be protected against climatic extremes and power surges, and must be maintained and repaired. If minimal environmental conditions are usually met in developed countries, this is not always the case in developing countries, especially in rural areas.

This is why we may confidently forecast a strong development of distance higher education, to the extent that, twenty years hence, a majority of the teaching will no longer be residential in most universities. This will allow these institutions to obtain an important part of their resources by charging higher prices for the courseware than for regular curricula. In the developing world, we can forecast the same evolution in semi-industrialized countries as can be seen in Asia. But those changes will come more slowly in the less developed countries, especially in Africa where distance teaching should preferably make use of the communication technology of the first generation rather than of the NTICs. Everywhere, however, the need will remain to extend some public support to the students themselves.

STUDENT AID

Students may contribute to the financing of their own studies, especially at the college level, from income earned from vacation and campus jobs. The latter should be provided and subsidized by institutions and government agencies responsible for student aid on the model of that which exists in the United States and should be made easier by the development of part-time study.

The burden on students and their families may also be spread over time through various education finance schemes. But students (or their families) should not be expected to finance the full cost of going to school. This statement leaves us with three fundamental problems:

First, should only the price of the educational services offered by the school system (the cost of schooling) be subsidized or should the total cost of obtaining an education, including living expenses while studying, be supported by the state (or other sources)?

Second, should students be helped through grants or through loans or some combination of both?

Third, should the aid be manipulated in order to orientate candidates towards certain disciplines?

Cost of educational services and living expenses

There are reasons for not separating completely the problem of subsidizing the cost of educational services and the living expenses of students. As students have to renounce gainful employment (at least full time) in order to go to school, they cannot support themselves; so long as university students who are above the legal adult age are officially classified as independent, their family should normally not be expected to provide for their needs. But, we should not lump the two questions together. The reasons why education should be subsidized are not exactly the same as those in favour of helping the students cover their living expenses.

Grants or loans?

Should students be helped through grants or loans? The aim of both types of support is twofold. From the standpoint of social efficiency, it is to maximize the enrolment of able students in order to maximize human capital formation. From the standpoint of equity, it is to make it possible for every able student to attend school whatever his or her economic circumstances.

The case for each type of aid should therefore be made keeping in mind these two aims.

Grants

The precise effects of grants also depend upon the way they are distributed and managed and upon their aim: covering all or part of the schooling cost (fee subsidies) or subsidizing living expenses (maintenance grants).

Fee subsidies are necessary so long as there is a shortage of skilled manpower, as few students (and/or their families) are able to pay the the cost of full tuition. Such grants can be paid to students or they can take the form of vouchers. An educational voucher is a coupon of prescribed purchasing power that can be cashed at any educational institution. The issuing of such coupons is supposed to reach two objectives simultaneously: enforcement of the right to education for all and freedom of choice. This could be achieved with a much lower administration cost by subsidizing institutions according to the number of students enrolled in order for them to charge no fee or very low uniform fees provided that students can freely choose between institutions.

Maintenance grants can be given either in kind (subsidized accommodation, food and transport) or in cash. In the former case, it is obvious that they can only be given to the institutions that offer those services. In the latter case, it is better that they be given to the student rather than to his parents as it is difficult to make sure that the parents will actually spend the whole amount to cover the living expenses of their children. Uniform grants clearly increase participation rates but they can be considered as inequitable as they help the rich as much as the poor. They may even amount to a regressive distribution of income if the tax structure is not very progressive and if participation rates are much higher for the children of well-to-do families. Furthermore, they are less efficient in boosting participation rates than income-related subsidies.

Criteria-bound grants may be of two kinds. Income-related grants are clearly meant to increase equality of opportunity. They should be chosen if equity is the main criterion. Ability-bound subsidies are given according to academic performance; they increase efficiency in that they maximize human capital formation but their effect on equity is probably nil and may even be negative.

It is still considered important to promote equity in education though few people still believe that educational expansion fosters a more equal income distribution. Equality of opportunity in education means that all students with a minimal level of competence should be able to participate beyond the compulsory level regardless of their other characteristics. Need-based student financial aid is meant to remove at least the financial barrier, often considered as the most potent one.

Student aid has clearly increased the rate of participation of poor students in higher education, allowed more of them to attend relatively costly and prestigious institutions and to stay at school longer. But it is also clear that it has not succeeded in eradicating the effects of social environment. Its effectiveness in promoting equity is linked with the way in which it is offered. We must keep that in mind when considering student loans.

Loans

The most striking and extensive recent changes in the pattern of financial sources for post-secondary education have involved private sources. In most countries with a tradition of 'free' post-compulsory education, users – that is, students and their families – have been increasingly asked to contribute to the cost of education.

First, support towards living expenses has gradually shifted from the state to students: aid-in-kind, through provision or subsidization of food, lodging, transportation and welfare, did not follow the pace of enrolments, leaving the students to foot a larger share of the cost of these services. In many countries, these services are largely self-financing, students-in-need being increasingly supported directly through grants or subsidized loans.

Second, some of the educational costs of PCE have been transferred to the students by resorting to specific fees for additional equipment or services (laboratory, computer, library fee) which, being easily identified, were more acceptable to students and their families. In a number of countries (Belgium, Spain, the Netherlands, Switzerland), general tuition fees have been increased to levels that are no longer nominal (ranging from \$200 to \$800).

The ever-increasing costs of PCE could not be met by families out of their pockets or by the state out of its budget, so there appeared a need for another major source of funds which was found in the development of student loans which were increasingly advocated for the following reasons.

Since education is a profitable investment for most students even in countries where a high proportion of each age-group goes beyond compulsory education, there is no reason why society should bear its total cost. If graduates earn more than non-graduates, they should be able to devote part of their extra income to repay a loan.

Furthermore, students who borrow to pay for their studies are more inclined to choose wisely their field of study and to try to go through the curriculum as fast as possible in order to minimize the amount they have to borrow. Contrary to income contingent grants that leave students from well-to-do families dependent upon the goodwill of their parents, loans enable all students to make their own choices, according to their capacity and their own preferences. Broadly, three main types of loans should be distinguished.

Commercial loans. These are organized like a mortgage or an ordinary bank loan. The interest rate is that of the market, the repayment period is fixed. Such a method has several drawbacks, however. As a way of financing education it is more risky for both the borrower and the lender than most other loans. Not only does a student who borrows not know with any degree of accuracy what will be the eventual return on his degree since it depends upon future labour market conditions and other unpredictable factors, but he cannot be even sure that he will graduate.

Contrary to those who borrow to buy a house, he cannot offer collateral. The result is that banks are very reluctant to offer such loans without a government guarantee, and hence tend to charge high interest rates. For the same reasons, they will tend to offer only relatively short term loans which raises the amount to be repaid at each period.

Public student-loan programmes. Public involvement in student loans can take the form of a public subsidy, allowing the lender to offer lower interest rates and deferred repayments (grace period). But it can also consist of a guarantee against default.

Owing to the great uncertainty about the future, commercial lenders tend to charge a premium to protect themselves from default on the part of a fraction of the borrowers who, having wrongly anticipated their future income, will be unable to pay back. This makes the cost of studies much higher for those who have to borrow than for those who can count on financial support from their family. A public guarantee or a subsidy high enough to eliminate this cost difference would, so to speak, re-create a 'perfect market' situation and correct the distortion in resource allocation. Such a guarantee or such a subsidy obviously creates a burden on the public budget, but it is likely to be a lighter one than is the case with outright grants.

But loans are actually often much more subsidized than is necessary to correct market imperfections. These large subsidies are justified by arguments of efficiency and equity.

If there are positive externalities, that is, if education has positive effects on society at large, over and above the benefits it confers to each graduate, students should not be made to pay the full cost of tuition. To offer them subsidized loans would be a way to shift part of the cost of tuition. But if teaching institutions are already subsidized by the state in order to charge lower tuition fees, subsidizing the loans above that required to correct market imperfections would amount to subsidizing the same good twice, which seems to complicate the administration of the system without improving efficiency.

On the side of equity, the high subsidy can be justified only if it is limited to 'poor' students. Besides the fact that it is difficult in most countries to measure the true ability to pay, it seems more logical to try to reach the same goal through a third type of loan: income-related repayment loans.

In any case, subsidized loans have obvious drawbacks. First, as they represent recurrent costs for the public budget, they tend to be rationed in periods of financial constraint, thus limiting access to education, as shown recently by the heavily subsidized German scheme (BA-FöG). Second, they do not help solve the problem of the so-called 'negative dowries', that is, the transfer to spouses of the repayment of loans contracted by non-working married graduates. This latter problem disappears with the third type of loan.

Loans with income-related repayments. Uncertainty about the return to the educational investment may deter prospective students from continuing their studies even when the investment would turn out to be profitable. This uncertainty leads to inefficient decisions and therefore to misallocation of resources. This can be prevented by setting up some sort of insurance against the risk of an individual not reaching a level of income that makes his investment in education profitable. Insurance of this sort can be achieved by a loan scheme where repayment is related to the actual income of the borrower. There are two possible kinds of relations between repayment and income.

First, repayment could be increased or reduced according to the income level reached. This procedure provides each individual borrower with an insurance against the risk of income fluctuations. If his or her income goes down due to unfortunate or unforeseen circumstances, he or she will automatically see repayment instalments decrease. It also makes the 'rich' pay back more than the poor and possibly much more than they borrowed. There are two drawbacks to such loans with income-related repayment, well known to insurance specialists.

The first one is called 'moral hazard' and involves the conscious or unconscious behaviour of insured individuals to increase the occurrence of the events against which they are insured, to the extent that they have control of them. If more students having borrowed under such a scheme drop out or choose to live on a small income, the scheme will incur losses that will have to be borne by the public purse. The other drawback is referred to as 'adverse selection'. If it is possible to 'opt out' of a loan scheme with income-related repayment, those students who have higher income expectations will choose to finance their education by borrowing from banks or with the help of their family and the source for potential excess repayments will dry up. Only those who expect to do less well will borrow under the scheme, which is bound to create another source of imbalance that would have to be made up by budgetary appropriations.

Second, the loan could be repaid more or less rapidly according to the income level of the borrower. 'Rich' individuals would repay more per year than 'poor' individuals, but repayment would stop for everyone when the full amount of the loan had been paid back with interest. This would considerably reduce the risk of adverse selection but probably would not eliminate moral hazard. Unemployed and other non-working people would not have to repay, unless they secured unearned income, and those in very low income brackets might repay only part of the loan before retirement. But, of course, the longer the period of repayment, the more interest will have to be paid, so that the poor would pay more interest than the rich.

If loans replaced grants, pure income-contingent loans would reduce the public budget by the amount of the grants except for two problems. First, the initial loans, before repayments start coming in, should probably be financed out of public money or at least subsidized in order for the scheme to get off the ground. Second, even after the launching period, such a system is bound regularly to bring about a deficit, whatever the solution chosen, as shown above.

In any case, a 'forgiveness clause' that waives repayment of a loan, can be used by governments as an incentive to attract students to specific jobs that are in particular need of manpower (as an alternative method to bonding, that is, financing students with the obligation to serve the government for a certain period after graduation). Other objectives can also be aimed at through such clauses as rewarding academically outstanding students or encouraging rapid completion of degrees.

In sum, there is a strong case to make in favour of loans. When local circumstances make them feasible, these loans should be of the income-related repayment type so as to provide mutual insurance. The amount to be repaid should not exceed – or at least not by much – the amount borrowed plus interest and service charges. Richer graduates should repay faster than their less successful colleagues and an income threshold should be set below which repayment could be suspended.

Subsidization of the scheme by the state, although inevitable, should be as small as possible in order not to distort the free choice of students. It should mainly consist of a public guarantee of the loans (which lowers the cost of borrowing by eliminating the risk component of the interest rate) rather than directly subsidizing the interest rate.

But a sudden switch from maintenance grants to loans is not acceptable. It would certainly meet with strong resistance from students or their unions, and is it objectively unsatisfactory. In particular, it would affect equity negatively, as the poorest would never be able to borrow enough to see themselves through long courses of study, and, more generally, it would discourage a growing number of students to enrol, especially for long courses.

The conclusion is that a combination of guaranteed loans for all students and means tested maintenance grants for the poorer would be the optimal solution. In order to make students more responsible and to lessen the financial burden on the public budget, extending maintenance grants only to students who take a loan of a minimum amount could be envisaged.

To sum up, the optimal financial setting for

higher education, which could be extended with some important qualifications to upper secondary education, seem to be the following:

Public financing, which should be predominant and should consist of a mixture of: (a) a basic unrestricted block grant to institutions ensuring a minimum of security and continuity; (b) specific grants negotiated between each institution and one or several public bodies, phased over a period of several years, subject to interim evaluation and renegotiation; (c) income-related grants to students, helping covering both tuition fees and maintenance; and (d) guarantee to student loans.

Private financing, in the shape of: (a) fees (basic tuition fees, uniform and substantial) and additional specific fees for special services, freely set up by institutions, within limits; (b) business contributions, which should be limited, in the public and publicly subsidized sector, to the financing of continuing education and training, practical training included in the curriculum of regular degrees and applied research, and which could be made compulsory in part through a payroll tax earmarked for education; and (c) gifts and endowments, which could be made easier by changes in tax regulations (but are likely to remain nominal in the short run for countries where they are not rooted in tradition).

For most Western European countries and for other countries with a similar higher education funding system this would mean: (a) in most cases, a drastic rethinking of the relationship between public authorities and institutions; (b) a progressive phasing out of the various subsidies to students services; (c) the phasing out of tax relief for dependent students; (d) a substantial increase in tuition fees; (e) the setting up of a guaranteed student loan system; and (f) increased participation by business.

Of course, each of these countries will have to make its own choice according to its own constraints and political stance, but the logic of the present situation should lead them all to broadly similar choices. ∎

Bibliography

BLAUG, M. 1970. *An Introduction to the Economics of Education.* Harmondsworth, Penguin.

COOMBS, P. 1985. *The World Education Crisis: The View from the 1980s.* New York, Oxford University Press.

GEIGER, R. L. 1988. *Privatization of Higher Education: International Trends and Issues.* New York, ICED.

HUSEN, T. 1979. *The School in Question.* Oxford, Oxford University Press.

LESLIE, L. L.; BRINKMAN, P. T. 1988. *The Economic Value of Higher Education.* New York, American Council on Education/Macmillan.

MONK D. H. 1990. *Educational Finance.* New York, McGraw-Hill.

PSACHAROPOULOS G.; WOODHALL, M. 1985. *Education for Development.* New York, Oxford University Press.

WOODHALL, M. 1990. *Student Loans in Higher Education.* IIEP Dissemination Programme. Paris, IIEP. (Educational Forum, Series 1.)

PART II

Case Studies

French-speaking universities in sub-Saharan Africa

A critical impasse

François Orivel

Administrators of French-speaking sub-Saharan African universities are faced with a cruel dilemma: with the passing years, their dwindling budgets have made it increasingly difficult for them to guarantee the proper functioning of their establishments; hence a decline in the level of competence of graduates and in research standards. At the same time, some studies show that unit costs are too high and that higher education receives an inordinate amount of educational funding. They recommend that the squeeze on university budgets be sustained and tightened.

The primary aim of this article is to provide evidence to support these two seemingly contradictory assessments. It is true that while French-speaking universities in sub-Saharan Africa are short of funds, they still manage to spend too much; however, it is equally true that solutions to this problem exist and that strategies compatible with both observations can be found.

François Orivel (France). *Director of IREDU (Institut de Recherche sur l'Économie de l'Éducation), a laboratory of the CNRS (National Centre for Scientific Research) at the University of Burgundy in Dijon. Author of numerous books and articles on the sujet of the costs, financing and efficiency of education systems. He is also a consultant to international organizations (UNESCO, IIEP, UNDP, OECD, World Bank, ILO) and governments, particularly in sub-Saharan Africa.*

Student enrolments

In spite of the persistent economic crisis characterized by shrinking budgets and bleak job prospects for graduates, student numbers continue to grow. (See Table 1.)

In the French-speaking countries, the annual growth-rate was 9.6 per cent from 1980 to

TABLE I. Student numbers in higher education in sub-Saharan Africa (thousands)

Group	1960	1970	1980	1983	1986
French-speaking countries	4	33	148	179	212
English-speaking countries	17	69	250	335	406

Source: World Bank, 1988, 1990, p. 13.

TABLE 2. Expenditure per university student (1986 dollars)

Country	1970	1975	1980	1983	1986
Burkina Faso	–	5 046	6 275	3 046	2 465
Cameroon	7 614	–	3 233	3 400	–
Central African Republic	–	4 667	3 638	2 458	1 630
Congo	2 616	7 307	3 634	–	4 218
Côte d'Ivoire	8 403	10 942	6 189	3 654	–
Madagascar	3 861	1 276	1 617	668	599
Mauritania	–	–	8 276	19 976	16 193
Niger	–	–	4 967	–	–
Senegal	–	2 781	2 916	–	–
Togo	–	–	3 271	2 792	2 182

Source: World Bank, 1990, pp. 42–3.

1983, and 7.1 per cent between 1983 and 1986, as compared with the growth-rate in primary-school enrolments, which barely kept pace with demographic growth (3.5 per cent). In English-speaking Africa, university enrolments increased less rapidly (7.3 and 5.7 per cent respectively over the same two periods).

Overall, the number of students in the two groups is roughly proportional to their respective populations. However, it would be logical to expect slower growth-rates for higher education in French-speaking Africa for two reasons: access to primary education is less developed (in 1986, 64 per cent compared with 74 per cent for English-speaking Africa), and the level of economic development is, on average, lower.

We cannot ignore the fact that, in a world – and regions – of limited resources, a boom in higher education is inevitably being achieved at the expense of other levels of education. On the other hand, the priority assigned to basic education at Jomtien should logically lead to a reversal of these trends until the objective of education for all has been achieved.

Budget

Budget growth has not been proportional to enrolments. The figures in Table 2, which concern public expenditure only (universities in this re-gion obtain nearly all of their funding from this source), were reached by dividing the total higher education budget by the number of students (in constant 1986 dollars).

Although these figures are incomplete and do not cover all the countries of sub-Saharan Africa, a general downward trend in spending can be observed beginning in 1980, which gathered speed in 1983. This downturn occurred somewhat earlier in Côte d'Ivoire, Cameroon and Congo, and later in Mauritania, where it began in 1983. It has been particularly marked in Madagascar, the Central African Republic and Côte d'Ivoire, with figures dropping to one third of their original level.

The sharp fall in unit costs is in most cases attributable to two factors: one positive and one negative. On the one hand, it is due to the economies of scale made possible by increased enrolments; numbers of teaching staff and classrooms thus rise more slowly than numbers of students. But, on the other, it is a consequence of the financial difficulties experienced by many countries obliged to implement structural adjustment programmes, forcing government funding agencies to curtail their spending. Educational facilities are the first to suffer from these budget cuts (investment budgets having all but disappeared), followed by outlay on equipment. Shortages are the most acute in these areas, and here, too, the negative impact on educational standards is the most alarming. In the scientific disciplines, universities are turning out (World Bank, 1988, p. 75):

chemists who have not done a titration; biologists who have not done a dissection; physicists who have never measured an electrical current . . . agronomists who have never conducted a field trial of any sort; engineers who have never disassembled the machinery they are called upon to operate.

No less alarming is the shortage of funding available for the acquisition of books and periodicals by university libraries, for this affects not only students but also teachers and researchers, who as a result find themselves increasingly cut off from the international scientific community and less able to participate in international scientific research.

The paradox of budget cuts and overspending

Authors who speak of overspending base their claims on two criteria, both of which point to the conclusion that the cost of higher education in sub-Saharan Africa can be considered too high.

The first criterion is derived from a comparison with primary-school pupil costs. In other continents, primary-school pupils cost only one-and-a-half to three times less than students in higher education. In sub-Saharan Africa, the same comparison reveals shocking discrepancies: in Burkina Faso, $37 was spent on every primary-school pupil in 1986, as opposed to $2,465 (67 times less); in Togo, these amounts represented $31–2,182 (70 times less); in the Central African Republic, $48–1,630 (34 times less); in Mauritania, $80–16,193 (202 times less); and in Congo, $84–4,218 (50 times less). The median value of this gap ranges from 1 to 60, which bears no relation to ratios to be found in the rest of the world.

The second criterion is based on per capita GNP. There is, in fact, a strong correlation between per capita GNP and expenditure per student at the international level, attributable to the fact that education is an activity where salaries are the main input, whereas per capita GNP is closely linked to the median salary level. This statistical connection is reflected, in the rest of the world, by costs per student ranging between 30 and 100 per cent of per capita GNP. Here again, sub-Saharan Africa departs from this norm, as each university student costs anywhere from three times the per capita GNP (in Congo) to thirty-eight times the per capita GNP (in Mauritania).

The result of this situation is that unit costs in sub-Saharan Africa are in fact closer to those observed in the richer countries than to those in countries having comparable levels of per capita GNP. For example, the countries shown in Table 2 had per capita student costs in 1980 amounting to an average of $4,400, which is slightly higher than the same costs observed over the same period in France, where they were roughly $3,000. While costs dropped significantly in 1986, they remained within the $2,000–4,000 range, while costs in Asian and Latin American countries with levels of development comparable to or even higher than sub-Saharan Africa, were all below $1,000, or even $500. It is therefore reasonable to conclude that there is some truth to the claim that unit costs are excessive.

Some reasons for abnormally high unit costs

Several factors explain this phenomenon. The most frequently mentioned – and criticized – is the exorbitant cost of student welfare subsidies; the second is the level of staff salaries compared with the income of the majority of the population; the third is linked to the size of the universities; and the fourth to the impact of foreign aid.

STUDENT WELFARE SUBSIDIES

Student aid makes up an average of 55 per cent of the higher education budget in French-speaking Africa as opposed to 15 per cent in English-speaking Africa. In the rest of the world, this proportion can vary widely, but in those countries – developed or less developed – which espouse progressive social policies, that proportion rarely exceeds 20 per cent. Most French-speaking universities unnecessarily provide two forms of financial aid at the same time: scholarships and board-and-lodging subsidies. Scholarships are lavishly granted and are seldom means-tested on the basis of family income. They represent a level of income far superior to the national average, and are in fact considered to be the first rung on the public service ladder. This brings them more into alignment with modern sector incomes than with those of the traditional sector which, we should point out, accounts for the overwhelming majority of the working population (80–90 per cent). This results in practices which may appear unusual when viewed from outside the sub-Saharan African context. In the rest of the world, students' families meet their welfare needs either wholly or in part, but in sub-Saharan Africa it is scholarship-holders who help their families by giving them part of their grants, or take in a younger school-age sibling or cousin. Students are more likely to be married and heads of households here than elsewhere in the world, for the simple reason that, in terms of income, the grant represents a more enviable situation than that enjoyed by the average citizen. Even more surprisingly, it is revealed in a study of student costs conducted in Côte d'Ivoire (Yao, 1986) that the concept of private costs has been given a rather unusual definition in the literature on the subject, since it is considered to include financial transfers made by the grant-holder to his or her extended family. It can be argued that scholarships are public costs, but if they are redistributed within a group of private individuals, they do not become private educational costs. Such a transfer should, on the contrary, be treated as a 'social' source of re-venue from the public to the private sector, for non-educational purposes, and would normally be deducted from national educational expenditure.

SALARIES OF UNIVERSITY STAFF

The argument that the salaries of university staff, particularly those of professors, are inordinately high does not meet with the general agreement of those concerned. University staff are painfully aware of the steady decline in the purchasing power of their salaries over twenty years and more. We should nevertheless bear in mind that at the time of independence in the early 1960s, the salary scales adopted were similar to those in force in the former metropolitan country. This level proved impossible to sustain economically in the long term for the newly independent countries whose per capita GNP was, and still is, depending on the country, thirty to sixty times lower. The establishment of a franc area and fixed parity between the French franc and the CFA franc has partially protected these salaries from even faster devaluation. For evidence of this, we need only observe what has occurred in countries that have relinquished these protective mechanisms for a period of time. Guinea, Madagascar and Mali, where this is the case, have much lower salary levels than other French-speaking countries, owing to the fact that market forces indifferently set the salary level of government employees according to domestic production and the fiscal capacity of the taxpayers. In other continents, developed or developing, the overall level of civil service salaries, and of primary-education teachers in particular, ranges from one to three times GNP per capita, (closer to three in the least developed countries, one in the industrialized countries). In sub-Saharan Africa, and particularly in the French-speaking countries, this ratio is much higher, representing 14 in Mali, 13 in Burkina Faso, 7 in the Central African Republic, and 5 in Togo to name just a few. Similar discrepancies are observed, proportionally, with teaching staff in higher education. This implies, all things being equal, that higher taxes are levied on a larger number of taxpayers when this ratio is closer to 1 rather than to 5 or 10. If the rate of taxation remains the same, this means that a smaller number of teachers can be paid out of the taxpayers' money, which in turn results in lower enrolment rates.

LOW ENROLMENTS IN CERTAIN CYCLES AND DISCIPLINES

Like their counterparts in the former metropolitan country, French-speaking universities in sub-Saharan Africa tend to have high student enrolments the first two years, falling off to only a handful of students enrolled in the many options of the second-degree cycles (third and fourth years). Of the 250 students enrolled in a first-degree science course, only 50 will go on to the second level, and be divided among four options of mathematics, physics, chemistry and biology. In some cases, the ten mathematics students will be further divided between the traditional course leading to a Bachelor's degree and a course leading to a secondary-school teaching degree at a teacher-training college. The same mathematics teacher thus gives the same lecture consecutively to two groups of five students in two separate institutions on the same campus.

This type of organization results in higher unit costs, as has been observed in Mauritania, which has the smallest university in this group (600 students) and the one with the highest unit costs ($16,000). Immediately after African independence, interregional university co-operation became quite prevalent, and nationals from any country in the region could enrol at the university of a neighbouring country if the training they sought was not available in their own country. This regional co-operation has suffered reversals too numerous to mention here, and the net result has been a serious balkanization of higher education, accompanied by spiralling unit costs.

FOREIGN AID

It may seem odd to speak of foreign aid as a factor in rising costs, especially as one would expect it to have just the opposite effect. A study of foreign aid flowing into the region (Millot et al., 1988) revealed a number of heretofore little-known facts. For example:

French-speaking sub-Saharan Africa receives more foreign aid for education than any other region in the world, both per student and per capita.

Most of this aid goes to higher education, representing nearly $1,000 per student, as opposed to only $1 per primary-school pupil.

A large proportion of that aid goes towards the salaries of foreign teachers who are expensive to hire, when compared with local staff and also with their counterparts in their home country, which is most often France.

The $1,000 in foreign aid per student is in addition to the local expenditure for education mentioned above. It does not include the indirect aid provided in the form of free board and lodging for African students at universities in some industrialized countries.

Such aid produces well-known knock-on effects on local costs. A local professor earning a monthly salary of $500 or $1,000 will feel that this is inadequate if his or her expatriate colleague is earning $5,000 for the same work. Taken to extremes, this means that a professor at a Chinese university is quite content to earn only $100, when he knows that his colleagues are all in the same boat.

Moreover, foreign aid brings with it technology more suited to the context of the donor country than to that of the recipient country, such as teaching aids, apparatus, spare parts and supplies. It does not encourage improvising alternative solutions, which, although they may be of inferior quality, are more in keeping with local resources. In India, for example, Western scientific texts can be reprinted at ten to twenty times lower cost than in New York and London. The presentation may be of poorer quality than the original but the content is identical. French-speaking Africa has not really attempted this type of approach. Expensive science books are imported from France and sold in Dakar and Abidjan at even more exorbitant prices, placing them completely beyond the range of students, professors or even university libraries. Foreign aid unwittingly perpetuates the myth that reference material must necessarily come from Europe or North America, even if this means that it is incomplete through lack of funding.

Dubious efficiency and unemployed graduates

Assessing the 'academic' excellence of graduates of French-speaking universities in Africa is a delicate task, in the absence of objective evaluation criteria. Several alarming trends are discernible, however. The local élite tends to send its children to universities abroad, and foreign diplomas have an over-inflated reputation on the employment market compared with the same diplomas obtained from local universities. The above-mentioned shortage of important inputs, such as properly functioning laboratories and well-stocked libraries, is hardly a guarantee of consistent educational quality. Finally, the dearth of articles published by professors in sub-Saharan African universities is a fairly good indication that research activities have fallen off, as it is generally acknowledged that the quality of higher education is low in the absence of high-level research.

These convergent observations prompt us to question the quality of today's graduates of French-speaking universities in sub-Saharan Africa. Even more unsettling is the fact that a large number of graduates can no longer find employment appropriate to their qualifications. Countries accustomed to recruiting all graduates who so desired into public service have, one by one, had to submit to the demands of structural adjustment programmes which block further public spending. In most countries, the private employment market has proved to be an unsatisfactory substitute for the former public sector, and many graduates have been waiting unsuccessfully many years for jobs corresponding to their qualifications. This situation has given rise to a number of surprising forms of job conversion. In one Central African town, we met someone with a Ph.D. degree in sociology who grew tomatoes, and an aeronautical engineer who managed a small 'itinerant' drinking-water concession. While these are perfectly respectable occupations, it is questionable whether the country concerned is justified in allocating its limited resources to higher training if these are the only job opportunities awaiting its graduates.

How, given the precarity of the job market, can the persistent demand for higher education be explained? The answer is simple: higher education remains advantageous to the individual for two reasons. The first is that employment prospects for secondary-school graduates are even less promising; not only do the latter face the same problems in finding employment as do university graduates, but, when competing for the same job, the university graduate is more likely to get it. In terms of expenses, university grants make up most of the loss of income that could have been earned had students decided to seek gainful employment instead of continuing their studies. All these factors thus tend to encourage individuals to embark on courses of higher study that do not lead to corresponding openings in the employment market.

It would be an exaggeration, however, to claim that there are no openings on the employment market for graduates, whatever their discipline. Jobs are particularly scarce in fields of training where French-speaking universities have the highest number of enrolments, such as law, economics, the arts, languages and the humanities. One Central African university has trained several thousand English-language specialists who all compete for the two or three English-language teaching posts available each year in secondary schools. This is by no means true of graduates in the fields of science and technology, the shortage of which is lamented by potential employers. This shortage is in fact felt worldwide, and is not confined to Africa, which means that African graduates in these fields are much in demand and often accept jobs in the industrialized countries where they can make a better living. France, for example, which helps many French-speaking countries to make up their chronic deficit of maths teachers, cancels out – intentionally or otherwise – any beneficial effects it may have created by recruiting back many of the graduates it has trained. More generally speaking, the world market, especially the international organizations, systematically siphons off all of Africa's best talent, particularly at the Ph.D. level. Unfortunately, little can be done to halt this kind of trend without at the same time compromising the individual's freedom of choice.

A similar problem arises with regard to medical and pharmaceutical training, which would seem to provide for the country's most urgent needs in this area. However, in this same sector, underemployment of graduates exists, not because demand has been met, but because in those countries that have a nationalized health service, the state no longer has the resources to recruit all the newly qualified doctors and pharmacists leaving university: and in countries with a private medical system, viable employment for such professionals is not guaranteed.

Strategies for French-speaking universities in sub-Saharan Africa

To find a way out of the crisis by cutting expenditure, while at the same time certain basic needs are not being met, may seem like trying to square the circle. Solutions do exist but they call for a degree of political fortitude and the assurance that the sociological obstacles believed to be insurmountable can in fact be overcome, as recent events in Eastern Europe have proved.

The first such obstacle is the unwillingness to establish a *numerus clausus* at university-entrance level based on the twofold criterion of the need for qualifications and the level of competence of the candidates. French-speaking universities have carried on the French tradition of granting baccalaureate-holders automatic access to higher education, but have overlooked the fact that an important condition is attached to this principal: namely, that the ruling class is not trained at the state universities but in the *grandes écoles*, whose entrants are rigorously selected.

The second obstacle concerns student welfare subsidies. The latter were originally devised to facilitate and speed up the training of national managerial personnel at the time of African independence, when potential candidates were few and far between and came from modest backgrounds. There is no longer any need for this: a shortage of candidates has given way to a glut, and needy families have been replaced by the local nomenklatura.

The third obstacle lies in the difficulty of reactivating regional co-operation, which is the only means of achieving the economies of scale necessary in order to develop top-level, state-of-the-art training. However, such co-operation comes up against legitimate national pride and the feeling that national sovereignty is at stake.

This being said, the average size of the French-speaking countries of sub-Saharan Africa, which is roughly equivalent to that of a French region, does not warrant the ruinous duplication of having separate institutions to meet every training need in each country. Each year, high-level training should be provided for cohorts of at least thirty students, and ideally as many as 100. It is no more expensive to hire an eminent professor for several hundred students than it is for five, and the difference in unit costs between the two is enormous. Respect for national sovereignty should be able to suffer this modest affront without too much difficulty. Renovation of the higher education system throughout French-speaking sub-Saharan Africa will be possible only if it is agreed that these three obstacles can and should be overcome.

Two sectors could be created: first, a prestige sector whose aim would be to gain international academic recognition and, second, one that would be regulated by demand. The first would recruit students from the entire region, irrespective of nationality, on the basis of their eligibility. For some sorts of training, a joint admissions system based on national quotas and on merit could be set up, on the understanding that quotas should be the exception, not the rule. This prestige sector would combine foreign aid, the best teachers and the best students in a given field. Student aid would be provided either by the students' home countries or through international aid organizations. The sector would not have supranational status, but each institution would be administered and financed primarily by the host country (international status would necessarily entail an upward trend in costs). The extra financial effort would be counterbalanced by the fact that students from the host country would be admitted, under comparable conditions, to advanced training centres in other countries. Some states may have more higher training centres than others, thus creating an imbalance in their geographical distribution, but the favourable impact of these centres will probably compensate for the extra financial burden.

International aid at this level of higher training should be processed through a central assessment body designed to rationalize support and prevent any reference to criteria other than those of academic excellence.

Institutions in this network could take on a variety of forms, such as specialized public or private schools, or university departments enjoying relative autonomy within the university. The number of such institutions and the form they take will depend on the initiative of their host countries, the enterprising spirit of existing institutions, recommendations from the central assessment centre, and the identification of potential centres in existing universities.

The average number of students in these institutions would be about 300 (divided into cohorts of sixty for a five-year course). Ten centres of this type could be set up in the short term, increasing to thirty centres catering for 3,000 students in the next ten to twenty years, and eventually reaching the level of 10,000 students in the medium term (representing the equivalent

of 5 per cent of current university enrolments in the region).

The sector regulated by demand would essentially comprise existing universities. The system of scholarships would be abolished and a student loan system set up. Part of the savings thus made could be reallocated to essential inputs such as operating budgets, libraries, and the equipment and maintenance of laboratories.

Admissions policies would be determined by the context. Wherever the number of candidates obviously exceeded the number of places available in the institution, and/or the market outlets for a specific type of qualification, selective admission criteria would have to be established.

Spending less but more effectively, and training perhaps fewer but better candidates is the challenge that French-speaking universities in sub-Saharan Africa must take up. This will be the price for putting French-speaking Africa on the map of the international academic world in the twenty-first century.   ∎

References

MILLOT, B.; ORIVEL, F.; RASERA, J. B. 1988. *L'aide extérieure à l'éducation en Afrique sub-Saharienne.* Washington, D.C., World Bank.

ORIVEL, F. 1987. *Costs, Financing and Efficiency in the French-speaking Universities of Sub-Saharan Africa.* Victoria Falls (Zimbabwe).

WORLD BANK. 1986. *Education Policies for Sub-Saharan Africa, Discussion Draft.* Washington, D.C., World Bank.

——. 1988. *Education in Sub-Saharan Africa. Policies for Adjustment, Revitalization and Expansion.* Washington, D.C., World Bank.

——. 1990. *Education in Sub-Saharan Africa. Updated Statistical Tables.* Washington, D.C., World Bank. (AFTED Technical Note, 1.)

YAO, J. 1986. Financement de l'Université Nationale de Côte d'Ivoire: Qui perd? Qui en bénéficie? Paper presented at the International Symposium on the Economies of Education. Dijon, IREDU.

Latin America

Higher education in a lost decade

Simon Schwartzman

The lost decade

The 1980s will be remembered in Latin America as the lost decade. Almost without exception, all countries faced political deterioration, economic stagnation, worsening living conditions, and cultural perplexity. The feeling in the early 1990s is that all roads have been travelled, all possibilities tested, and nothing really worked. In the 1950s and 1960s it was still possible to put the blame on the local oligarchies and their international allies, and hope that a new era could be produced through increasing political mobilization and participation. In many countries, populism led to military regimes, which begot revolutionary guerrillas, which in turn begot military repression and widespread violence. As the military regimes exhausted their cycles, they were replaced by shaky and unconvincing democracies, unable to control their budgets, check corruption and face the mounting pro-

Simon Schwartzman (Brazil). *Professor of political science, Faculdade de Filosofia, Letras e Ciências Humanas, University of São Paulo; Scientific Director, Nucleo de Pesquisas sobre Educação Superior (NUPES, University of São Paulo); President, from 1989 to 1991 of the Brazilian Sociological Association. Author or co-author of numerous articles and publications, among them:* Universidade Brasileira: organização e problemas; A pesquisa universitaria em questão *and* The Development of the Scientific Community in Brazil.

blems of economic obsolescence and urban decay.

Economic stagnation shook a central tenet of past decades, that progress would inevitably follow social and economic modernization. No region modernized so rapidly in the last twenty years as Latin America. Almost everywhere, traditional agriculture was replaced by mechanized agro-industries, and the rural population flocked to the cities. Mass communications reached every corner, spreading the language, consumption patterns and values of urban life. Improvement of basic health conditions led to a dramatic fall in infant mortality and a large increase in life expectancy, resulting in a population explosion that is only now slowing down through generalized access to birth-control devices. Education, even if still not universal, reaches more people, proportionally, than it ever did, from basic to graduate levels. Latin America is very unequal, and many countries and regions still face the traditional problems of rural poverty, illiteracy and lack of access to basic health and sanitary services. But the problems of the 1990s are very modern: urban overcrowding, environmental pollution, poor education, mass culture, youth unemployment, organized crime, urban violence, drug and alcohol abuse, alienation, swollen public bureaucracies and the growing inability of established governments to deal with these problems.

The key question is whether the lost decade was just a transitional period or will remain as a permanent fixture of Latin American societies. The current crisis affects some countries and regions more than others, and some authors are beginning to distinguish between 'viable' and 'non-viable' countries, believing that the latter are facing the same processes of economic, social and political degradation that affect so many sub-Saharan African countries. This may prove true in some extreme cases, but it is in an unacceptable simplification. To replace the old, naïve belief in economic development and progress with wholesale pessimism and gloom will not lead very far. A much closer look at past and present experiences is needed, to find out not only why so many hopes and projects have failed, but also why others seem to work better, and to point toward more positive roads.

Higher education is just one element of this broad picture, and its recent changes and current dilemmas cannot be understood without the full picture of the lost decade in our minds. There would be no point in looking at higher education in detail, however, if we took it as just another instance of a picture of global pessimism. Our assumption is the opposite. In spite of its obvious difficulties, higher education is one among other areas in which there are still opportunities to be explored, and hopes to be found for a broad, positive role in the region's predicaments.

The origins

Latin American higher education, as it exists today, was organized during the period of independence, in the early nineteenth century, grew slowly for about 150 years, went through a period of explosive growth in the 1960s and 1970s, and levelled off again in the 1980s. Before independence, where they existed, higher education institutions were run by the Catholic Church of the Counter Reformation, as part of the Spanish colonizing enterprise. The struggle for political independence was coloured by the ideals of secularism, the appreciation for technical knowledge, and a general attack on the traditional university institutions.

Throughout, the rhetoric was about tradition and present times, scholastic and practical knowledge, general and professional education, the colonial tradition and the building of modern nation-states. Universities were a natural place for these confrontations to take place. Conservative and liberals, Catholics and positivists fought each other through the following century, creating new public institutions, closing down Catholic universities, opening them up again, supporting them with public money or cutting off their lifelines. In Mexico the Catholic universities disappeared, in Chile the two coexisted, in Brazil the Catholic institutions appeared only in the 1940s, in Argentina still later.

Political independence did not mean much in terms of social and economic transformations. Enlightened Latin American élites spoke French, travelled to Europe and handled French concepts, including their democratic and rationalist ideals; yet, their societies remained restricted to the limits of their economies, based on a few export products, large pockets of traditional or decadent settlements, one or two major administrative and export centres, and, in Brazil, a slavery system that lasted almost to the end of the nineteenth century. There were not many jobs requiring specialized knowledge and skills, except for handling the tangled legal systems inherited from Iberian baroque legislation, for military work and health care. Law, military engineering and medicine were main fields of study, none of them demanding enough to put special premium on innovation and achievement.

To the prevalence of rhetoric, feeble intellectual and technical competence and reduced social impact, should be added centralization and bureaucratic control. There was a matter of symmetry, new states organizing their educational institutions against the centralizing traditions of the past; then, most of the education business dealt with bestowing honours, titles and privileges, rather than with knowledge as such, formal goods that can only exist if regulated from above. More generally, the whole colonial enterprise, both in Portuguese and Spanish America, was carried on through centralized authority and control, and the local élites did not know otherwise.

Centralization did not go unchecked. The landmark of the reaction was the student rebellion at the University of Córdoba, Argentina, in 1918, which led to joint academic governance by faculty, students and alumni. The Córdoba movement – the Reforma – soon spread its word throughout the continent, leading to the adoption of similar governance rules in national universities in most countries. The Reforma movement was incendiary in its rhetoric against the university establishment but conservative in its accomplishments. Where it succeeded universities became less subject to daily interferences from central government, but did not incorporate new social groups nor improve the quality of teaching. Self-governance meant that decisions had to be taken by vote, and no place could exist for institutional leadership. It is not a coincidence that the Reforma started in Córdoba, an Argentine province that was declining in face of the intense economic and political growth of Buenos Aires. Even where economic development did not occur, cities were growing, populations increased, and traditional power arrangements were difficult to maintain. The Latin American reformed universities became the place where the children of the traditional élites expressed their frustrations against the decadence of their elders, and their hopes for the future.

In the early 1960s, the contrasts between the modernization drives of Latin American societies and the narrowness of their political regimes led to intensified political activism, followed by unprecedented levels of repression. Political repression came from the confrontation of student, and sometimes teacher, activism against the military regimes that emerged more or less at that time in many countries: Argentina after 1966, Brazil at first in 1964, but intensifying in 1969; Chile in 1973; not forgetting the massacre of students in Mexico City of 1968. For the military, at the beginning, the problems of higher education were a matter of police and discipline. With different emphasis in one place or another, elected rectors were replaced by colo-

nels, teachers were dismissed, students arrested, the social sciences were banned, mandatory civic education was introduced. Large sectors of the universities were destroyed and demoralized, while hundreds of students took up guerrilla warfare. The cycles of expansion, repression and insurrection came together to their end in the late 1970s and early 1980s. It was then time to pick up the pieces, see what remained of higher education from the past years and decide what could be done about it. By then political mobilization of students had lost its virulence, to be replaced by the unionization of teachers and employees. In most public institutions the traditional part-time professor had been replaced by a new professional, the full-time teacher (who had been very often the militant student of ten years before) and sometimes by the academically oriented researcher, educated abroad and expecting his institution to become like the research university where he received his degree. Most military regimes had by then disappeared, but a new scourge was already looming – economic stagnation.

The uncertain future

Published in 1983, Juan Carlos Tedesco's study of the tendencies and perspectives of development of higher education in Latin America and the Caribbean is an unsurpassed gathering and organization of the available information, and a reasoned and scholarly reflection on why higher education reached the problems and difficulties it faced. Following Tedesco's study, it is possible to travel in time from the traditional élitist Latin American universities to the current mass education systems, and see how the traditional interpretation of Latin American universities as training grounds for political élites gave way, after the 1950s, to the human-capital approach, which was replaced, in turn, by a much more sceptical view of its role in socio-economic development and modernization. We can trace the evolution from the times when reformed and expanded universities were expected to become landmarks of democratization, to a time when education came to be perceived as little else than the reproduction and consolidation of old patterns of social stratification and social inequality; the transition from a period of optimism about the academic communities' ability to find their own ways on the road of competence and social relevance, if given enough freedom and resources, to a reluctant return to the need of governmental planning and oversight.

Expansion

Tedesco (1983) starts by showing the extraordinary expansion of higher education in Latin America since the 1960s, coinciding with the growth of urban centres and the replacement of

TABLE 1. Enrolment in higher education in Latin America, 1985

Country	Enrolment	Women (%)	rate[1]
Argentina	846 141	53	36.4
Bolivia	95.052	–	19.0
Brazil	1 479 397	48	11.3
Colombia	391 490	49	13.0
Costa Rica	63 771	58	23.0
Cuba	235 224	54	21.4
Chile	197 437	43	15.9
Dominican Republic	123 748	–	19.3
Ecuador	277 799	39	33.1
El Salvador	70 499	44	13.8
Guatemala	48 283	–	8.4
Haiti	6 289	–	1.1
Honduras	30 632	42	9.6
Mexico	1 207 779	36	15.7
Nicaragua	29 001	56	9.8
Panama	55 303	56	25.9
Paraguay	33 203	–	9.7
Peru	443 640	35	23.8
Uruguay	87 707	–	35.8
Venezuela	347 618	–	26.4

1. Higher education enrolment as percentage of the population in the 20–24 age bracket, for 1985 or the closest available year.
Source: Brunner, 1990; based on UNESCO, 1988.

the old oligarchic political regimes with different systems of mass politics, in alternation with periods of authoritarian rule. Writing on the same subject a few years later, Winkler (1990, p. xii) noted that

higher education enrolments in Latin America increased tenfold between 1960 and 1985, resulting in levels of access approaching those found in many industrialized countries. Private institutions absorbed more than their share of this growth and now represent one-third of total enrolments in the region.

The expansion is to be explained by broad social and political trends, and was stimulated by the huge wage differentials that still exist in Latin America across educational levels. In 1950, only Uruguay, Argentina and Cuba had around 5 per cent of the age group enrolled in universities; in 1980 only Honduras, Guatemala and Haiti had less than 10 per cent. Table 1 gives the picture for the whole region in the middle of the 1980s.

In no country was this growth the product of government planning or decision. In all regions, expansion was related to the massive incorporation of women in higher education, and led to the prevalence of 'soft' fields of knowledge, like the social sciences and humanities, over the traditional careers of law, medicine and engineering. It came also from older people hoping to improve their educational credentials and gain access to, or promotion in, public jobs in the region's expanding public bureaucracies. For the first time, most of the students came from families with no previous experience of higher education.

In their drive for higher education, students got into the careers they could, rather than to those they preferred. The predominance of the social sciences and humanities stems from their lower costs and less demanding academic requirements, not by a sudden preference of young Latin Americans for such topics. But it was compatible with large increases in tertiary occupations that were occurring at the time, typical of Latin American modernization. While the countries' economies supported it, expansion of higher education was largely financed

TABLE 2. World expenditure on education, 1975–85

Year	Total ($ millions)	% of GNP	Per capita ($)
World total			
1975	330 117	5.5	84
1980	618 195	5.5	144
1985	681 195	5.6	144
Developing countries			
1975	40 433	3.6	14
1980	93 384	3.9	29
1985	95 846	4.1	27
Latin America and the Caribbean			
1975	13 477	3.5	43
1980	31 397	3.9	88
1985	25 392	3.8	63

Source: Brunner, 1990; based on UNESCO, 1988.

Number	Year midpoint
0	1880
3	$1887^1/_2$
9	1895
8	$1902^1/_2$
28	1910
23	$1917^1/_2$
11	1925
49	$1932^1/_2$
111	1940
138	$1947^1/_2$
211	1955
436	$1962^1/_2$
1419	1970
1091	$1977^1/_2$
663	1985

Number of courses (0, 300, 600, 900, 1200, 1500)

Valid cases: 4.200
Without information: 100

FIG. 1. Number of higher-education courses created by year in Brazil (by 7.5-year intervals). After: ME/SEEC, 1988.

from taxation, and university-level employment was provided by an expanding public sector and by the creation of professional privileges for the holders of educational credentials.

Economic stagnation in the 1980s caught educational expansion at full speed, constraining the job market, limiting the universities' budgets and causing widespread perplexity and frustration (see Table 2). The problem was aggravated by the time it took for the education sector to react to economic expectations. Data from Brazil show that the creation of new courses peaked in the early and mid 1970s, reflecting the economic expansion of those years, and was still going strong in the 1980s, when the signs of crisis were already visible (Fig. 1).

Differentiation

One effect of expansion was the development of a large private sector, which in some countries, such as Brazil and Colombia, accounts now for more than half of current enrolments, and reaches about a third of the enrolments in the region. The growth of private higher education is

the subject of a book by Daniel Levy, for whom private institutions have 'remolded the relationship between higher education and society's multiple classes, groups, interests, and they have remolded the relationship between higher education and the State' (Levy, 1986, p̃. 334). This is the more visible, but by no means the only differentiation that took place in recent years: universities have become internally stratified, non-university sectors have grown in many countries, and significant regional decentralization occurred everywhere.

The issue of public versus private education has its roots in colonial times, when the only universities in the continent were those organized by the Catholic Church, in close alliance with the Spanish Crown. Political independence, in the early nineteenth century, led to the establishment of secular higher-education institutions, usually based on the Napoleonic model of state-controlled professional 'faculties' or schools. Levy gives the details of this transformation. By the end of the colonial period,

Spanish America had about twenty-five universities (the Portuguese, however, always refused to establish higher-education institutions in Brazil). A century later, only Colombia and Chile had private Catholic universities (Levy, 1986, pp. 28–32). In the 1930s the Church moved to recover its role in higher education, trying in some cases to re-establish its association with the state, as in Colombia and Brazil (see Levine, 1981; Schwartzman et al., 1984) or, more frequently, creating their independent institutions. Catholic universities were to provide the students with the traditional religious, moral and humanistic education they thought the public universities neglected, and in their defence of educational freedom they joined hands, unwillingly, with the liberal students who, starting with the Córdoba movement, unfolded the banner of university autonomy from the state.

The second wave of privatization, following Levy's chronology, was a backlash from sectors of Latin American élites against the deterioration of public education. As the public universities absorbed the growing demand for higher education in the 1960s and 1970s, they changed from an élite to a predominantly middle-class constituency, their academic standards deteriorated and they became the focus of permanent political agitation. In many countries the élites decided to move away to their exclusive institutions, a role taken up by Catholic institutions, newly created private universities or special élite institutions established with government support.

The third wave happened mostly in response to situations where the public sector did not open widely enough to absorb the demand for large quantity, low-quality mass education. Brazil, Costa Rica, Colombia, the Dominican Republic and Peru are the major examples. The new institutions kept their costs down by paying their teachers by the hour, teaching in the 'soft' fields where no special equipment and technical support was needed, opening evening classes for working students, and packing them into large classrooms.

With expansion and privatization, higher education remained homogeneous horizontally but became increasingly stratified vertically. Expansion could be expected to lead to different institutions doing different things, responding to the varying needs of different people. However, this tendency tended to be checked by strong pressures for equal rights and status to all educated persons, which resulted at the end in increased, if barely disguised, forms of discrimination. Horizontal homogeneity came from a blurring of the frontiers between religious and lay, public and private, technical and professional institutions, careers and courses. Today in Latin America few students go to Catholic universities through religious conviction, and few Catholic institutions manage, or even try, to infuse their students with the religious and moral teachings that led to their organization as independent entities. Direct and indirect public subsidies to private institutions, on one hand, and the administrative autonomy, the ability to raise money and even to charge tuition in public universities, on the other, make the distinction between public and private less straightforward than in the past. A final convergence is among what could be considered 'university proper' institutions and those like teachers' colleges, technical institutes and vocational schools. In the past, as in Europe, higher education was the privilege of the few, with a narrow access path provided by education in the liberal arts or in basic sciences, to be obtained at secondary school. Now, in most countries, any secondary-school diploma can lead to university, and no course programme taught at the tertiary level, from medicine to nutrition, from economics to hotel management, from physics to production engineering, can be denied 'university' status.

Horizontal homogeneity has not led to more equality, but to increased stratification: there is little incentive for less prestigious careers like teaching and technical work, and extremely high rates of failure and frustration in the competition for the most prestigious degrees, now supposedly accessible to all. Where, in the past, a secondary-school diploma was an achievement, today anything less than a four-year university degree is a failure. Careers and institutions are strongly stratified and socially selective, whether it be in Brazil, where difficult entrance exams screen out the less qualified students from the more prestigious careers, or in Argentina, where there is a policy of open admission, but the less qualified students are screened out after one or two years of schooling.

Efficiency, equity and costs

Latin American higher education is in obvious need of improvement, and evaluations and proposals abound. The issues of efficiency, equity and costs are the central concerns of the discussion paper prepared by Donald R. Winkler (1990) for the World Bank, another trove of useful data.

Efficiency in Latin American universities, that is, the ratio between input and output within an educational institution, is low by almost any indicators one wishes to take: students per faculty, administrators and staff; percentage of funds allocated to non-personal categories of expenditure; faculty salaries; teaching loads; scientific output. The reasons pointed out by Winkler for this situation include: (a) the prevalence of political over performance criteria in academic governance; (b) the emphasis on university autonomy, which rejects policy directives from government; (c) the lack of a tradition of careers in university administration; and (d) a lack of norms on efficiency measures.

A deeper problem is that nobody knows what social benefits higher education can really bring, beyond the private gains of graduates. Winkler approaches this problem with the concept of 'external efficiency'. If it were possible to know how many medical doctors, engineers, sociologists and managers a society needs, it would be possible to compare the figures with what the education institutions produce, evaluate their efficiency in meeting the needs, and steer them in the proper direction. Manpower forecasts, however, are now in disrepute, and economists prefer to resort to estimations of 'rates of return', which is a comparison of earnings of degree hol-

ders with the costs of their education. If society is willing to pay a given amount for a professional's work, this could be taken as an estimate of how useful this work is. Educational efficiency could then be measured and improved by comparing the rates of return of higher with those of lower education, or the returns of one profession with those of another. Exercises of this kind show that returns of higher education in Latin America are higher than in other countries, but still lower than those of other levels, and seem to have been coming down in recent years, and that some professions pay substantially higher salaries and have more employment opportunities than others.

Is it possible to use this information to derive policy recommendations such as to redirect public investment from higher to lower educational levels, and from ill-paying to better paying fields and specialities? Besides its technical difficulties (Leslie, 1990), the problems with policies based on social rates of return are not very different from those coming from the now out-of-fashion manpower planning approach. Except under near pure market conditions, which are very far from what exists in Latin America, earnings obtained by different professional groups depend on a combination of professional privileges, market monopolies, legal benefits, corporatist arrangements and social biases that have little connection with the skills supplied by the specialist.

The thrust of the World Bank recommendations is to shift investments from higher to basic education, to charge tuition and to reduce the public sector's investments in higher education. Winkler's suggestions for improvement are more topical. They include: (a) the introduction of modern information management systems, to allow for the assessment of costs and productivity; (b) the introduction of performance criteria in allocation of resources among units within the universities; (c) the establishment of evaluation mechanisms; and (d) the training of university administrators in the use of these tools. Winkler does not discuss the reasons why these management tools have not been adopted more extensively. It is not a question of ignorance;

most universities have courses in administration and economics where these issues are taught. The answer lies in the contrast between Winkler's diagnosis, which is political and institutional, and the recommendations, which are technical and managerial. Is it possible to improve administrative efficiency without tackling the political and institutional issues?

Public universities are autonomous regarding governments; departments and schools are autonomous within the universities, and their priorities are seldom those of improving efficiency and performance. There are no incentives to improve internal efficiency in public or government financed institutions, and universities are no exception. Budgetary allocations are usually based on past expenditure, if not on political patronage, and money saved this year can mean a lower budget next time. Beyond some very gross indicators like students per faculty or articles published, there are no consensual indicators of what good performance really is. Does it mean teaching more students with a little less quality, fewer students with more quality, reducing the teaching load to allow time for research, or investing in useful technical assistance at the expense of academic publications? There are advocates and vested interests for each of these and many other alternatives. The establishment of evaluation procedures and the introduction of performance criteria in the internal allocation of resources would require to take sides on these issues, and could lead to painful conflicts between departments, teachers, researchers and students. Instead of in-fighting, why not try to come together and pressurize the government for more money? While it was possible to keep expanding the public budget, this strategy worked well. Now that the money is drying up, for many institutions it is still better to cut expenditure across the board than to make painful decisions on priorities and preferences.

Would a professional body of university administrators change the situation? Latin American public universities are typically governed by professors elected or appointed to administrative offices, and controlled by all kinds of collective bodies formed by delegates from professors of all ranks, students and employees. They hold very different and often contradictory notions of the role of universities, what goals are worth pursuing and how priorities should be established. They go from small groups of research-minded scholars, who can only think of universities as places for scholarship, to many ill-trained and unionized full-time teachers, who see themselves as just another branch of the civil service; from students eager to get their degrees in prestigious fields and move on to high-paying careers, to those in the 'soft' and less prestigious fields, lacking the qualifications and professional perspectives of the former, and expressing their frustrations through collective agitation or anomic behaviour. They lack a common academic culture and ethos, which would accept what the goals of higher-education institutions should be. Good managers could hardly tip the power from these networks of widely contradictory interest groups towards the administration, and could not provide their institutions with the cultural traditions they lack.

The professional privileges and salary differentials granted to degree holders, discussed neither by Winkler nor Tedesco, are in themselves an important dimension of inequity in Latin American higher education. Winkler shows that access to higher education is socially biased – children from lower-income families are less likely to be admitted – and government subsidies benefit high income more than lower-income groups. This situation is particularly serious in Brazil, where private secondary schools function as filters selecting middle- and high-income students who later gain admission to wholly subsidized public universities. The inherent inequity of higher-education access was not perceived as a problem when social mobility was high and educational opportunities were increasing for everybody, but it has become evident now that the economy is stagnating, and that those who go up do so at the expense of others going down.

Now, as Tedesco says, it is impossible to continue to pretend that higher education is an unqualified boon to everybody. The income differentials obtained by university degree holders came to be perceived as the product of social transfers, rather than the consequence of increased productivity. Public expenditure in higher education, which used to be considered good and self-evident investments in human capital, started to be seen as subsidies to private consumption and personal privilege. The issues of financing of higher education ought to be seen as political questions, linked to the social dispute over the appropriation of economic surplus, rather than as purely technical matters. Political considerations should not preclude efforts to devise financing mechanisms able to achieve the requisites of social equity, efficiency and reduction of public expenditure, and the educational usefulness of the money spent, but those considerations cannot be set aside (Tedesco, 1983, p. 19).

Modernization and reform

aa Contemporary attempts and proposals to improve the condition of Latin American universities have usually come from outside, whether piecemeal or comprehensive, through incentives or forceful imposition, and have seldom produced the expected results.

Incentives were typical of gentler times, when it was believed that better trained scholars, technical assistance and exchange programmes could do wonders. For many years, in the 1960s, the Universidad de Chile developed a comprehensive co-operative programme with the University of California, with support from the Ford Foundation. Large projects like this were rare, but thousands of students from Venezuela, Brazil and other countries went to get their advanced degrees in the United States and Europe, with money provided by national and foreign agencies. Most of these co-operation projects hoped to train students in the modern sciences and bring scientific research to Latin American universities. In Brazil, in the 1970s, millions of dollars were poured into the organization of a new tier of graduate education in public universities. In the 1960s and 1970s, research councils were created in most countries, and their money went usually to researchers in universities, allowing them to rise above the limitations of their institutions.

Thanks in part to these efforts, it was possible to form a sophisticated and modern scientific élite in many countries, and to develop a series of research institutions that strive to keep Latin America abreast with what is happening in the world of modern science and technology (Schwartzman, 1991). This was not enough, however, to affect higher education more profoundly, because Latin American universities were going through two contradictory modernization tendencies. One was in the direction of making them more scientific, more competent and internationally more up-to-date, and, in this sense, more élitist; the other was pulled by the expansion of enrolments, which would require a set of educational and pedagogic skills and priorities which were not in the minds of this élite. The better educated found it increasingly difficult to deal with their universities, and took refuge in their laboratories, research institutes, international networks, and even whole new institutions, leaving the broader problems of their universities untouched. To this relative failure should be added another, which was the inability of most scientific and technological research to contribute more effectively to the countries' social and economic needs. In consequence, there is today a feeling in some circles that Latin American countries should not really try to develop scientific competence, but put their resources to the service of more humble and pressing problems (Vessuri, 1990).

Comprehensive reforms have been unusual and often traumatic. The Brazilian reform of 1968 was carried out under a military government, which made it difficult to distinguish its political from its truly academic intentions. Its inspiration was the American research university. The old chair system was replaced by the department structure, together with American entities such as the credit system, the central institutes and the graduate programmes. In practice, the new system was superimposed on the traditional one, and there was no provision to account for the expansion of demand which was already on its way. In 1985, with the military out of power, a national commission was created to reorganize the whole system. It was to be a democratic commission, representative of all political parties and interest groups. Incredibly, it managed to produce a coherent blueprint for reform, based on the recognition of institutional differentiation, the introduction of evaluation procedures and autonomy and increased accountability for results. None of it, however, was implemented (Schwartzman, 1988).

The Chilean reform of the 1980s was very different from anything ever tried in the region. Between 1973 to 1980 the Chilean universities were kept under military control, which led to the dismissal of about a quarter of its faculty and the closing of many departments in the social sciences and the humanities (Cox, 1989). In 1981 the military government started to implement a policy which was the opposite of that of Brazil in the 1960s. Instead of a single university model, differentiation; instead of trying to improve quality through graduate education and research, the introduction of market mechanisms; instead of the reliance on the traditional, public universities to set the pattern, the creation of new private, universities. Tuition was introduced in all institutions, government subsidies were given to a limited number of institutions, private or public, and competitive mechanisms were introduced to stimulate quality and efficiency.

The reform did not produce the expected results, but it would be naïve to dismiss it as just another nasty attack by the military against the academy. In 1991 the new civilian government in Chile established a national commission to set a policy for its higher-education sector, and, in its proposal, several innovations from the 1981 reforms were retained, among them the demarcation lines between universities, professional institutes and technical schools, mechanisms for competition and accountability, including indirect subsidies, and the principle that students who can should pay for their studies. The new project introduces a National University Coun-cil responsible for supervising the whole system and to establish mechanisms for evaluation, accreditation and budget allocation, and there is a clear commitment to improving quality, assuring equity and stimulating the development of research and graduate education.

It is still too early to know what will happen with this project, which, as of this writing, is being submitted for approval to the Chilean Congress. If it succeeds, it can become an inspiration for other countries, showing that there is still hope for higher education in Latin America, and that the lost decade was not completely wasted, if it left the region with some lessons for the future.

The first lesson should be that no single model of higher-education institutions can account for the complexity of current needs and demands. The traditional Napoleonic model geared to certification for the liberal professions left little room for research, technical education, distance learning, continuous education, short-term vocational courses and liberal arts programmes. The indiscriminate adoption of the university research model may have helped to solve the first of these problems in some places, but made the others still more intractable. Whenever a single model is adopted, very often in the name of egalitarianism, a few institutions set the pace while the rest become just a series of fading shadows of a vanishing ideal. Differentiation is unavoidable, and it cannot be understood as just a series of strata in a ladder of social prestige.

The second lesson is that governments will be increasingly less able to maintain, supervise and care for the quality of higher education. There are many reasons for this, from budgetary restrictions to the impossibility of central bureaucracies to lead institutions driven by the spirit of initiative, involvement and enthusiasm of their members to set its goals and work for their fulfilment. Academic autonomy and decentralization are unavoidable, and they are likely to blur still further the dividing lines between private and public institutions, leading to a continuum going from proprietary, profit-making operations to publicly funded, national universities, with all gradations in between. A corollary for content and institutional differentiation is the gradual development of a competitive market for higher education, both through actual competition for students and resources and the establishment of reliable and public mechanisms of evaluation and institutional accreditation.

The third lesson is that it would be naïve to expect Latin American higher-education institutions to make these changes on their own, but it would be still worse to pretend that these changes could be introduced through government imposition or management patches. With all its problems and limitations, higher-education institutions are still a repository of competent and motivated people, and no reform that begins by demoralizing them would have any chance of succeeding. The quandary is only apparent, since there are enough people in Latin American higher-education institutions aware of the current difficulties and needs, and willing to participate and co-operate in any well-conceived and academically legitimate reform project.

The fourth lesson is that the scientific, technological and educational competence that exists in the region's higher-education institutions is a precious asset, which should not be depleted in the name of narrow, pragmatic or egalitarian concerns. Good universities and competent scholars, scientists and technologists are essential for whatever Latin American countries hope to do in the future, in basic education, higher education and in other fields. There is not assurance, of course, that they will do what should be done, or succeed in their undertakings, and it is certain that they can do little alone by themselves. But the fifth, and probably more important lesson of the lost decade should be to reject the anti-intellectual, 'no-nonsense' attitude that have accompanied so many of the frustrated reforms and reform proposals of those years. ∎

References

BRUNNER, J. J. 1990. *Educación superior en América Latina: cambios y desafíos*. Santiago de Chile, Fondo de Cultura Económica.

CLARK, B. C. 1986. *The Higher Education System – Academic Organization in Cross-National Perspective*. Berkeley/Los Angeles/London, University of California Press.

COX, C. C. 1989. Autoritarismo, mercados y conocimiento: evolución de las políticas de educación superior en Chile en los años '80'. *Educação e Sociedade*, Vol. 32, April, pp. 27–50.

LEVINE, D. 1981. *Religion and Politics in Latin America: The Catholic Church in Venezuela and Colombia*. Princeton, N.J., Princeton University Press.

LESLIE, L. L. 1990. Rates of Return as Informer of Public Policy: with Special Reference to the World Bank and Third World Countries. *Higher Education*, Vol. 20, No. 3, pp. 287–300.

LEVY, D. C. 1986. *Higher Education and the State in Latin America – Private Challenges to Public Dominance*. London/Chicago, University of Chicago Press, 1986.

TEDESCO, J. C. 1983. *Tendencias y perspectivas en el desarrollo de la educación superior en América Latina*. Paris, UNESCO. 43 pp.

SCHWARTZMAN, S. 1988. Brazil: Opportunity and Crisis in Higher Education. *Higher Education*, Vol. 17, No. 1, pp. 99–119.

——. 1991. *A Space for Science – The Development of the Scientific Community in Brazil*. University Park, Pa., The Penn State Press.

SCHWARTZMAN, S.; BOMENY, H.; COSTA, V. 1984. *Tempos de Capanema*. Rio de Janeiro/São Paulo, Paz e Terra/Editora da Universidade de São Paulo.

UNESCO. 1988. *Statistical Yearbook*. Paris, UNESCO.

VESSURI, H. M. C. 1990. O Inventamos o Erramos: The Power of Science in Latin America. *World Development*, Vol. 18, No. 11, pp. 1543–53.

WINKLER, D. R. 1990. Higher Education in Latin America – Issues of Efficiency and Equity. Washington, D.C., World Bank. 147 pp. (Discussion Paper, 77.)

The problems
of higher education
in the Arab States

Raji Abou-Chacra

Background

Before embarking on this study of higher education and the problems it faces in the Arab countries, I shall briefly sketch the historical background. Through a period of decline that lasted several centuries, Arab civilization stagnated in most fields of science, arts and culture. For 800 years, the Arab people remained oppressed, the last four centuries of this era being spent under the Ottoman Empire, which destroyed the spirit of creativity and innovation among the Arabs, isolating them from developments elsewhere, particularly from the West and its industrial revolution.

Islam, however, played a significant role in preventing the total extinction of Arab thought during these dark days. If only to a limited extent, the religious schools continued to provide

Raji Abu-Chacra (Lebanon). Dean of the Faculties of Science and Education, the Lebanese University, where he is professor of particle physics. Member of the Lebanese Association for the Advancement of Science and member of various national education committees. Author of Ashi'a al-lizar wa-tatbiqatiha (Lasers and their Applications); participated in the translation into Arabic of the McGraw-Hill Dictionary of Scientific and Technical Terms.

the Arab people with a measure of intellectual stimulation. Up to the beginning of the nineteenth century, intellectual endeavour was limited to a few centres for linguistic, religious and literary studies. The Western industrialized countries then began to find new interests in the Arab world and this was the motivation behind the establishment in Beirut of such missionary institutions as the American University (1886) and the French Jesuit University (1881). This came as a severe intellectual shock to the Arabs, who were still living off their past glories. Their backwardness became apparent to them through their contacts with the West, when they measured their own situation against the scientific knowledge brought by the missions and the military prowess demonstrated in military campaigns such as Napoleon's.

These contacts with the West led to the production of books and studies, which dealt with ways of reconciling the new sciences and Islam. We must conclude, however, that this was not their true aim, since this reconciliation was not the real problem. In fact, it should be seen as the expression of the psychological trauma suffered through eight centuries of oppression, by a people who, in times past, had led the world in fields such as medicine, algebra, geometry, astronomy and chemistry but who now found their existence devoid of everything but a few spiritual comforts. Rather, such writings were an attempt to establish a link between the Islamic heritage and modern scientific development in order to encourage this development.

In my view, the root of the problem of Arab higher education lies in the imbalance between the need to catch up with the rapidly changing modern age and the limited academic resources available. Necessity has dictated specialization in various fields – and nowhere more so than in science – transforming traditional schools and institutes into technical ones and creating new universities capable of meeting contemporary requirements and the needs of society. However, this desire to catch up, particularly during the post-independence period, led the countries of the Middle East to hasten the establishment of educational institutions without paying due attention to quality, with the population explosion adding to this sense of urgency.

Today, Arab higher education institutions are spread over 14 million km^2 in twenty-one countries, stretching from Turkey to the Horn of Africa, from the desert heat of the Arabian peninsula to the Mediterranean. Many of the establishments benefit from modern means of communication which greatly facilitate their work.

After independence, although the university system developed, things remained much as they had been in colonial days. State universities were established alongside their private counterparts and they, too, were imbued with the spirit of colonialism, whether through the subjects taught, the language used or the reliance on teachers from the former colonial powers. Meanwhile, technical institutes at secondary and tertiary level have been established in the Arab world only over the past twenty years. Thus, it can be said that most institutes of higher education in the Arab world are still fledglings by comparison with their counterparts in the West.

The Arab States are divided into two groups: the rich oil producers and the countries with medium or low incomes. Naturally, this situation is reflected in education, where some universities have the most modern equipment while others are lacking in technical resources of many kinds (Osman, 1983) and are reliant on foreign aid, which influences educational policy and makes it intellectually accountable to the donors. Public policy in every Arab state is, for the most part, directly connected with the ruler and his family, entourage or party. The policy changes with the ruler and this, in turn, has an impact on education.

We shall be considering these matters in detail later. For the present, I should like to stress the great geographical area of the Arab world, the diversity of climate and economic circumstances, the considerable co-operation between political regimes and the disparities between the spoken dialects of Arabic. All these factors can be obstacles to co-ordination between the various Arab universities and institutions. We shall therefore confine ourselves to looking at the problems experienced by the majority of the universities.

The main problems

The definition of the aims of higher education is a subject much talked about, particularly in Europe, with emphasis being placed on certain aspects such as the transfer of knowledge, scientific research, technological development and so on, the focus depending on the needs of the country and the attitude adopted towards the society for which it is intended. However, during the past few years, a general and comprehensive definition of the goals of higher education has come to be adopted by many international conferences, that is, 'to disseminate and develop knowledge, to form the intellectual personality of the student and to prepare him for a vocation which will benefit the society to which he belongs' (Council of Europe, 1984).

This is a definition that we must bear in mind when we come to consider the situation of higher education in the Arab world. It is a standard by which to measure the shortcomings of educational establishments in disseminating knowledge, whether in setting the curricula or in developing them through teaching aids or teacher training and supervision. It is one way to determine whether such establishments have fulfilled their duties in forming the personality of the student and ensuring that he is a benefit to his society rather than a burden upon it.

THE CURRICULUM

The curriculum varies from one Arab country to another in terms of level, content and means of application. The principal deficiencies may be attributed to the following causes.

The higher-education curriculum bears no relation to the major issues affecting Arab society. Rather than deriving from the needs of that society, the curriculum is copied from what has been taught for years in foreign universities. When on occasion the curriculum is amended but not completely transformed, the gaps and distortions are even more evident and the objective is not achieved.

Arab universities lack the central apparatus needed to lay down curricula, to ensure that they are applied and to develop them in the light of government policy, taking into account local requirements and academic changes. Neither in the Arab world as a whole nor in the individual countries are there any central bodies to define the goals of higher education and to appoint supervisors to ensure that they are properly implemented. This chaotic situation with regard to curricula has led to a multiplicity of programmes and the squandering of resources. Thus, in the end, it is the administrator and the teacher who play the main role in laying down the curriculum and, as their ideas vary according to the countries in which they received their education, there is no harmonization.

There are foreign universities and institutes in the Arab world which follow curricula different from those of national universities. Students graduating from them have a different intellectual and cultural outlook and may not be able to serve their society. Because of their political influence, foreign universities have had a negative effect on the growth of national universities. The best example of this chaos is the situation of higher education in Lebanon, where there are eight universities and institutes of higher studies teaching in Arabic, French and English. The curricula are, for the most part, taken from abroad and because they are not co-ordinated with each other, it is difficult for a student who has begun studying in one of them to transfer to another. There is, furthermore, no central control over the curricula of these private institutions, despite the fact that they receive financial support and other kinds of help from the state.

Let us now consider the content of these curricula in relation to the growth and development of the Arab student's personality. In curricula deriving from the French system and in science courses, for example, we note the absence of languages and other arts subjects which develop the mind and round off the student's general culture. In this system, the award of a degree requires the student to pass a set of courses within a given scientific specialization. In the Anglo-Saxon system, on the other hand, there are also socio-cultural and pedagogical subjects to develop the student's personality. Curricula in the Arab world fall between these two systems. Whichever system is chosen, it will not be on the basis of research findings or from the standpoint of the needs of society (Klansner, 1986).

LANGUAGE OF INSTRUCTION

Universities in the Arab world do not all teach in the same language. Even within a single country, the language of instruction will vary, for the most part between Arabic, French and English. The use of disparate languages in universities clearly poses problems of co-ordination, even within a single country. One such problem can be seen when we examine the terminology used in scientific translations. The fact that terms are translated differently, depending on the reference work or the translator, causes problems of co-ordination between universities and higher-education institutions in general (Ibn Abdullah, 1976).

Moreover, translators are no longer able to

cope with the sheer volume of works to be translated. By the time a book can be translated and published, the original will often have been superseded by newer works which render the basic information it contains obsolete. Whereas in the past, when the world changed more slowly, translation was successful in transmitting knowledge, today the translator is condemned to trail further and further behind modern scientific developments.

In addition, for obvious reasons, the Arabs have been unable to standardize scientific terminologies. For the most part, this is due to the fact that the Arabs feel that a terminology established in one particular country would in some way lose its identity if it were replaced by another.

These linguistic problems are not confined to higher education. At secondary and primary level the language of instruction for science in some Arab countries – especially private schools – may be English, French or Arabic. These schools produce a mix of students who, on entering university, may feel alienated because the language of instruction in the university of their choice is different from the one in which they were taught scientific subjects at school. This is one of the reasons why some students drop out.

There is nothing new in saying that language is an intellectual mould and that the mode of thinking in one language differs from the mode of thinking in another. Thus, the problem is deeper than mere terminology – it concerns the way people think and this is reflected in the intellectual decline of university graduates. It is all too easy for us to tell which students were taught in English and which in French or Arabic. We might ask if it is possible to achieve any co-ordination between education systems in the Arab countries. An attempt was made recently to standardize scientific terminology in a scientific dictionary, compiled by a number of eminent linguists under the auspices of the Libyan-financed Arab Development Institute, and McGraw-Hill, in Beirut. However, because of the problems referred to earlier, there is no sign of the terminology being adopted in the various Arab countries.

EDUCATIONAL MATERIALS AND METHODOLOGY

In the same way as the curricula, methodology varies with the language of instruction selected. The methods adopted where French is the language of instruction differ from those adopted by universities using English or Arabic, because those responsible for determining the programmes imported their attendant methodologies without adapting them to the specific conditions of the Arab world and to the needs of the Arab student.

Moreover, many teachers who have themselves studied abroad return to teach in Arab universities, using the same methodologies as those they are used to. Thus, within the same university, one teacher will prefer a theoretical approach and another a practical one, a third tending towards research and a fourth relying on group work. The result is that the student, torn between different teachers and different methods, does his best to learn but lacks a clear method to enable him to reach his goal.

It is obvious that educational materials and methods are part of education itself. The aim of higher education is not so much to provide students with a complete corpus of knowledge but to impart a clear method of learning by which it may be acquired. The university, therefore, is the place where learning begins rather than the end of the road. Standardizing teaching methods in accordance with curricula and educational objectives will produce a generation of graduates who share a common way of thinking. This objective of higher education, however, will not be realized without planning of the standardization of materials and methodology in Arab universities.

Yet, no matter how much methodologies are developed and improved, they will remain insufficient so long there is overcrowding in the schools. In some universities, especially in the first years, 400 or more students may be packed into a single lecture room (Za'rour, 1988). How can a teacher faced with such numbers have any control over students or any means of assessing understanding and modes of thinking? First-year examinations, therefore, must serve as a massive screening process, filtering through only about 10 per cent of the students – those who have worked hardest to absorb the syllabus.

In the poorer countries universities are often short of laboratories, and the sciences are taught only as theory, which of course falls short of the desired aim. Students fail to gain the required experience and, upon graduation, are incapable of doing serious applied work in their field of specialization. The libraries of many Arab universities lack important reference materials and documentation needed for research or to supplement theoretical and practical lessons.

The result of all this is that students in most Arab universities have to make do with dictated notes or hand-outs. They have no opportunity to benefit from laboratories and do not learn how to conduct proper documentation and library research owing to lack of materials, leaving considerable gaps in their overall education.

THE IMBALANCE BETWEEN SPECIALIZATIONS

There is an obvious imbalance between specializations in Arab universities, with students at faculties of arts, politics and law far outnumbering those in the pure and applied sciences. This distribution is contrary to the needs of the states in question and means that the local market is not supplied with the experts required in such fields as energy and electronics, for example.

The reason for this situation is the failure of the state to intervene and direct young people into areas where job opportunities exist in their countries. Students opt for the easiest routes to a degree but then find there is no job available for them after graduation, since there is an oversupply of graduates in such fields as the arts and the humanities, while the demand for scientists remains unsatisfied. Part of the problem is that entry standards are too low in some faculties encouraging students to follow courses of study their countries do not need. For example, in Algeria, Morocco, Tunisia, Egypt, Lebanon and Iraq, anyone with a secondary school certificate

can enrol in an arts course, while these countries require very high grades for entry into science faculties like medicine and engineering. The result is that students whose applications are rejected by the science faculties turn to the humanities (Jones, 1981). The problem is exacerbated by lack of standardization – the standards required to obtain a science degree are determined by contemporary requirements whereas those for the humanities vary from place to place. All these factors contribute to the imbalance between student numbers in various specializations.

SELECTION AND TRAINING OF UNIVERSITY STAFF

It is often assumed that the most important element in achieving the desired level of university education is the quality of the staff. The unevenness that exists at present is due to a number of factors, the most important of which is the nature of qualifications, PhD degrees being as variable as the universities that award them.

Moreover, those responsible for awarding contracts to staff at Arab universities and institutes do not always look closely at the level of a degree but, in deciding between various candidates, may well be more influenced by personal or political connections. Clearly, this attitude does nothing to enhance academic standards and results in different levels of teaching in the same institution or course.

In most higher-education institutions in the Arab world, moreover, the selection of staff is based solely on degrees and titles and the choice does not take into account other qualities such as personality and creativity, teaching ability and enthusiasm. Though academic qualifications may be a necessary condition for appointment, they are not the only criterion for choosing university teachers. Despite the fact that personality is a crucial factor, people are still being appointed to faculty posts purely on the basis of correspondence and the submission of official documents. In the Arab world, personal interviews are rare while in any European country no contract would be concluded without an interview to find out what the candidate is like.

One regrettable consequence is that all sorts of people are finding their way into higher education, with contracts being handed out indiscriminately. And before we even mention productivity, it should be noted that some of them are so devoid of professional conscience that they will even take bribes (Safi, 1986).

These problems could be overcome if the universities concerned took action to train staff properly. However, as long as there are no training programmes, no valid system of equivalences, no systematic interchange of experiences between Arab universities, no Arab educational meetings and conferences to make sure that staff is kept up-to-date on international issues, no recognition of the principle of reward for merit, the Arab lecturer will be left completely on his own in what and how he teaches, without regard to his university's policy – if indeed it has one.

As a result, the energies of the faculty are dissipated instead of being focused around a clear common goal. Because of the failure to select and train staff adequately, students' development is impaired and they find themselves unable to articulate information systematically with a given objective in mind.

Educational democracy

In this context, democracy means education open to anyone with the ability to follow any course he wishes, given the needs of society, regardless of race, religion, class or sex, without any form of political or other discrimination.

If we focus our attention simply on higher education, we find that student numbers are growing continuously from one year to the next, as more universities and institutes are being established, even in the middle of the Sahara (e.g. Sebha in the Libyan Arab Jamahiriya). In Iraq, Lebanon and the Syrian Arab Republic, the student population has quintupled and in Saudi Arabia, Jordan and the Libyan Arab Jamahiriya

it has grown twentyfold (Za'rour, 1988). These figures show that most Arab states are attempting to provide higher education for the largest possible number of young people even if, at times, standards are low. The question of democracy in higher education presents a contradiction: the solution is not to limit the number of students nor to allow them to enrol in the subject of their choice without guidance; rather, it must be to direct students into fields of specialization that match both their intellectual abilities and the needs of society.

A further distinction may be drawn between democracy in higher education and the elementary and secondary levels. Children coming from remote villages and poor families are at a disadvantage compared to town dwellers. In the villages, the schools that do exist leave much to be desired. Moreover, compulsory primary education is not respected and poor children have to begin work at an early age to earn their living.

In the oil-rich countries, higher education presents a completely different picture. Here, university degrees are a matter of title rather than substance, of personal pride, family recognition and social status rather than a key to mobilizing the energies of society. So great is the rush into higher education that there are attempts to buy degrees, whether through cash bribes or the offer of services to lecturers (Khashan, 1984).

Scientific research

Just as higher education is, for the most part, an import from Europe rather than the product or creation of local knowledge, much academic research tends to be a replica of foreign work or to derive from work which the Arab researcher had been involved in during his higher studies abroad. As a result, such research often seems amateurish, particularly when it does nothing to advance the development of the country concerned.

In addition, there is an enormous gap between the researcher and an educational bureaucracy, which largely ignores research or accords it little importance or attention. Research, therefore, tends to be a solitary task, performed by specialists who are trying to keep up with what they had studied abroad receiving neither direction nor encouragement. As far as the state is concerned, it is of no significance whether researchers continue their studies or not. According to one estimate, 40 per cent of the articles published by Arab researchers in foreign journals originate from the Arab world while the other 60 per cent comes from Arabs working in the United States and Europe (Qubaysi, 1981).

These remarks do not apply to research into law, religion and letters, fields that may be flourishing but have little effect on the development of science and technology, which is needed right now. When benefits do accrue from solid scientific research carried on in the Arab world, they invariably go to the West.

For all its deficiencies and shortcomings, however, it is better to have some scientific research rather than none at all. While waiting for a comprehensive programme to organize and exploit work for the benefit of the Arab States, at least it keeps up the intellectual powers of research workers and maintains some kind of ongoing connection with developments in the technologically advanced countries.

Some of the main problems facing Arab research are as follows:

As research has such a low priority in budgets, there is a lack of financial resources to enable researchers to attend international or even Arab conferences for exchanges of ideas.

Poor scientific and technical preparation and failure to provide and modernize structures (Abd Al-Wahab, 1987).

Unstable conditions of the research worker, whose earnings are too low for a decent standard of living and who leaves the laboratory in search of better pay, leaving the equipment unused.

The lack of full-time research assistants and technicians to maintain equipment means that whenever any material breaks down, the researcher has to turn to outside experts for repairs and is at the mercy of administrators and the bureaucracy.

Not enough reference is available and library services are inadequate.

In many of the poorer Arab countries, the location and condition of laboratory buildings make them unsuitable for teaching or research.

Finally, there is the crucial problem of the brain drain. This can take two forms: on the one hand, teachers and researchers go to other Arab countries for more money, leading to instability and reduced productivity; on the other – and this is the greatest loss – they quit the Arab world permanently for North America and Europe.

Proposals and future prospects

Educational reform is urgently needed in the Arab world. However, it is scarcely possible to conceive of a radical reform of higher education without a review of teaching methods and objectives at primary and secondary level, where the root of the problem lies. The student's talents and abilities and his social and moral personality are all formed in school. University training must have a sound basis to work with, directed towards the service of society.

Even if pre-university education were better organized, reform at the tertiary level could not miraculously come about overnight. It would first be necessary to create a suitable political and economic climate in which the reform of higher education would be part of a comprehensive reform of society. Without such a socio-economic renaissance in the Arab world, any step forward would be followed by two steps back. Nevertheless, the institutions of higher education cannot wait for reform to be complete throughout the various Arab states. Governments and institutions must deal with matters as best they can, since the interaction of the graduate population with society is one of the factors that would accelerate the overall development process. In view of this, I shall now suggest some short-term proposals, as well as others requiring co-ordination between various Arab bodies.

CURRICULA

Curricula must be reviewed on the basis of the numbers and types of graduates required.

There must be a close connection between the subjects studied, and overlapping should be avoided. The student's pre-university background must be taken into account so that there are no gaps when he moves from secondary to tertiary level.

Finally, evaluation methods must be revised and students tested regularly to check intellectual development and the extent to which the curriculum is appropriate and being absorbed. Units should be established in every country and even in every university to work on the continuous development of the curricula.

LANGUAGE OF INSTRUCTION

The Arabic language must be used in all public institutions of higher education in the Arab world since, no matter what level the student may achieve in other foreign languages, he will always be most at home in Arabic. At present, we find some students having to spend a year learning English before they can start work in their major field (Safi, 1986).

At least one foreign language – English or French – must be taught in secondary school up to a level that will enable the university student to use textbooks, journals and other reading matter required in his field of specialization.

Serious consideration must be given to translating basic scientific reference works into Arabic and standardizing Arabic scientific and technological terminologies. Ideally, this work should be carried out under the auspices of the Arab League so that such terminology is made compulsory (Abiyad, 1987).

To facilitate translation work and to keep science graduates in contact with what is going on in research and education in the Arab world, I consider, based on my personal teaching experience in a number of Arab countries, that the Arabic language should be used for explanation and discussion with students but that the formulae and equations should remain in Latin characters as they are found in foreign textbooks. At the same time, scientific terms should be repeated in the foreign language, even after agreed translations have been established. This practice should enable students to follow the subject in foreign reference works (Ibn Abdullah, 1976).

TEACHING MATERIALS AND METHODOLOGY

It is essential to get away from rote learning, to find ways to encourage students to understand their subject and write about it in their own words. One way to do this is to use modern techniques, such as language and science laboratories so that students reinforce their theoretical knowledge of a subject by putting it into practice. At the same time, this will require teachers themselves to be thoroughly trained in the use of these teaching aids.

Although the emphasis today is on the sciences, because they relate directly to production, we must not neglect literature, language and art. Study abroad is essential for Arab students of literature and the arts. Languages, for example, cannot be properly understood in isolation from customs and ways of life, so students who are studying, let us say, English or German should visit the country concerned as part of their university course.

During the past few years, technical advances have made possible the development of open universities, even though these are still in their infancy (Kamhawi, 1988). It is now possible to present lectures on television, for students who are unable to follow a full-time academic course. This system has been successfully applied in the United Kingdom, for example. It would be highly advantageous if the Arab world had a television station to transmit to the various countries for the same purpose. This would be much more effective in standardizing scientific language and terminology than the present piecemeal approaches. Such a system would also help to modernize adult, continuing and postgraduate education.

THE IMBALANCE BETWEEN SPECIALIZATIONS

The present situation in the Arab universities must be reversed. Although the study of the humanities will be maintained, universities must give every possible encouragement to the study of the sciences, especially the applied and technical branches. To this end, the media must send the message to secondary-school leavers that the sciences offer good job prospects and benefit society. Making it easier for these students to enter science faculties does not mean automatically giving them a degree but rather applying the principle of selection at the end of the first year of study. Then, the best students could go on to study science at a higher level, while the less successful could pursue a shorter course more in keeping with their abilities. The Arab world today is sorely lacking people with intermediate technical skills, that is, those who have completed a two-year post-secondary course.

Entry to the humanities should be determined by competition so that only a small minority of gifted students would study literature, law and the like while the rest would be directed towards scientific and technical branches. Once a large percentage of the student population are engaged in scientific studies, a redistribution will take place between faculties on the basis of inclination and ability.

Although this process might result in an over-supply of labour with intermediate skills, the Arab labour market will be able to absorb them more easily and more usefully than large numbers of graduates from the humanities.

Meanwhile, the state, co-operating with the universities through ministries of education and planning, must study the country's short and medium term needs for graduates, in order to decide which branches of higher education need to be developed.

SELECTION AND TRAINING OF STAFF

With regard to the appointment of staff, our proposals are as follows:

University staff appointments should be made on the basis of ability and experience, free of political pressures. No member of staff should be dismissed on other than academic or moral grounds.

In every educational institution, staff should work as a team in which everyone has his role rather than as separate individuals. Specialized committees should be set up to carry out studies and make proposals for any changes that may be needed in respect of methodolody, curricula or equipment.

In-service training centres should be organized for staff, whether in a single country or on a shared basis between a number of universities. Staff should be encouraged and financially assisted to visit foreign universities in order to keep abreast with scientific and educational developments.

Arab educational conferences should be organized to seek solutions to common problems in higher education.

A general agreement should be drawn up to promote interaction through the exchange of staff between Arab universities so that teachers do not move solely for financial gain in response to the pressures of supply and demand.

Staff should have properly paid full-time employment to avoid having to take on a second job. This would improve their abilities and reduce the brain drain.

The universities should co-operate with industry, agriculture, etc., concluding contracts to bring the problems of the productive sectors before research committees composed of academic staff and gradually eliminate dependence on foreign experts.

EDUCATIONAL DEMOCRACY

Putting educational democracy into practice means opening higher education of all kinds and levels to the greatest possible number of students, while maintaining a suitable, uniform standard. Everyone should be given the necessary opportunity to pursue higher education in accordance with his academic ability. In any screening process, those who are not selected should be directed into fields where their abilities will be of use. The experience of the Lebanese University provides a good example. There, after an initial preparatory year in the faculty of science, students sit a competitive examination to determine who will proceed to study medicine. Those who do not pass go on to study biology, botany, geology, etc. However, the educational authorities in Lebanon are still failing to recognize and plan for the needs of society in various fields of specialization.

In countries where there are private universities and institutes, these bodies must be subject to official supervision to ensure that standards are maintained and that the numbers graduating in different areas are in line with government planning.

It is evident that the Arab world lacks technicians with the background of a two-year course at an institute of higher education. We propose that more institutes of this kind should be established to attract students who want a relatively short period of study with guaranteed work upon graduation.

We are all aware that constant efforts must be made and that the situation must be kept under continuous review if we are to maximize the benefits of this potential in accordance with the needs of society. This is a task that must be addressed by those in charge of education.

At the same time, we must emphasize the need to direct women towards specializations that are in keeping with their role in the Arab world as wives and mothers but also ensure that they feel they are contributing to the development of society on an equal footing with men (Ramdas, 1989).

SCIENTIFIC RESEARCH

I would not claim that every lecturer should also be an eminent researcher as well, but I do insist that institutions of higher learning cannot continue to exist unless some of their staff are involved in genuine research. If this is not the case, they will be no better than secondary schools and the information contained in lectures will be obsolete.

Starting from the proposition that well-targeted research is essential to benefit society and improve productivity, we propose the establishment of a research directorate in every Arab country to provide local planning and determine priority areas. It would be responsible for monitoring allocations and concluding contracts with institutions of higher education specifically for research projects to raise levels of production and to improve living standards. It would also be beneficial if such centres were each represented on a council at top levels in the Arab world, possibly through the Arab League or the Organization for Education in the Arab States. The council would give guidance on research topics concerning a group of Arab countries, for example, in relation to oil, the environment, wildlife, etc. The council would also serve to integrate the roles of both rich and poor countries. Thus, Arab research projects would be financed by Arab funds and carried out by Arab brains.

The purpose of this proposal is not to bind Arab researchers to one specific research topic and no other. All that is intended is to encourage attention to certain subjects which the states concerned feel are of common benefit and which should be treated in greater depth. As research – even in arts subjects – is exceedingly expensive, it is necessary to try to ensure finance to attract Arab experts back from research work abroad.

We must set up proper workshops that initially, will be capable of servicing the scientific equipment used by researchers and, subsequently, of manufacturing parts and apparatus for the laboratory. There will soon be no scientific research done, if researchers continue to be at the mercy of foreign suppliers for spare parts.

General conclusion

We have reviewed the various failings of higher education in the Arab world, and the picture is indeed a gloomy one. On the positive side, some modest attempts are being made to apply scientific research, to bring education to all sections of society and to encourage researchers and academics abroad to return home. However, for the most part, these efforts have been inadequate and inconsistent.

The chronic disease affecting education and the source of all its problems is politics in all its forms, from the international arena all the way down to partisan and individual interests. We have only to look at the internal situation in any Arab country to see that educational decisions are made by a small group of individuals united by ties of blood or party. Only if a project is in their interests will it be approved. When power changes universities suffer, projects are stopped and researchers, academics and other staff are dismissed or transferred to places where they are of no use. Teachers and researchers feel no sense of security and are in fear of dismissal at any moment. For this reason, we can see no place for long-term planning at the present moment.

In Europe and the United States, researchers are under much less political pressure, whereas in the Arab world, they are dominated by political patronage. In the West, officials come and go; in the East, when an official goes, the institution often goes as well.

It cannot be said that the domestic politics of the various Arab states exist in isolation from regional and international disputes. How could it be otherwise when they have only recently achieved their independence? The Middle East is a focus of attention for its natural resources; the internecine struggles between Arab leaders are the result of outside interference. The resulting climate of political instability affects educa-

tional planning. How can new institutions be established in areas disputed by neighbouring countries? What kind of education are peoples who live in such areas to receive? This situation is perfectly illustrated by recent events in the Gulf. Can we say that the Iraqi government is as eager to develop education and the infrastructure in the Kurdish areas in the north of the country as in the rest of Iraq? What kind of educational relations are there going to be between Iraq and Kuwait for the foreseeable future? Will they be any better than the present relations between Iraq and the Syrian Arab Republic?

Who knows whether the friendly relations between Egypt, Saudi Arabia and the Syrian Arab Republic will continue for long enough to carry out educational planning? How often have we seen so-called 'unity' between Arab countries degenerate into hostility within a few years? Today, Egypt and the Libyan Arab Jamahiriya say that there is no border between them, but how long will this last?

Given the existing political situation, how can we speak of co-ordination between Arab states, exchange of experiences and the establishment of integrated educational institutions designed to serve Arab society? As long as the bitter conflicts now existing continue, there is no hope of standardizing scientific terminologies, of exchanging technical knowledge and academic staff and planning for decades to come.

The one ray of hope is that the Arab world may learn the lesson to be drawn from the events in the Gulf and establish a new system for security in the region, settling the outstanding issues of the Middle East and ensuring stability for future generations.

This does not mean that we can just fold our arms and wait for a miracle solution to appear. On the contrary, all of us – in education, government and administration – must do everything we possibly can in word and deed to improve matters until higher education can eventually play an effective role in developing Arab society.   ■

References and bibliography

ABD AL-WAHAB, H. S. 1987. The Role of Technical Institutes in Changing Arab Society. *Arab Journal of Higher Education Research* (Damascus), Vol. 6, July.

ABIYAD, M. 1987. Arabization at Damascus University. *Damascus University Journal for the Humanities* (Damascus), Vol. 2, No. 7, September.

AL-BADER, H. 1987. The Rationalization of University Education Admission Policies in the Gulf States. *Arab Journal of Higher Education Research* (Damascus), Vol. 6, July.

ALGIERS. 1981. Higher Education and Development in the Arab Countries. First Conference of Arab Ministers of Higher Education.

AMIDEAST. 1986. *A Guide to University and Technical Programmes in Certain Countries of the Middle East and North Africa.* Washington, D.C., Amideast, 1986.

ASSAYH, A. H. 1982. The University Problem in the Arab Countries: A Historical and Social Analysis. *Arab Journal of Education* (Tunis), Vol. 2, No. 2, September.

COUNCIL OF EUROPE, 1984. *U2000. Higher Education and Research Policies in Europe Approaching the Year 2000.* Strasbourg, Council of Europe.

IBN ABDULLAH, A. A. 1976. Problems of Arabization in Science. *Impact of Science on Society,* Vol. XXVI, No. 3, pp. 151–9.

JONES, H. T. 1981. Allocation of Students in North African Universities. *Higher Education,* Vol. 10.

KAMHAWI, W. 1987. *Higher Distance Education in the Arab World.* Amman, Al-Quds Open University.

——. 1988. The Al-Quds Open University Project. *Prospects,* Vol. XVIII, No. 2, pp. 239–47.

KHASHAN, H. 1984. A Study of Student Perceptions in a Saudi Arabian University. *Research in Higher Education,* Vol. 21, No. 1.

KLANSNER, S. Z. 1986. A Professor's-eye View of the Egyptian Academy. *Journal of Higher Education,* Vol. 57, No. 4.

OSMAN, O. M. 1983. *Perspectives of the Development of the University in the Arab Region from the Present to the Year 2000.* Paris, UNESCO.

QUBAYSI, H. 1981. An Introductory Study about the Geographical Distribution of Arab Scientific Researchers. *Proceedings of a Seminar on the Arab Brain Drain.* Beirut, BCWA.

RAMDAS, L. 1989. Women and Literacy: A Quest for Justice. *Prospects,* Vol. XIX, No. 4, pp. 519–30.

SAFI, A. Q. 1986. Student Evaluations of Courses and Instructors at Kuwait University. *Higher Education Review,* Vol. 18, No. 3.

UNEDBAS. 1986. *Les systèmes d'enseignement supérieur à distance: planification, gestion et évaluation.* Amman, UNESCO Regional Office for Education in the Arab Countries.

UNESCO. 1990. *Compendium of Statistics on Illiteracy.* Paris, UNESCO. (Statistical Reports and Studies, 31.)

YUSIF, A. 1984. Priorities and Alternatives in Higher Education for the Palestinian People. *Arab Journal of Higher Education Research* (Damascus), Vol. 1, June.

ZA'ROUR, G. 1988. *The University in Arab Countries.* Washington, D.C., World Bank, Population and Human Resources Department.

Higher education
and development

The experience of four newly

industrializing countries in Asia

Jasbir Sarjit Singh

Since the 1970s a number of economies in Asia have successfully upgraded their industrial base and strengthened their capacity to adopt, adapt and create new technologies. Among these countries, the Republic of Korea, Taiwan and Singapore have already demonstrated significant industrial achievement while Malaysia is pursuing the same path. Commonly referred to as newly industrializing countries (NICs) they possess limited natural resources but have recognized the importance of the knowledge and skills composition of their labour force as the key to their productivity and national develop-

Jasbir Sarjit Singh (Malaysia). *Chief Project Officer, Education Programme, Commonwealth Secretariat, London, with responsibility for higher education. Until 1990 she was Professor of sociological studies, Faculty of Education, University of Malaya, where she also served as Dean, Institute of Advanced Studies. Her principal interests in teaching and research are education and social mobility, education, learning orientation and work in developing societies. Author of numerous articles in her fields of competence.*

ment transforming them from agricultural to industrial export economies.

Impressed by the success of the NICs in structural adjustment and industrial development other developing countries look to the NICs for lessons on how to stimulate their growth. The principal concern is with the role of human-resource development, in particular with investment in different levels and types of education as a generator of growth. Investment of scarce resources in higher education proves especially problematic; as the most expensive sector of education it is imperative that the higher-education system produces the right mix of manpower pertinent to national needs. Of special interest to developing countries are the higher-education strategies that have enabled NICs to produce a scientific and technological capacity to support industrialization.

Successful restructuring and development in these countries may be attributed to a number of factors, two of which have a direct bearing upon higher-education institutions: (a) the quantity and quality of scientific and technological manpower, and (b) the research and development environment which enables the achievement and sustainability of indigenous industrial development.

TABLE I. Contribution to GDP and employment distribution, Republic of Korea, Malaysia, Singapore and Taiwan (percentages)

Country	Year	Contribution to GDP			Distribution of employed		
		Agri-culture	Manufac-turing	Services	Agri-culture	Manufac-turing	Services
Republic of Korea	1970	26.5	22.4	51.1	50.4	14.3	35.3
	1980	14.9	31.0	54.1	34.0	22.5	43.5
	1988	10.5	33.2	56.2	20.7	24.4	50.9
Malaysia	1970	30.8	13.4	41.9	53.5	8.7	35.2
	1980	22.2	20.5	45.1	40.6	15.8	36.7
	1988	21.1	24.4	45.0	31.3	16.6	45.5
Singapore	1970	3.0	20.2	71.5	3.5	22.0	67.5
	1980	1.3	29.1	66.7	1.6	20.1	61.5
	1988	0.4	38.0	61.0	0.4	28.5	62.5
Taiwan	1970	18.0	26.2	47.5	36.7	20.9	35.3
	1985	6.9	35.8	48.2	17.5	33.5	41.1
	1988	6.1	38.1	47.7	13.7	34.5	43.7

Sources: Republic of Korea, 1990; Taiwan, 1990; Singapore, 1971/72, 1986, 1990; Malaysia, 1989.

Higher-education institutions play a singularly important role in the training of scientific and technological manpower because they are often the sole suppliers of high-level scientific and technological personnel. Research and development activity, though shared with other research and specialized institutions is a crucial part of higher education as it strengthens and enhances their training capacity. Of central concern to the analysis is the extent to which higher-education systems of NICs provide support to their industrialization policies.

This article will portray higher-education developments in selected NICs – the Republic of Korea, Malaysia, Singapore and Taiwan – to assess their role in each country's progress towards industrialization. It will sketch briefly the nature of industrialization and the degree of structural adjustment achieved. The higher-education policies and developments that have helped shape these countries' remarkable industrial growth will be identified and reviewed primarily from the perspective of the role of higher education in developing and strengthening their scientific and technological capacity. The experiences of these countries will illustrate higher-education developments which may be vital to the growth and development of NICs.

Structural adjustment

The NICs' annual growth rate of 6–10 per cent since the 1970s has been paralleled by structural adjustment policies that have sought to reallocate the factors of production to bring about improved products or services. They have replaced agriculture with manufacturing as the key factor in promoting and sustaining economic growth, gradually shifting from import substitution industries to export-oriented and selected high technology heavy industries. To achieve this, the NICs have pursued 'corrective and directive structural adjustment' clearly intended to move away from low-wage, low-productivity and unskilled labour-intensive activities and have created for themselves growth niches which lie in high-technology and high value-added activities. (Chowdhury et al., 1986, p. 61)

Singapore's experience in structural adjustment is quite typical. In its first phase of industrialization, efforts were concentrated on a small number of industries – chemical processing, metal engineering and machinery, heavy engineering and electric and electronic engineering (Lim, 1984, pp. 33, 41). Since 1979, seeking to bring about a second industrial revolution, Singapore has directed its industrial sector towards the production of goods that require more skill, pay higher wages and generate more value added. Recognizing its comparative advantage in promoting knowledge-based industries Singapore set in motion measures to become an international centre for exporting software technology to world markets.

In all the NICs changes in sectoral distribution of the employed labour force as well as broad shifts in sectoral contributions to gross domestic product (GDP) are evident (see Table 1), reflecting the slowing down of agricultural production and expansion in the industry, manufacturing and the service sectors. In the Republic of Korea from 1960 to 1985 agricultural production growth averaged 3 per cent and during the 1980s 3.7 per cent, but from 1965 to 1980 industry grew by 16.4 and 12.4 per cent respectively during the 1980s, while manufacturing recorded a growth of 18.7 per cent during the period 1965 to 1980 and 13.5 per cent in the 1980s. Singapore experienced a decline in agricultural production during the 1980s (minus 5.1 per cent) while industry and manufacturing showed a marked growth-rate of 11.9 and 13.2 per cent respectively from 1965 to 1980 and 4.5 and 4.8 per cent respectively in the 1980s. (World Bank, 1990, pp. 180–1).

The adjustment policy has been greatly facilitated by the consciously formulated and far reaching policies for manpower development, education and training (Chowdhury et al., 1986, p. 11). The correspondence between structural adjustment and human-resource development has been evidently directed at obtaining the mix of skills needed to sustain the planned industrialization. As the demand for skills built up, the proportion of enrolments in secondary and higher education increased. To accommodate the demand for technicians and engineers, enrolments in schools, colleges and universities were tilted in favour of science entrants. The outcome is clearly evident: the shape of the educational pyramid in all the countries has been transformed (see Table 2) with clear implications for the qualifications structure of the labour force.

TABLE 2. Enrolments in educational institutions in the Republic of Korea, Malaysia, Singapore and Taiwan

Country	Population (1988) (millions)	GDP (1988) ($)	Year	Primary (%)	Secondary (%)	Higher (%)
Republic of Korea	42.0	3 600	1970	73.1	24.3	2.6
			1980	54.2	40.1	5.7
			1988	44.4	42.6	13.0
Malaysia	16.9	1 940	1970	75.0	24.3	0.6
			1980	63.8	34.7	1.5
			1988	59.1	37.1	3.8[1]
Singapore	2.6	9 070	1970	68.9	28.5	2.6
			1980	58.1	37.4	4.5
			1988	48.2	43.1	8.7
Taiwan	19.9	6 302	1970	65.9	29.0	5.1
			1980	57.6	34.9	7.5
			1988	56.9	33.5	9.6

1. Estimate for 1990: Malaysia, 1986, p. 485.

Sources: Republic of Korea, 1990; Taiwan, 1990; Singapore, 1971/72, 1986, 1990; Malaysia, 1989.

Targeted higher-education priorities

Since the 1970s the NICs have planned for higher education within the framework of national priorities set for the larger education system under the control of the Ministry of Education. Higher education is seen as a vital component of the process of nation-building, expected to bring about socio-economic and political development of the country. As part of the national education system a tight rein has been kept on all developments in higher education. However, as has been argued for the Republic of Korea, despite serious flaws, strains on students and parents, and denial of opportunities for individual personal development, the education system managed to contribute to the country's economic progress. (Selth, 1988, p. 16).

There is evidence of a high degree of co-ordinated control which is exercised through large subsidies comprising frequently around 95 per cent of the development and recurrent costs of these institutions or legislative enactments that have empowered these governments to moderate the expansion and direction of higher education. During the period from the 1960s to the 1980s, the Republic of Korea's five year development plans prompted the government to regulate the establishment of new departments and set student quotas for different universities and disciplines, influencing the curriculum and university appointments (Bom Mo Chung, 1988, p. 52). The government stipulated the number of courses, the combination of subjects to be taken, the bestowing of doctorate degrees and regulation of overseas students (Selth, 1988, p. 11). Malaysian higher education has been closely guarded by the Ministry of Education as one of the principal actors in national development. The Universities and Colleges Act, 1971, stipulates that no higher-education institution with the status of a university shall be established except in accordance with the provision of this Act (Isahak Haron, 1988, p. 6). The government also exercises full authority over student enrolments, staff appointments, curricula and financing. Consecutive five-year plans have set out targets for readjusting higher education and a strict policy of quotas is adhered to through a central admissions unit. Singapore has closely co-ordinated the development of technical institutes, polytechnics and universities as the producers of the appropriate type and quantity of manpower for the economy. Access to universities and colleges has been prompted by objective criteria and not individual need, and enrolment levels have been pegged to a ten-year manpower plan. The government actively influences career choices and it encourages students to enter fields where there are shortages and stay out of others that have become competitive. Expanding faculties are encouraged with a proper supply of qualified skills (Pang Eng Fong, 1982, p. 157). Taiwan proves no exception in relation to the regulation of access, structure and content of higher education. All decisions, from the appointment of presidents, the establishment of new departments, colleges or universities, the number of students enrolled in a department to the curriculum, the number of teachers per faculty, the teaching load, tuition fees and faculty salaries are approved by the Ministry of Education. (Hsieh, 1989, p. 179). The government has maintained a ratio of 3:7 in favour of vocational schools to keep the level of output at the technician level high. Recent changes to allow more students to move up to comprehensive schools have been influenced not by student or parental pressure but by the concern to upgrade the labour force to meet the demand for high level manpower (Yi-Rong Young, 1991, pp. 6–7).

Investment in higher education

Recognizing the higher-education system as the valued producer of high-level manpower NIC governments were willing to invest large amounts in it. In all the NICS the percentage of expenditure on education increased steadily as a part of the GNP, and of higher education as a

Jasbir Sarjit Singh

TABLE 3. Expansion of higher education in selected NICs, for both university and college sectors, 1970–90

Country	Enrolments						
	1970	1975	1980	Average annual increase 1970–80 (%)	1985	1990	Average annual increase 1980–90 (%)
Republic of Korea	201 436	297 219	615 452	20.5	1 062 195	1 529 244[1]	14.8
Malaysia	10 995	25 420	32 280	19.4	359 346	75 178[2]	13.3
Singapore	13 683	18 078	22 633	6.2	39 913	50 742[3]	12.4
Taiwan	203 473	289 435	342 528	6.8	428 576	535 064[4]	5.6

1. 1988 data, from UNESCO, 1990.
2. 1990 estimate.
3. 1989 data (includes Institute of Education).
4. 1989 data.

Sources:
REPUBLIC OF KOREA: Kim Jong Chol and Hung Sah-Myung, 1984, Table II, p. 7; Kim Shin Bok, Table 1, p. 66;
Lee Sungho, 1989, p. 58, Table 2.1.
MALAYSIA: Malaysia, 1986, p. 264; Malaysia, 1989, p. 95.
SINGAPORE: Singapore, 1971/72; Singapore, 1990a, p. 32.
TAIWAN: Taiwan, 1990, pp. 283–4.

part of the total education budget. The Republic of Korea's educational expenditure in the 1980s has been 5.5 per cent of GNP of which 30 per cent has been allocated to higher education. The government considers that one of its major roles 'is to see to it that the maximally possible, if not sufficient expenditure is secured' (Bom Mo Chung, 1988, p. 53). Malaysia in 1985 was spending 6.9 per cent of its GNP on education with 15.6 per cent of it on the higher-education budget (compared with 7.1 per cent in 1970). Singapore, in 1989/90, similarly spent about 22 per cent of its education budget on its universities and polytechnics (Singapore, 1990b, p. 33). At the same time Taiwan's education expenditure has increased from 1.73 per cent in 1985 to 5.3 per cent of the GNP in 1985 with 20 per cent to higher education (Taiwan, 1990, pp. 39, 43).

Higher-education structures

The high expenditure is paralleled by increased enrolments (Table 3). Since the 1970s, the NICs have experienced rapid growth in higher education: an annual increase of around 20 per cent in

Malaysia and the Republic of Korea and 6.2 and 6.8 per cent respectively in Singapore and Taiwan between 1970 and 1980; and an annual growth-rate of 14.8 per cent in the Republic of Korea, around 13.3 per cent in Malaysia, 12.4 per cent in Singapore and 5.6 per cent in Taiwan during the 1980s.

The size and structures of the higher-education systems in these countries are varied. Singapore has only had the National University of Singapore, the Nanyang Technological Institute (upgraded to the status of a university in 1991), two polytechnics and the Institute of Education with a total enrolment in 1989 of 50,742, of which 22,094 were in universities, 27,106 in polytechnics and 1,542 in teacher-training colleges (Singapore, 1990b, p. 32). Malaysia has six national universities, one international university, MARA Institute of Technology, Tengku Abdul Rahman College and four polytechnics with an estimated enrolment in 1990 of 75,178. Higher education in the Republic of Korea, begun by American missionaries, underwent rapid reconstruction and expansion following the Korean War designed largely on the United States model. By 1986 there were 111 colleges and universities with an enrolment of 992,233 students, with another 69,962 students in graduate schools but nearly 70 per cent of these institutions are private (Altbach, 1989, p. 16). By 1988 a higher-education enrolment of 1,529,244 was recorded (UNESCO, 1990, pp. 3–356). This represents a third of the college age cohort, but the government is directly involved in only a quarter of the students with less than 2 per cent subsidy to private colleges (Bom Mo Chung, 1988, p. 54). In Taiwan by 1989 there were 535,064 students enrolled in 116 higher-education institutions comprising 21 universities, 20 independent colleges and 75 junior colleges.

Despite these differences a number of common features are discernible. The systems that developed in the Republic of Korea and Taiwan more closely resemble the American university system with a range in the quality of institutions and a clear 'social pecking order' (Lee Sungho, 1989, p. 36). There clearly emerged in the Republic of Korea and Taiwan a two-tiered hierarchy with the majority of students aspiring to enter the state financed colleges – placing great pressure on entrance for coveted places. In Malaysia and Singapore the institutions are of more uniform quality, reminiscent of British higher-education institutions. The universities are at the apex with specialized institutes awarding diplomas and certificates.

The NICs provide useful lessons in the structuration of higher education. Recognizing that they cannot take all applicants into a high technology and capital intensive system, the Republic of Korea and Taiwan have evolved a two-tier system, one lower-level, low-cost and localized tier and one high-level specialized tier. They have successfully expanded and diversified their higher-education systems to meet national skills requirements as well as satisfy to some extent the aspirations of the population by providing all who desire access to some level of higher education and avenues to move from one level of higher education to another. Thus, nearly 30 per cent of this age cohort have access to higher education. Following the British trend, Malaysia and Singapore have retained a few élitist institutions almost fully subsidized by the government leading to credentials that enable employment in the upper echelons of the occupational structure. A small group of polytechnics and institutions of technology provide training to technicians. However it is unlikely that this can be maintained and the indications are that as the pressure for more higher education builds up in these countries, it is the lower tier that will have to be expanded.

Science and technology manpower

The countries under review had inherited an imbalanced development in the levels and type of manpower: over-production of managerial and under-production of para-professional and vocational as well as an oversupply of arts and social science graduates and a shortage of natural science and technical graduates. During the last thirty years the NICs concerned themselves with the task of enlarging their pool of scientific and research personnel; evidence can be adduced from all the countries of the strategies they have pursued to sharpen the focus on science and technology manpower and research (see Table 4).

The government of the Republic of Korea was prompted to control all non-development-related aspects of higher education. The First Five Year Economic Development Plan in 1962 emphasized higher education in the natural sciences and engineering. The government moderately increased the enrolment quotas in science and engineering every year while limiting social science and humanities intakes. In 1967 a Ministry of Science and Technology was created and a series of laws were enacted to promote developments – the Electronics Industrial Promotion Law in 1969 and the Eight-year Development Plan for the Electronics Industry (1969–76), while a number of science-and-technology institutes were established around the country (Sanyal, 1990, p. 20). New departments in social sciences were restricted and research grants were made available more readily to projects with practical application than to basic research. The government exerted considerable

TABLE 4. Enrolments in higher-education institutions by field of study in Selected NICs (percentages in italics)

Country	1970			1980			1989/90		
	Arts	Science	Technical	Arts	Science	Technical	Arts	Science	Technical
Republic of Korea	115 230	36 422	49 784	312 250	93 566	209 636	1 021 622	218 019	289 603
	57.2	*18.1*	*24.7*	*50.7*	*15.2*	*34.1*	*66.8*	*14.3*	*18.9*
Malaysia	6 245	3 297	1 453	14 790	11 325	6 165	42 500	17 408	15 269
	56.8	*30.0*	*13.2*	*45.8*	*35.1*	*19.1*	*56.5*	*23.2*	*20.3*
Singapore	2 708	541	4 769	6 850	1 630	8 000	13 589	5 209	30 650
	33.7	*6.7*	*59.6*	*41.7*	*9.8*	*48.5*	*27.5*	*10.5*	*62.0*
Taiwan	122 434	31 153	49 886	185 365	41 977	115 186	294 700	60 869	179 495
	60.2	*15.3*	*24.5*	*54.1*	*12.3*	*33.6*	*55.1*	*11.4*	*33.5*

Sources:
REPUBLIC OF KOREA: UNESCO, 1972, p. 384; 1987, pp. 3313; 1990, pp. 3–356.
MALAYSIA: Malaysia, 1986, p. 264; 1989, pp. 94–95.
SINGAPORE: Singapore, 1971/72, p. 167; data represents students admitted into these disciplines for the year 1970.
TAIWAN: Taiwan, 1990, pp. 283–4.

effort to encourage students towards vocational and technical schools and colleges. Graduate education which in the past was limited largely to medicine and limited to a few prestigious universities such as Seoul National and Yonsei has been extended to science and engineering and greatly strengthened through the establishment of more graduate schools, in particular the establishment of the Korea Institute of Science and Technology (KAIST) in 1981. Its principal objective is to educate and develop high-calibre and competent manpower in both abstruse theory and practical applications in the field of science and technology and to develop the nation's science and technological potential (Lee Sungho, 1989, pp. 42–3). Enrolment in scientific fields has wavered between 40 and 50 per cent during the 1960s and 1970s, though in 1985 it was reported to be only 33.1 per cent (UNESCO, 1990). At postgraduate level more than 50 per cent have been enrolled in these discipline; in 1986 there were 12,018 Master's degree students and 3,871 doctoral science-and-engineering students out of a total of 30,265 graduates representing 52.5 per cent of the total graduate student population (Lee Sungho, 1989, pp. 39, 59–60).

As Singapore's industrialization took off, its education system was also adjusted to produce knowledge-based graduates and technicians for its specific industries. In the 1970s engineering, accounting and business management/administration were given more emphasis in the university sector. As new priority industries required a high level of skills and technology, the Nanyang Technological Institute and the polytechnics produced practice-oriented engineers. The Report of the Economic Committee in 1986 endorsed the assumption that the government should create the infrastructure and environment conducive for science-and-technology development goals for Singapore's high-technology policy which would allow industry to exploit and advance new technologies, develop competence in new technologies and move into high-technology industries which would help Singapore's growth and carried implications for the expansion of programmes to train manpower needed to carry out R&D in industry. At all the institutes of higher education less than 30 per cent are in arts and humanities studies. Both at the National University of Singapore and at the Nanyang Technological Institute Master's programmes with specialized focus have increased (Pang and Gopinathan, 1989, p. 140).

Malaysia has gradually shifted from overemphasis on the social sciences and humanities to science and technology, achieving a ratio of three science to two arts students in secondary schools, by deliberately adjusting the admission quotas and concentrating on the development of specialized science-and-technology institutions. In the 1970s from the one comprehensive university, the University of Malaya, Malaysia established a university of science, upgraded the agricultural and technical colleges to universities and began to develop postgraduate courses in science, medicine and engineering. To focus on applied research and courses with developmental bias, the Institute of Advanced Studies was founded in 1980 at the University of Malaya. As a result the share of arts students shrank from 56.8 per cent in 1970 to 45.8 per cent in 1980, while the proportion of science and engineering students increased from 43.2 to 54.2 per cent. Since then the proportion of arts and humanities enrolments has increased but this has been largely in business and accountancy studies.

The importance Taiwan placed on science and technology is apparent from the predominance of technological and engineering colleges and universities established during the 1970s and 1980s, enabling a great push for science and engineering as well as postgraduate education. In 1975 only 47.5 per cent of undergraduate degrees and 4 per cent of the Master's and doctoral degrees were granted in science and engineering. In 1982 the government launched a special programme to train more graduate students seeking significant expansion of graduate programmes in strategic areas such as information, materials, electronics, automation and biotechnology, increasing faculty and the number of scholarships for students. As a result in 1985 Master's and doctoral graduates in science and engineering increased from 54 per cent (in 1980) to 64 per cent and from 18 to 48 per cent respectively. Since then the level of science and engineering enrolment has tapered off, with about 44 per cent of all students in public and private universities and colleges in 1990 enrolled in science-and-technology courses. In the public sector at first-degree level 51 per cent were in science and engineering. Science and engineering graduate enrolments now comprise 57 per cent of the total graduate population, that is, 60 per cent of all Master's and 28 per cent of all

Ph.D. enrolments were in scientific and technological fields.

Strengthening engineering and technological studies

As industrialization became more prominent the need was not merely for undifferentiated scientific manpower but for specialized engineers rather than natural scientists, and for technicians to support their work. In this respect, a clear relationship is evident in NICs between the proportion of technology students and the level of industrialization (see Table 3). The Republic of Korea, Taiwan, Singapore and, to a lesser extent, Malaysia concentrated in their prestigious universities on the production of engineers relevant to their targeted industries. The Republic of Korea and Taiwan multiplied their electrical and electronic engineering departments and students, while Singapore concentrated on training specialists in computer hardware and software and in biotechnology. At the same time the higher-education system was diversified, providing opportunities for large numbers to study technology at a lower level, in the two- to five-year junior colleges and polytechnics which enabled their graduates to work at practical levels in industry, while allowing a small proportion to move on to institutes of technology for more specialized studies.

During the 1980s Singapore clearly shifted emphasis in favour of engineering students, with an accelerated output of engineering graduates. Engineering enrolments in higher education in 1980 comprised 8,000 out of a total of 16,480, or 48 per cent of tertiary students. By 1989 out of a total of 49,448, 62 per cent of all universities and college students were enrolled in engineering. By 1980 Singapore also enrolled 10.2 per cent of its students in postgraduate studies which since then have been considerably increased through the establishment of key specialized centres to provide excellent opportunities for postgraduate education: the Institute of Molecular and Cell

Biology, Institute of Systems Science and the Centre for Advanced Studies. It has instituted prestigious research awards to draw the best students into postgraduate studies and has targeted 10 per cent of its university population to be research students by 1990 (Pang and Gopinathan, 1989, p. 147). It has added prestige to its engineering studies by establishing in 1990 a postgraduate school of engineering 'to strengthen and to give focus to the postgraduate programmes' and to assist the faculty in developing into a centre of excellence for postgraduate training and research in engineering.

The story in the Republic of Korea is somewhat similar. Structural change from light to heavy industry in the 1970s led to an increased demand for engineers and research scientists in the academic system. The primary goal in the 1960s and early 1970s was to produce technicians and engineers who could absorb or initiate foreign technology. The mid-1970s saw a change to capital- and technology-intensive industrial sectors. The new industries needed scientists and research engineers who could promote creative assimilation of foreign technology as well as invention and innovation. The academic system was now required to expand its mission to move away from basic research to expand indigenous sources of scientific and technological creation through promotion of production, assessment and validation of ideas (Lee Sungho, 1989, p. 55).

The influence of the new developments was sharply felt in the electrical and electronics departments whose student numbers increased rapidly to keep pace with developments in these industries which led the industrialization process. The number and variety of courses in electronics leading to Master's and doctoral degrees increased. In the electronic industries courses ranged from semi-conductor and electronic material, digital systems, communications, automatic control and measurement, electronic circuits and systems, and computers. Master's degree students increased from 2,259 to 5,504 and Ph.D. students from 462 to 1,026 during the six-year period from 1985 to 1991. Similarly, the number of electronic departments increased

from four in four-year colleges in 1965, to thirty-six in 1975 and 100 in 1988, while in graduate schools the numbers rose from three in 1965 to twenty-one in 1975 and seventy-five in 1986. Enrolments in electronic departments rose in four-year colleges from 279 in 1965 to 6,042 in 1975 and 35,873 in 1984, and the number of graduate students increased from 4 in 1965 to 125 in 1975 and 1,659 in 1984 (Sanyal and Hyun, 1989, pp. 92–102).

Taiwan has a high proportion of engineering students among its science enrolments. The proportion of engineering students has gradually increased from 24.5 per cent in 1970 to 33.6 per cent in 1980 and throughout the 1980s engineering enrolments comprised around 33 per cent of total higher-education enrolments. In comparison pure science enrolments have remained at around 11 per cent. By 1989, of the total enrolment in science and engineering, 47.1 per cent were enrolled in engineering courses. More importantly in the public sector day session engineering students constituted 56.8 per cent of the total science and engineering students.

Compared with the Republic of Korea, Taiwan and Singapore, Malaysia's output of science-and-technology graduates has been slower and the focus has until recently been on the basic science courses – biology, chemistry, physics and mathematics. Between 1981 and 1988, 45 per cent of all science students graduated in these fields. Graduates in the applied sciences have remained low at between 2 and 3 per cent of all enrolments. Generally, technology-oriented graduates from the engineering faculties accounted for only about 24 per cent of the graduates of whom the largest proportion had graduated in civil engineering. The level of enrolments in post-graduate studies by the mid-1980s was still only around 4 per cent of total enrolments and there were few graduate centres. In postgraduate studies too, the concentration of science and engineering studies had made little headway accounting for barely 19 per cent of the postgraduate population (Singh, 1989, pp. 91, 120–1).

Ensuring quality

While quantitative expansion provided the basic pool of scientists, technologists and craftsmen for industry, attention was also turned to the type and quality of higher education to produce an élite corpus of science-and-technology manpower. Malaysia and Singapore have maintained a tight grip on access to higher education and especially in the scientific fields – requiring better A-level results to enter science and engineering courses than the arts and humanities. The number of applicants far exceed the places offered allowing only the best to enter these courses. The Republic of Korea and Taiwan followed a more open entry system allowing large numbers to enter the higher-education sector but within that sector a small prestigious, difficult of access, competitive and publicly funded group of universities emerged that produced the highly skilled manpower needed for research and industry. Both groups of countries were selective and promoted a small élite group of scientific manpower: one through limited entry along the British lines and the other through keenly contested entry into the key institution along American lines.

The experience in the Republic of Korea bears illustration. The harsh Korean education system, which forces students to undergo a rigorous regime to reach the higher levels of education permits only the fittest and best qualified to survive (Selth, 1988, p. 17); there is a process of natural attrition that allows only 7–8 per cent of those who entered primary school to attain college and university education. Quality has been further augmented by regulating entrants into departments and particularly into the premier institutions. With the top colleges – Seoul National University, Yonsei University and Ewha Women's University – allowed to accept less than a quarter of the entrants into higher-education competition into these institutions became fiercer. The key institutions in the Republic of Korea have been nurtured and given facilities and funds above the others. Their staff have bet-

ter qualifications, they have more funds, they are encouraged to do research and publish, and are provided with a more conducive research environment. Further improvements were effected during the 1980s through reform of college entrance examinations and entrance to be based on a combination of school record and national achievement tests. A 30 per cent larger enrolment than expected to pass was permitted – setting a graduation quota (Park Yungchul, 1983, p. 6). This further placed pressure on the students to perform well while in university or college. They were rewarded in turn with easy access into the key jobs encouraging more to try the difficult route into these institutions.

While the higher-education systems may be viewed as quite contrary to the traditions of freedom of access and scholarship that are extolled in many developed countries they did serve national needs to produce a breed of technologists that were the best within the country.

Research structures and environment

As intellectual centres and producers of knowledge universities in the NICs present a paradox: they remain on the periphery of a world system of knowledge; yet within their own countries they represent the most important centres of knowledge and indigenous research geared to national development needs. At one level these researchers and scientists of developing countries are influenced by the knowledge, training, patents, innovations and research agendas generated in the research centres of the industrialized world. Working in small scientific communities and lacking the personnel, equipment or funding to enable them to work independently they orient their research and writing to issues of international concern and for recognition by the international forums. The orientation is reinforced from within their universities where recognition and promotion is accorded to those who meet the international criteria. At another level there is plenty of evidence that they have succeeded in creating an indigenous base and they have demonstrated their faith in their own capacity by committing considerable resources to the development of local research and development. They recognize that locally rooted research and knowledge development will contribute to a mature academic system as well as promote scientific developments to assist local technology for industry and provide the key personnel for further research and industrial development (Altbach, 1989, pp. 4–6).

While the universities are important in the research and development plans of the NICs, the extent to which they are central to the R&D of countries varies. The National University of Singapore plays a central role in the scientific research in the priority areas identified by the Singapore Government and carried out within the university departments or specialized institutions such as the Institute of Systems Science, which concentrates on research related to computer application. With its large number of academic staff and scientific facilities, the National University is the largest scientific agency in the country. It has achieved close collaboration for research and training with local industry (Pang and Gopinathan, 1989, p. 145). Malaysian universities on the other hand have only recently begun to sharpen their focus on scientific research for development purposes. Most of the earlier research in natural products was undertaken by specialized research institutes with the universities playing the role of trainers and teachers of scientific manpower. The development of the specialized science-and-technology universities and the setting up of the Institute of Advanced Studies point to an enhanced role for universities in development-oriented research. With the launch of the Industrial Master Plan, 1986–91, and the identification of research priorities universities are expected to play a greater role in the training of postgraduate researchers, a function that is viable only when it takes place in conjunction with a lively research environment. Nevertheless, the teaching and training function retains importance with universities expected to carry out about 22 per cent of the national R&D. The universities are themselves keen to increase this research profile and have specifically directed their research agenda to national priorities. Interdisciplinary and multidisciplinary collaborative research have mushroomed and a number of consultancy agencies within universities have sprung up to undertake research on a scale and range of problems not possible within existing academic structures (Singh, 1989, pp. 87–8).

In the Republic of Korea the private sector with its large industrial corporations plays a significant role in the sponsorship and execution of research. The government has tried to give the universities an important role through the establishment of the Korea Advanced Institute of Science and Technology (KAIST), which is to provide leadership in the training of élite scientists as well as in research. However, support for university research remains low. Research expenditure on university scientists is 15 per cent of that of business and industry. The role of universities is perceived largely to train the R&D personnel and to conduct all the basic research (Lee Sungho, 1989, p. 55).

In Taiwan, the universities and the Academia Sinica represent the two agencies involved in scientific research. The universities engage in both applied and basic research but research is limited to the prestigious public institutions. They receive research money from the National Science Council but this is usually inadequate for large-scale efforts (Hsieh, 1989, pp. 189–90). With the establishment of the Science-based Industrial Park, located close to several important universities, more university researchers have become involved with high-technology research (Altbach et al., 1989, p. 25).

All countries have attempted to improve the motivation and the conditions for local research. Research was recognized as a team effort to be effectively carried out in a co-operative effort. If the problems of developing countries were to be advanced, multidisciplinary teams working in close collaboration were most likely to succeed. Hence we see the setting up of such teams and project groups to carry out research in strategic development areas – marine ecology, agricultural processing, natural disaster mitigation, increasing crop and annual production, and finding alternative uses for traditional products like tin and rubber. All such projects have greatly enhanced the productivity of these countries. In countries where professors' salaries were low, efforts have been made to raise their incomes and status, as in Taiwan where the National Research Council paid supplementary research stipends. Outstanding scientists and their work are given recognition by the instituting of outstanding research awards by the professional bodies and research councils.

Singapore has introduced a package of reforms to make for a more conducive research environment. It has improved staff/student ratios, tripled the research budget, increased the ties with prestigious foreign universities in developed countries, and improved university and industry ties which have benefitted both parties. In particular excellence in research and scholarship has been paraded as an ideal to be upheld. Visiting scholars and advisory panels of outstanding calibre internationally are invited to dialogue with local scholars, advise the government and the Science Council, give directions and often set standards for research. Within the university, research and publication in respected international journals are highly regarded for promotion, and staff are given an orientation and training that leans towards research. To some extent these measures exist in other countries. All vie for international standards while maintaining a local thrust and validity in their research.

Universities clearly play a prominent role in the development of scientific research which provides the stimulus to indigenous development. By stressing research and publications for promotion they have brought scientific research into prominence. Through funding managed by national research councils, governments have managed to orient their research agendas to problems of national priority. Most importantly, universities provide the training for all technologically skilled manpower that flows into industry and other research institutes. They represent in these countries the core of highly skilled manpower to which emerging new functions can be added. Universities fulfil multiple roles in their development which no other institution has the capacity to fulfil.

The language of science

The approach the NICs have adopted to the language question in higher education is instructive. All function in the international knowledge and research system by using English, which enables them access to English-language journals and research networks, the largest pool of international scientific knowledge.

In Singapore despite official recognition of four languages – Malay, English, Mandarin and Tamil – English is in effect the only language of post secondary and higher education. All scientific journals are published in English and the government has adopted a policy of using English to be part of the international economy in trade and scientific knowledge exchange. As such, language is not an issue. A high proportion (close to 50 per cent) of the teaching staff at the National University of Singapore are foreign and teaching materials from abroad are commonly used. The other three countries have a more interesting approach to language, with lessons for other developing countries. All have used a foreign language prior to independence, all have an indigenous language as the principal medium of instruction, all have to varying degrees made provision for instruction in and the use of English in higher education and all have made tremendous efforts to develop and adapt their indigenous language capacity and vocabulary for scientific purposes.

Malaysia has gradually changed the medium of instruction from English to Bahasa Malaysia. At present all undergraduate and a high proportion of graduate courses are conducted in Bahasa Malaysia. This has been accompanied by massive efforts to provide textbooks and instructional materials in Bahasa Malaysia, spearheaded by a government-funded agency, Dewan Bahasa dan Pustaka (Language and Literature

Agency), which has promoted writing, translation and publication of texts and scholarly journals in Bahasa Malaysia. At the same time, the need for English as a language of international communication and science and technology is recognized and it is a second language for all university students ensuring that they possess at least the capacity to read and understand foreign journals and texts. Over the last few years the requirements for English have been increased and a pass in English made a condition for graduating. A considerable amount of postgraduate teaching, research and writing of theses, which are externally validated, continue to be in English. Many academic staff are competent in English and write both locally and for international publications in English. More than 90 per cent of scientific writing is in English – both locally and overseas, compared with 70 per cent, which is the norm for all the faculties (Singh, 1989, pp. 130–1).

After their bitter experience with Japan, followed by nationalist governments strongly influenced by the United States, Taiwan and the Republic of Korea made the indigenous languages the principal media of instruction at all levels of the education system while English was adopted for communication with the rest of the world. In the Republic of Korea, most of the journals are published in Korean but Taiwan has promoted a number of scientific journals for international circulation. Both countries provide English for advanced training in science and technology as many of the reference materials are in that language. Professors in the prestigious universities are rewarded by better promotion prospects if they write in English and publish in international journals.

Altbach et al. (1989) conclude that 'all four countries function in an international scientific system dominated by English and all have made adjustments to this fact'. The Republic of Korea has the longest indigenous scientific infrastructure with journals and texts published largely in Korean. In Taiwan, teaching is done in the indigenous language but texts and other materials for advanced work are largely in English. Malaysia has gone a long way to indigenization of

teaching but shortages of materials and the need to be part of an international scientific network have prompted a high degree of advanced scientific teaching, research and publication in English. Singapore's scientific teaching and research activities function wholly in English. All depend on the international scientific community for validation of their courses and postgraduate education. All place a value on publications in international journals for promotion. Such a focus keeps the link with English as a language of science and technology and also with the values and concepts of the international scientific community (Altbach et al., 1989, p. 8).

The NICs that have been examined here – the Republic of Korea, Malaysia, Singapore and Taiwan – have over the last two decades achieved quite remarkable industrial growth as a key component of overall national development. All have been imbued with the belief that education is an agent for development and in the absence of many national resources investment in education is of primary importance as the engine for change and progress. They have identified targeted growth areas within industry and manufacturing and structured their education systems to supply the necessary levels of skills for their proper functioning. In particular the higher-education systems have been developed in tandem with their industrialization policies demonstrating many of the characteristics of planned economies, with fixed growth targets and manpower forecasting aligned to intended growth patterns.

The NICs have demonstrated their ability to enforce and implement their plans through legislation and regular development plans. A number of features are pertinent: all the countries at some point in their development adopted specific measures that increased their science-and-technology capacity. Initially science enrolment and subsequently engineering and technology rather than natural science and medical enrolments were given priority; specialized institutes and centres of science and engineering, advanced study and research were established; the areas of study and research were targeted to maximize the heavy investment of scarce resources; postgraduate education was given a boost with the award of research scholarships, establishment of graduate schools in these fields and improved staff/student ratio. The Republic of Korea, Singapore and Taiwan demonstrate these qualities to a higher degree than Malaysia, but the trend in the latter is clearly towards the same pattern. Within their institutions research has gained prestige and is the most highly regarded activity of university staff. Universities are cognisant of this function and the support and environment for research has gradually improved. Mindful of their constituents, university researchers devote considerable time to consultancy and publication locally, but also remain aware of the need to maintain an international profile and standards and keep up their contacts with these research and scientific colleges. They have received encouragement from a large number of measures their institutions have introduced to stimulate and raise the quality of their research. The international dimension has been easy to maintain in these countries because they have retained an international language, in this case English, either as the primary medium of instruction as in Singapore, or as a second language, as in Malaysia, or as the language of scientific research and publication as in the Republic of Korea and Taiwan.

Higher-education systems have been shown to fulfil two essential prerequisites for industrial development. First, higher education has supplied adequate manpower quantity and quality to work at the different levels of the economy. Two clear strata have developed – one high-level scientific and professional layer for top research, managerial and executive positions in industry and a second layer that supplies the practitioners. Secondly, the specialized research institutions and universities have been able to adopt, adapt and improve the technology that has been imported. Considerable effort has been made to use technology for local development and there is evidence of fairly active scientific activity which partly interfaces with the international community but at the same time provides a focus for technology transfer and adaptation

for local developmental needs. The success of the NICs in structural adjustment and development draws attention to the role of human-resource development in development. In particular interest is focused on the contribution that higher education may make to this process. Discussions on human-resource-led development present conflicting conclusions about the crucial role of education in the take-off for industrial development. While little conclusive evidence has been adduced by research proving that higher education is a sufficient condition for development, the evidence from the NICs points to the need for higher education as a necessary condition. As has been shown, the NICs have made large investments in higher education and shaped their higher-education systems and institutions to suit their particular needs both quantitatively and qualitatively. The role of higher-education institutions as the principal producers of the scientific and technological know-how and manpower contributing to national goals and development cannot be overlooked. ∎

References and bibliography

ALTBACH P. G., et al. (eds.). 1989. *Scientific Development and Higher Education: The Case of Newly Industrializing Nations.* New York, Praeger.

BOM MO CHUNG. 1988. The Role of Government in Higher Education. Country Report: Korea. In: *The Role of Government in Asian Higher Education Systems: Issues and Prospects.* Hiroshima, Reports from the Fourth International Seminar on Higher Education in Asia, Research Institute for Higher Education, Hiroshima University.

CHOWDHURY A.: KERKPATRICK, C.H.; ISLAM, I. 1986. Structural Adjustment and Human Resources Development in ASEAN. Asian Network of Human Resource Development Planning Institutes Technical Workshop, Bangkok, 16–18 December 1986. ILO–ARTEP.

HSIEH, S. H. 1989. University Education and Research in Taiwan. In: P. G. Altbach et al. (eds.), *Scientific Development and Higher Education: The Case of Newly Industrializing Nations,* pp. 177–214. New York, Praeger.

ISAHAK HARON. 1988. The Role of the Government in Higher Education in Malaysia. *The Role of Government in Asian Higher Education Systems: Issues and Prospects.* Hiroshima,

Reports from the Fourth International Seminar on Higher Education in Asia, Research Institute for Higher Education, Hiroshima University.

KIM JONG-CHOL; HONG SAH-MYUNG. 1984. *Higher Education in Korea.* Seoul, Korean Educational Development Institute. (Contract Research Report, 84-1.)

REPUBLIC OF KOREA. NATIONAL BUREAU OF STATISTICS, ECONOMIC PLANNING BOARD. 1990. *Major Statistics of Korean Economy, 1990.* Seoul, National Bureau of Statistics.

LEE SUNGHO. 1989. Higher Education and Research Environments in Korea. In: P. G. Altbach et al. (eds.), *Scientific Development and Higher Education: The Case of Newly Industrializing Nations,* pp. 31–82. New York, Praeger.

LIM, David. 1984. *Industrial Restructuring in Singapore.* Bangkok, ILO-ARTEP. (Asian Employment Programme Working Papers.)

MALAYSIA. 1986. *Fifth Malaysia Plan, 1986–90.* Kuala Lumpur, National Printing Department.

——. 1988. *Third Malaysia Plan .* Kuala Lumpur, National Printing Department.

——. 1989. *Mid-Term Review of the Fifth Malaysia Plan 1986–90.* Kuala Lumpur, National Printing Department.

PANG ENG FONG. 1982. *Education, Manpower and Development in Singapore.* Singapore, Singapore University Press.

PANG ENG FONG; GOPINATHAN, S. 1989. Public Policy, Research Environment and Higher Education in Singapore. In: P. G. Altbach et al. (eds.), *Scientific Development and Higher Education: The Case of Newly Industrializing Nations,* pp. 137–76. New York, Praeger.

PARK YUNGCHUL. 1983. *South Korea's Experience with Industrial Adjustment in the 1970's.* Bangkok, ILO-ARTEP. (Asian Employment Programme Working Papers.)

SANYAL, B. C. 1990. *Technological Development and its Implications for Educational Planning.* Paris, International Institute for Educational Planning. (Research Report, 85.)

SANYAL, B. C.; HYUN-SOOK YU. 1989. *Technological Development in the Micro-electronics Industry and its Implications for Educational Planning in the Republic of Korea.* Paris, International Institute for Educational Planning. (IIEP Research Report, 72.)

SELTH, A. 1988. *The Development of Public Education in the Republic of Korea: An Australian Perspective.* Nathan, Queensland, Centre for the Study of Australian–Asian Relations, Division of Asian and International Studies, Nathan, Queensland, Griffith University. (Research Paper, 46.)

SINGAPORE. DEPARTMENT OF STATISTICS. 1971/72, 1986, 1990a. *Year Book of Statistics.* Singapore, Department of Statistics.

——. MINISTRY OF EDUCATION. 1990b. *Education Statistics Digest, 1990.* Singapore, Ministry of Education.

SINGH, J. S. 1989. Scientific Personnel, Research Environment and Higher Education in Malaysia. In: P. G. Altbach et al. (eds.), *Scientific Development and Higher Education: The Case of Newly Industrializing Nations,* pp. 83–136. New York, Praeger.

TAIWAN. COUNCIL FOR ECONOMIC PLANNING AND DEVELOPMENT. 1990. *Taiwan Statistical Data Book, 1989.* Taiwan, CEPD.

UNESCO. 1972–90. *Statistical Yearbook* (varied years).

WORLD BANK. 1990. *Development Report.* New York, Oxford University Press.

YI-RONG YOUNG. 1991. Higher Education and National Development in Taiwan. Paper delivered at the 1991 Bristol Conference on Higher Education and Development, Bristol (United Kingdom), 7–9 January.

The development of higher education in Eastern and Central Europe in the aftermath of recent changes

Jan Sadlak

Marxist-Leninist ideology's argument of historical determinism and its claim to conceptual superiority were put forward as the main rationales for the political legitimacy of the communist socio-economic system in the countries commonly referred to as Eastern Europe.[1] This pretended superiority was also behind profound changes in higher education and the organization of science, which were introduced in somewhat se-

Jan Sadlak (Poland/Canada). *President of the international consulting firm EastEuroConsult in Toronto and a visiting scholar with the Ontario Institute for Studies in Education. Former Executive Secretary of the Standing Conference of Rectors, Presidents and Vice-Chancellors of the European Universities (CRE) and staff member of UNESCO–European Centre for Higher Education (CEPES) in Bucharest. First editor of the CEPES journal* Higher Education in Europe, *his publications cover such issues as policy, planning, financing and governance of higher education in Eastern Europe and various OECD countries as well as relations between higher education and industry.*

rial reforms in the 'newly socialist' countries after 1948. Another characteristic feature of those reforms was that they used the organizational patterns and practices of higher education in the Soviet Union as a model, at least during the first few years. Generally speaking, the new educational policy represented a rejection of the 'old' – the so-called 'liberal-bourgeois' – idea of education and its replacement with a vision of education that would correspond to the principles of the 'new' socio-political order. Even the professional and intellectual training carried out predominantly in the higher-education institutions was perceived as 'training of cadres for the construction of socialism'. The implementation of the social policy of 'construction of socialism' led to the abolition of the previous class structure and privileges, including those of the intelligentsia. The introduction of centrally planned economies and forcefully imposed collectivization of agriculture gave the state total control over employment opportunities for higher-education graduates.

Generally speaking, the situation that higher

education had to face was to a great extent a consequence of adherence by the state to a single ideological doctrine – Marxism-Leninism – and a vision of societal organization based thereon. Higher education was made an integral part of the political system through subjecting essential decisions to the Party's ideological and political objectives. At the same time, it was also considered a part of the economic system, through subjecting admission and staff policies to centrally set manpower objectives. Pragmatically oriented research was also part of this role in fostering economic modernization. It can also be pointed out that higher education was expected to be an agent of social change – by forming a so-called 'socialist' or 'people's' intelligentsia. Implementation of this vision of higher education was frequently accompanied by the repressive behaviour of the political and state authorities towards academia. It resulted in substantial limitations of academic freedom and university autonomy, whose bottom line is the freedom to research, teach and publish without being subject to punishment because of the nature or content of what is studied or researched. Another consequence of an instrumental approach towards higher education was excessive politicization and bureaucratization in such matters as curricula, student life, research content, the process of academic appointments and international academic relations.

Recent changes in Eastern and Central Europe represent not only a rejection by the people of this region of Marxism-Leninism as the dominant ideological framework for the organization of society but also the abandonment of the concept of a state that adheres to one specific ideological order. In its place, a majority of the countries in this region are unambiguously committed to the process of democratic change based on the adoption of principles of respect for individual and group aspirations for freedom, political pluralism and a market economy. As history shows, calls for profound transformation of education have always been a part of revolutionary change, and those we are witnessing in Eastern and Central Europe only confirm this principle. Current reforms and developments in

education, especially those in higher education, represent a significant passage in the process of shaping new democratic societies which are currently burgeoning in this historically diversified part of Europe. This article looks into the direction, content and results as well as the fragility and obstacles of these changes – turning-points in higher education, with implications for whole systems of university-level education and the organization of science as well as the collective and individual interests of academics and students.

The 'socialist' model of higher education and its legacy

The interplay between the obligation to harness science and education to the ideological and political ambitions of the regime, and the pre-requisite of commitment to genuine learning and scholarship, which represent the 'ethos of university', was a general framework in which higher education functioned until very recently in Eastern Europe. This combination of diverse and sometimes contradictory expectations and tasks resulted in a relatively unstable educational policy, which led to frequently modified regulations that consequently resulted in considerable damage, impeding or retarding development of science and learning. The assumption that everything was related to the class struggle brought about a vision of education as a kind of a 'mass political arena' which made politicization of the curriculum and scholarship, especially in the humanities and social sciences, almost inevitable. For a similar reason, it was also argued that not only the state but also the Party had to participate in regulating the policy-making, governance and functioning of higher education and science. The acceptance by some academics of this new system of governance of higher education was justified by the following arguments (Rosca, 1966, p. 78):

When the orientation of the state constituted an

obstacle to the general evolution of society or to the interests of the people, the exercise of university autonomy, from a progressive standpoint, has a particularly important practical value. But when the state itself is the promoter of progressive social development, state direction does not clash with the advanced spirit of autonomy.

It is quite evident that the 'socialist' model of higher education was not an entirely static concept. There had been some relaxation of political control over higher education, for example, in Poland in 1956 and in Romania in the mid-1960s. Some advisory bodies, such as the Main Council on Higher Education in Poland, tried genuinely to represent the interests of higher education. But co-opting policy towards academia was short-lived and quickly followed by return to ideological orthodoxy and close supervision over the academic community, for example, in Poland in March 1968 and again after the imposition of marshal law in December 1981, and in Czechoslovakia after the foreign intervention and the termination in mid-1968 of the 'Prague Spring' and its aim to introduce 'socialism with a human face'. Even when new attempts at modernization were undertaken in Eastern Europe in the early 1970s in the context of the so-called 'advanced socialism' and the accompanying 'scientific and technological revolution' which resulted in substantial increase of student enrolment and some improvement of funding, the basic policy-making concepts and solutions towards higher education remained unchanged. Therefore, despite a certain degree of national variation within the original dogmatic model of 'socialist' higher education of the late 1940s and early 1950s, higher education under communism with which those countries entered the late 1980s had a number of common characteristic features. Reiterating them here will allow us a better understanding of the shared intellectual experience of the academic community in Eastern Europe as well as the scope of the present process of reforms. Generally speaking, the 'socialist' model implied the following.

First, higher education was not only a functional instrument for academic and professional training and development but also a means of political education within the ideological framework of Marxism-Leninism. Monitoring by the academic community of conformity to political and ideological objectives was an essential part of the relationship between the state and party bureaucracy and academia. Public discussion of objective academic analysis which did not fit in with official 'thinking' was considered counterproductive or even subversive. It was also a system that allowed periodic outbursts of anti-intellectualism, ideologically motivated fabrication of research as well as the application of political orthodoxy in teaching.

Secondly, policy-making and governance in the universities were co-ordinated and supervised by central political/state bodies. It was achieved through such mechanisms of control as inclusion of top academic and administrative positions within a nomenklatura system and the need of adherence to a top-down party discipline principle of 'democratic centralism'.[2] It is true that some academics played an important advisory role or occupied high positions in political and state institutions, but it cannot be said that this type of close relationship actually served the general interests of higher education. The Polish sociologist, Jan Szczepański, who was involved in political life in Poland in the 1970s, saw that the generally ineffectual role played by the academic community was very well reflected by the fact that 'professors in governments or in ruling party groups are there not as higher-education representatives' and that 'political usefulness of institutions of higher learning is not measured by internal criteria developed by them' (Szczepański, 1986, pp. 72-3). But the paradox of the functioning of universities under a communist regime was that the Party played an important, sometimes even a decisive, role in the initiation, formulation and implementation of such 'internal criteria'. The representatives of the Party were ex-officio members of the academic senate and other decision-making bodies in the academic institutions.

Thirdly, student enrolment and graduate employment were correlated with narrowly interpreted and centrally established manpower plans, while place and duration of employment of graduates were often bureaucratically assigned by the state. The argument in favour of such arrangements was based on the need to avoid regional shortages of specialists with higher-educational qualifications. The almost regular deviation from the established targets, in terms of both number of students and graduates, would indicate that these plans not only took into consideration genuine manpower needs but were no less importantly used as an instrument and expression of control by central political and administrative authorities over higher education and the intelligentsia. In arguing for the need for such a system, the state administration pointed out that higher education was 'free' and those benefiting from such a system should be obliged to respond to such employment requirements.

Fourthly, the propagation of educational equity and democratization of access to higher education was carried out as a part of the ideologically determined social policy of the Party and the state which has been artificially stressing the peasant/working-class composition of the student population. This top-down approach to social change, used as a basis for educational policy, overlooked the concealed existing differences in the preceding levels of education and the fact that social and cultural background can play a significant role in pointing to higher-education studies. As the rector of one Soviet university observed (Zhdanov, 1977, p. 144):

A child born into a family of Moscow intellectuals growing up among cultivated people will, all things being equal, have a better chance of developing his abilities on entering the university, though an attempt is made to give all new entrants an equal chance by organizing special preparatory courses, direct contacts between universities and schools, educational series on television, and so on.

Equally underestimated in policies relating access to higher education with those directed towards a 'desired' modification of the social composition of the student population was the issue of individual cost of study. Certain Polish empirical studies found that, in the case of full-time students living away from home, the parental contribution was quite high and it could even exceed a quarter of the family budget. Contributions 'in kind' by parents for students living at home, however, reduced the cost burden associated with university-level studies to around 6 per cent of the family budget (Paszkowski, 1987).

The institutional structure of higher education was modified by separating major groups of disciplines such as medicine, agriculture, etc., from the general type of universities, which were dominant before the Second World War, into more specialized institutions. The creation of national academies of sciences, based on the Soviet model, weaken even further the position of higher education with regard to research. The newly created academies – the so-called 'working academies' – were given three functions: as research centres, corporations of eminent scholars, and as state bodies supervising the conduct of research carried out in higher-educational institutions.

The elimination of the theological faculties from the universities was one of the consequences of the new institutional model of higher education. At the same time the so-called 'Party schools', which were directly run by the central committee of the Communist Party, were also made an integral part of the institutional, professional and academic network of higher education.[3] In some areas of training and research the Party schools, like the Academy of Social Sciences in Warsaw, did not only meet the needs of the Party but virtually became centres that concentrated, and to a certain extent co-ordinated, Marxist research workers in various scientific institutes in such fields as religious studies, history of the workers' movement, empirical research on living conditions, agricultural policy and theoretical and empirical research on the Communist Party (Maciszewski, 1986, p. 91). Some of them even monopolized academic and professional training, as in the case of Romania where the Stefan Gheorghiu Academy for Training and Development of Cadres was the only institution in the country with advanced programmes in the political sciences and journalism.

Academic appointments, and in some countries (e.g. Romania and the Soviet Union) also higher academic degrees, required a final acceptance by central screening and accrediting bodies. All of them resembled the Soviet proto- type – the Supreme Attestation Commission. The advocates of this system argued on the basis of the unequal quality of higher-educational in- stitutions. However, there should be little doubt that in the course of the lengthy and complex procedures, involving a variety of institutions and organizations at different levels, not only academic but also political criteria played a sig- nificant role in the outcome of such processes.

International relations of academic institu- tions and individual scholars were co-ordinated and strictly supervised by political and state bo- dies. Positive political recommendations were often a prerequisite for participation in interna- tional academic events or international research programmes. To a great extent, all international academic relations involve some concern for op- timalization of national interests and as such are subjected to economic and foreign-policy con- siderations. However those of the socialist coun- tries of Eastern Europe were carried out predo- minantly from the 'class-struggle' view of the international scene. This was particularly visible with regard to recruitment, admission policy and allocation of scholarships for foreign stu- dents. Another important aspect of international academic co-operation was the desire to expand intrabloc co-operation within the Council of Mutual Economic Assistance (CMEA) and the Conference of Ministers of Higher Education of the Socialist Countries that was founded in 1966.[4] It was argued that such an approach would accelerate the process of integration of educational and scientific potential to meet the common needs of the socialist member states. Overall, international academic relations were greatly formalized leaving only minimal scope for non-formal scholarly and student contacts.

Of course, the above picture of higher edu- cation's socialist past in Eastern Europe can be criticized as being too generalized, since it scar- cely reflects its achievements such as, for ex- ample, that despite adverse political conditions and financial restraints, many academic institu- tions were educating their countries' profession- al and intellectual élites and developing genuine high-quality research in a number of disciplines. These accomplishments definitely should not be omitted in a comprehensive study of the past de- velopment of higher education in this region. It should also be stressed that an educated pop- ulace is one of the few assets that these countries possess as they enter a new political and eco- nomic reality. At the same time, the overall in- efficiency of the 'socialist' model of higher edu- cation is nowadays generally recognized. The examples of its political, ideological and perso- nal abuses are plentiful. The part of the legacy that should particularly worry present-day re- formers of higher education is the intellectual damage done through encouragement – espe- cially in teaching – of mediocrity and the pre- sent general miserable state of the academic in- stitutions. The persistently poor economic situation and the restraints on public spending at the time of current transformation from a cen- trally planned to a market economy make the re- forming of higher education even more difficult than is usually the case with major educational reforms, such as those that are inevitable in East- ern and Central Europe.

Changes, opportunities and challenges

A critical comment made by the German philo- sopher Eric Voegelin about the relativity of long-term adherence of any higher-educational establishment to a particular concept of the 'un- iversity' can be extended to the outcome of the 'socialist' model of higher education. He warns that more than any other institution the 'un- iversity' is not 'a structure that is established once and for all, but a process in time whose course of development under certain circum- stances can deviate considerably from the in- tention of its founders' (Voegelin, 1985, p. 24).

The disappearance of the Marxist-Leninist ideological framework of higher education is the most dramatic such 'deviation' from the original 'socialist' model. The political and intellectual bankruptcy of communist ideology as defined by Marxist-Leninism, brought almost instant calls for profound conceptual and administrative transformations of higher education. The overall de-ideologization of academic life also pointed out the need to embark on a search for a 'post-socialist' model of higher education.

It is still too early to speak about the new system but it is already clear that all countries of Eastern and Central Europe are trying, albeit in different degrees and ways, to depart from the previous system. It can be stated that present higher-education systems in all the countries of the region differ from the 'socialist' model at least in one area: Marxism-Leninism no longer serves as the policy-making framework and conceptual base for setting goals towards higher education and science. It has been entirely abandoned, even in the Soviet Union. One of the first changes was a removal of unbalanced ideologization of social studies and research. At present, Eastern European universities are no longer required to teach Marxism-Leninism, which Vaclav Havel called 'the arrogant and intolerant ideology, which denigrated man into a production force and nature into a production tool' (Havel, 1990, p. 42). They also dropped previously compulsory courses of 'dialectical materialism' and replaced them with intellectually balanced social-studies courses.

Further de-ideologization of policies, governance and academic life is related to the fact that the Communist Parties in Eastern Europe not only lost their 'leading political force' status that allowed them to exercise one-party rule but, in a prevailing number of countries in the region, they have been dissolved or altogether disappeared from the political scene. As a consequence the Party 'schools' and 'academies of social studies' as well as the special research institutes, departments and chairs of Marxism-Leninism were closed or dissolved. Only a small part of their staff was re-appointed to other institutions or departments. This created substantial professional, administrative and personal problems, especially in the case of staff with tenure. Yet the breathtaking pace with which those changes have been introduced in some countries has given rise to criticism among some members of the academic community about high-handedness of the new policy-makers and administrators towards higher education. They also point out that the top-down bureaucratic way of handling these problems is contravening the process of reclaiming university autonomy. There is of course the problem of intellectual and moral credibility of the academic staff who uncritically supported, through their teaching and research, the undemocratic policies and practices of the previous regime. In fact, a relatively small part of the academic community reproach themselves for not criticizing openly the communist regime's policies.

After the enthusiastic celebrations of the disappearance of communist ideology from higher education, staff and students have to come to terms with the emerging new free-market system. There is little doubt that this new economic reality will dictate the direction and outcome of the major reforms and equally badly needed improvements of the infrastructure and facilities of higher-educational institutions. If the process of de-ideologization of academic life stresses a need for intellectual integrity, the new economic conditions of functioning of higher education in Eastern and Central Europe will inevitably result in the emergence of a more competitive and more market-oriented academic environment. This will not only bring substantial changes in rules of financing of higher education and science, relations with the state bureaucracy and the general public, but will increasingly affect the structure of higher education, organization of enrolment and distribution of students among various fields of study and staff policy. There already are observable significant changes and developments in higher education in the region.

The admission system is beginning to reflect the public and academic community's preference for meritocratic criteria for student selection. It is based on the overall negative experience with the policy measures and bureaucratic regulations favouring access to higher education based on non-academic considerations. Such opinion prevails even with regard to those measures that aimed at favouring students from disadvantaged family backgrounds, such as the so-called 'preferential point system' which functioned in Poland, with various modifications, in the years 1965–88.[5] It is assumed that the problem of educational equity has to be seen in the context of existing structural and cultural constraints which requires long-term policy directed towards elimination of selectivity at the lower levels, earlier reduction of disproportions in educational provision as well as diminution of socially based differences with regard to the choice of the type of higher-education institutions. Access will be developed, more than ever, in the context of the social demand for a particular type of higher education and greater autonomy of higher-education institutions with regard to academic standards for student admissions. At the same time, labour-market conditions are playing a much greater role in the individual decision to undertake university-level education, at what type of institution or in which particular field of study. The first signs of this new approach became already apparent with regard to part-time studies. Their number has dropped substantially. For example, the number of part-time students in Poland at the end of the 1980s dropped by more than 50 per cent in comparison with the mid-1970s. There are even those who consider that extramural or correspondence study is not legitimate for modern higher education.

The organization and content of study programmes no longer depends on central guidance. It is the responsibility of the higher-educational institution and its faculty. The rebuilding of higher education based on a market approach and the need to prepare new generations of graduates for changing economic requirements implies the reassessment of teaching priorities. In this process the less practical subjects are losing out. It is also in this context that academic schools organize remedial courses for students and faculty members to make their

training and teaching more adequate for present economic and social transformations. Another important change in study programmes is represented by various independent or private 'business schools' in which teaching is conducted mainly in English and the instructors are free-market liberal economists and internationally experienced practitioners, for example, in the International Business School in Warsaw. As students in a growing number of institutions now have a choice with regard to the subjects they are studying, it has become necessary to make rapid changes with regard to the organization of studies and conditions for graduation. Some academic schools in Czechoslovakia, Poland and the Soviet Union have already introduced a credit system as well as undergraduate and graduate degrees based on the model used by American research universities. This new system will most likely facilitate, better than the traditional one, such things as national and international mobility of students and graduates. The number of specializations, especially in the technological studies, has been reduced, which is understandable when we take into account that, for example, there used to be more than 500 specializations in Soviet engineering studies.

The return to principles of academic freedom and university autonomy which eliminated the nomenklatura system for senior academic and administrative positions has been accompanied by the substantial increase and diversity in collective representation of academics and students. Some of the bodies and organizations have merely to be reactivated, such as, for example, the Rectors' Conference of the Academic Schools, which played an important role in representing interests of Polish higher education before the communist era, or various student fraternities. In the countries where such autonomous self-representation hardly existed, new organizations are to be founded. For example, in October 1989, the Association of Universities of the USSR was established, which represented the country's twenty-eight major universities. At its second congress, held in May 1990, it was deemed necessary to deal with such problems as

Jan Sadlak

the role of universities in the new economic conditions prevailing in the transition to a market economy and the means of enhancing university autonomy, which implies the complete independence of the universities in accordance with the rights guaranteed by federal and republican constitutions and in accordance with individual university statutes.[6] This agenda has not been accidental, as these two issues – autonomy and adaptation – are the current watchwords of present structural changes concerning higher education in Eastern and Central Europe.

The recently achieved right for self-organization and liberalization of the administrative regulations for founding associations have affected even more the open forms of student activism. At present, the number and type of student associations are becoming hard to keep up with. There is a great variety of student organizations, and the majority of them represent or relate to the religious liberal economic or political philosophy as well as those representing ecological and pacifist movements. The present diversity of student organizations in each country is probably even greater than that in the society as a whole.

The long-term inefficiency of the centrally planned economic system has resulted in the general underfunding of higher education. There is hardly a country in the region that does not require major improvements of outdated research facilities in higher-education institutions, libraries, student residence halls as well as a reduction in financial hardship that affects both students and academics. The existing salary structure in academic institutions and the conditions on the labour market for higher-education graduates have to be modified; otherwise there is a risk that an excessive number of highly trained academics will search for employment abroad or leave academic institutions altogether. There is also a possibility of a decline in applicants in those fields of study that are intellectually demanding but not financially rewarding (e.g. engineering and natural sciences). Such developments do not go unnoticed, and the dominant view is that, in order to countervail this trend,

economic – not administrative – measures will have to be devised. It is also in this context that political accountability has been replaced by economic accountability in higher education. As a consequence many aspects of funding of higher education will require a major overhaul. The often inaccurate concept of so-called 'free education' will also have to be redefined. Even if academic institutions are encouraged to take their financial matters into their own hands and to look for improvements through such initiatives as charging for special programmes or language courses, consulting services and even commercial land development on which they are situated, public funding will remain the principal source of financing of higher education.

Various initiatives like the launching of 'private' universities such as the Ecological University of Bucharest or the initiating by the Soros Foundation, a University of Central Europe, which is planned to operate as a multi-campus network of colleges in academic centres of Central Europe (its colleges were already established in Prague, Bratislava and Budapest), all show that there is no shortage of local and international initiatives to invigorate the institutional diversity of higher education in Eastern and Central Europe. But their actual impact on higher education is still to be seen. It is quite likely that existing institutional structures within higher education systems will prevail, except that of the former German Democratic Republic, which is being integrated into that of a unified Germany. After several rapidly introduced administrative and organizational reforms, we can observe a relatively slower period of constructive co-existence and the introduction of various transitional programmes in teaching and research. Bearing in mind the amount of needed improvement in quality of teaching and research as well as the need for modernization of infrastructure of the academic institutions in the former German Democratic Republic, it is estimated that the whole process of merging the two systems could take up to five years.

Overall, it is only a matter of time before the academic vitality of the academic institution

– a 'critical mass' of excellence in teaching, research and services – will also affect the financial conditions of the particular institute or department. In the Soviet Union industry is already being asked to share the institutional cost of engineering studies. The cost, which varies from 3,000 to 25,000 roubles, is stipulated in the agreement between the particular institution and the industrial enterprise. Under such conditions, industry will be more and more concerned with the quality of graduates, while institutions with highly prized graduates will receive higher benefits.

A certain number of institutions, especially those created mainly for political reasons or those lacking academic vitality, will have to be transformed or even closed. For example, it is estimated that at least 10 per cent of Poland's higher-educational institutions will be closed for such reasons in the next ten years.[7] It is very likely that institutional and individual programme evaluation will be carried out through the external accreditation process. But it is still too early to say how this process will be organized and administered. It appears that the benefits of the accreditation that were proposed in the Soviet Union go beyond academic privilege. 'Strong institutions', those that will get federal accreditation for five years, will receive 'good state financial backing', have the right to enter joint ventures with Soviet and foreign companies and their diplomas will also carry a 'special mark'.[8]

Probably the most visible transformation with respect to the aftermath of recent changes in Eastern and Central Europe took place with regard to international academic relations. They are no longer dependent on political approval or subjected to ideologically determined foreign-policy objectives. Development of international co-operation has gained additional significance as many institutions and academics see it as an important venue to catch up with international scholarly standards. Therefore, it is not surprising that universities, academics and students in Eastern and Central Europe so eagerly embark on reinvigorating existing programmes such as those carried out by the German Academic Exchange Agency, DAAD (Deutscher Akademischer Austauschdienst), or the British Council, and entirely new initiatives of the West to aid 'newly emancipated' higher education such as those funded by the European Community's TEMPUS (Trans-European Mobility Scheme for University Studies). There are also a number of new smaller programmes such as short study visits sponsored by the American Collegiate Consortium for East–West Cultural and Academic Exchanges, which acts on behalf of a group of thirty-five private colleges in the United States. It can even be said that there is an entirely new mechanism of international academic relations in the region. For example, such a body as the Conference of Ministers of Higher Education of Socialist Countries, which was founded in 1966 and whose aim was the co-ordination and promotion of the 'socialist' model of higher education, lost both political and practical significance. Its last session took place in October 1989 in Bucharest. Its journal *Sovremennaya Vysshaya Shkola* (*Contemporary Higher Education*), published since 1973 in Russian with short English summaries and, since 1976, also in a Spanish version, was devoted to higher education in 'socialist countries' and 'communist' education of students. Its editorial policy has been changed to that of an international journal to be opened to 'the largest international scholarly community concerned with higher education'.

Another international organization affected by the de-ideologization of international academic relations is the International Union of Students (IUS) whose headquarters are located in Prague. It was a stronghold of the official student organization in Eastern Europe and radical student organizations in other parts of the world, but many of its activities appeared to be closely correlated with Soviet-bloc foreign policy.

Even if only indirectly related to research activities carried out in Eastern European higher-education institutions, the research institutes created mainly in the 1970s within the CMEA's ambitious programme of co-operation in science and technology, played to some extent a positiven role in fostering international co-operation between researchers in academic institutions. The new situation in the region and the probable dissolution of CMEA, will lead to the closing of those programmes. It is still to early to say what kind of bilateral or regional co-operation will come in their place.

At a time when old, ideologically motivated and greatly inefficient forms of co-operation are disappearing, new organizations and programmes are emerging. The new form of regional co-operation is represented by the Conference of Baltic University Rectors, which was founded in March 1990, with a particular focus on academic co-operation in the area of environmental problems among the countries of the Baltic region. The new Western-modelled academic institutions are endowed as well. A good example of such development has been the recently established Collegium Budapest, which is an international institute of advanced studies similar to Princeton University and the Wissenschaftskolleg in Berlin, where scholars concentrate on internationally relevant research themes. Predictably, pan-European academic organizations are gaining new significance and their membership growing due, *inter alia,* to the increased participation of East and Central European countries that see it as a re-affirmation of their European links with academic institutions in the West. For example, the Standing Conference of Rectors, Presidents and Vice-chancellors of the European Universities (CRE) which in 1988 had some 350 members – the heads of major university-level institutions, in 22 countries – now has some 470 members in 28 European countries, out of which 40 members are from former Eastern-bloc countries.

Conclusions

The previous 'socialist' model of higher education which tried to combine educational and professional activity, increased acquisition of knowledge and loyalty to Marxist-Leninist ideology, has failed. The bureaucratic governance of education and science inflicted many ills and problems on to higher education in Eastern and Central Europe, which are not going to be cured overnight. However, even if some of these countries are still in the throes of democratization and the effectiveness of new governments is sometimes questioned, the new political and economic reality in this region is quite evident. The developments in higher education discussed in this article show that every Eastern and Central European country has abandoned the 'socialist' model of higher education, but by no means has this rid higher education of problems of the past and dilemmas concerning the future. The repudiation of the political and ideological straitjacket has resulted not only in the rise of democratic expectations but also the need to address new issues. The key to successful coping with the complex process of change is the search for the appropriate vision for each society in this region of the democratic and active society – a society willing and able to be its own master. It is as much an educational problem as an economic, political and cultural one.

The profound transformations in higher education in this region are part of this desired course of development. Unfortunately, the point is sometimes overlooked that universities and other academic institutions have an important role to play in the democratization process and functioning of the 'civic' state. Higher education as a whole has status and responsibilities that can have a lasting effect on society. Universities have a large audience. Academia possesses an expertise over vast areas of knowledge that stretch from the past to the future. It can be particularly effective and credible, especially if it remains consistently constructive in being critical of reality, where fallacies in thinking are quickly revealed, and by being adept at solving problems. Even if academic institutions compete between themselves for scarce resources and prestige, their main interests, both nationally and internationally, are more often common than exclusive. However, some caution is advised, too. Traditionally, the academic community possesses more passion than power. This could be observed during the events that followed recent democratic revolutions in Eastern and Central Europe. Resentment towards intellectuals and students, as was demonstrated during the miners' intervention in Bucharest in June 1990, does not give unqualified confidence in public support for the academic community. Despite the general decline in student enrolment, it is not unusual to encounter the view that higher education is overdeveloped in relation to the countries' ability to provide adequate employment and existing budgetary resources. Low demand for new technologies from a greatly antiquated industry undermines even further public support for more generous financing of research activities in higher education.

As I have tried to show, higher education in Eastern and Central Europe has, despite numerous difficulties, made an auspicious start in the direction of modernization. Many of the abnormalities and anachronistic features of the former model of higher education have been eliminated. But we should also bear in mind when evaluating the ongoing transformations that typically the final outcome of the major educational reforms reflect a balance between high idealism and pragmatic compromise. No less important for the pace of reforms are the economic difficulties that higher education in this region is facing today. There is also a real danger that the rapid transition to a market economy, which according to some economists resembles a 'rush towards capitalism', might impoverish academic life even further. Therefore, the advice given by J. K. Galbraith (1990, p. 51) that 'moderation, not ideology, must again be the rule' is probably even more valid for higher education than economic systems, especially if we take into consideration how sensitive educational and academic activities are with regard to the human factor.

The disappearance of communism as a unifying element in the region unleashed a number of centrifugal forces, one of them being a revival of nationalism. Its repercussions are also observable in academic life. The most recent one is the unsuccessful effort to re-establish the Hungarian University in Romania.[9] It is not in the interest of higher education in this region to become entangled in this type of conflict as it would hamper the efforts to regain a 'European dimension'. The chant 'Europe is with us' by students demonstrating in Bucharest in December 1989 has been a call for support as much as a declaration of belonging to a certain, even if somewhat amorphous, concept of Europe and its cultural identity.

It is also appropriate to see recent changes in Eastern and Central Europe, as well as those in higher education, in the context of rapidly advancing economic integration of Western Europe, and inevitably following the new political and social reality of Europe. The forthcoming Western European integration after 1992 can be seen both as an opportunity but also as a danger for the division of Europe within new boundaries. In such a context international academic relations gain additional significance. At present, when the societies in Eastern and Central Europe and their academic institutions struggle to rebuild their economies, establish working democratic mechanisms, and reclaim their place in the international arena, international co-operation is rightly perceived as an important way of overcoming constraints of meagre financial resources. But all parties participating in such co-operation should also keep in mind that promotion of knowledge and science through international academic co-operation is primarily pursued by the promotion of excellence. Thus international co-operation should avoid, especially in the long run, one-way traffic in implementing this vital form of academic dialogue.

Altogether, the reforming process of higher education in Eastern and Central Europe should allow it to reaffirm and embrace its European humanistic traditions, show its constant readiness and desire to attain universally valid knowledge and seek inspiration from a dialogue of different cultures, as well as confirm its observance of universal principles of academic autonomy and academic freedom. These are only the major elements of the scenario for the modernization of higher education in the region. As it has been presented above, the first steps have already been taken. Others' experience offers some examples of mistakes to be avoided and solutions to be adopted. But there is no perfect or universal model of higher education, and it is worth bearing in mind that searching for its own model of the 'modern university' is an important part of building the vision of a democratic society.   ∎

Notes

1. Europe itself sometimes being called a *géométrie variable*, implies difficulty in making precise and unbiased regional divisions. Therefore in order to counterbalance an arbitrary bipolar geopolitical division of Europe into 'Western' and 'Eastern', it is now argued that the term 'Eastern and Central Europe' better reflects the cultural and economic diversity of this part of Europe.
2. The characteristic feature of 'democratic centralism', the organizational principle of the communist parties, has been described as 'the electivity of all executive bodies from top to bottom, their accountability to their party organization and to higher bodies, subordination of the minority to the majority, and the obligation of lower bodies to observe the decisions of higher ones. Democratic centralism also forms the basis of the organization of the state apparatus, economic management bodies, and all social organizations in a socialist society'. See D. Dmiterko and V. Pugachev, 'Democratic Centralism', *What is the Working People's Power?*, p. 217, Moscow, Progress Publishers, 1986.
3. A particular situation that existed in Poland were universities that were state-recognized but administered by the Roman Catholic Church – Lublin Catholic University and two small academies of theology. The Faculty of Protestant Theology remained part of the former German Democratic Republic's Humboldt University in Berlin.
4. The composition of this body varied. In the 1980s the following countries took part in its work: Afghanistan, Angola, Bulgaria, Cuba, Czechoslovakia, the Democratic People's Republic of Korea, Democratic Yemen, Ethiopia, the German Democratic Republic, Hungary, Mongolia, Mozambique, Nicaragua, Poland, Romania, the USSR and Viet Nam.
5. The additional points for 'social origin' were important for only a small percentage of applicants from working-class or peasant backgrounds to gain admission to higher-education institutions, especially the more prestigious ones like polytechnics and medical academies (estimated to be between 1 and 2 per cent). The remainder in any case would have been either admitted or failed on the basis of their entrance examinations results alone. See, for example, B. Witkowska, 'Doskonalenie systemu rekrutacji na studia wyzsze [Improvements in the Admission System to Higher Education]', *Zycie Szkoly Wyzszej*, Vol. XXXVII, No. 4, 1989, pp. 165–77.

6. 'Resolution of the Second Congress of the Association of Universities of the USSR', *CRE-Action*, No. 3, 1990, pp. 86–7.
7. B. Bollag, 'Universities in Poland Face New Financial Trouble', *The Chronicle of Higher Education*, 9 January 1991, pp. A45, A48.
8. See the presentation of the proposed accreditation system in the Soviet Union made by V. Severtsev from the State Committee for Public Education in S. Massey, 'Soviet Union: Giving Autonomy to Soviet State University . . .', *The Chronicle of Higher Education*, 13 February 1991, pp. A39–40.
9. For an analysis of this issue, see J. Sadlak, *Higher Education in Romania, 1860-1990: Between Academic Mission, Economic Demands and Political Control*, Buffalo, N.Y., State University of New York at Buffalo, Graduate School of Education Publications, 1990.

References

GALBRAITH, K. J. 1990. The Rush to Capitalism. *The New York Review of Books*, 25 October, pp. 51, 58.

HAVEL, V. 1990. President Vaclav Havel's New Year's Address (excerpts). *Newsweek*, 15 January, p. 42.

MACISZEWSKI, J. 1986. Research and Teaching in the Academy of Social Sciences. *Zycie Szkoly Wyzszej* (English edition), Vol. XXXIV, pp. 91–98.

PASZKOWSKI, J. 1987. W sprawie indywidualnych kosztów ksztalcenia (On the Issue of Individual Costs of Study). *Zycie Szkoly Wyzszej*, Vol. XXXV, No. 2, pp. 99–105.

ROSCA, A. 1966. Address at the Session on the University's Autonomy. *Report of the Fourth General Conference of the International Association of Universities*, pp. 78–9. Paris, International Association of Universities.

SZEPAŃSKI, J. 1986. Institutions of Higher Education and Economic and Social Crisi. *Zycie Szkoly Wyzszej* (English edition), Vol. XXXIV, pp. 65–76.

VOEGELIN, E. 1985. The German University and the Order of German Society: A Reconsideration of the Nazi Era. *The Intercollegiate Review*, Vol. XX, No. 3, pp. 7–27.

ZHDANOV, Y. A. 1977. Training Graduates as Innovators and Agents of Change. *The Contribution of Higher Education in Europe to the Development of Changing Societies* (Proceedings of UNESCO–CEPES Symposium. Bucharest, 21–23 September 1976). Bucharest, UNESCO–CEPES, pp. 143–48.

Changing higher-education policy

Three Western models

Osmo Kivinen and Risto Rinne

Two fundamental characteristics of universities are autonomy and internationalism. Kerr (1990) has argued that for 2,000 years higher learning maintained its character as a community transcending national and other boundaries; only 500 years ago did this international community of learning begin to split into national institutions, serving the functions of reinforcing nationality and training national élites. The nation-states needed the universities' support. Nowadays, while on the one hand research is increasingly international, national governments are also increasingly interested in using the universities to promote national wealth. Kerr

Osmo Kivinen (Finland). *Sociologist. Director of Research Unit for the Sociology of Education (RUSE) and Docent in Sociology at the University of Turku. Recently author of research on higher-education policy and author of several books and articles on the sociology of education, the history of education systems and questions of educational deviances and inequality.*

Risto Rinne (Finland). *Associate Professor of the Sociology of Education and Planning and the Chair of the Board of the Research Unit for the Sociology of Education (RUSE) at the University of Turku. Specialist in the sociology and history of education, recently in the fields of higher-education and adult-education policy and author of numerous books and articles in the field.*

(1990, p. 5) has called this relationship one of 'dual identity', poised between a mythical academic heaven and an actual earthly hell. On the other hand, signs are also becoming visible of a new reconvergence, and the emergence of the 'cosmopolitan-national' university.

With increasing internationalization, competition is taking on more and more significance as a means of control of higher education. Whatever fiction may be preached concerning the nominal equality of different components in the higher-education system, intensifying competition inevitably means the formation and reinforcement of institutional hierarchies (Neave, 1989, p. 360).

The markedly hierarchical systems in countries such as the United Kingdom, France or Japan produce towering peaks of excellence, but simultaneously close the doors of advancement to the masses, and even exclude large sections of the higher-education institutions themselves outside the inner élite. In contrast, the gentle rolling landscapes of higher education in Italy encourage openness and social mobility, but discourage the emergence of summits of excellence (see Clark, 1983, p. 256). On the one hand, institutional hierarchy offers a form of quality control: responding to the evaluations by both public and expert opinion, it rewards competent operation with status, prestige and resources. On the other hand, although the American system, with its openness and free market mechanisms, can produce a few centres of excellence, these are far outnumbered by the merely average, indeed mediocre, colleges.

As long ago as the beginning of the twentieth century, Max Weber (1974, pp. 20–1) pointed out that there was no more guarantee that the interests of science or the academic community would be met through the means of universities financed or maintained by the state than through those formerly under the control of the Church. Weber was seriously concerned about the danger that the role of the state, as the vehicle of political power, could lead to the castration of academic freedom.

By the end of the century the question at the centre of debate on universities (in Europe, at least) would appear to concern the tug-of-war between market attraction and state governance in steering the future development of higher education. In the last instance, however, the most important question is how can the academic community preserve its autonomy, its identity, and its vitality amid the turbulent changes currently under way at both the national and international levels?

Size and integration: structural factors in higher education

'In every advanced society, problems associated with higher education are problems associated with growth', argued Trow (1974, p. 55) in his OECD report in the mid-1970s. For a more carefully focused analysis, however, we need to distinguish between three factors: (a) the rate of growth of higher education; (b) the size of the university system; and (c) the rate of population growth in the generation entering higher education at any given time. Rapid growth and the scale of the higher-education system create problems in terms of integration and governance. The growth in the size of the generation entering higher education, on the other hand, raises questions related to the changing societal role of the university. The impact of this form of

growth has in fact made the university more central in society, and contributed to the formation of social stratification.

Trow's division of universities into three stages in terms of recruitment is familiar. In the élite university phase, entry to higher education was open to a small minority, below 10 per cent of the age-group. An academic education was the privilege of the minority, and those who received it were able to move on in positions of privilege within society, as judges, physicians and schoolteachers. Once more than 15 per cent of each generation gains access to the university, however, we enter the age of the mass university. The third phase, that of the universal university, is defined by Trow as occurring when more than half of each generation enters higher (or perhaps 'tertiary') education; and this stage has now been reached both in the United States and in a few other countries. Finland, however, with 20 per cent entering higher education, is still far from this point.

Alongside institutional size, student numbers, and the proportional recruitment within each generation, a further central structural factor in the higher-education system is the degree of integration (Teichler, 1988): that is, the extent to which any particular national system is in-

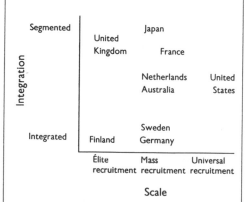

FIG. 1 National higher-education systems in terms of scale and integration. After: Lane 1989, p. 45; see also Teichler, 1988.

tegrated or segmented. Scale and integration thus furnish the two dimensions of a field in terms of which the structural differences between various national higher-education systems can be classified. In the following, this field will be simplified into three contrasted models of the university.

American, West European, and Nordic higher-education models

Any attempt to discuss higher education in the United States or Western Europe inevitably involves considerable generalization and simplification. The substantial differences that exist between the universities and colleges throughout the United States and in the many nations of Western Europe must not be forgotten. Nor within the countries of Northern Europe, represented in this article by Finland, organized on a standardized model. None the less, it may be fruitful to consider these as constituting three distinct types: the university in the United States, Western Europe and Northern Europe.

THE UNITED STATES

It is argued by Trow (1979, p. 191) that in Europe, with the expansion of higher education, and especially of the non-university sector, supply is currently in excess of demand. The situation is extremely different in the United States, where both the market and competition operate on a completely different scale. Not only does the United States have an extensive private university sector, but even within the public sector, each university's or college's budget is closely linked to the number of students it trains. If a college's student enrolment falls, so does its budget. Higher education in the United States is thus characterized by severe competition, powerful specialization, and major differences in status between institutions.

Similarly, American higher education is analysed by Rhoades (1987) in the context of a consumer society: its major distinguishing characteristic in comparison with European systems, he argues, is the fact that it is market-driven and open (based on student demand). Neither the Federal nor the state governments attempt to control higher education in detail; operations are strongly steered through the consumers' financial choices, rather than the politicians' political priorities, although many of the private universities and colleges are also heavily financed by public money.

The number of students in higher education in the United States is today around 13 million, that is, approximately the same as the total combined populations of Norway, Denmark and Finland. The numbers of teaching and research staff in the United States amount to around 800,000: a number similar to the total student enrolment in higher education in the United Kingdom (and eight times the student enrolment in Finland). These figures provide some idea of the scale of the higher-education markets involved (Clark, 1990; Trow, 1989).

The American universities are able to recruit their personnel from a wide labour market, which in turn offers a wide range of employment to the students who graduate. Mobility among the graduate population is evidently high in comparison with other societies; and the labour markets decide many questions.

The student body in a universal higher-education system such as that in the United States is obviously not highly selected, as it is in Europe, though there is intense competition for entrance to the élite universities. No central legislation or organization is in charge of American higher education. Almost 2,000 private universities and colleges operate under boards of lay trustees, and the 1,500 or so public institutions under the supervision of state or local authorities are also, in many cases, governed by lay boards. Higher education in the United States is thus both the most extended, and the most decentralized system of post-secondary education in the world today (Trow, 1989, p. 369).

Moreover, the higher-education system in

the United States is in a constant state of flux. Under the combined impact of market forces, the law of supply and demand, the birth and mortality rates for colleges are high. Between 1974 and 1986, for example, approximately 500 new colleges were created, and over 100 closed down (Trow, 1989, p. 376).

In the United States, the operation of a free market in higher education means, first of all, that the output of the universities is not the result of centralized planning or decisions. Secondly, since there are so many rival producers, their operations are dominated by competition for clients. This also means that academic standards, curricula, and modes of operation are free to develop in literally hundreds of different directions (Trow, 1989, p. 377).

The central market mechanism consists of factors affecting the status of departments or colleges. Market shifts are thus based not merely on profit, but on prestige. Status is an important commodity and bargaining counter. Relative prestige steers not only the choices of consumers and employees, but also a wide range of attitudes and behaviour affecting the institutions. Universities and departments that have acquired high prestige have a clear effect on others. They provide models for academic operation, trends and modes, which academic drift then pressures other institutions to follow (Clark, 1983, 1990).

Clark (1990) lists five features as fundamentally characteristic of higher education in the United States:

Large size, creating vast markets handling millions of students.

Radical decentralization of control, with virtually no governance exercised by either Federal or state authorities.

Extreme institutional diversity, with the parallel existence of public and private institutions of many distinct types, and the clear formation of status hierarchies.

Intense competition, one of the major points of contrast with European institutions of higher education.

High institutional initiative, since conditions of intense competition and extreme decentralization promote an entrepreneurial spirit-

and the taking of initiatives among the staff of the colleges and universities.

When something takes place under state control, argues Clark, the characteristic mode of thinking is based on the statistics of 'adding up': 'OECD reviews themselves are exercises in adding things up'. The American experts were constantly asked by the OECD panel: 'How do you plan this, how do you plan that, how do you integrate everything into a meaningful whole, how do you make things add up?' (Clark, 1990, p. 18). Where a field such as higher education is operating in a market context, however, it becomes by definition decentralized. Things can no longer be added up and collated under a single heading: they have to be left where they are, in their functional context. The whole concept of system therefore becomes radically different.

In the American system, in fact, the major co-ordination takes place not through government, but through (a) the activities of a network of voluntary associations, and (b) the operations of the market (Clark, 1990; Rhoades, 1987).

The American decentralized system predicates the existence of autonomous contacts and links between the individuals affiliated to the various universities, colleges, departments, etc., for example, those working in a particular disciplinary field. It is claimed that the values and preferences of the American academic public make them much more willing to participate as activists in the work of voluntary associations than as organization men or women in a bureaucracy. Voluntary associations, for Americans, represent a means of keeping the bureaucracy at bay; but at the same time, they provide the administration of the universities with a mechanism for avoiding the dangers that rampant competition presents (Clark, 1990).

Voluntary, autonomous co-ordination is thus an integral element in American academic life and in its institutional development. When a need for links is perceived, the bonds are brought into being; when the challenge has passed, redundant links can be allowed to wither away. Voluntary associations thus promote flexible, constantly changing, even once-off co-ordination on a scale not met with in other societies.

WESTERN EUROPE

In Europe, market forces have not steered the development of education so profoundly. Education has partly been seen as a component in state-led social policy, and higher education has mainly been built under state funding and control. Trow (1989, p. 382) goes so far as to argue that Europeans (in contrast to the populist Americans) consistently aim at preventing the unqualified masses from exercising influence over the field of higher education and thus over the direction of high culture, and at maintaining this field in the hands of an élite. This élitism, he argues, can be seen in the way that higher education is structured so as to exclude market forces and consumer pressures from questions of access, content or modes of operation. In European universities, the establishment of a new discipline typically comes about only after careful deliberation by central authorities as to needs and standards, whereas in the United States, new academic subjects can emerge as a result of the laws of supply and demand (Trow, 1989, p. 384).

In the context of European integration, the central tension in higher education is that between harmonization and diversification. Since the 1960s, the national higher-education systems in Europe have been developing in centrifugal directions partly spontaneously, partly as a consequence of deliberate policy. Each nation-state has built up its own system of higher education. Under the pressure of increasing student flows, these have then fragmented in distinct ways into differentiated levels and sectors (Cerych, 1989; Neave, 1989). Alongside the traditional university, dedicated to science and scholarship, there has thus come into being an expanding non-university sector, comprising a wide variety of more vocationally oriented colleges, open university institutions, post-experience training, etc. (Teichler, 1990). National governments have become increasingly keen to make use of higher education in the pursuit of economic growth and national welfare. Paradoxically, in countries which traditionally operated highly centralized systems of governance in

higher education, this has led to decentralization: the granting of increased autonomy, together with direct measures of Government policy, in order to promote competition and market sensitivity (Cerych, 1989). On the other hand, in the 1980s universities have been increasingly called to account for their results, with the consequent need to create of evaluation systems by which such results can be assessed.

In most European countries, access to higher education is restricted by means of matriculation examinations at the end of secondary education, by entrance selection procedures, and by student quotas laid down by the central authorities. Despite the shrinking size of the generations now reaching university age, there seems to be little evidence of cuts in student quotas or of any abandonment of the monitoring of student quality or quantity (Neave, 1989, p. 353). Belief in the rationale of state governance and control of higher education continues to prevail in Europe, despite the beginnings of a reliance on consumer- and market-driven forces.

With the growth of the non-university sector in Western Europe, however, a significantly new situation has come into being. There can be no doubt that the university has opened up, taken on new tasks, entered into closer relations with industry and business, taken up the development of extramural training. Not only have the colleges in the non-university sector, and the quasi-professional occupations associated with these, set out under the pressures of academic drift in quest of university-like status for themselves; but the university itself, too, has set out along new paths, and surrendered its role as the ivory tower of pure science and scholarship (Neave, 1989; Kerr, 1982, 1987).

Cerych (1985, pp. 7–8, 1989) believes that the attitudes towards the relationship between higher education and industry has changed fundamentally in Western Europe since the 1970s: 'Today, all governments, irrespective of political allegiance, are calling for this kind of co-operation and introducing such measures as they regard appropriate in order to facilitate it.' Hence the rise all over Europe of science parks and other joint ventures between universities and industry: shared facilities, consultancies, training courses, research contracts, etc. And this in sharp contrast to the way in which such co-operation occurs in the United States. Behind it all, in Europe looms what Neave (1984) has called the 'evaluative state'.

FINLAND: THE NORDIC MODEL

The nations of Northern Europe share a high standard of living and a strong welfare system, in which education is awarded a central role in the creation of national welfare and identity. The state has taken on responsibility for the maintenance and supply not only of welfare and health services, but of educational services also. The state is the major source of funds for higher education. Student flows, curricular organization, in fact the entire higher-education system, are governed through an extensive machinery of parliamentary and supplementary legislation, rules and regulations, and (not least) the state budget.

In Finland, higher education proper includes neither a private sector nor (strictly speaking) a non-university sector. There are perhaps few Western countries in which higher education is organized entirely in state institutions each of which, in principle, is intended to perform all the formal functions of a university: to engage in research, and on the strength of this to provide teaching at both undergraduate and postgraduate levels (up to and including the doctorate).

The Finnish university model has emerged in its present form out of the interacting pressures of expansion, central planning, and regional policy during the 1960s and 1970s. In three decades, the numbers of students have tripled, and the twenty institutions of higher education now have a joint enrolment of just over 100,000 students. Administrative reforms have led to an explosive increase in administrative personnel, who now clearly outnumber the professoriate. As a result of curricular reforms, studies have been reorganized on the basis of more vocationally oriented 'degree programmes', in-

cluding some not previously represented within the university, and the lower B.A. degree was (against the universities' own wishes) abolished (Kivinen and Rinne, 1991).

The central principles running through Finnish higher-education policy during the 1960s and 1970s were linked to the social theses of regional policy and educational democracy. In the 1980s, however, effort switched to harnessing the universities to the pursuit of national welfare and competitiveness on international markets. Fences between higher education and business and industry were pulled down; universities and departments were urged to compete with each other, and an enterprise culture was encouraged. Management by results, evaluation and managerialism are all familiar terms in the Finnish higher-education debate. A variety of technology centres, post-experience training, industrial retraining, and a wide range of commercial operations are all expanding rapidly (Kivinen and Rinne, 1990).

Competition between universities in Finland, therefore, where it exists at all, operates under centralized state supervison. It is the state that decides on the universities' budgets, on building projects, on the establishment of senior posts, on the acquisition of large-scale equipment, on student quotas or on the establishment of new curricular degree programmes. In the absence of any private sector of higher education, the 'market' in Finland is therefore very limited.

Consumer demand has very little impact on shaping higher education; indirectly at best, from political pressures and interests operating through the state's machinery. In Finland it is not normal practice to close down or transfer colleges, departments, or even individual posts. University entrance is restricted. On the other hand, cracks have appeared in the public image of a unified, consistent university system. Plans are afoot for the establishment of vocationally oriented colleges; and the encouragement offered to the competition principle will inevitably lead to the increasing hierarchicization of higher education and to increasing market impact.

The proposals for a shift towards freer markets and for the partial dismantling of state control run into many problems, however. One of the most serious is that in a country with a total population of only around 5 million, the markets are too small. The northern and eastern periphery of the country is thinly settled, with a powerful attraction of population towards the south; for the universities in the north and east of the country, it may prove difficult to maintain an adequate supply of qualified staff, or indeed of willing students. Radical deregulation could possibly lead to a situation where only a few of the present twenty universities, scattered around the country, would survive; but this would be incompatible with the principles of regional and social planning which have so far steered higher-education policy.

The higher-education system in Finland could therefore be characterized as an inverted mirror-image of that in the United States:

Small size, creating restricted markets.

Strict centralization of control of resources.

Formal institutional uniformity, with no hierarchy ostensibly recognized.

Restricted competition, exercised with respect not to markets, students, or business, but to state-controlled resources.

Low institutional initiative, since conditions of strict centralization inhibit the taking of initiatives, the challenge of bureaucratic rule in the universities, or the development of an entrepreneurial spirit.

Finland thus exemplifies at least in some respects the Nordic model of a planned economy and a welfare state, characterized by the belief that society's political and administrative élite (in principle, the people's elected representatives) are better equipped than the market to govern higher education. Pressures for a modification of this model are however increasingly apparent.

Universities and Europe in the 1990s

In addition to pressures for increased market sensitivity, a further factor affecting the future development of the universities is the constantly expanding number of adult students, both as mature students on degree programmes and on a wide range of short-term training courses. Postgraduate training is also becoming increasingly central to the tasks of the university (Neave, 1985).

Neave (1985) and van Vught (1990) have identified five trends characteristic of governments' higher-education policies during the 1980s, permeated by a contradiction between the continuation of powerful state interventionism, and the move towards granting increased autonomy to the institutions of higher education (van Vught, 1990):

Budget cuts, partly against the background of ageing populations throughout the Western world, and the consequent shift towards investing more on the needs of senior citizens. In some countries (e.g. the United Kingdom), the implementation of the cuts is being left to the universities themselves; in others (e.g. France), the government is taking the decisions. In either case, the implications for higher education are serious.

Pressures for efficiency, including demands for reduced durations of study, fewer dropouts, and in general more results for less funding.

Managerialism, involving increased recognition of external interest groups, the introduction within the universities of strategic management geared towards the achievement of pre-stated objectives and the monitoring of results, and an emphasis on the values of enterprise culture.

Conditional contracting, that is, the replacement of block funding by an on-going process of negotiation between the universities and the state, under which funding is tied to specific objectives and to the monitoring of results.

The introduction of evaluation systems into higher education as part of normal procedure, with a shift from a priori to post facto assessment not of objectives but of results.

It may be presumed that all of these trends will continue powerfully during the 1990s.

It is frequently argued that Europe needs to learn from the United States. By this is meant, in the first place, the recognition of the priority of competition. Unless a country is also prepared to courses. Post-graduate training is also becoming it will be unable to apply the American lesson. A shift to intense competition, with its institutionalized consequences, requires that the state must be prepared to surrender control to the markets of higher-education demand and of competitive prestige between rival universities and departments (Clark, 1990).

The second crucial factor would be a shift from state-led co-ordination to a more flexible voluntary system. A market system of higher education is able to promote operations founded on expertise instead of propping up bureaucratic authority. In this way, it can create a network of bonds and contacts permeating the whole nation, but which originate in the academic community. Co-ordination of this type is more 'secretive', perhaps, than state control; but it is far more flexible.

There is also one further lesson to be learnt from the American model which not every country will be able to adopt easily: the doctrine of many masters. Control over higher education should not be in the hands of any single authority. Today, where such a single master exists, it is virtually without exception the government. In the American model, multi-based sources of funding are an indispensable condition for reliable, lasting institutional autonomy. They would also appear to be an essential condition for universities and colleges to be able to adapt quickly and flexibly to a rapidly changing environment. 'Diversify! Diversify!' is the fundamental lesson that the American model preaches. A wide base of funding is essential, in order to reduce the risk of destruction implicit in dependence on the power of any single master. The capacity of national governments to adopt predatory behaviour towards their own higher-education systems can only too easily be documented in recent years, the Australian and British examples being merely two of the most dramatic (Clark, 1990).

The Finnish university model is that of a po-

werful national state. In a strongly centralized, comparatively rigid system, change is cumbersome. It would appear more than probable that Finnish higher-education policy will continue to be dominated by regional policy considerations. Where the markets are small, with few people and few resources, decisions are made centrally about many other matters as well as university policy. This regional emphasis in higher-education policy, and adherence to the principle of parity of esteem between institutions, are likely to continue to provide the social force by means of which the central authorities in Finland will decide on the fates of individuals and regions.

Neither in the government in general nor in the Ministry of Education in particular has there been evidence of the political will or mechanisms to bring about radical reorganization of higher education, or for instance the transfer of departments, posts, or individuals from one place to another. The top-down chain of bureaucratic command is in any case too cumbersome to achieve change, even if the will were there.

The most probable future source of inducement to radical change lies therefore in international pressure. If Europe is genuinely integrating, if national higher-education policy practised by sovereign nation-states weakens, if the needs of the minor regions are subjected to the needs of the greater ones, then the Finnish model of the university will inevitably change. Moreover, since the structures of the New Europe do not, apparently, incorporate powerful centralized authority, it seems likely that it will be through market mechanisms that change will be forced on the Finnish universities. International student markets, employee markets, job markets and status markets will eventually and inevitably also come to dominate even the universities of the European periphery, and the national government will be forced to withdraw from the stage. At that time, possibly, the American model may become a seriously viable alternative. In the worst event, this could lead to the demise of the university ideal, as the distinctive nature of the university is swallowed up within the labour market; but in the best event, it may provide the room needed for the university to retain, and promote, its own autonomy. ∎

References

CERYCH, L. 1985. Collaboration between Higher Education and Industry: An Overview. *European Journal of Education*, Vol. 20, No. 1, pp. 7–17.
——. 1989. Higher Education and Europe after 1992: The Framework. *European Journal of Education*, Vol. 24, No. 4, pp. 321–32.
CLARK, B. 1983. *The Higher-Education System. Academic Organization in Cross-national Perspective*. Berkeley, University of California Press.
——. 1990. Is California the Model for OECD Futures? Paper presented at the Conference on Policy Change in Higher Education, 4 June. University of Turku.
KERR, C. 1982. *The Uses of the University*. Cambridge, Mass., Harvard University Press.
——. 1987. A Critical Age of the University World: Accumulated Heritage versus Modern Imperatives. *European Journal of Education*, Vol. 22, No. 2, pp. 183–93.
——. 1990. The Internationalisation of Learning and the Nationalisation of the Purposes of Higher Education: Two 'Laws of Motion' in Conflict? *European Journal of Education*, Vol. 25, No. 1, pp. 5–22.
KIVENEN, O.; RINNE, R. 1990. The Limits for the Expansion of Higher Education? The Case of Finland. *European Journal of Education*, Vol. 25, No. 2, pp. 147–55.
——. 1991. Mapping the Field of Stratification in Higher Education: The Finnish Experience. *Journal of Higher Education*, Vol. 21, No. 4, pp. 521–49.

NEAVE, G. 1984. On the Road to Silicon Valley? The Changing Relationship between Higher Education and Government in Western Europe. *European Journal of Education*, Vol. 19, No. 2, pp. 111–28.
——. 1985. The University and State in Western Europe. In: D. Jaques and J. Richardson (eds.), *The Future for Higher Education*, pp. 27–40. Milton Keynes, Open University Press.
——. 1989. On Articulating Secondary School, Higher Education and 1992. *European Journal of Education*, Vol. 24, No. 4, pp. 351–63.
RHOADES, G. 1987. Higher Education in a Consumer Society. *Journal of Higher Education*, Vol., 58, No. 1, pp. 1–24.
TEICHLER, U. 1988. *Changing Patterns of the Higher Education System. The Experience of Three Decades*. London, Kingsley.
——. 1990. *Europäische Hochschulesysteme: Die Beharrlichkeit vielfältiger Modelle*. Frankfurt/Main, Campus.
TROW, M. 1974. Problems in the Transition from Elite to Mass Higher Education. *Policies for Higher Education*, pp. 51–104. Paris, OECD.
——. 1979. Elite and Mass Higher Education: American Models and European Realities. *Research into Higher Education: Process and Structures*. pp. 183–220. Stockholm, National Board of Universities and Colleges.
——. 1989. American Higher Education: Past, Present and Future. In: T. Bybom (ed.), *Universitet och samhälle*, pp. 369–96. Stockholm, Tidens Förlag.
WEBER, M. 1974. On Universities. *The Power of the State and the Dignity of the Academic Calling in Imperial Germany*. Chicago, Chicago University Press.
VAN VUGHT, F. 1990. Recent Developments in Higher Education Governance. Paper presented at the Conference on Policy Change in Higher Education, 4 June. University of Turku.

Higher education
in the United States
in the year 2000

D. Bruce Johnstone

Current and retrospect

A prospective view of higher education in the
United States in the year 2000 must begin with
the features that best define American higher
education in the present, the early 1990s. Although any list of defining features will be to
some degree arbitrary, the following characteristics set higher education in the United States

D. Bruce Johnstone (United States). *Chancellor of
the State University of New York, a sixty-four-cam-
pus system headquartered in Albany, New York.
Formerly President of the State University College
at Buffalo, and Vice-president for Administration at
the University of Pennsylvania. Author of numerous works on the economics and finance and the
planning and management of education. Among his
recent works are:* Sharing the Costs of Higher Education: Student Financial Assistance in the United
Kingdom, the Federal Republic of Germany,
France, Sweden and the United States *(1986). He
contributed 'The Costs of Higher Education' to*
International Higher Education: An Encyclopedia
*(Philip G. Altbach (ed.), 1991) and 'Tuition Fees'
to* The Encyclopedia of Higher Education *(Burton
Clark and Guy Neave (eds.), forthcoming in 1992).*

apart from its counterpart institutions in other
countries.

LARGE SCALE

Higher education in the United States by the
1990s has become an enormous enterprise,
whether measured by the number of institutions, number of students, or number of dollars
committed to its operation. Furthermore, this
large scale holds up even when the United
States' relatively large population and overall
wealth are controlled – that is, as in higher education's enrolments per 100 high-school graduates or per number of eighteen- to twenty-year-
olds, or higher-education expenditure per
$1,000 of gross national product (GNP).

For example, in 1990 American higher
education:

Consisted of nearly 3,400 degree-granting institutions, further categorized in Table 1 by
public or private control and by predominate degree orientation. Under the broader
rubric 'post-secondary education' may also
be included more than 7,000 non-colle-
giate schools, usually proprietary, or profit-
making, which grant highly specialized, vocational training, generally for short cours
es of a year or less (NCES, 1990b, p. xvi, Table 3, p. xxvii, Table 14).

TABLE I. Degree-granting institutions of higher education in the United States, 1987, by control and predominating degree orientation

Type of institution	Public	Private	Total
Doctorate-granting universities	134	79	213
Comprehensive universities and colleges	331	264	595
Liberal arts colleges	32	540	572
Two-year institutions	985	382	1 367
Specialized institutions	66	576	642
TOTAL	1 548	1 841	3 389

Source: Carnegie Foundation for the Advancement of Teaching, 1987, p. 5. Table 4.

Enrolled nearly 14 million degree-seeking students, nearly 8 million full-time and just over 6 million part-time (NCES, 1990c). This number includes 2.4 million first-time students, who are about 37.3 per cent of the most recent high school graduating class. Just over 30 per cent of students in the 18–24-year-old age-group are enrolled full or part time and some 46 per cent of Americans by the age of 34 have had some higher education (United States, 1990a, p. 5, Table 1; NCES, 1989a, p. 16, Table 9).

Consumed approximately $120 billion in total institutional current fund expenditure (NCES, 1989b, p. 95, Table 38). This was about 2.5 per cent of 1990 GNP.

PERVASIVENESS

The place of higher education in the United States is measured not just in enrolments and dollars, but in the degree to which colleges and universities pervade American culture. Whether young people actually go to a college or university or actually complete a degree, the experience of college has become a virtual expectation of American youth and their families. The American college or university has become the major launchpad to social mobility and to most occupations, or at least to most well-paid positions of authority within most occupations.

Higher education in the United States is expected to play: (a) the leading institutional role in the social transition of youth to young adulthood; (b) to teach what high schools have failed to teach; (c) to advance the status of minorities; (d) to uphold technological supremacy for the advantage of American industry, agriculture, defence and medicine; (e) to upgrade the skills of the American worker; and (f) to entertain the nation through intercollegiate athletic competitions.

THE BACCALAUREATE DIVIDE:
UNDERGRADUATE, GRADUATE
AND ADVANCED
PROFESSIONAL STUDY

The first four years (or the equivalent period of time with only part-time study) of tertiary-level education in the United States is termed 'undergraduate', and culminates with a baccalaureate degree. The word 'college', albeit with shades of meaning, most often refers either to an institution that offers only a baccalaureate degree (or perhaps also a Master's, but not a doctorate) or to the undergraduate school, undergraduate years of a university or university education.

Students may be awarded an Associate of Arts or Associate of Science degree after two years if attending a community college and may then complete the baccalaureate degree in approximately two more years by transferring to a four-year college or a university as an upper-division undergraduate. Four-year colleges and universities do not generally, however, award associate degrees and a student who drops out of a four-year college or university after two or three years, but short of the length of time necessary to receive the baccalaureate – even in good academic standing – is not entitled to an associate degree as any kind of consolation award.

The classical professional fields of study in the United States – medicine, dental medicine, veterinary medicine, pharmacy and law – take place overwhelmingly as advanced professional study, entered after completion of a baccalaureate. Other significant advanced professional degrees at the Master's level – e.g. business, city planning, architecture and education – often build upon professional baccalaureate majors, but may also be entered with a baccalaureate degree in a range of arts and science disciplines, frequently – with the exception of architecture – after some years spent since completion of the baccalaureate practising in the field.

Advanced graduate study in the disciplines culminating in the Ph.D. is the province primarily of approximately 200 major doctorate-granting universities, nearly all of which also have large undergraduate programmes as well. The same departments and faculties are generally given responsibility for both undergraduate and graduate study and professors who are rewarded mainly for their research and graduate teaching may also teach some undergraduate courses. Professorial time and attention, however, is drawn towards graduate-level courses, thesis supervision and, increasingly in the sciences, towards the mentoring of post-doctoral students. Many American universities that are not particularly selective in their undergraduate admissions and that have large amounts of financial and political resources remaining accessible, diverse and 'non-élitist' at the undergraduate level, have nevertheless built, with the same faculty and governance structures, some of the most distinguished, selective and avowedly élite graduate programmes and research institutes in the world (Clark, 1990, p. 27).

OPENNESS AND EGALITARIANISM

Higher education in the United States, at least at the undergraduate level, is available to almost everyone. Some kind of collegiate experience is offered to, and partaken by, individuals at levels of academic aptitude that would be considered far too low for higher education in most other countries. The United States is exceptionally tolerant of the underachiever, even the academic failure, and there is always some college to which virtually anyone can gain admittance.

Furthermore, there are few 'dead ends' or irreversible academic decisions. Undergraduate students can change academic majors any number of times, albeit sometimes with some loss in progress, and they may enter, exit and re-enter degree programmes almost at will. All this is costly and indicative to some observers of insufficient rigour and discipline. But it reflects the nation's allegiance to opportunity and egalitarianism, to the 'late bloomer', and to the perpetual 'second chance'.

COURSES AND CREDITS

Most instruction, even at the graduate level, takes place in 'courses', conducted by a single professor (albeit frequently with assistants) and a number of students (anywhere from five or six to several hundred) who meet for formal instruction for a defined number of hours a week (usually three to four or more) for an American semester (about fifteen weeks). Students do written assignments and are usually also examined, sometimes several times, for a final grade for the course. Undergraduate degrees are given for an accumulation of 'course credits', generally with the stipulation that a certain number, and certain specific ones, must be earned within the student's 'major', or academic speciality, and a certain number must be earned outside the major, often from special courses representing either introductions to, or examples of, the basic concepts or systems of thought identified with broad domains of knowledge – as in literature and the fine arts, mathematics and science, or the social sciences.

American undergraduates are generally not comprehensively examined or otherwise held accountable for the learning that has already been ascertained as 'learned' through a satisfactory grade in a particular course. Even at the graduate level, where comprehensive examinations and theses are often the capstones to learning, a prerequisite to these examinations is the accumulation of a generally well-defined number of courses or 'credit units' (the typical course usually carrying three or four such credit units, corresponding roughly to the weekly hours of formal instruction).

An important consequence of the course-credit-accumulation method of ascertaining learning is that it is especially compatible with withdrawal and re-entry and with transfer from one institution to another, provided only that a student's past accumulation of credits are accepted at the institution to which he or she is applying for admittance or re-entry.

THE PRIVATE SECTOR

The early American colleges were private corporations, developing their policies and standards and procedures quite independently from the state. As recently as 1950, 49 per cent of all college and university students were enrolled in private institutions (NCES, 1989a, p. 10, Table 3). Since then, the growth of the public community college and the public comprehensive college has shifted the enrolments to about 78 per cent public and 22 per cent private (NCES, 1990c, p. 6, Table 1). Nevertheless, some 47 per cent of the United States' approximately 3,400 degree-granting institutions of higher education are private charitable corporations, owned by trustees, generally prominent alumni and other lay supporters of the institutions, who serve without personal gain (NCES, 1990b, p. xxvii, Table 14). Their principal responsibilities are the selection of a president, the assurance of financial viability and good stewardship, and the establishment, upon recommendation of the president and generally with substantial input from the faculty, of broad policy guidelines and plans for the institution's future.

The private sector in the United States contains many of the most prestigious research universities (Harvard, Stanford, Yale, Chicago, for example) and most of the most prestigious and selective undergraduate colleges (Williams, Swarthmore, Carleton), all of which enjoy substantial endowments as well as reputations that allow them to charge high tuition fees and other charges, well in excess of $20,000 in the early 1990s. But the private sector in the United States also includes many colleges that are virtually 'open admission' (that is, they admit nearly everyone who applies), that have minimal endowments, and that are, by most measures, financially and academically precarious.

ABSENCE OF A NATIONAL MINISTRY

Education, including elementary, secondary and higher levels, is a matter left by the 'Powers Reserved' clause of the United States Constitution to individual states. There is a United States Department of Education, the Secretary of which holds cabinet rank. But its powers are minimal, and its principal significance to American colleges and universities lies in the amounts of, and conditions attached to, granting Federal student financial aid and in its central role in the compilation of statistics and in reporting on the condition of higher education in the United States (see NCES 1990a). Of much greater significance to universities are the major Federal research granting agencies: the National Science Foundation, the National Institutes of Health, the Department of Defense and the Department of Agriculture.

In fact, governmental control even at the state level and even over the states' public institutions is minimal. Although the dependence of the public university on state funding obviously makes public higher education at least vulnerable to state governmental interference, American higher education enjoys an enormous and robust measure of autonomy. Government, both Federal and state, imposes a myriad of regulations on everything from occupational health and safety to the racial and gender compositions of faculty and staff to the satisfactory degree progress of students receiving financial assistance. But with few exceptions, there is neither Federal nor state control over the curriculum, over standards for student admissions or for the awarding of a degree, or over the qualifications for, or terms of employment of, the faculty.

INSTITUTIONAL GOVERNANCE

The governance of American colleges and universities is marked by lay boards of trustees and by relatively powerful presidents selected by, and answerable directly to, the trustees and only indirectly (albeit importantly) to the faculty. Public colleges and universities are increasingly parts of large state systems, usually with a central board of trustees and a chief executive officer who exercises co-ordination, leadership and budgetary authority over the member campuses.

Faculty influence is exercised through faculty or school and campus-wide senates, with faculty influence greatest over appointment and promotion of colleagues, curricula, standards for admission and requirements for degrees. The more prestigious research university and private college faculties tend not to be unionized, whereas faculty at community colleges as well as at many public four-year colleges and universities frequently are.

THE CURRICULUM

The four-year American baccalaureate curriculum is considerably less specialized than equivalent curricula elsewhere, with typically only a little more than a third of the courses being within the major, and those concentrated in the third and fourth years. Much of the first two years, and about one-third to one-half of the total courses, will be in what is loosely termed 'general education', which may consist either of distribution requirements that force each student to take a course or two in each of several broad domains of knowledge (e.g. the humanities), or of core courses that all must take, traditionally emphasizing cultural heritage, but more recently oriented to 'current issues' such as multiculturalism or personal ethics. Many but not all colleges require proficiency in a second language. Some require either courses, or demonstrated competency, in 'basic skills' such as writing, mathematics and the ability to use a personal computer. Depending on the college and on the students' pattern of course selection, 10 to 25 per cent of the courses may be in totally 'free electives', in which students are encouraged to experiment with hitherto unfamiliar fields of knowledge, often before selecting their majors, or simply to acquire learning in fields they are likely never again to study formally.

RESEARCH

Research is the special province of the universities, more so than of the country's many predominantly undergraduate colleges, particularly research which is costly (e.g. in the physical, biological and biomedical sciences) and which therefore requires the presence of costly space and equipment, graduate students and a critical mass of similarly trained colleagues. Such research is mainly sponsored, or supported by grants from foundations or governmental agencies, generally awarded to a faculty 'principal investigator' through a process of peer review. The grants many buy some or all of the faculty member's time – that is, release him or her from course-teaching duties – though the professor will generally continue to teach advanced graduate students in their thesis research as well as to mentor post-doctoral scholars. Total college and university spending on research and development in the United States in 1988 was $13 billion, 68 per cent of which was basic as opposed to applied research or development and 60 per cent of which was sponsored by the Federal Government (United States, 1990*b*, p. 583, Table 986). The annual output of Ph.D.s in the early 1990s is approximately 38,000 (NCES, 1990*c*, p. 12, Table 7).

The United States employs stand-alone, or non-teaching, research institutes less than most other countries, though such institutes are still significant centres of research and trainers of post-doctoral scientists. Direct expenditure by industry on research in 1988 was $20.1 billion, only $2.8 billion of which was basic research of the kind traditionally conducted in academic settings (United States, 1990*b*, p. 583).

STUDENT SERVICES

American undergraduate higher education emerged under the influence of the English college, stressing residential life and substantial attention to the students' intellectual and social development outside the classroom. The much more recent priorities on expanding access and on retaining more students, especially racial minorities, who often enter with insufficient academic preparation, has brought new emphasis to the need for a range of supportive student services in such areas as advising, counselling, career guidance, financial services and special ethnic group advisers. Around these services have grown entire new professions and career ladders, as well as resource expectations and inevitable budgetary competition with the more traditional needs of the instructional faculty, libraries and other infrastructure.

ORIENTATION TO THE STUDENT
AS CONSUMER

The very large (possibly excess) physical capacity of American colleges and universities, the near saturation of the market of traditional college-age youth, coupled with the sharp decline from the mid 1970s to the mid 1990s of the size of this age cohort, the financial dependence of all institutions on maintaining or expanding enrolments, the great diversity of institutional types and curricula, and the general absence of government-imposed standards or controls have all encouraged and permitted very aggressive competition for students among colleges and universities. This competition includes intense advertising and marketing, much of it by direct mail to students during their junior and senior years of high school. Colleges employ extensive staffs of recruiters, who visit high schools and 'college fairs' where competing recruiters from dozens of colleges and universities hawk their academic wares with the aid of handsomely designed, multi-coloured brochures, video tapes and attractive young students who testify to the academic quality and the good fun to be had at their particular college. Colleges unable to maintain enrolments have, at times, entirely reorientated their curricula and marketing strategy – for example, a church-related liberal arts college for traditional-age youth in full-time attendance transmogrifying to a career-oriented school emphasizing business and other applied studies and catering to older students who may attend primarily in the evenings and on weekends. Financial aid, too, has become a major recruiting device, with grants (i.e. tuition-fee discounts) being offered in carefully measured amounts to fill the class and meet the requisite revenue goal, but also to attract as many as possible of the most desired students – for example, the very bright, the outstanding athlete, the promising minority student.

By the early 1990s, concerns were being expressed that this marketing orientation was eroding standards, consuming too many scarce institutional resources, and at times misleading students, who might thus attend inappropriate institutions for the wrong reasons. At the same time, their aggressive marketing orientation has made most American colleges and universities more responsive than universities in other countries to the needs, interests and comforts of students, as well as to the needs of the economy and of the graduate and advanced professional schools. Arguably, the quality of teaching, the currency of the curriculum, and the cost-effectiveness of the institution (presumably reflected in its tuition) are all enhanced by the 'consumer' orientation of American higher education.

SOURCES OF REVENUE

Higher education in the United States, more than in any other country, depends on revenue from other sources than taxation. Tuition and required fees, covered both by students (from savings, term-time earnings and loans) and by parents (from savings as well as current income) cover on average about 25 per cent of educational costs in the public sector and up to 80 or 90 per cent in private colleges with little endowment or current giving. Endowment income is significant in much of the private sector, and current donations from alumni and friends, totalling some $8.9 billion in 1988/89 (Chronicle of Higher Education, 1990, p. 26), is increasingly important for public as well as private colleges and universites. Services to students such as room, board, books, health care and even some academic expenses such as special equipment are generally provided at cost, even in public institutions, and are often operated under contract by private profit-making companies. Universities are even becoming more aggressive and entrepreneurial in licensing patents, leasing real estate and marketing high-priced executive services – all to gain more income.

COMMUNITY ORIENTATION

American colleges and universities have deep roots of community service, stemming from the Land Grant tradition of the late nineteenth-century state-owned universities of agriculture and applied arts; through the 'Wisconsin tradition' of academic and intellectual service directly to state and local government and to progressive social agendas; more recently from the community college movement of the 1960s, 1970s and 1980s; and, finally, from more recent themes such as enhanced university assistance to business and industry or increasing offerings of recreational and non-credit courses to the burgeoning senior citizen population. This community orientation is characteristic of most private as well as public institutions, and reflects, in turn, some of the features of American higher education mentioned above: pervasiveness, egalitarianism and student-as-consumer orientation.

Towards the year 2000: the economic, demographic and social context for American higher education

What higher education will become in the future depends very largely on what becomes of the key economic, demographic and social variables of which a country's colleges and universities are very much a function. American higher education in the year 2000 is likely to be influenced by the following trends.

THE ECONOMY

The economic base of the United States will continue to shift from heavy manufacturing to lighter, smaller-scale and more technologically dependent manufacturing and services, including the export of higher education and knowledge. Agriculture and natural resources will continue to be the mainstay of export earnings. The changing American and world economy by the year 2000 will call upon higher education to continue, and desirably to enhance, its university-based basic and applied research and its training of Ph.D.s. It is unclear whether or not the economy alone will need a greater percentage of workers with university degrees; but it is clear that all workers, and therefore all youth, will need solid grounding in technology and communication skills beyond levels now being taught in American high schools. Business and industry will look to higher education for the continuous upgrading of their work-forces at all levels through regular degree-credit, part-time, short-cycle and self-paced courses.

DEMOGRAPHICS

The remarkable decline in births during the 1960s and 1970s, which in turn caused such a precipitous decline in the traditional college-going age cohort from the mid-1970s to the mid-1990s has ended, and the number of eighteen-year-olds leaving high school will soon stabilize. The American population will become older, with a 50 per cent increase in persons 45 and older from 1990 to 2010. Racially and ethnically, the 18–24-year-old population in 2000 will show a slightly higher proportion of Afro-Americans (not of Hispanic origin) and Asians as well as a significantly higher proportion of Hispanic-origin youth: from just under 11 per cent in 1990 to nearly 14 per cent in 2000 to an estimated 18.5 per cent in 2010 (United States, 1986, pp. 48–51, 1990b, p. 16, Table 18; see also unpublished summaries from the 1990 Decennial Census).

Demographics will force American higher education to be even more adept at handling students with diverse cultural, linguistic and socioeconomic backgrounds. More and more higher education will be oriented to what in the early 1990s still may be called 'non-traditional' and 'minority' students – who by the year 2000 will be virtually 'traditional' and 'majority', or at least no longer aptly described by their current labels.

SOCIAL AND POLITICAL BELIEFS

Hardest to predict are changes in values, ideologies, behaviour patterns and ways of life which are almost certain to affect higher education, in some ways, in the decade ahead. For example, the American electorate in the 1980s and into the early 1990s demonstrated a vague unhappiness with government spending, taxation and the public sector generally, including publicly supported higher education, sufficient to create some real austerity, curtail trajectories of growth, and shift some burden from taxpayers to students, parents and donors. The tax resistance did not, however, materialize into the kind of full-scale, anti-government, taxpayer revolution that was sought by some of the political far right and that could have virtually privatized much of American public higher education, leading to full-cost tuitions, reductions in enrolments, the closure of some institutions, and the near elim-

ination of distinctions between public and private colleges and universities.

Because 'no profound change', however unimaginative, is often, nevertheless, the best single prognostication of social behaviour, it is at least not unlikely that states will continue through the 1990s to support their public higher-education sectors, but to do so reluctantly and with some deterioration of, for example, faculty compensation, faculty-student ratios and infrastructure, and that the Federal Government will likewise preserve the basic financial assistance and sponsored research programmes, supporting both public and private sectors, but with little or no real enrichment.

Attitudes towards government generally and to a willingness to be taxed are related to attitudes towards the domestic agenda of the American political left. While this agenda is not without its own internal conflicts and inconsistencies, the classic liberal agenda in the early 1990s continues to include: a concern for poverty and the increasingly unequal distribution of income and wealth, together with a desire to ameliorate it in part through governmental intervention; a concern about discrimination and racial injustice and a determination to reduce such inequities, again through governmental and institutional actions; and a priority on civil liberties and individual freedoms. In general, this 'social agenda' receded during the 1980s, and there does not appear at present any great reawakening in the United States of liberal social consciousness or activism. The safest prediction of American social and political values for the duration of the 1990s is a continuation of a basically conservative orientation, with relatively mild social and political pressure upon colleges and universities to perform more effectively, to teach 'good values', insist on responsible behaviour and to be instruments of social cohesion and a common culture.

Towards the year 2000: pressures for reform of American higher education

'Prediction is risky business,' quipped futurist Alvin Toffler, 'especially about the future.' A common mistake among those who dare to predict the future is to confuse that which everyone seems to want to happen – the generally accepted reform agenda – with that which is statistically most likely to happen. Thus, for example, if the improvement of undergraduate education is on virtually everyone's agenda, it is difficult not to assume that there will, in the future, be a significant change in higher education in the direction of better teaching, changed institutional policies regarding the criteria for promotion and tenure, and a different drumbeat – superior teaching – to which professors will soon begin to march. Similarly, as 'enhanced retention' or 'more attention to learning and to its assessment' appear with increasing frequency on university agendas and in reports for the reform of American higher education, it is natural to assume that the future will, indeed, bring about changes, perhaps profound ones, that will enhance the realization of these goals.

Unfortunately, although a reform agenda may signal some changes to look for, it may not always yield good predictions, and may at times even be a source of predictions that are actually among the least likely to materialize. For example, calls for 'better teaching' and for changes in higher educationss reward system have been around for decades. In fact, the American professoriate is more pedagogically sophisticated and more oriented to the student, as a general rule, than the professoriate in most other countries. Furthermore, the unrelenting pressure for research, conventionally thought to be that which turns the professor's attention away from teaching, is a truly significant diversion only in the research universities, which educate only about 20 per cent of all undergraduates and only 17 per cent of first-time students (NCES, 1991).

Finally, the fact that a dominant orientation in the American University towards research and towards one's colleagues outside of one's own institution have persisted for so many decades – in the face of consistent complaints and determined efforts to substitute student and institutional orientations – should suggest that there are extremely powerful and robust factors at work maintaining the current reward system, and that something much like the status quo, rather than any major change, however seemingly attractive, should be considered by far the most likely pattern of faculty rewards and incentives into the foreseeable future.

Nevertheless, the higher-education and reform agenda in the 1990s is a source of certain possible and other probable, trends and must be considered in any prospective view of higher education in the year 2000. Most such reform lists in the early 1990s would contain the following:

The need for more attention to effective teaching in the awarding of tenure, promotion and merit pay, as well as more of the Ph.D. preparation devoted to developing teaching skills.

More attention to, and better evidence of, the results of higher education.

More effective recruitment and retention of currently underrepresented minorities and more attention to the values of pluralism, diversity and tolerance.

More academic rigour, especially in mathematics and in the use of the English language and higher standards generally for graduation.

(To some) more attention to a common core of knowledge, particularly emphasizing Western history and cultural heritage.

(To others) more attention to non-Western history and cultural heritage and to curricula that is Afro-, Islamic- or other than Euro-centred.

Greater productivity and cost-containment.

All these presumed reforms, and undoubtedly others, will continue to press upon higher education in the United States as the year 2000 approaches. Some progress towards certain goals will undoubtedly be made. It is also likely, though, that much the same list, with some of its same internal contradictions, will be presented in the year 2000 as the then-current reform agenda and as goals to be realized, it will then be hoped, by the year 2010.

American higher education in the year 2000

From what we have discussed above, and with the overarching caveat that American higher education is an especially diverse and robust institution, most likely in the year 2000 to be much as it was a decade earlier, some trends and predictions can nevertheless be expounded.

ACCESS AND PARTICIPATION

Participation rates among eighteen-year-olds may increase slightly, tracking increases in completion of secondary schooling and thus yielding noticeable increases in Hispano-, Afro- and Native Americans and in children of recent immigrants, especially from Asia and the Caribbean. Retention rates and rates of post-baccalaureate study are likely to increase slightly as retention programmes take hold and as competition for jobs continues to inflate the requisite educational credentials.

ENROLMENTS

As these factors come into play upon a slightly larger cohort of eighteen- to twenty four year olds, higher-education enrolments can be expected to rise. The United States Office of Education's high, middle and low projections of enrolments in the year 2000 are shown in Table 2. Actual data for autumn 1990 enrolments would seem to lend most credence to the 'high' projections (NCES, 1990d, pp. 6–7, Table 3).

TABLE 2. Higher education enrolments, actual 1990[1] and projections to the year 2000 (in thousands)

Year	Public	Private	Total
1990 actual early estimates	10912	3039	13951
1990 projected (high series)	10757	3082	13839
2000 projected (low series)	10067	2861	12928
2000 projected (middle series)	11171	3155	14326
2000 projected (high series)	11935	3399	15334

1. Projections were done in March 1990. Actual autumn 1990 data show enrolments to be tracking closest to the high-projection series.

Sources: Actual – NCES, 1990c; projections – NCES, 1990d.

STRUCTURE AND GOVERNANCE

The balance of enrolments between the public and private sectors will tip more towards the lower-tuition, public institutions and a number of private, regional colleges will probably close their doors during the 1990s, though the selective, well-endowed, high-tuition private institutions will remain at least as healthy as the most selective and well supported of the public institutions, most of which will have experienced a decade or more of austerity and a steadily diminishing proportion of their resources coming from tax revenues. More public colleges and universities will come under large State systems, embracing research universities and comprehensive colleges under a single board and chief executive officer (as, for example, in Georgia, Florida, Maryland, New York, North Carolina and Wisconsin), occasionally including community colleges.

THE CURRICULUM

Trends observable in the early 1990s will probably continue, so the American college curriculum in the year 2000 will likely be somewhat more structured, with most students having to demonstrate proficiency in mathematics and English, and more students required to demonstrate both minimal computer skills and some proficiency in a foreign language. Tensions will continue over the sanctity of the traditional literary and historical canons, particularly over attempts to diversify them by the inclusion of more female and minority perspectives; but the general education core in the year 2000 will be not unlike that in the early 1990s.

TESTING AND EVALUATION

The United States will continue its passion for testing and evaluation, with two separate movements of the 1990s likely by the year 2000 to converge in powerful and extensive evaluations. One movement is the quest for excellence and the political pressure upon universities, stemming largely from state and Federal Government, to demonstrate what it is that students are actually learning and thus to be held more accountable for successes and failures in teaching and learning. The object of such assessment is the university, not the student, and might be satisfied with periodic assessments or samples, rather than universal and comprehensive evaluation of students.

The other pressure for evaluation and testing stems from a need for better assessment and sometimes evaluation of prior learning, a more effective diagnosis of individual learning difficulties and knowledge gaps, placing students at more appropriate levels of challenge, and allowing them to progress more at their own speed through self-paced learning modules, with the assistance of video technology and personal computers. These advances in the technology and use of evaluation may also, by the year 2000, cause a better integration of secondary and tertiary levels of instruction, sharpening expectations of each level upon the other and reducing duplication of coverage.

TEACHING AND LEARNING

Increasing competition for students and increasing public and political pressure for more attention to the undergraduate student and to the craft of teaching will probably, by the year 2000, yield some results in the form of, for example, better supervision and mentoring of apprentice faculty during their graduate studies, as well as more attention to, and more explicit rewards for, teaching performance during the period before the award of tenure. The dominant methodologies – lectures, discussions, periodic examinations and term papers – are not likely to change, with the exception of a probable increase in the use of instructional technologies. Some colleges, schools or departments within universities and individual faculties are by the year 2000 likely to be deeply immersed in instruction through video tape and interactive computer software, allowing more of the professor-student interaction to be genuinely personalized, while more of the sheer content is transmitted, learned and evaluated through self-administered and self-paced learning technologies.

CONNECTIONS AND COLLABORATION WITH BUSINESS AND INDUSTRY

American business and industry throughout the 1980s and early 1990s has been lamenting the inadequate preparation of undergraduates, particularly in the written and oral use of English, in basic mathematical and technological literacy and in study skills and work habits. At the same time, many businesses have been looking to nearby universities and colleges for assistance in upgrading work-place skills and reorienting managers to the new perspectives needed to compete for global markets. Higher education in the year 2000 will see more internships and practical experiences for students in business, together with more two-way exchange between the professoriate and business practitioners.

FINANCING HIGHER EDUCATION

Higher education in the United States by the year 2000 is likely to cost some $136–152 billion in 1987/88 dollars by United States Office of Education projections of total current fund expenditure (NCES, 1989*b*, p. 95, Table 38). All projections assume real (that is, inflation-adjusted) increases in expenditure due to the twin assumptions of (a) some increases in scale and in overall employment due to increases in enrolments and in research activity, and (b) real increases in unit costs due to a tendency of such costs to track increases in wages and salaries generally rather than increases in retail prices. Pressure will continue, from state government on the public sector and from parents and students on the high-tuition private sector, to reduce costs or at least to hold per-student cost increases down to levels reflecting either the increase in prices generally (i.e. the prevailing rate of inflation) or the increase in wages and salaries generally (i.e. inflation plus real wage increases). Even this would reflect, for most colleges and universities, a lower trajectory of cost increases than experienced in the 1980s, and would require some or all of the following economy measures: (a) increasing selectively some teaching loads, particularly for research university faculty no longer interested or productive in substantial original scholarship; (b) eliminating some under-enrolled courses or programmes; (c) increasing the intensity of use of space; employing more part-time (and thus lower cost) faculty; contracting out more custodial or service functions; and (d) reducing or at least holding the line on the employment of administrative and instructional support staff. For most community colleges, public comprehensive colleges and regional (i.e. minimally selective) private colleges, however, most of these productivity measures have already been employed, and it is not clear that their unit cost profiles can be lowered significantly beyond those reached in the early 1990s.

Costs will continue to be met through a combination of revenues from parents, students, taxpayers and business or institutional philanthropists (Johnstone, 1991, pp. 73–5). The year 2000 will, in the public sector, see a slightly higher proportion of costs born by parents and students in the form of higher tuitions, particularly in the south and west, where tuitions in the late 1980s were significantly below average.

In sum, higher education in the United States in the year 2000 will be just a little larger, a bit leaner in per-student costs, even more diverse in student profiles and more technologically oriented than at the start of the present decade. In its basic structure and degree configuration, in the way professors teach and students learn, and in its prominent role within American society, colleges and universities at the turn of the millennium will look much as they did a decade or two earlier. ■

References and bibliography

AMERICAN COUNCIL ON EDUCATION. 1990. *U.S. Higher Education: An International Visitor's Guide.* Washington, D.C., American Council on Education.

CARNEGIE FOUNDATION FOR THE ADVANCEMENT OF TEACHING. 1987. *A Classification of Institutions of Higher Education.* Princeton, N.J., The Carnegie Foundation.

CHRONICLE OF HIGHER EDUCATION. 1990. Facts About Higher Education in the Nation, the States, and D.C. *Chronicle of Higher Education*, 5 September.

CLARK, B. R. 1990. Higher Education American Style: A Structural Model for the World. *Educational Record*, Fall, pp. 24–7.

JOHNSTONE, D. B. 1991. The Costs of Higher Education. In: P. G. Altbach (ed.), *International Higher Education: An Encyclopedia*, Vol. I, pp. 59–89. New York, Garland Publishing.

JONES, L. W.; NOWOTNY, F. A. (eds.). 1990. *An Agenda for the New Decade.* San Francisco, Jossey-Bass. (New Directions for Higher Education, 70.)

MILLER, R. I. 1990. *Major American Higher Education Issues and Challenges in the 1990s.* London, Jessica Kingsley Publishers.

NCES (NATIONAL CENTER FOR EDUCATIONAL STATISTICS). 1989a. *Digest of Education. Statistics 1989.* Washington, D.C., US Department of Education, Office of Educational Research and Improvement.

——. 1989b. *Projections of Educational Statistics to 2000.* Washington, D.C., US Department of Education, Office of Educational Research and Improvement.

——. 1990a. *The Condition of Education 1990.* Vol. 2: Postsecondary Education, p. 8. Washington, D.C., US Department of Education, Office of Educational Research and Improvement.

——. 1990b. *1989-90 Directory of Postsecondary Institutions.* Washington, D.C., US Department of Education, Office of Educational Research and Improvement.

——. 1990c. *Early Estimates National Higher Education Statistics: Fall 1990.* Washington, D.C., US Department of Education, Office of Educational Research and Improvement.

——. 1990d. *Projections of Educational Statistics to 2001. An*

Update. Washington, D.C., US Department of Education, Office of Educational Research and Improvement.

——. 1991. *1989 Fall Enrollment in Postsecondary Institutions.* Washington, D.C., US Department of Education, Office of Educational Research and Improvement. (Data tape.)

UNITED STATES. BUREAU OF THE CENSUS. 1986. *Projections of the Hispanic Population: 1983 to 2080.* Washington, D.C., US Government Printing Office. (Current Population Reports, Series p–25, No. 995.)

——. 1990*a. School Enrollment – Social and Economic Characteristics of Students: October 1988 and 1987.* Washington, D.C., US Government Printing Office, (Current Population Reports, Series p–20, No. 443.)

——. 1990*b. Statistical Abstract of the United States: 1990,* 110th ed. Washington, D.C., US Government Printing Office.

Promoting higher education's contribution to the developing European Community*

Hywel Ceri Jones

The late 1980s and the first years of the current decade have been a remarkably fertile period for higher-education co-operation in the European Community (EC). After ten years of preparatory work within the 1976 Community Action Programme in the field of Education,[1] there emerged a new political consensus about the importance of education and training for the development of the Community. This consensus was based on a recognition that in the 1990s deep-seated and fundamental changes in every aspect of European society would occur. These changes are being brought about by the increasing pace of European integration following the planned completion of the Internal Market in 1993 and accelerated advances towards European economic and monetary as well as political union. At the same time, the inexorable advance of science and technology will continue to produce new knowledge and, in its applications, continue to pervade every facet of economic life and the day-today living of virtually every citizen. The closer identity of purpose with its European and world neighbours defines for the Community a larger sphere of interest which has already resulted in increased opportunities for co-operation, partnership and mutual support. A European Community, growing in strength and confidence, will affirm its unity and identity on a world stage and define new areas of

Hywel Ceri Jones (United Kingdom). *Director of the Commission of the European Communities' Task Force for Human Resources, Education, Training and Youth, which includes responsibility for a number of Community programmes, notably ERASMUS, COMETT, LINGUA, FORCE, EUROTECNET, TEMPUS and the European Training Foundation for Co-operation with Central and Eastern Europe. Author of numerous articles on education and training in Europe and co-author of several works, among them:* Teaching and Learning: An Introduction to New Methods and Resources in Higher Education *and* Planning and Management of Universities: A Study of British Universities.

* This article has been prepared in close co-operation with E. Prosser (Director, COMETT Technical Assistance Office), Alan Smith (Director, ERASMUS Bureau) and Finbar O'Callaghan (Expert, Task Force Human Resources).

interaction with all third countries, that is, non-members of the European Community.

The acceleration of the integrative process within the EC will result in more frequent and more intensive mobility and enhanced interaction of Europeans with one another at the economic, social, political and cultural levels. It will bring about a consciousness of the ability to use the vast and varied resources of the Community to the solution of Community problems and will promote in the member states a heightened awareness of each other's development strategies and of the desirability of adopting compatible directions when new initiatives are required.

The challenge of science and technology is central to European competitiveness and economic progress and requires that the continent be in the forefront, not merely in the generation of new knowledge, but also in its dissemination and exploitation in economic life. The enlargement of the Community through the reunification of Germany, its probable future enlargement by the accession of new members, as well as the growing co-operation with the EFTA countries[2] and with Central and Eastern Europe provide the opportunity where European countries working together can make outstanding scientific and cultural contributions to the world of the twenty-first century.

At the global level, the European Community will have to formulate and participate in active world strategies which will support peace and stability as well as the evolution of economic progress and of democracy in developing countries. Concern for the environment will also lead to difficult choices about the optimal routes towards economic development.

Higher education and human-resource development

All the factors mentioned above call for the devotion of greater efforts to the achievement of European excellence in the development of human resources, particularly in the areas of higher education and advanced training. These efforts should be designed to:

Provide the extended knowledge and skills requirements needed to exploit fully the economic advantages of the internal market.

Strengthen Europe's position in the global economy by the application of scientific and technical innovation to business and industry.

Take account of the particular demographic position which exists in the European Community and its influence on the labour market over the next two decades.

Provide a distinctive contribution to the affirmed policies of the Community in regard to economic and social cohesion.

Recognize the extent to which co-operation in the field of higher education and advanced training is becoming more and more a feature of the Community's relationships with third countries.

Affirm the importance of safeguarding and strengthening Europe's cultural and linguistic heritage in all its diversity.

Promote understanding across national boundaries so as to reinforce the concept of the Citizen's Europe and to strengthen among young people in particular the basis for further political development and for European integration.

Higher education and advanced training is a vast and complex enterprise. Throughout the European Community there are more than 3,500 institutions of higher education serving approximately 6.75 million students. The higher-education systems represent an enormous investment and expenditure on the part of the member states, regional authorities, individuals and latterly of the Community itself. The systems are characterized by a high degree of diversity, differing in: (a) the languages used and the cultural background of participants; (b) the duration, level, content and academic structure of the courses; (c) the degree and nature of their involvement in research; and (d) the resources available to them, which reflects the levels of social and economic development in the regions of the Community. Practically all these systems were designed primarily with regional or national purposes in mind, to meet the requirements of labour markets at these levels and to maintain and transmit national cultural positions. The graduates were prepared to meet the expectations of regional and national employers and equipped to live active civic and social lives in the communities. At the same time, however, it is natural that universities and higher-education institutions should take a lead in forging strong European bonds since universities especially have always taken a great pride in their international role and responsibilities. Building stronger cross-national links within Europe in teaching and research has emerged as a natural extension of their previous international connections. The Community is seen as a new source both of innovation and intellectual inspiration and also, inevitably, of some financial backup.

With the mutual recognition of professional qualifications, the mobility of labour and the development of a European labour market, we are witnessing the emergence of a 'European' expectation by employers of future employees as well as on the part of young people taking up higher education. As European opportunities become available, those members of the European Community are demanding a 'European' education, or at least one with a significant European dimension to it. A European dimension, in the broadest interdisciplinary sense of the term, is now a necessary part of the educational experience of all young people growing up in the Community. This is not an argument in favour of establishing a common or harmonized policy on education, but rather for much stronger, large-scale co-operation at Community level in the education field – as education provides the binding force for co-operation and partnership in all other sectors in order to make a success of the post-1993 possibilities and master the challenges that lie ahead.

The concern for the nature and quality of higher education and training has also been reflected in recent studies by the Community's In-

dustrial Research and Development Committee (IRDAC). Its recent work on skills shortages in the Community[3] highlights the relationship between education and training and industrial competitiveness and advocates a strongly European approach towards ensuring that the EC has a sufficient high-quality work-force.

The question for policy-makers in the Community has been whether this huge diverse system of higher education – or rather assembly of systems – can be given a European focus in order to realize European objectives, including those of sharing Europe's cultural wealth among European citizens and promoting a European identity and commitment that can co-exist alongside national and regional allegiances. The major EC action programmes launched since 1986 may be looked upon as providing basic European infrastructures to assist the member states to make more rapid progress in this direction. The basic objectives and content of four of the key programmes in the higher-education field are set out in Table 1. A brief comment on each of these programmes follows, prior to identifying what common factors link them.

COMETT: co-operation between higher education and industry

COMETT is about changing attitudes regarding co-operation between higher education and industry, and about creating lasting change in behaviour. It can be simplified into three basic types of university-industry collaboration which the Community supports:

University-industry structures in the form of regional or sectoral consortia providing a focus for dialogue and action to meet training needs. In COMETT I, there were about 120 such consortia throughout the member states, and this number has risen to 160 in COMETT II from 1990 onwards. About two-thirds of them are regionally based, the other third in a range of technology sectors

Four key European Community programmes in higher education

Programme	Main objective	Duration	Budget 1991 (ecus millions)	Actions supported	Key actors	Notes
COMETT	Promote co-operation between higher education and industry in training for technology	1986–94	46.4	Higher education-industry consortia Transnational student placements in industy Transnational exchange of personnel between higher education and industry Higher-education-industry projects to develop training courses and networks (especially for continuing education) Visits and studies	Higher-education institutions Companies (especially SMEs) Professional organizations Chambers of commerce	Since 1990, open to participation of EFTA countries Most funding given under cost-sharing contracts COMETT consortia act as decentralized agents for implementing COMETT projects
ERASMUS	Boost student mobility within the Community and promote co-operation between higher-education institutions	1987–	74.0	Inter-university co-operation programmes Transnational student mobility Transnational mobility of higher-education personnel Joint course and curriculum development European Course Credit Transfer Scheme (ECTS) Support for European associations Visits and studies	Higher-education institutions Associations related to higher education and the professions	From 1992, open to participation of EFTA countries (subject to ratification) Student funding distributed through National Grant-Awarding Authorities in the member states
LINGUA	Promote improvement of foreign-language competence	1990–94	23.1	In-service training of language teachers Inter-university co-operation programmes Transnational student mobility Transnational mobility of higher-education personnel Joint course and curriculum development Projects promoting foreign-language competence in economic life Exchanges of young people aged 16–25 Visits and studies	Higher and further education institutions Associations in the foreign-language field Companies (particularly SMEs)	Higher education part of programme is implemented in conjunction with the ERASMUS programme
TEMPUS	Promote the development of higher-education systems in Central and Eastern Europe	1990–92	55–70	Joint European projects designed to promote the development of the higher-education systems in Central and Eastern Europe Transnational student mobility and youth exchanges Transnational mobility of higher-education personnel Joint course and curriculum development Support for European associations and publications Visits and studies	Higher-education institutions Associations related to higher education and the professions Companies	Programme implemented within G24[1] framework, and therefore offering co-operation possibilities for non-European countries also Eligible countries in Central and Eastern Europe are: Bulgaria, Czechoslovakia, Hungary, Poland, Romania and Yugoslavia

1. G24 is the group of twenty-four countries that participate in the 'PHARE operation' of assistance to Central and Eastern European countries.

from high-tech areas of information technology and telecommunications through applications areas such as the automobile or wood industries to general sectoral areas such as agrobusiness, environment and energy.

University-industry exchanges of both personnel and students undertaking work placements. The Community is currently funding about 4,000 such student placements and 100 such personnel exchanges each year.

University-industry joint training projects, where transnational groupings of firms and universities elaborate training materials and courses (including in particular multimedia-based approaches) to meet industry's training needs (especially in continuing training). These joint training projects cover: (a) support for *crash training courses* with a European dimension designed for the rapid dissemination of the results of research and development in the field of new technologies and their applications, as well as for the promotion, particularly for small and medium-sized businesses, of the transfer of technological innovation to sectors in which it was not previously applied; (b) support for work on devising, developing and testing at European level more extensive *joint training projects* initiated jointly by different industries in association with the universities concerned; and (c) support for multilateral arrangements aimed at establishing systems for *distance learning utilizing new training technologies*. There are currently about 350 such projects underway, ranging from short-sharp courses in highly specific fields such as DNA *in situ* hybridization or third-generation application-specific integrated circuits (ASICs) design to Europe-wide satellite-based training structures for high-tech firms or for traditional professional sectors such as veterinary practitioners. The multimedia projects include initiatives concerning the training of trainers for the use of multimedia techniques. The prominent partners in many of these projects include the main European

actors in the distance and open learning fields, such as the European Association of Distance Teaching Universities (EADTU), SATURN (the consortium of open universities for technological updating) and EUROSPACE (the consortium for satellite-based training for high-technology firms).

Overall, COMETT is an ambitious programme given its relatively short time-span. It was an important new departure for the Commission, being the first higher-education programme of any significant scale. This meant that the new programme had to respond to a wide range of expectations, especially given that its scope went far beyond the education and training sector as such and also concerned an area of activity, university-industry co-operation, which was unevenly developed across the Community as a whole. In those circumstances, the optimum approach was to remain flexible and experimental and to use the limited funds as widely as possible. COMETT has therefore provided well-prepared foundations upon which further building is occurring in the second and larger phase of the programme that began in 1990. Those foundations are serving not only needs at member-state level, but also Community development needs in so far as human-resource development is increasingly an important feature of all Community efforts. COMETT is like the technology itself: an integrating force that challenges existing forms of co-operation and organization but that offers outstanding opportunities for ever higher levels of performance.

ERASMUS: higher-education co-operation

Named to remind us of the ease with which scholars could move around European universities in medieval times, accumulating their study achievements, the ERASMUS programme is the centrepiece of Community action to promote inter-university co-operation and the organized mobility and exchange of students and staff.

The basic idea of ERASMUS is to promote the formation of partnerships between universities in offering programmes of study so that students have the opportunity of taking a recognized component of their courses in another higher-education institution in another member state. ERASMUS scholarships for students are awarded only if there is some advance guarantee that the period of study spent abroad will be fully recognized as an integral component of the student's final degree, and the Commission emphasizes that it should be explicitly presented as such in the diploma so that prospective employers can see the added value of such European experience.

Unlike COMETT, which is restricted to technology and its applications, the ERASMUS scheme is open to all disciplines, though demand is stronger in certain disciplines – for example business studies, foreign languages, engineering – than others. The idea is to ensure that future professionals in all fields and walks of life will be able to act as multipliers of further European co-operation and contribute to a long-term process of building stronger foundations of inter-cultural understanding. In this way too, we hope to encourage a new form of professionalism gained through experience of working and studying in another country and, of course, by the acquisition of at least one foreign language – the kind of professionalism that will have the capacity to exploit fully the opportunities of the Single Market. In 1990, some 30,000 ERASMUS student scholarships were awarded, as well as the seed-grant money for co-operation between the thousand or so participating institutions and the several thousand academic staff members involved.

ERASMUS has also provided the basis for the launch of the European Community Course Credit Transfer System (known as ECTS), which is a six-year voluntary and experimental scheme in which students may receive credit for training undertaken at universities in other Community countries. Some 84 higher-education institutions and organizations are participating in this challenging venture, ranging across all member states and five selected subject areas

(business administration, history, medicine, chemistry and mechanical engineering). The system relies substantially on mutual trust and respect between the participating institutions and systems, and promises to become a milestone in the quest for more flexible academic recognition across the Community as a whole.

LINGUA: foreign-language competence

The year 1992 has put the spotlight on the Achilles' heel of many of our common endeavours: our lack of ability to communicate with each other. The lack of people capable of working through the medium of at least one other European language is a severe handicap in completing and exploiting the internal market. It was against this background that the Council of Ministers of the Community approved the LINGUA programme in July 1989. The LINGUA programme puts the highest premium on the acquisition of communication skills which young people and adults need to take advantage of the new European employment and business opportunities.

Through the catalytic contribution of LINGUA, the Commission hopes to contribute to a de facto requirement in member states that all future language teachers should, as part of their professional preparation for teaching, have spent a recognized period in a country where the language they propose to teach is the vernacular language. It is intended also that practising teachers should have a similar entitlement with respect to a refresher period in the country whose languages they are teaching. Such periods abroad should provide them with the opportunity to build an exchange project for their school or class through their in-service project abroad. In these ways the language teaching policies of the member states are being assisted and supported with the aim of achieving substantial improvement in foreign language competence among young people leaving school. LINGUA will also provide support for firms to analyse their future language needs and the relative importance of linguistic expertise for their future recruitment and personnel policies.

Since the 1987 signature of the Single Act, this trio of Community initiatives, ERASMUS, COMETT and LINGUA has put inter-university and higher-education co-operation in Europe on a much larger scale than previously. The more than 600 million ecu now agreed by the Council for these three schemes over the next five years complements the substantial training resources tied up in the European Structural Funds. The Community R&D programme, which is now moving into its third phase (1990–94) also places a high premium on the mobility and training of researchers.

under ERASMUS and COMETT, the projects are addressing longer-term structural questions for higher-education institutions in the so-called 'new democracies'. They are providing timely and substantial assistance at a time when the higher-education institutions in Central and Eastern Europe are using their new freedom to bring their teaching and research across the board to competitive levels. Furthermore, it is already apparent after just one year's operation that TEMPUS will be a major agent in enabling the higher-education institutions in the Central and Eastern European countries to forge the links with partners elsewhere in Europe, which will be a springboard for their re-entry into the mainstream of the academic community worldwide.

TEMPUS: co-operation with Central and Eastern Europe in the field of higher education

The education-and-training field has now been given further impetus by the pace of political developments in Eastern Europe, which has resulted in the decision of the Council of Ministers in May 1990 to set up a European Training Foundation – to act as the clearing-house for the transfer of training know-how and expertise initially to Poland and Hungary, but then extended to Czechoslovakia, Bulgaria, Romania and Yugoslavia[4] – and, in particular, to launch, for the academic year 1990/91, the TEMPUS scheme, modelled on ERASMUS and CO-METT, tailored to meet the needs of the countries of Central and Eastern Europe, in adapting their higher-education systems through co-operation with Western European institutions.

At the time of writing, the first round of TEMPUS projects has been underway for not quite a year, but they represent a selective and high-quality group of joint European projects with their own distinctive character. Not simply carbon copies of the types of projects developed

Common factors

Both in terms of objectives as well as at the practical and operational level, there are many common factors that characterize the various programmes. These characteristics have been refined over the periods of programme implementation. The Commission has underlined clearly, especially in recent years, two specific guiding principles: (a) the respect for diversity of the member state' education and training systems, and (b) the concern for subsidiarity, whereby the Community should not assume responsibilities that are more effectively exercised by or within member states. Against this background, it is possible to pinpoint a number of characteristics that have given the European higher-education programmes their special quality.

EUROPEAN DIMENSION AS 'VALUE-ADDED'

The actions supported either have in themselves a European character or are designed to serve purposes that extend beyond a single national frontier. This is often referred to as 'European value-added' by analogy with one of the European Community's favoured taxation approaches. It is not for the Community to duplicate activities that are being or could be undertaken perfectly well by the member states themselves. On the other hand, the Community plays a vital role in ensuring the multilateral networking between several member states which is a powerful feature of all the Community programmes in the higher-education field and can also provide the stimulus and incentives for activities that any individual member state might not itself wish or be able to afford. To that extent, this principle is closely allied to the subsidiarity question mentioned above.

The classic examples of actions in the higher-education field are:

Mobility of people (both students and personnel) between countries.

Development of *transnational study programmes* that feature such exchange (and where no international student or staff mobility is involved, an internationalized curriculum can provide the European element).

Linked to the above, *transnational systems* for providing *recognition/academic credit* for study periods and industrial placements undertaken abroad. These can be either 'micro-systems' such as those in individual Inter-University Co-operation Programmes in ERASMUS (typically involving groups of three to ten universities in various countries) or 'macro-systems' such as the European Course Credit Transfer Scheme (ECTS) initiated by the Community across all the member states.

When considering the programmes from the point of view of their 'European dimension', it should also be noted that in selecting the projects for support within the respective programmes the Commission attaches particular importance to ensuring that participation encompasses all the Community's member states in as judiciously balanced a manner as possible. In this way, the higher-education programmes may be regarded as contributing, in their specif-

ic manner, within this particular field of policy, to the overarching objective of achieving greater economic, social and political cohesion within the Community as a whole.

FUNDING CONCENTRATES ON 'EUROPEAN' COSTS

The funding granted by the Community is by priority concentrated on the 'European' elements of the project in question. Where mobility of students and staff is concerned, this is obvious. Where we are dealing with the development of training courses and materials, the creation of new associations, the funding of meetings and conferences, and so on, the Community is at its most effective where it is complementing what can be funded at national level.

The most common cases of this are where the organizations in the member states may meet the basic salary costs of the personnel engaged in project development, but are unable to meet costs incurred through transnational co-operation, notably cost-of-living differentials when abroad, travel costs and language preparation for both students and staff. A more specific example might be where the Community will direct its funding, within an overall project budget, to specific interpretation or translation costs. An enormous amount of the Community's investment is going towards those types of extra cost, given that transnational co-operation has its own cost, as anyone with any experience of aircraft projects such as Concorde or the Airbus will know.

VOLUNTARY CO-OPERATION AND A DIRECT LINE TO BRUSSELS

The collaborative activity promoted is voluntary and 'bottom-up'. the projects supported under the programmes emerge as a result of open and published Calls for Applications. Those organizations wishing to participate are able to apply directly to Brussels for the financial support available, and, with few exceptions, such as the use of national grant-awarding authorities for the disbursement of student grants within ERASMUS and various forms of support within LINGUA, the support comes in the form of a direct contract with the Commission or its agents. In certain programmes, furthermore, decentralized programme implementation is occurring through the medium of the projects supported, albeit within an overall policy framework. The clearest examples are: (a) in COMETT, where the COMETT university-industry consortia received decentralized funding for student placements and short course development that they themselves disburse, and (b) in TEMPUS, where the Joint European Projects provide the framework that handles a large share of the student and staff mobile grants that TEMPUS makes available.

This is not to say that the national and regional authorities are not involved. The national authorities, which are represented on the official committees that assist the Commission in implementing the programmes, are closely involved in the overall strategic direction of the various initiatives, but decision-making responsibility regarding individual projects generally lies ultimately with the Community. This has been an illuminating experience for certain higher-education institutions accustomed to close State control within all their sectors of activity. The opening up of alternative channels of support has been both stimulating and challenging, even though the existing administrative and accounting rules in member states may not always provide the ideal framework for dealing with this new revenue from Brussels.

The voluntary aspect of co-operation has also been essential. The complexity and diversity of Europe's higher-education systems are such that co-operation potential can never be taken for granted if it is based on simplistic typologies of higher-education institutions.[5] In fact, one of the greatest satifactions emerging from programmes such as ERASMUS and COMETT has been to see small and new colleges forging genuine partnerships with larger and older institutions, given that the common base was a shared vision of course development in a specific area. In the area of higher-education-industry co-operation, the need for the voluntary approach is even more self-evident, given the dichotomies that divide and, arguably, should divide, these two worlds, which are often considered to have fundamentally different strategic objectives, though they are deeply complementary. In a very simplified form, on the one hand, one is dedicated to knowledge in all its forms and branches, its long-term development and its dissemination. On the other hand, the industrial partner must be concerned with immediate innovation and exploitation of this new knowledge, short- and medium-term economic return and thereby legal and commercial constraints on the distribution of that new knowledge.

This being so, industry is none the less simultaneously developing more and more into a major provider and organizer of training at all levels. The centrepiece of European strategy in the 1990s will be to widen access to and participation in continuing education and training throughout a person's working life. This is now not only a demographic necessity – with fewer young entrants due to enter the labour market in the next decade – it is widely recognized as a vital factor in the economic strategy of firms concerned to achieve for themselves a competitive edge: better performance and productivity as a pay-off from investment in training. With companies in some countries now spending more together on training than their governments spend on their university and higher-education sector, it is essential to map out a new European strategy for training in the 1990s forging a much stronger and explicit partnership between the public and private sectors.

PROMOTION OF EUROPEAN NETWORKS

By far the most striking and successful aspect of the EC programmes is their networking potential. This was already hinted at above in relation to the European dimension. Each of the programmes is a network in itself, for example: ERASMUS and LINGUA with together about 1,800 inter-university co-operation programmes, many of which embrace higher-education institutions from all member states, working together in their specific discipline; COMETT, with its network of 160 university-industry training partnerships acting as structures for exchange of training, trainees and training needs assessment across the key sectors of European industry; and TEMPUS, with its 150 Joint European Projects linking higher-education institutions (and in some cases industry) in at least two Community member states with partners in Central and Eastern Europe.

The best may be yet to come. ERASMUS has already laid the foundations for transnational arrangements for the academic recognition of higher-education qualifications, whether through joint and co-operative degree arrangements or through the ECTS, and has given rise to the spontaneous creation of an increasingly wide and varied array of networks, consortia and associations; COMETT has provided internationally oriented companies with a student placement (internship) system that will allow them to intensify their international recruitment of engineers in an increasingly intensive labour market for engineers and technologists; both COMETT and ERASMUS have supported the emerging network of open and distance teaching universities in Europe as well as assisting the emergence of other distance-learning networks (e.g. for high-tech industry or for veterinary practitioners). LINGUA and TEMPUS remain in their first years of implementation, but already promise to yield networks of activity that will represent the best long-term output from the Community's energies and financial investment.

SUPPORTING POLICY DEVELOPMENT AT ALL LEVELS

These myriad actions serve a policy-development purpose that goes beyond the actions in themselves. While in the first phase of development, the main aim was to develop the European character of higher-education systems through exchanges, joint degrees, transfer of credit and academic recognition of qualifications, information exchange, etc., it can be argued that the overall volume of activities has developed to such an extent that the programmes themselves represent significant testbeds of experience and action networks and provide tangible bases for policy analysis and implementation. This is all the more accentuated by the enthusiastic and widespread response of the higher-education sector to the 1993 debate and the move towards the Single Market. The higher-education institutions participating in the programmes – their students and staff – have themselves been a strong motor towards co-operation. The recent period has seen the emergence of European-level associations and fairs concerned with European co-operation and exchange, as well as clearer organizational focus in individual universities as they establish offices and services specifically designed to develop collaborative linkages with counterparts elsewhere in Europe an aspect that, of course, is having a positive impact on institutions' orientation towards and capacity to handle international links in general. This interest has also been underlined by the employers and trade unions, who – meeting regularly within the Community social dialogue – have passed a number of joint opinions pinpointing the pivotal role of education and training within European Community development.

In this context, it is important to note that experience of the European programmes has led to a significant policy review and new legislation at national level in order to respond to the new requirements of the European marketplace. National legislation on student financial support for, and on recognition of, study abroad has been amended in several countries as a direct result of ERASMUS ventures. Similarly, the academic arrangements for student placements abroad have also evolved because of pressure from interested and satisfied customers having experience in COMETT placements. The debate about foreign languages has had an enormous stimulus as a result of LINGUA, both at national level (for example, in relation to how well prepared the member states are to meet the foreign-language challenges of the European Single Market) and in individual higher-education institutions, some of which have now developed institution-wide policy targets in language competence for the first time.

Conclusions: into the future

It is possible to discern a spectrum of development through which the EC programmes are going. These stages of evolution are quite consistent with the changing political and legal framework within which EC policies have developed over the last fifteen years. Five broad stages could be identified:

1. An initial stage of information gathering and exchange, increasing mutual awareness of the various education systems.
2. Launch of financial support for preparatory actions towards creating co-operation.
3. Launch of programme on concertation basis with member states.
4. Launch of programme with substantial direct EC funding.
5. Strategic programme continuation.

Such typologies always carry the risk of over-simplification. Here the intention is not to develop a rigid schema but to illustrate the broad characteristics of programme development over the last fifteen years. However, as the range of programmes increases and thereby the experience of the ground conditions for making them a success, and given the strong programme interrelationships, the newer programmes can be said to some extent to have leap-frogged over the earlier stages.

The main purpose of developing such an evolution typology is to illustrate how the higher-education programmes are reaching a much more advanced state, as they become integral parts of overall Community human-resource strategy. It is difficult and contentious to speculate on this passage between what is described as Stages 4 and 5 and – who knows? – into any further state. Prior to knowing this, we must await the outcome of two significant exercises, the first and more significant of which will be the decisions on the legal and political position to be ascribed to human-resource development within revised treaty arrangements currently under discussion in the Inter-government Conference on Political Union. The second major exercise, which had already been launched prior to those discussions, is one of re-examining the overall pattern of EC education and training programmes and examining any desirable re-alignment that may make them more effective and indeed 'user-friendly' to the institutions they are serving. In that respect, it is fairly certain that after 1994, when the major higher-education programmes reach the end of their current phases, we shall see some structural adjustments, though the types of action supported are likely to remain largely of the same character. As part of the continuing process of review, the Commission is also currently preparing a Green Paper on the contribution of higher education and advanced training to the development of human resources within the Community as a means of further exploring the implications for higher education of the changes taking place in Europe and of facilitating and promoting dialogue between the various actors concerned with the planning and development of higher education.

A further vital factor which will determine the future patterns of development is of course monitoring and evaluation. With the emergence and extension of the Community's efforts, there is a corresponding responsibility to pay great attention to the results of programme evaluation, into which ever-increasing resources are being invested, including, for example, major research of the impact of study abroad. This activity is a shared challenge for both the Community as a whole and for each member state, since both parties stand to gain enormously from the benefits of what is fundamentally a joint collaborative venture.

The principal message to emerge from the experience alluded to in this article is that the EC's co-operation programmes have had a major influence in causing higher-education institutions to review their European role in the accelerated process towards a strong European Community. For higher-education institutions, this is a double process. First, the outward dynamic of assessing how they can contribute to the process of building this Europe, through education, training, scientific creativity, social and intellectual leadership. In this context, the potential and increasing contribution of the higher-education programmes to implementing the sectoral policies of the Community should clearly be noted. Then, the inward dynamic of taking stock of the impact of the new internal market on the requirements of their institutions, the courses, qualifications, curricula and above all their inter-connection to the broader European marketplace.

Through the evolutionary process described above, the EC's programmes have been recognized as having their primary value in the catalytic process of process of putting institutional adaptation firmly on the agenda at all levels, local, regional, national and Community, and by dealing with that agenda through partnership activities mounted on a voluntary basis. The overwhelming response which all the European Community's higher-education programmes have received from higher-education institutions in all member states, demonstrates that the need for this partnership is not merely a postulate of policy uttered by the higher-education

Notes

1. On 9 February 1976 the European Council approved an Action Programme in the field of Education (OJ C 38, 19/2/1976) which addressed a small number of broad policy objectives, among which were the promotion of closer relations between education systems in Europe and co-operation in the field of education. Although the resources devoted to this action programme were extremely limited, the activities undertaken were of great influence in the design of later programmes and stimulated the development of many of the co-operation networks that were to emerge in later years.

2. European Free Trade Association countries (Austria, Finland, Iceland, Liechtenstein, Norway, Sweden, Switzerland).

3. *Skills Shortages in Europe, IRDAC Opinion*, Brussels, Commission of the European Communities, 1991.

4. In the first year of TEMPUS, the then German Democratic Republic (GDR) was also included in the programme for an interim period. The subsequent reunification of Germany meant that the new Länder from the former GDR were fully eligible under the other EC co-operation programmes such as ERASMUS, COMETT and LINGUA.

5. It should be noted that all the European Community's programmes are based on the same, extremely broad definition of what constitutes an eligible higher-education institution, namely: 'all types of post-secondary education and training establishments which offer, within the framework of initial and/or continuing training, qualifications or diplomas of that level, whatever such establishments may be called in the member states' (OJ No. L 13/28, 17/01/89, p. 3.)

Index